THE REVELATION OF BAHÁ'U'LLÁH

Baghdád, 1853–63

By the same author

THE REVELATION OF BAHÁ'U'LLÁH, VOL. 2
Adrianople 1863–68

THE REVELATION OF BAHÁ'U'LLÁH, VOL. 3
'Akká, The Early Years 1868–77

THE REVELATION OF BAHÁ'U'LLÁH, VOL. 4
Mazra'ih and Bahjí 1877–92

THE COVENANT OF BAHÁ'U'LLÁH

THE CHILD OF THE COVENANT
A Study Guide to the Will and Testament of 'Abdu'l-Bahá

TRUSTEES OF THE MERCIFUL
An introduction to Bahá'í Administration
(Bahá'í Publishing Trust, London, 1972, second edition 2009)

To those brilliant souls
the Bahá'í Pioneers and Teachers in every land
who have expended their lives and their substance
in the path of Bahá'u'lláh.

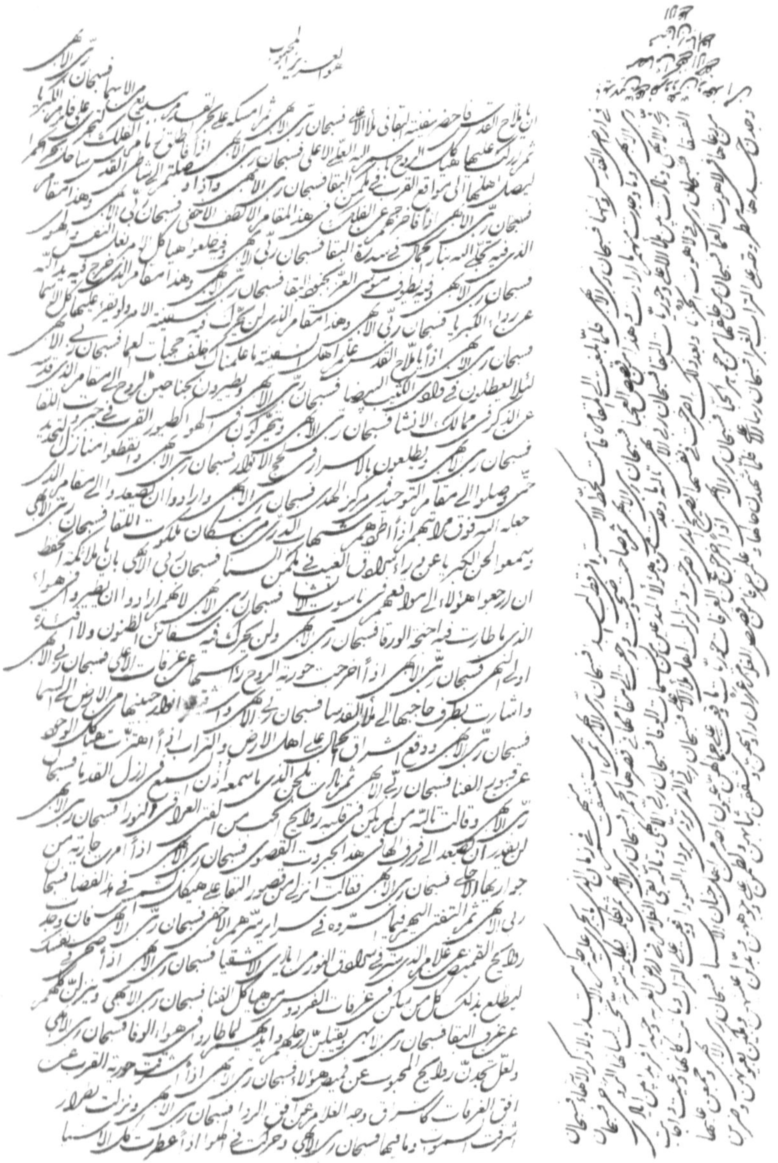

TABLET OF THE HOLY MARINER

Revealed by Bahá'u'lláh in Arabic
In the handwriting of 'Abdu'l-Bahá

THE REVELATION OF Bahá'u'lláh

Baghdád 1853–63

Adib Taherzadeh

GR

GEORGE RONALD
OXFORD

GEORGE RONALD, Publisher
www.grbooks.com

Revised edition 1975
First paper edition 1975
Revised edition 1975
Reprinted 1980, 1988, 1996, 2001, 2007, 2011

ISBN 978–0–85398–057–5

Printed and bound in Great Britain
by the MPG Books Group

CONTENTS

page

FOREWORD xv

INTRODUCTION: The Manifestations of God 1

1. THE BIRTH OF THE REVELATION 7

2. BAHÁ'U'LLÁH IN EXILE 12

3. THE WORD OF GOD 18
The Word of God Is Independent of Acquired Knowledge 18
The Nature of Bahá'u'lláh's Revelation 21
The Creative Power of the Word of God 30
The Word as the Source of Knowledge 32
The Most Exalted Pen 34
The Authenticity of the Word of God 40
True Knowledge 42

4. THE FIRST EMANATIONS OF THE SUPREME PEN 45
The Poem of *Rashḥ-i-'Amá* 45
The City of Ṭihrán 46
The Sisters of Bahá'u'lláh 49
A Prayer on Leaving Persia 51

5. THE EARLY TABLETS IN 'IRÁQ 53
Circumstances of Their Revelation 53
Lawḥ-i-Kullu'ṭ-Ṭa'ám 55
Some Tablets Revealed in Kurdistán 60
The Day of God 64
Bahá'u'lláh's Return to Baghdád 67

page

6. *THE HIDDEN WORDS* 71

7. SOME EARLY BELIEVERS 84
Mullá Riḍá of Muḥammad-Ábád 84
Nabíl-i-Akbar 91

8. *THE SEVEN VALLEYS* 96
Siyyid Ismá'íl of Zavárih (Dhabíḥ) 101
The Four Valleys 104

9. SOME OUTSTANDING TABLETS 105
Ṣaḥífiy-i-Shaṭṭíyyih 105
Madínatu'r-Riḍá 108
Madínatu't-Tawḥíd 109
Súriy-i-Qadír 119
Ḥurúfát-i-'Állín 122
Lawḥ-i-Ḥúríyyih 125
Lawḥ-i-Áyiy-i-Núr 125
Lawḥ-i-Fitnih 128
Súriy-i-Nuṣḥ 137
Shikkar-Shikan-Shavand 147
Javáhiru'l-Asrár 149

10. *THE KITÁB-I-ÍQÁN* 153
Circumstances of Its Revelation 153
The Importance of the *Kitáb-i-Íqán* 160
Major Themes of the *Kitáb-i-Íqán* (Part One) 162
The reasons for man's opposition to the Prophets of God 163
The signs of the return of Christ 165
Interpretation of symbolic terms 166
Further reasons for man's rejection of the Prophets 171
Major Themes (Part Two) 175
The nature of God and His Manifestations 175

page

The sovereignty of the Prophets 180
The meaning of 'life', 'death' and 'resurrection' 183
The veil of knowledge 185
The true seeker 186
Proofs of the Báb's Revelation 189
Bahá'u'lláh anticipates His own Revelation 194

11. OTHER EARLY BELIEVERS 198
Ḥájí Mírzá Muḥammad-Taqíy-i-Afnán 198
Nabíl-i-A'ẓam 202
Companions of Bahá'u'lláh 206

12. BAHÁ'U'LLÁH'S APPROACHING DECLARATION 210
Subḥána-Rabbíya'l-A'lá 211
Lawḥ-i-Ghulámu'l-Khuld 213
Ḥúr-i-'Ujáb 218
Az-Bágh-i-Iláhí 218
Halih-Halih-Yá-Bishárat 219

13. FRIENDS AND FOES 221
Ḥájí Siyyid Javád-i-Karbilá'í 221
Some Powerful Enemies 225

14. *TABLET OF THE HOLY MARINER* 228
Other Tablets of This Period 244

15. MÍRZÁ YAḤYÁ AND SIYYID MUḤAMMAD-I-IṢFAHÁNÍ 246

16. THE DECLARATION OF BAHÁ'U'LLÁH IN THE GARDEN OF RIḌVÁN 257
His Influence on the People of Baghdád 257
The Festival of Riḍván 259
Lawḥ-i-Ayyúb 263

Page
The Significance of Riḍván 273
Three Important Statements by Bahá'u'lláh 278
The Báb's Prophecies Fulfilled 280
Bahá'u'lláh's Departure from the Garden 281

17. THE JOURNEY TO CONSTANTINOPLE 283

18. 'HIM WHOM GOD SHALL MAKE MANIFEST' 294

Appendix I: Mírzá Áqá Ján 315
Appendix II: Ḥájí Muḥammad-Ṭáhir-i-Málmírí 320
Appendix III: Vaḥíd 325
Appendix IV: Ḥájí Mírzá Karím Khán 332

Bibliography 337
References 341
Index 351

ILLUSTRATIONS

TABLET OF THE HOLY MARINER *frontispiece*
Revealed by Bahá'u'lláh in Arabic
In the handwriting of 'Abdu'l-Bahá

facing page

'ABDU'L-BAHÁ 14
The Centre of the Covenant of Bahá'u'lláh
A photograph taken in Adrianople

BAHÁ'ÍYYIH KHÁNUM 15
The Greatest Holy Leaf, daughter of Bahá'u'lláh
A photograph taken circa 1895

MÍRZÁ MÚSÁ, SURNAMED ÁQÁY-I-KALÍM 46
A most faithful brother of Bahá'u'lláh
And foremost among His Apostles

MÍRZÁ MUḤAMMAD-QULÍ 47
The youngest half-brother of Bahá'u'lláh
Devoted to Him and steadfast in His Cause

THE SEALS OF BAHÁ'U'LLÁH 78
Displayed in an ornamental Persian design
(As reproduced in *The Bahá'í World*, vol. V, p. 4)

MULLÁ ZAYNU'L-'ÁBIDÍN 79
A noted scribe and Apostle of Bahá'u'lláh
Surnamed by Him Zaynu'l-Muqarrabín

ONE SHEET OF 'REVELATION WRITING' BY MÍRZÁ ÁQÁ JÁN 110
(reduced from the original size of 35 × 22 cms)
Only the first few words are sufficiently legible to identify the passage as the third Tajallí of the Tablet of Tajallíyát

between pages

A FEW LINES OF THE 'REVELATION WRITING' 110–11
From the Tablet illustrated on the previous page *(actual size)*

facing page

MÍRZÁ ḤUSAYN-I-IṢFAHÁNÍ 111
Entitled Mishkín-Qalam
An Apostle of Bahá'u'lláh and distinguished calligrapher

ḤÁJÍ MUḤAMMAD-ṬÁHIR-I-MÁLMÍRÍ 142
Historian and teacher of the Faith, father of the author
Some of his memoirs concerning Bahá'u'lláh are quoted in this book

TABLET OF BAHÁ'U'LLÁH 143
In His own handwriting
Intended for Ḥájí Muḥammad-Ṭáhir-i-Málmírí (*see page 39*)

MULLÁ MUḤAMMAD-RIḌÁ OF MUḤAMMAD-ÁBÁD 174
An outstanding and heroic exponent of the Faith

MULLÁ MUḤAMMAD-I-QÁ'INÍ 175
An erudite teacher and Apostle of Bahá'u'lláh
Surnamed by Him Nabíl-i-Akbar

SHAYKH SALMÁN 206
The indefatigable special messenger of Bahá'u'lláh

ḤÁJÍ MÍRZÁ MUḤAMMAD-TAQÍY-I-AFNÁN 207
A cousin of the Báb
And a renowned follower of Bahá'u'lláh

MULLÁ MUḤAMMAD-I-ZARANDÍ 238
Historian, Apostle of Bahá'u'lláh and His poet-laureate
Surnamed by Him Nabíl-i-A'ẓam

ḤÁJÍ SIYYID JAVÁD-I-KARBILÁ'Í 239
One of the 'Mirrors' of the Bábí Dispensation
And an outstanding follower of Bahá'u'lláh

NOTES AND ACKNOWLEDGEMENTS

The extracts from the Writings of the Báb and Bahá'u'lláh contained in this book are from the matchless translations by Shoghi Effendi, the Guardian of the Bahá'í Faith, and their published sources are acknowledged in the references and bibliography. There are many other quotations from Persian manuscripts and publications, and these I have translated, unless otherwise indicated. The footnotes are mine, except for one which is identified. Verses taken from the *Qur'án* are numbered in accordance with the Arabic text, although their numbering may differ from that given in English translations. Persian and Arabic names are transliterated in accordance with the system adopted for books on the Bahá'í Faith, but quotations are reproduced in their original form. To assist the reader, I have sometimes referred to certain well-known Persians by their titles instead of their full names; however, the interested reader may find their names in brackets in the index.

The early followers of Bahá'u'lláh seldom sought to be photographed. Occasionally, group photographs were taken, from which it has been possible to obtain many of the individual photographs which I have included, in the belief that their historical interest outweighs the fact that some are faded and out of focus. I am deeply indebted to the Audio-Visual Department of the Bahá'í World Centre for supplying most of these photographs; one has come from the National Spiritual Assembly of the Bahá'ís of Írán and Mr. Ruhi Shakibai has skilfully reproduced another.

I wish to acknowledge with sincere thanks the co-operation of the National Spiritual Assembly of the Bahá'ís of Írán, the Bahá'í Publishing Trust, London, and the Bahá'í Publishing Trust, Wilmette, Illinois, in permitting me to quote extensively from their publications. I am also most grateful to Madame

Laura Dreyfus-Barney for permission to quote from *Some Answered Questions*.

For the editing of the book I desire to record my warm appreciation to Mrs. Marion Hofman, whose advice at every stage has enriched its quality. I am also grateful to Mr. Joseph Watson for reading most of the manuscript and offering valuable suggestions, to Miss Rosemary Magill for meticulously checking the quotations and rendering many other services including proof reading, to Mr. Paul Reynolds who has prepared the index with efficiency and resourcefulness, to Mrs. Jacqueline Mehrabi who patiently converted my scribblings into neatly typed manuscript, to Mrs. Frances Beard for additional typing assistance, and to Miss Mary Perkins and Mr. John Coates for so carefully reading the proofs.

To one friend, in particular, Mr. O. Z. Whitehead, I am deeply indebted for his constant interest and encouragement.

And last but not least, I wish to express my heartfelt thanks to my wife Lesley, for her selfless enthusiasm and unfailing support without which the writing of this book would have been much more difficult.

Adib Taherzadeh

Bray, Co. Wicklow
April, 1974

FOREWORD

This book is an attempt to describe, in language however inadequate, something of the supreme spiritual phenomenon of this age, namely, the Revelation of Bahá'u'lláh.

The creative Word of God in every Dispensation is vouchsafed to mankind through the intermediary of His Prophets and Messengers. Bahá'u'lláh, Whose innumerable followers throughout the world believe Him to be the most recent in the succession of these Messengers or Manifestations of God, has revealed the Word of God for today. His recorded utterances and writings in Persian and Arabic, authenticated by Himself, are viewed by Bahá'ís as their Scripture. In English these are often referred to as Tablets.

In order to indicate the manner of, and the background to, the revelation of some of Bahá'u'lláh's Writings during the forty years of His ministry, it has been felt essential to recount part of the history of His life, and also of the lives of some of His companions and followers whom He addressed, or who were affected, directly or indirectly, by the outpouring of His words or served Him by recording His utterances, transcribing and disseminating His Tablets, or propagating His Message in the land of His birth and in adjoining countries. The author has drawn on narratives which they have left us, in most cases providing the translations.

This volume is the first of four which will survey the better-known Writings of Bahá'u'lláh throughout the period of His ministry. It deals only with a number of Tablets which He revealed in 'Iráq during the ten years of His sojourn in that land, the majority of them unavailable in Western languages. Obviously, it is not possible to describe every Tablet which was revealed by His Pen in this or any other period, for the outpouring of His Revelation was so prodigious that such an attempt would be tantamount to trying to capture an ocean within a cup.

Moreover, since Bahá'u'lláh's Writings, for the most part, have not yet been translated from the originals, the present writer has been faced with the task of conveying in his own words something of their true spirit and feeling, a task which is rendered supremely difficult—and indeed in its entirety impossible—both by the limited vision of man, and by the vast range of the utterances of Bahá'u'lláh and their limitless potency and significance.

If even a small measure of the power and beauty contained within these Writings is imparted here, this book will have gone some way towards achieving its purpose.

FOREWORD TO THE 1976 REVISED EDITION

Recently I have received some authentic material which was not available to me when I wrote this book. It chiefly concerns two of Bahá'u'lláh's Tablets revealed in Baghdád and, as a result, I have revised some paragraphs between pages 147 and 151.

Adib Taherzadeh

Through the movement of Our Pen of glory We have, at the bidding of the omnipotent Ordainer, breathed a new life into every human frame and instilled into every word a fresh potency. All created things proclaim the evidences of this world-wide regeneration.

BAHÁ'U'LLÁH

The world of being shineth in this Day with the resplendency of this Divine Revelation. All created things extol its saving grace and sing its praises. The universe is wrapt in an ecstasy of joy and gladness. The Scriptures of past Dispensations celebrate the great jubilee that must needs greet this most great Day of God. Well is it with him that hath lived to see this Day and hath recognized its station.

BAHÁ'U'LLÁH

Centuries, nay ages, must pass away, ere the Day-Star of Truth shineth again in its mid-summer splendour, or appeareth once more in the radiance of its vernal glory . . .

'ABDU'L-BAHÁ

INTRODUCTION

THE MANIFESTATIONS OF GOD

The Prophets and Founders of the world's great religions have assured Their followers of the existence of God and have led them to love and worship Him. Thus, for thousands of years, throughout the various ages until the present day man's efforts to understand his Creator have been illumined by the lives and teachings of these great Beings.

Never before in the history of religion, however, has so much light been thrown on this subject as in the Writings of Bahá'u'lláh. Here it is asserted that God as Creator stands above His creation, and that man, by virtue of having been created, can never ascend to such heights as to understand the essence of his own Creator. Any description, image or likeness which may be attributed to the essence and nature of God can only be described as man's imagination. For how can the infinite be comprehended by, and remain within, a finite mind?

'To every discerning and illumined heart', Bahá'u'lláh solemnly affirms, 'it is evident that God, the unknowable Essence, the divine Being, is immensely exalted beyond every human attribute, such as corporeal existence, ascent and descent, egress and regress . . . He standeth exalted beyond and above all separation and union, all proximity and remoteness.'[1]

But God, Whose essence is unknowable, clearly manifests His attributes in His vast creation, both physical and spiritual. The mineral—the lowest form of life and yet the pivot around which all other forms of life on this earth revolve—manifests some of the attributes of God: but this is the lowest form of their manifestation. For instance, cohesion, a characteristic of the mineral, is indeed the manifestation of God's attribute of love in this kingdom.

The vegetable, driving its roots forcefully into the soil and taking away the mineral for its own life and growth, stands above and dominates the mineral kingdom by its power of growth. The attributes of God manifested within the vegetable kingdom are fuller and more potent than those appearing in the mineral. The seed, the flower, and the fruit are all earthly manifestations of divine power.

The next degree of manifestation appears in the animal kingdom which rules over the vegetable and the mineral. In this kingdom some of the attributes of God find their expression on a higher level. To cohesion and growth is added the power of the senses, which are the manifestations of divine attributes within this kingdom. For instance, sight and hearing are inadequate reflections on this earthly plane of the attributes of the 'All-seeing', 'All-hearing' God.

Man, physically an animal, is endowed with all the attributes of God, manifesting them on a much higher level than the animal. He is the apex and purpose of creation and rules over the entire range of life in this world. Yet, although created in the image and likeness of God—meaning that all the attributes of God are manifested within him—man can never transcend the bounds of limitation which are imposed upon him by the Creator.

The manifestation of the attributes of God does not end here. The next degree of manifestation appears within the realm of the Prophets and Messengers of God. Though physically human, and possessing human souls like the rest of mankind, the Messengers of God are endowed, in addition, with the Divine Spirit and, consequently, manifest the attributes of God to the highest degree of perfection. In His Writings, Bahá'u'lláh has given Them the appellation of 'Manifestations of God'.

Throughout this vast creation a lower kingdom always remains blind to a higher one. The vegetable world cannot comprehend the existence or qualities of the animal, nor can the animal appreciate the manifold attributes of the human mind. In like manner, no man, however capable, can ever hope to attain through his own efforts the exalted station of the Manifestations of God, nor can any human mind, however brilliant, ever ascend to such heights as to comprehend Their essence and attributes.

The Manifestations of God, by virtue of the Holy Spirit which animates Them, dwell in a kingdom of Their own far above the world of humanity and dominate the destiny of mankind. Though basically human, They abide in the realms of the Spirit beyond the reach of man. Bahá'u'lláh has described this station as that of the Sadratu'l-Muntahá, which can be translated as 'the tree beyond which there is no passing'.

In the recorded history of mankind there have been only a few such Manifestations of God. They have appeared at intervals of about a thousand years. Krishna, Buddha, Zoroaster, Moses, Christ, Muḥammad, the Báb and Bahá'u'lláh—Each has founded a religion for the people of His own age and, like a perfect mirror, has reflected the light of God to them. His words are spoken with the authority of God. Each is the Lord of His age and His teachings, which become the spirit of the age, are promulgated in accordance with the capacity of the people among whom He appears. He releases to the world of humanity spiritual energies designed to advance the human soul in its journey to God.

All created things, whether tangible or intangible, come into being as a result of the intercourse between two elements which assume the functions of male and female. This pattern is followed throughout the whole of creation and the birth of a religion is no exception.

Consider a table which comes into being when a carpenter chooses a piece of wood to work on. In this operation, the piece of wood assumes a female role and is shaped to the carpenter's design. The table—the child born of the intercourse between the mind of the carpenter and the piece of wood—combines within itself the characteristics of both its parents. Its style, its beauty and proportions, its shape and construction all represent the art and craft of its father, the carpenter; whereas its colour, quality and consistency are inherited from its mother, namely, the piece of wood.

A similar principle governs the birth of a civilization whose founder, by imparting his ideas and principles to a society, plays the part of the male. The society, the recipient of his teachings, acts on the other hand as a female agent. The child of this mystical intercourse is a new civilization which reflects the characteristics of the founder as well as those of the society within whose womb it was conceived.

Religions are born as a result of the spiritual intercourse between God, on the one hand, and the person of the Manifestation of God, on the other. In His inscrutable wisdom, God chooses one of His servants from among humanity and makes Him the recipient of His Revelation. He releases within the soul of His chosen One the spiritual forces of His Revelation, while the person of the Manifestation, emptying Himself of self and human qualities and submitting Himself entirely to the will of His Creator, becomes a worthy recipient of these spiritual energies.

Once this relationship is established, as a result of the interaction between God and His chosen Mouthpiece, the child of a new religion is conceived and the Manifestation of God, in the fullness of time, by declaring His mission gives birth to this child and presents it to humanity. The Báb, the Forerunner of Bahá'u'lláh, declared His station about a year after the intimation of His sacred mission, but Bahá'u'lláh waited for ten years to make His mission known.

Every religion embodies within itself, on the one hand, the characteristics of God in the form of spiritual teachings which are eternal and, on the other, the characteristics of the Prophet in the form of human and social teachings which vary from age to age. The advent of the Manifestation of God is accompanied by the release of spiritual energies into human society. Like the rays of the sun in springtime which give new life to this physical world, these energies bestow a new capacity upon mankind and enable it to attain a higher state of spiritual and material development.

Through His Revelation, Bahá'u'lláh, the Manifestation of God for this day, has released in the world of man the forces of universality and of the oneness of mankind. These forces are exerting pressure upon humanity and their intensity increases day by day. Those who have recognized Bahá'u'lláh and followed Him are, in a mysterious fashion, propelled forward in the direction taken by these forces and are assisted, through His divine power, in their task of erecting the framework of His new World Order for mankind. Those who, whether consciously or unconsciously, oppose these forces—and they constitute the majority of mankind, its rulers and wise men—have set up, within their various societies, forces of reaction which by their very nature are destructive and are responsible for the breaking up of the old order.

Today the Revelation of Bahá'u'lláh has vouchsafed to humanity tremendous potentialities—potentialities which will, in the fullness of time, transform the human soul into a noble being and will establish, upon this earth, the Kingdom of God promised by the Messengers and Prophets of old.

1

The Birth of the Revelation

An infinitely precious, divinely-ordained Revelation, glorious in its essence, dramatic in the circumstances of its birth, majestic in the person of its Bearer, distinguished by the universality of its Message and incomparably rich in the vastness of its Scriptures, was vouchsafed to humanity over a century ago by Bahá'u'lláh, the Manifestation of God for this age. Its light broke upon the world, unnoticed by the vast majority of mankind, from the confines of a dark and pestilential underground dungeon, the Síyáh-Chál of Ṭihrán. Here Bahá'u'lláh, in company with a handful of the followers of the Báb and surrounded by over one hundred and fifty criminals and assassins, lay imprisoned during the latter months of 1852.

Bahá'u'lláh, Whose name was Mírzá Ḥusayn-'Alí, was a nobleman of the province of Núr in Persia. A great Bahá'í scholar, Mírzá Abu'l-Faḍl, through extensive historical research has verified that Bahá'u'lláh was descended from Zoroaster and the Sásáníyán kings of Persia, thereby fulfilling certain traditions that the great Redeemer of mankind would be of pure Persian lineage. Bahá'u'lláh was also descended from Abraham through His third wife Katurah, thus uniting in His own person two branches of the Aryan and Semitic religions. He was born in Ṭihrán in 1817 and His father Mírzá 'Abbás, known in royal circles as Mírzá Buzurg, was at the court of the Sháh.

Almost nine years before His imprisonment in the Síyáh-Chál, Bahá'u'lláh, through a special envoy, received a message from the Báb,* Who claimed to be the Herald of that Universal

* Siyyid 'Alí-Muḥammad (1819–50).

Manifestation of God foretold by the revealed religions of the world. Not long thereafter, Bahá'u'lláh arose to promote the Cause of the Báb, at first among His own relatives and close friends in the province of Núr, and then to others. As a result, several of them accepted the Báb and became active in making His Message known. Among these were some of Bahá'u'lláh's uncles, aunts, brothers, sisters and cousins, as well as certain notables and divines of Núr, a number of whom were later martyred.

To the noble qualities and virtues which had distinguished Bahá'u'lláh's life prior to the birth of the Bábí Revelation were now added the strength and radiance of a new Faith. Thus, inevitably, He attracted a great deal of public attention. His innate knowledge, His insight and wisdom, His indomitable faith, His open championship of the Báb, His irresistible eloquence when expounding the newly-born Faith to groups of learned divines and the public, together with His resourcefulness, His penetrating judgement, and His unobtrusive yet effective leadership of the Bábí community during the imprisonment of the Báb and after His martyrdom—all these brought Him the adoration and respect of that community. So highly did His fellow-disciples esteem Him that they refrained from mentioning His name and instead referred to Him in the plural as 'They'. At the conference of Bada<u>sh</u>t He was designated Jináb-i-Bahá,* an appellation which the pen of the Báb later confirmed.

The veneration shown to Him, coupled with His open proclamation of the Cause of the Báb, aroused the opposition of enemies who had already persecuted Him on various occasions and now awaited only an excuse, provided by the attempt on the life of Náṣiri'd-Dín <u>Sh</u>áh by a few irresponsible Bábís, to imprison Him in the Síyáh-<u>Ch</u>ál. He was arrested and forced to walk before royal horsemen and at their pace from Níyávarán to Ṭihrán, a distance of about fifteen miles, in the burning heat of a summer day, barefoot and in chains. To further humiliate

* His Honour Bahá.

Him they removed His hat which in those days was the very symbol of a man's dignity.

The Síyáh-Chál (Black Pit) was no ordinary prison, but a huge underground pit which once had served as a reservoir for one of the public baths of the city, and had only one entrance. It was situated in the heart of Ṭihrán close to a palace of the Sháh and adjacent to the Sabzih-Maydán, the scene of execution of the Seven Martyrs of Ṭihrán. This dungeon was occupied by many prisoners, some of whom were without clothes or bedding. Its atmosphere was humid and dark, its air fetid and filled with a loathsome smell, its ground damp and littered with filth, and these conditions were matched by the brutality of the guards and officials towards the Bábí victims who were chained together in that dismal place. The notorious chains of Qará-Guhar and Salásil, one of which was placed around Bahá'u'lláh's neck at all times, cut through His flesh and left their marks on His blessed body till the end of His life. They were so heavy that a special wooden fork was provided to support their weight.*

Through the kindness of one of the prison officials who was friendly towards Bahá'u'lláh, His eldest son 'Abdu'l-Bahá, then nine years of age,† was taken one day to visit His Father at the Síyáh-Chál. He had descended only half-way down the steps when Bahá'u'lláh caught sight of Him and ordered that the child be taken out immediately. He was permitted to wait in the prison yard until noon when the prisoners were allowed an hour of fresh air. When 'Abdu'l-Bahá saw His Father, He was in chains and tied to His nephew, Mírzá Maḥmúd. He walked with great difficulty, His beard and hair were unkempt, His neck bruised and swollen from the pressure of a heavy steel collar, and His back was bent with the weight of the chain. On witnessing this sight 'Abdu'l-Bahá fainted and was carried home, unconscious.

* Qará-Guhar, heavier than Salásil, weighed about seventeen 'man' (fifty-one kilos).

† According to the lunar calendar. He was born 23 May 1844 and was in His ninth year.

The fate of Mírzá Maḥmúd was tragic. Notwithstanding the many favours that Bahá'u'lláh bestowed upon him and the unique honour which was his, to share the same chain as Bahá'u'lláh, he betrayed Him some years later by joining hands with His half-brother, Mírzá Yaḥyá, the breaker of the Covenant of the Báb and Bahá'u'lláh's arch-enemy.

While breathing the foul air of the Síyáh-Chál, with His feet in stocks and His head weighed down by the mighty chain, Bahá'u'lláh received, as attested by Him in His *Epistle to the Son of the Wolf*, the first intimations of His station as the Supreme Manifestation of God—He Whose appearance had been foretold by the Prophets of old in such terms as the 'reincarnation of Krishna', the 'fifth Buddha', the 'Sháh Bahrám', the 'Lord of Hosts', the Christ returned 'in the glory of the Father', the 'Spirit of God', and by the Báb as 'Him Whom God shall make manifest'. These are Bahá'u'lláh's words describing this initial experience of the 'Most Great Spirit'* stirring within His soul:

> During the days I lay in the prison of Ṭihrán, though the galling weight of the chains and the stench-filled air allowed Me but little sleep, still in those infrequent moments of slumber I felt as if something flowed from the crown of My head over My breast, even as a mighty torrent that precipitateth itself upon the earth from the summit of a lofty mountain. Every limb of My body would, as a result, be set afire. At such moments My tongue recited what no man could bear to hear.[1]

While Bahá'u'lláh lay in the prison of Ṭihrán, Náṣiri'd-Dín Sháh ordered his Prime Minister, Mírzá Áqá Khán, to send troops to the province of Núr and arrest the followers of the Báb in that area. The Prime Minister—who also came from Núr and was related to Bahá'u'lláh by the marriage of his niece

* The Manifestations of God have used different terms to describe the descent of the Spirit of God upon Them. In Christianity, the term 'Holy Spirit' is used, while Bahá'u'lláh designates this as the 'Most Great Spirit', signifying thereby the Revelation of God in its fullness.

to Mírzá Muḥammad-Ḥasan, His half-brother—made efforts to protect Bahá'u'lláh's relatives in Núr, but failed.

Bahá'u'lláh's properties were confiscated by the Sh̲áh and His house in Núr was razed to the ground. Even the Prime Minister took advantage of the situation and, without recompense, transferred the deeds of some of Bahá'u'lláh's properties into his own name. The luxurious house of Bahá'u'lláh in Ṭihrán was plundered and its valuable furnishings were removed. Some unique articles, together with many more of great value, fell into the hands of the Prime Minister. Among them were part of a Tablet, inscribed on leather by the hand of Imám 'Alí, successor to Muḥammad, which was over a thousand years old and known to be priceless, and a rare manuscript of the poems of Ḥáfiẓ written by a celebrated calligrapher.*

Although most of the Bábís were taken from the prison, one by one, and martyred in the adjoining market square of Sabzih-Maydán, Bahá'u'lláh's life was providentially spared. After four months He was released, but was ordered to leave Persia within a month.

* Muḥammad Sh̲áh had once been eager to own this manuscript, but when he learned that for each of its twelve thousand verses he would have to pay one golden sovereign, he abandoned the idea.

2

Bahá'u'lláh in Exile

When Bahá'u'lláh came out of prison, stripped of His possessions, His back bent by the weight of the fetters, His neck swollen and injured and His health impaired, He did not intimate to anyone His experience of Divine Revelation. Yet those who were close to Him could not fail to witness a transformation of spirit, a power and a radiance never seen in Him before.

The following is an extract from the spoken chronicle of the Greatest Holy Leaf, the daughter of Bahá'u'lláh, recounting her impressions of Him at the time of His release from the Síyáh-Chál:

> Jamál-i-Mubárak* had a marvellous divine experience whilst in that prison.
>
> We saw a new radiance seeming to enfold him like a shining vesture, its significance we were to learn years later. At that time we were only aware of the wonder of it, without understanding, or even being told the details of the sacred event.[1]

Bahá'u'lláh spent the month preceding His exile in the house of His half-brother Mírzá Riḍá-Qulí, a physician. The latter was not a believer though his wife Maryam, a cousin of Bahá'u'lláh, had been converted by Him in the early days of the Faith and was one of His most sincere and faithful followers within the family. With great care and affection Maryam, together with Ásíyih Khánum, the wife of Bahá'u'lláh, nursed Him until His condition improved and, though not fully recovered, He had

* Literally, the Blessed Beauty, referring to Bahá'u'lláh.

gathered sufficient strength to enable Him to leave Ṭihrán for 'Iráq.

Throughout His exile, Bahá'u'lláh often recalled the loyalty and devotion of Maryam and showered His bounty and blessings upon her. To her, from 'Iráq, He addressed some of His Tablets known as the *Alwáḥ-i-Maryam* which are unique in their tone and sentiment. In language at once moving and tender He poured out His heart to her and recounted the afflictions heaped on Him by some of His unfaithful kinsmen and friends within the community:

> The wrongs which I suffer have blotted out the wrongs suffered by My First Name [the Báb] from the Tablet of creation . . . O Maryam! From the land of Ṭá [Ṭihrán], after countless afflictions, We reached 'Iráq, at the bidding of the Tyrant of Persia,* where, after the fetters of Our foes, We were afflicted with the perfidy of Our friends. God knoweth what befell Me thereafter! . . . I have borne what no man, be he of the past or of the future, hath borne or will bear.[2]

Maryam was devoted to the Cause of Bahá'u'lláh. She longed to attain the presence of her Lord again, but some members of the family who were ill disposed towards the Faith prevented her from leaving home and she died sad and disappointed. Bahá'u'lláh favoured Maryam throughout her life, honoured her with the appellation 'Crimson Leaf' and, after her death, revealed a special Tablet of visitation in her memory.

Bahá'u'lláh departed from Ṭihrán for 'Iráq on 12 January 1853. Among those who accompanied Him in His exile was His eldest son, nine-year-old 'Abbás, who later assumed the title of 'Abdu'l-Bahá (Servant of Bahá). He had such spiritual insight that, as a young boy, He intuitively recognized the station of His Father. So highly did Bahá'u'lláh esteem Him that in Baghdád He used to address Him, while still in His teens, as the Master—a designation which Bahá'u'lláh had also used for His own father while in Ṭihrán. He later conferred

* Náṣiri'd-Dín Sháh.

upon 'Abdu'l-Bahá such exalted titles as the 'Most Great Branch', the 'Mystery of God', the 'Limb of the Law of God', and 'He around Whom all names revolve'. Next to the Revelation itself, He may be regarded as Bahá'u'lláh's most precious gift to humanity. He was destined to succeed His Father as the Centre of His Covenant, to be fully entrusted with the Cause of God and to become, after Bahá'u'lláh's ascension, the fountain-head of the spiritual energies released by Bahá'u'lláh for the regeneration of mankind.

Another member of the Holy Family who accompanied Bahá'u'lláh on this journey was His six-year-old daughter Bahá'íyyih Khánum, titled Varaqiy-i-'Ulyá (The Greatest Holy Leaf). She occupies a unique position in the Bahá'í Dispensation and is regarded as the outstanding woman of this age. Her life was so filled with trials and tribulations that few within the Holy Family ever endured a comparable adversity with such resignation and fortitude. To the sufferings she bore with Bahá'u'lláh and 'Abdu'l-Bahá were added the sorrow and anguish she felt for the cruelties which were inflicted upon Them. No words can express adequately the degree of dedication with which this exalted Leaf* of the Abhá Paradise served Bahá'u'lláh and 'Abdu'l-Bahá, and no pen can depict the virtues of her saintly life.

The Greatest Holy Leaf renounced the idea of marriage in order to be free to serve her Father. Over the years she managed, by perseverance and the potency of her faith, to alleviate some of the hardships to which Bahá'u'lláh and the Holy Family were subjected. In her life she reflected the very qualities and attributes which distinguished her illustrious Brother 'Abdu'l-Bahá—the Exemplar of the Faith of Bahá'u'lláh.

The Greatest Holy Leaf played a unique part in the advancement of her Father's Faith. After the ascension of 'Abdu'l-Bahá, it was the Greatest Holy Leaf who, at an advanced age, held the

* Varaqih (Leaf) is a feminine designation which Bahá'u'lláh uses for His next of kin, although He has occasionally conferred this title upon someone outside His family.

ʻABDU'L-BAHÁ

The Centre of the Covenant of Bahá'u'lláh
A photograph taken in Adrianople

BAHÁ'ÍYYIH KHÁNUM

The Greatest Holy Leaf, daughter of Bahá'u'lláh
A photograph taken circa 1895

reins of the Cause of Bahá'u'lláh in her able hands for a short period and rallied the believers around Shoghi Effendi, whom 'Abdu'l-Bahá had appointed the Guardian of the Cause. She died in 1932 and is buried near the Shrine of the Báb on Mount Carmel.

Also accompanying Bahá'u'lláh on His journey was His wife, Ásíyih Khánum, surnamed Navváb and designated 'the Most Exalted Leaf' by the Pen of Bahá'u'lláh. Navváb was the daughter of a nobleman, Mírzá Ismá'íl-i-Vazír. She had a compassionate and loving nature and was endowed with noble qualities. Her daughter, the Greatest Holy Leaf, has described her in these words:

> . . . I always think of her in those earliest days of my memory as queenly in her dignity and loveliness, full of consideration for everybody, gentle, of a marvellous unselfishness, no action of hers ever failed to show the loving-kindness of her pure heart; her very presence seemed to make an atmosphere of love and happiness wherever she came, enfolding all comers in the fragrance of gentle courtesy.[3]

Her faith in Bahá'u'lláh, Whom she regarded as her Lord, was resolute and unshakeable. In the path of His love she suffered with resignation and patience the agonies and hardships of four successive exiles. Bahá'u'lláh in one of His Tablets, which was revealed after her death, in 1303 A.H. (about A.D. 1886), bestowed upon her the unique distinction of being His 'perpetual consort in all the worlds of God'.

On account of their love for Him, two others with the utmost willingness accompanied Bahá'u'lláh into exile. They were His younger brother Mírzá Músá, surnamed Áqáy-i-Kalím by the Pen of Bahá'u'lláh, and the youngest half-brother Mírzá Muḥammad-Qulí who was in his teens. Both brothers remained with Him and shared the hardships of repeated banishments from land to land.

Áqáy-i-Kalím, whose heart was awakened on that historic occasion when the envoy of the Báb delivered His message to

Bahá'u'lláh, was the most loyal of His brothers and a trusted supporter, staunch in his faith and indefatigable in his efforts to shield and protect Bahá'u'lláh. Until 'Abdu'l-Bahá assumed such functions, he would frequently deputize for Bahá'u'lláh in meeting ministers, government officials, notables and divines. His life of service and devotion elevated him to a rank foremost among the Apostles of Bahá'u'lláh.

The other brother Mírzá Muḥammad-Qulí, who was only about seven years older than 'Abdu'l-Bahá, had from childhood developed a strong attachment to Bahá'u'lláh, for their father had died soon after Mírzá Muḥammad-Qulí was born and he was, consequently, brought up by Bahá'u'lláh. He had a quiet disposition and a loving nature and, throughout his life, remained a true servant at the threshold of his illustrious Brother. He was accorded the honour of pitching the tent of Bahá'u'lláh on the way from Baghdád to Constantinople, as well as on other occasions, and often used to serve tea in His presence.

As for the eight remaining brothers* of Bahá'u'lláh, only one, Mírzá Muḥammad-Ḥasan, who was older than Bahá'u'lláh and much esteemed by Him, is known to have been a loyal follower. The others with the exception of Mírzá Yaḥyá, who became the arch-breaker of the Covenant of the Báb and a great enemy of Bahá'u'lláh, had either died before the Revelations of the Báb and Bahá'u'lláh, or remained untouched by the light of God's new-born Faith.

The journey to Baghdád, undertaken in the middle of a severe winter across the snow-bound mountains of western Persia, inflicted much hardship and suffering on the exiles. Bahá'u'lláh remained about ten years in 'Iráq, spending two years alone in the wilderness of Kurdistán and most of the remaining time in Baghdád.

The enemies of Bahá'u'lláh, among whom were the Persian Consul-General in Baghdád and certain divines, eventually succeeded in having Him banished again. As a result of representations made by the Persian to the Ottoman Government,

* One of these was by a former marriage of Bahá'u'lláh's mother.

the Sulṭán's decree was issued and Bahá'u'lláh was called to Constantinople. On the eve of His departure from 'Iráq in 1863, Bahá'u'lláh, outside the city of Baghdád, declared His station to His companions as 'Him Whom God shall make manifest', the One foretold by the Báb and anticipated by His followers.

After He had remained five months in the capital city of the Ottoman Empire, His enemies again sought to banish Him. They succeeded, and He was sent to Adrianople, a city called by Him 'the remote Prison'. There the Sun of His Revelation ascended to its zenith and He proclaimed His Message for the whole world. Having endured five years of tribulations in this city, Bahá'u'lláh was finally exiled to the prison-city of 'Akká in the Holy Land.

The last twenty-four years of Bahá'u'lláh's ministry were spent partly in 'Akká and partly in the surrounding countryside. The sufferings He endured during the first nine years of His imprisonment within the walls of 'Akká were so grievous that, as Bahá'u'lláh remarks in one of His Tablets, 'upon Our arrival at this Spot, We chose to designate it as the "Most Great Prison". Though previously subjected in another land [Ṭihrán] to chains and fetters, We yet refused to call it by that name . . .'[4]

3

The Word of God

The ministry of Bahá'u'lláh is characterized by two features, both unparalleled in the history of mankind: first, the suffering and persecutions which were inflicted upon Him, and second, the vastness of His Revelation. The contrast of light and darkness, of majesty and bondage, of glory and abasement is to be seen throughout His ministry. The history of His life can be described as a book whose pages are darkened by the cruelties inflicted upon Him at the hands of a perverse generation, but whose letters shine with the splendours of God's Revelation, shedding their lustre upon a world shrouded in ignorance and prejudice.

The spiritual energies latent within this mighty Revelation were released by Bahá'u'lláh during the forty years of His ministry. They were destined to revitalize the entire human race and create a divine civilization which has been heralded by previous Messengers as the 'advent of the Kingdom of God on earth'. The vehicle of these energies is the Word of God which He revealed for this age. This Word was not the fruit of learning and knowledge, for Bahá'u'lláh's education was an elementary one, but the emanation of the Holy Spirit.

The Word of God is Independent of Acquired Knowledge

In Persia in the nineteenth century most people were illiterate, under the domination of the clergy whom they blindly obeyed. There were two educated classes, divines and government officials, plus a small number of others. Only the religious leaders and divines, however, could be called learned. They used to spend decades of their lives applying themselves to theology, Islamic law, jurisprudence, philosophy, medicine, astronomy and, above all, the Arabic language and its literature. Since Arabic was the language of the *Qur'án*, the divines attached great importance to its study. Many would spend a lifetime mastering the language because of its vast scope and wealth of expression. They considered no treatise worthy of perusal unless it was composed and written in Arabic, and no sermon from the pulpit as moving or eloquent unless the mullá* preaching it had used an abundance of difficult and often incomprehensible Arabic words. By this means they excited the imagination of their often illiterate audiences who were fascinated by the apparently learned discourse of their clergy, despite the fact that they might not understand a single word. The normal yardstick for determining the depth of a man's learning was his knowledge of the Arabic language and the size of his turban!

The second class included government officials, clerks and some merchants, who received a certain elementary education in their childhood. This consisted of reading, writing, calligraphy, the study of the *Qur'án* and the works of some famous Persian poets. All this was usually accomplished within the span of a few years, after which many of them would marry, as was customary, in their late teens.

It was to this class that Bahá'u'lláh belonged. His father was a senior dignitary at the court of the Sháh and famous as a calligrapher—an art which carried with it great prestige in royal circles. Bahá'u'lláh as a child received a simple education for a brief period of time. Like His father, He excelled in calligraphy. Some specimens of His exquisite handwriting are kept in the International Bahá'í Archives on Mount Carmel.

When Bahá'u'lláh was about nineteen years old He married a lady of noble birth, Ásíyih Khánum. She bore Him seven children of whom only three survived—'Abdu'l-Bahá, the Greatest Holy Leaf, and Mírzá Mihdí, the Purest Branch.

* Muslim clergyman.

In those days government officials enjoyed all the benefits of a totalitarian régime, and were aggressive and arrogant. These men could, by their very presence, terrify innocent people. It was for this reason that many who met Bahá'u'lláh in His youth were surprised to see One Whose father had held a high position in the court of the Sháh, Who Himself stood high in the esteem of all the courtiers, especially the Prime Minister, but Who, although He was expected to lead an overbearing and tyrannical life was, on the contrary, the embodiment of love and compassion. To the orphan He was a kind father, to the downtrodden a helper, and to the poor and needy a haven and a refuge. These heavenly qualities manifested by Him from childhood made Him the object of adoration and love among people who heard His name and came in touch with His vibrant personality.

Although in this society it was the government officials who wielded authority, nevertheless, the all-powerful clergy looked down upon such men as inferior beings, unworthy to enter with them into the realms of knowledge and learning. Yet Bahá'u'lláh, on several occasions, expounded with simplicity and eloquence abstruse and mysterious traditions of Islám in the presence of divines, who were astonished at the depth of His knowledge and the profundity of His utterance.

The revelation of the Word of God has never been dependent on acquired knowledge. The Bearers of the Message of God in most cases were devoid of learning. Moses and Christ were not learned men. Muḥammad was not educated, but when Divine Revelation came to Him, He uttered the words of God. Sometimes His utterances would be recorded on the spot by one of His disciples and sometimes the words would be memorized and recorded later. The Báb and Bahá'u'lláh had an elementary education, yet their knowledge, which was derived from God, was innate and encompassed the whole of mankind.

In one of His Tablets known as the *Lawḥ-i-Ḥikmat* (Tablet of Wisdom), which contains some of His noblest counsels and exhortations concerning individual conduct, Bahá'u'lláh, in the course of expounding some of the basic beliefs of certain philosophers of ancient Greece, stated that He had entered no school and acquired no knowledge from men. Yet the knowledge of all that is, He asserted, was bestowed upon Him by the Almighty and recorded in the tablet of His heart, while His tongue was the one instrument capable of translating it into words.

In another Tablet Bahá'u'lláh revealed the source of His knowledge and the divine origin of His Mission in these words:

> O King! I was but a man like others, asleep upon My couch, when lo, the breezes of the All-Glorious were wafted over Me, and taught Me the knowledge of all that hath been. This thing is not from Me, but from One Who is Almighty and All-Knowing. . . . This is but a leaf which the winds of the will of thy Lord, the Almighty, the All-Praised, have stirred.[1]

The Nature of Bahá'u'lláh's Revelation

The mystical intercourse between God, as the Father, and His chosen Mouthpiece, the Prophet, as the Mother, gives birth to Divine Revelation which in turn brings forth the Word of God. It is not possible for man to understand the nature of this sacred relationship, a relationship through which God is linked with His Manifestation. Our limited knowledge in this field is derived from the words of Bahá'u'lláh, and words are inadequate tools for the expression of a spiritual reality.

The revealed Word has an inner spirit and an outer form. The innermost spirit is limitless in its potentialities; it belongs to the world of the uncreated and is generated by the Holy Spirit of God. The outer form of the Word of God acts as a channel through which the stream of God's Holy Spirit flows. It has its limitations inasmuch as it pertains to the world of man.

Like a mother who impresses on her child certain traits of her own character, the Bearer of the Message of God influences the outer form of the Word of God. For example, Muḥammad was born among the people of Arabia and spoke the Arabic language. Therefore, the Word of God recorded in the *Qur'án* took a form which is closely linked with His background. Because Bahá'u'lláh was a Persian, the Word of God in this age is revealed in both the Persian and Arabic languages. The personality of Bahá'u'lláh, the style of His Writings, the nature of the Persian language, its idioms and its proverbs, the stories He relates of the lives of His contemporaries in that country and the lands to which He was exiled, all contribute to the form of the revealed Word in this Dispensation.

Although Bahá'u'lláh did not attend any of the schools for the divines or learned classes, yet men of letters have testified that His Writings both in Arabic and Persian, viewed solely from the literary point of view, are unsurpassed in their beauty, richness and eloquence. Although unfamiliar with the Arabic language, its vast vocabulary and the complexities of its grammar, which normally took the divines a lifetime to master, Bahá'u'lláh has so enriched Arabic literature with His Writings that He has created, as Muḥammad did in His day, a style which has inspired Bahá'í scholars and writers ever since. The same is true of His Writings in Persian.

Not only will the reader be enchanted and uplifted by the beauty of His style, the eloquence of His words, the flow and lucidity of His composition and the profundity of His utterances, but he will also find that Bahá'u'lláh has originated a new terminology which contributes, in large measure, to a fuller and deeper understanding of the verities of the world of the spirit.

The Writings of Bahá'u'lláh, which are usually known as Tablets, are revealed in either Persian or Arabic and often in both. There are many Tablets which are partly in Persian and partly in Arabic. In one of His Tablets He has referred to Arabic as the 'language of eloquence' and to Persian as the 'language of light' and the 'sweet language'. His Arabic Writings are filled with power and authority and His utterances in this language appear in their greatest majesty and eloquence.

His Persian Writings are beautiful, warm and soul-stirring. Unlike other writers who seek to work in peaceful surroundings, Bahá'u'lláh revealed most of His Tablets while enduring the afflictions of four successive exiles.

In order to write, any writer must rely on his knowledge and learning. He will have to meditate on the subject and undertake research. After much work he may produce a book in which always there will be ample room for improvement, and not infrequently he will feel it necessary to rewrite the entire book. This is not so in the case of the Manifestations of God Who do not rely on Their own human accomplishments.

When revelation came to Bahá'u'lláh, the Word of God poured forth from His lips and was recorded by His amanuensis or, occasionally, was written by Himself. His words flowed with such rapidity that, as attested by Himself in one of His Tablets, His amanuensis was often incapable of recording them.

The *Qur'án*, the Holy Book of Islám, consists of approximately six thousand three hundred verses. It was revealed by Muḥammad during the course of twenty-three years. In this Dispensation, however, the outpouring of Divine Revelation has been vouchsafed to humanity in such profusion that, within the span of one hour, the equivalent of one thousand verses was revealed by Bahá'u'lláh. 'So great is the grace vouchsafed in this day', Bahá'u'lláh testifies, 'that in a single day and night, were an amanuensis capable of accomplishing it to be found, the equivalent of the Persian Bayán* would be sent down from the heaven of Divine holiness.'[2]

As if the gates of heaven were flung open, the Word of God for this age enveloped humanity. During the forty years of Bahá'u'lláh's ministry, this earth was immersed in an ocean of Revelation, which released enormous spiritual energies whose potentialities no one can as yet apprehend. The Writings of Bahá'u'lláh, which constitute the Holy Scriptures for the whole of mankind, are so vast in their range that, as attested by Him-

* The Mother Book of the Bábí Dispensation, revealed by the Báb.

self, they would, if fully compiled, amount to no less than one hundred volumes.

The person who for most of Bahá'u'lláh's ministry acted as His amanuensis was Mírzá Áqá Ján of Káshán, entitled Khádimu'lláh (Servant of God). Apart from being His amanuensis, Mírzá Áqá Ján also used to wait on Bahá'u'lláh and was often addressed by Him as 'Abd-i-Ḥáḍir (Servant in Attendance). He did not belong to the learned class. He had an elementary education and in his youth used to make soap and sell it for a living in Káshán. He came to 'Iráq soon after the arrival of Bahá'u'lláh in that country and his first meeting with Him took place in the house of a friend in Karbilá. It was there that he sensed a great spiritual power emanating from Bahá'u'lláh, a power which transformed his whole being and filled him with a consuming love for his Beloved. He was the first one to whom Bahá'u'lláh gave an intimation of His station, later honouring him with the responsibility of serving as His amanuensis.

Notwithstanding this bounty, Mírzá Áqá Ján, who for almost forty years was so intimately associated with Bahá'u'lláh and His Revelation, ultimately betrayed his Lord. After the ascension of Bahá'u'lláh he rebelled against 'Abdu'l-Bahá, the Centre of His Covenant, and joined hands with the arch-breaker of that Covenant. During the ministry of Bahá'u'lláh, however, Mírzá Áqá Ján assiduously served Him in his capacity as amanuensis and would make himself available to Bahá'u'lláh at any time of the day or night.

Whenever revelation came to Bahá'u'lláh, whether in His humble dwelling in Baghdád, or in the bitter cold of Adrianople, whether sailing by sea or travelling by land, whether in the prison cell of 'Akká or in His spacious Mansion at Bahjí, Mírzá Áqá Ján was invariably ready with quantities of paper, some ink-pots and a bundle of reed pens to record the utterances of Bahá'u'lláh as they streamed from His lips. Owing to the rapidity with which His words were revealed, the first recordings were not easily legible and had to be transcribed again. After approving these Tablets Bahá'u'lláh sometimes authenticated them with one of His seals.*

Apart from one seal which bore His name, Ḥusayn-'Alí, Bahá'u'lláh had altogether ten seals which were made at different times during His ministry. Only one of them bears the inscription 'Bahá'u'lláh'. A few contain passages which describe Him as a Prisoner and the One Whom the world has wronged. Others declare in majestic language and unmistakable terms His incomparable authority, His transcendent majesty and His glorious station as the Supreme Manifestation of God and His Vicegerent on this earth.

Among those who took part in the transcription of the Tablets was 'Abdu'l-Bahá, Who was occupied with this work from His early teens in Baghdád to the end of Bahá'u'lláh's ministry. Many of the original Tablets of Bahá'u'lláh are in the handwriting of 'Abdu'l-Bahá.†

Once the Tablet was written, several copies had to be made for the purpose of disseminating them among the believers. There were times in Bahá'u'lláh's life when the outpourings of Divine Revelation were so profuse that even a number of scribes, working day and night to transcribe His Tablets, were still unable to cope with them all. Some have left to posterity volumes of compilations in their own handwritings.

Notable among these was Mullá Zaynu'l-'Ábidín, surnamed Zaynu'l-Muqarrabín (the ornament of them that are nigh unto God) by Bahá'u'lláh. Before his conversion to the Bábí Faith, he was a learned mujtahid (doctor of Islamic law) and an outstanding figure in his native town of Najaf-Ábád. He became an ardent Bábí about the time of the imprisonment of Bahá'u'lláh in the Síyáh-Chál, and was bitterly opposed and persecuted by those very people who were once his admirers and followers. Later he travelled to Baghdád and eventually attained the presence of Bahá'u'lláh after His return from the mountains of Kurdistán. As a result of this meeting and of receiving some

* See plate facing p. 78.

† See frontispiece.

Tablets from Bahá'u'lláh, his soul was transformed and attained such heights of faith and dedication that he is numbered among the outstanding Apostles of Bahá'u'lláh. After his release from a long period of exile and imprisonment in Mosul, 'Iráq, he made his way to 'Akká where he spent the rest of his days in Bahá'u'lláh's service, mostly as a scribe.

He was meticulous in transcribing the Writings of Bahá-u'lláh and took great pains to ensure that they were correctly recorded. Any Tablet in the handwriting of Zaynu'l-Muqarrabín is considered accurate. He has left to posterity, in his exquisite hand, many volumes comprising most of Bahá'u'lláh's important Tablets; today Bahá'í publications in Persian and Arabic are authenticated by comparison with these.

Another work associated with his inquisitive and brilliant mind is the book *Questions and Answers* by Bahá'u'lláh. Being a mujtahid and thus highly qualified in the application of Islamic laws, Zaynu'l-Muqarrabín received permission from Bahá'-u'lláh to ask any questions he might have regarding the application of the laws revealed in the *Kitáb-i-Aqdas*. The answers given by Bahá'u'lláh provide further elucidation and expansion of His laws and this book is regarded as a supplement to the *Kitáb-i-Aqdas*.

The story, however brief, of the life of Zaynu'l-Muqarrabín will not be complete without referring to his great sense of humour which always cheered the believers. At times he used to make amusing remarks in the presence of Bahá'u'lláh, some of which are even recorded in certain narratives.

Another person of outstanding qualities who performed distinguished services in the field of transcription was the celebrated calligrapher Mírzá Ḥusayn, surnamed Mis͟hkín-Qalam, a native of Iṣfahán who, like Zaynu'l-Muqarrabín, was endowed with the gift of humour.

Before embracing the Faith, Mis͟hkín-Qalam was closely associated with the court of Náṣiri'd-Dín S͟háh in Ṭihrán where he held a position of some eminence. Once the S͟háh allowed him to pay a short visit to his home in Iṣfahán; it was on this occasion that he met a Bahá'í and as a result accepted the Faith. He did not return to the court of the Sháh, but travelled instead to Adrianople where he attained the presence of Bahá'u'lláh. From that time he dedicated his life wholly to the Cause. Later, Bahá'u'lláh sent him on an important mission to Constantinople to counter the misrepresentations which had been spread abroad in royal circles by the notorious Siyyid Muḥammad-i-Iṣfahání.* After some time, through the intrigues of Siyyid Muḥammad and his associates, Mishkín-Qalam and a few other Bahá'ís were imprisoned in Constantinople. They were later sent to Gallipoli to await the arrival of Bahá'u'lláh and His companions on their way to 'Akká. It was in Gallipoli that the fate of Mishkín-Qalam was determined by the authorities; he and three other disciples of Bahá'u'lláh were sent to Cyprus in company with Mírzá Yaḥyá, the breaker of the Covenant of the Báb and the arch-enemy of Bahá'u'lláh.

Mishkín-Qalam was an exile in Cyprus for about nine years, but the influence of Bahá'u'lláh had so permeated his soul that, notwithstanding his long association with the perfidious Yaḥyá, he remained steadfast in the Cause, indomitable in faith, and unswervingly loyal to his Lord.

As soon as freedom came to him in 1294 A.H. (*circa* A.D. 1878), he left for 'Akká; there he attained the presence of Bahá'u'lláh Who permitted him to reside in that city. He was a companion, a devoted servant and one of the Apostles† of Bahá'u'lláh, an artist of remarkable talent, unsurpassed as a calligrapher, and a genius in the creation of exquisite designs from letters and words. Among his works of art are some which have been made merely by the impression of his finger-nails on a sheet of blank paper.

Mishkín-Qalam spent many years of his life transcribing the Tablets of Bahá'u'lláh and 'Abdu'l-Bahá. There are several

* A Bábí who was the embodiment of wickedness. He opposed Bahá'u'lláh and was the 'Antichrist of the Bahá'í Revelation'.

† The nineteen Apostles of Bahá'u'lláh are listed, with illustrations, in *The Bahá'í World*, vol. III, pp. 80–81.

volumes of these in his beautiful writing, and his name is immortalized by his signs and symbols and his design of the 'Greatest Name'.

One of the major features of the Revelation of Bahá'u'lláh is the authenticity of its revealed Word. Unlike the Dispensations of the past, when the words of the Prophet were not recorded at the time they were uttered, the words of Bahá'u'lláh were written down as He dictated them. In many cases the circumstances in which He revealed His Tablets are recorded by His amanuensis, or by other trusted companions and pilgrim disciples who at one time or another were privileged to be in His presence.

The onrushing force of the Holy Spirit produced, at the time of revelation, awe-inspiring physical effects on Bahá'u'lláh. An ordinary human being becomes overwhelmed when he receives news of exceptional import: how much more, then, would the human temple of the Manifestation of God be affected when it becomes the channel through which the Holy Spirit of God flows to mankind.

No one except His amanuensis was allowed to be present at the time of revelation, but occasionally some of the believers were permitted to remain for a short time. Those who received this privilege witnessed a special glory and radiance which emanated from Him. So dazzling was His transfiguration that many found themselves unable to gaze on His face.

One such was Ḥájí Mírzá Ḥaydar-'Alí, a native of Iṣfahán, who embraced the Faith soon after its inception. He first attained the presence of Bahá'u'lláh in Adrianople. From there he was sent by Bahá'u'lláh to Constantinople where he acted as a channel of communication between Him and the believers in Persia and 'Iráq. Later, he was sent to Egypt where he was arrested by the enemies of the Faith and dispatched as a prisoner to the Súdán. The persecutions which he suffered there for many years served only to strengthen his faith and intensify his love for Bahá'u'lláh. After his release, he went straight to

'Akká where he was privileged to remain for some months in the presence of his Lord. Then, directed by Him, he went to Persia where he served the Cause as an outstanding Bahá'í teacher for many years. Ḥájí Mírzá Ḥaydar-'Alí played a major role in the promotion and protection of the Covenant of Bahá'u'lláh after His ascension, defending it most ably against the onslaught of the unfaithful band of Covenant-breakers who were determined to undermine the edifice of the Cause of God and to uproot its institutions. The latter part of his long and eventful life was spent in the service of 'Abdu'l-Bahá in the Holy Land. He died in Haifa and is buried in the Bahá'í Cemetery on Mount Carmel.

It was during one of his visits to 'Akká that Ḥájí Mírzá Ḥaydar-'Alí was allowed to enter the presence of Bahá'u'lláh at the time of revelation. He has left to posterity the following brief account of that memorable occasion:

> . . . When permission was granted and the curtain was withdrawn, I entered the room where the King of kings and the Ruler of this world and the next, nay rather the Ruler of all the worlds of God, was with great authority seated on His couch. The verses of God were being revealed and the words streamed forth as in a copious rain. Methought the door, the wall, the carpet, the ceiling, the floor and the air were all perfumed and illumined. They all had been transformed, each and every one, into ears and were filled with a spirit of joy and ecstasy. Each object had become refreshed and was pulsating with life . . . To which worlds I was transported and in what state I was, no one who has not experienced such as this can ever know.[3]

It has been said that one of the effects of the revelation of Tablets on Bahá'u'lláh was that He would remain for some time after in a state of excitement and, as a result, would be unable to eat.

The Creative Power of the Word of God

The Word of God is the noblest form of the creation of God and it stands far above the comprehension of man. Bahá'u'lláh has warned us in a Tablet never to compare the creation of the 'Word' with the creation of other things. He states that each one of the words of God is like a mirror through which the attributes of God are reflected, and that through the Word of God all creation has come into being. In Islám it is stated that God created the universe through the utterance of one word 'Be', which brought into existence all created things. The Revelation of Bahá'u'lláh which is the Word of God for this age is, in like manner, creative. Bahá'u'lláh has, in some of His Tablets, referred to the word 'Be' as the cause of creation. For instance, in the *Tablet of Visitation* which was compiled after His ascension,* He says: 'I testify, moreover, that with but a movement of Thy Pen Thine injunction "Be Thou" hath been enforced, and God's hidden Secret hath been divulged, and all created things have been called into being, and all the Revelations have been sent down.' Another example is the following passage in the *Long Obligatory Prayer* revealed by Bahá'u'lláh: '. . . He Who hath been manifested is the Hidden Mystery, the Treasured Symbol, through Whom the letters B and E (Be) have been joined and knit together.'[4] When the letters B and E are joined together, they make the word 'Be' which calls creation into being.

The following passages, taken from Bahá'u'lláh's Writings, refer to the creativeness of His words:

> Every word that proceedeth out of the mouth of God is endowed with such potency as can instil new life into every human frame, if ye be of them that comprehend this truth. All the wondrous works ye behold in this world have been manifested through the operation of His supreme and most exalted Will, His wondrous and inflexible Purpose. Through the mere revelation of the word 'Fashioner', issuing forth

* See p. 206.

from His lips and proclaiming His attribute to mankind, such power is released as can generate, through successive ages, all the manifold arts which the hands of man can produce. This, verily, is a certain truth. No sooner is this resplendent word uttered, than its animating energies, stirring within all created things, give birth to the means and instruments whereby such arts can be produced and perfected. All the wondrous achievements ye now witness are the direct consequences of the Revelation of this Name. In the days to come, ye will, verily, behold things of which ye have never heard before. Thus hath it been decreed in the Tablets of God, and none can comprehend it except them whose sight is sharp. In like manner, the moment the word expressing My attribute 'The Omniscient' issueth forth from My mouth, every created thing will, according to its capacity and limitations, be invested with the power to unfold the knowledge of the most marvellous sciences, and will be empowered to manifest them in the course of time at the bidding of Him Who is the Almighty, the All-Knowing. Know thou of a certainty that the Revelation of every other Name is accompanied by a similar manifestation of Divine power. Every single letter proceeding out of the mouth of God is indeed a mother letter, and every word uttered by Him Who is the Well-Spring of Divine Revelation is a mother word, and His Tablet a Mother Tablet. Well is it with them that apprehend this truth.[5]

In another Tablet, speaking of the potency of His words, Bahá'u'lláh reveals:

Every single letter proceeding from Our mouth is endowed with such regenerative power as to enable it to bring into existence a new creation—a creation the magnitude of which is inscrutable to all save God.[6]

The words which the Manifestations of God utter are the outer form of spiritual forces born of the Revelation of God. The innermost reality latent within the Word is limitless in its potentialities. It belongs to the world of God and is not fully comprehended by man, whose finite mind is only capable of grasping to a limited degree the meaning, the power and the creativeness of the Word.

The Word of God can be likened to the rays of the sun which carry its energy. Their intensity in close proximity to the sun is so great that no living creature can sustain their energy in outer space. Yet the same rays, traversing space and passing the atmosphere and layers of cloud, shed a limited portion of their energy on the surface of the earth. Similarly, in this world, the Word of God reveals a limited measure of its spiritual truth and meaning to the mind of man, who, by reason of his finite form is not capable of comprehending these in their fullness.

The innermost reality, the power, the efficacy and the creativeness of the Word acquire greater significance as the soul, after its separation from the body, progresses in the spiritual worlds of God. Although the meanings and latent spiritual truths of the Word of God remain somewhat obscure to the mind of man, yet the Manifestations Who reveal this Word are aware of its full potency and significance.

The Word as the Source of Knowledge

In response to a request by a certain Shaykh Maḥmúd, a Muslim divine of 'Akká who later embraced the Faith,* Bahá'u'lláh revealed a Tablet in which, commenting on the 'Súriy-i-Va'sh-Shams' in the *Qur'án*, He disclosed heavenly vistas of knowledge concerning the Word of God. Every word sent down from the heaven of Divine Revelation, He stated, is filled with soft-flowing rivers of divine mysteries and wisdom. Bahá'u'lláh also gave in detail, in response to the questioner, several meanings pertaining to the word 'sun', adding that this word has so many other meanings that if ten secretaries were to record His explanations for a period of one or two years, He would still not exhaust its significance.

* He made a compilation of all the traditions attributed to the Prophet of Islám concerning the sacredness of the city of 'Akká.

The following verses are taken from this Tablet to Shaykh Maḥmúd:

Know assuredly that just as thou firmly believest that the Word of God, exalted be His glory, endureth for ever, thou must, likewise, believe with undoubting faith that its meaning can never be exhausted. They who are its appointed interpreters, they whose hearts are the repositories of its secrets, are, however, the only ones who can comprehend its manifold wisdom. Whoso, while reading the Sacred Scriptures, is tempted to choose therefrom whatever may suit him with which to challenge the authority of the Representative of God among men, is, indeed, as one dead, though to outward seeming he may walk and converse with his neighbours, and share with them their food and their drink.

O, would that the world could believe Me! Were all the things that lie enshrined within the heart of Bahá, and which the Lord, His God, the Lord of all names, hath taught Him, to be unveiled to mankind, every man on earth would be dumbfounded.

How great the multitude of truths which the garment of words can never contain! How vast the number of such verities as no expression can adequately describe, whose significance can never be unfolded, and to which not even the remotest allusions can be made! How manifold are the truths which must remain unuttered until the appointed time is come! Even as it hath been said: 'Not everything that a man knoweth can be disclosed, nor can everything that he can disclose be regarded as timely, nor can every timely utterance be considered as suited to the capacity of those who hear it.'

Of these truths some can be disclosed only to the extent of the capacity of the repositories of the light of Our knowledge, and the recipients of Our hidden grace. We beseech God to strengthen thee with His power, and enable thee to recognize Him Who is the Source of all knowledge, that thou mayest detach thyself from all human learning, for, 'what would it profit any man to strive after learning when he hath already found and recognized Him Who is the Object of all knowledge?' Cleave to the Root of Knowledge, and to Him Who

> is the Fountain thereof, that thou mayest find thyself independent of all who claim to be well versed in human learning, and whose claim no clear proof, nor the testimony of any enlightening book, can support.[7]

Not only do the words uttered by the Manifestations have inner meanings but even a single letter contains divine mysteries and significances. There is a well-known tradition in Islám—attributed to 'Alí, the first Imám and the lawful successor of Muḥammad—that the essence of all the Scriptures of past Dispensations is to be found in the *Qur'án*, that the *Qur'án* itself is contained in the opening chapter, that this chapter is embodied in the first verse, that the first verse in its entirety is included in the first letter (B),* and that all that is within this letter is condensed in the dot beneath it. This clearly indicates that the Word of God is transcendental in its nature and far beyond the comprehension of men.

The Báb, the Forerunner of Bahá'u'lláh, has revealed voluminous Writings on the interpretation and the inner significances of some individual letters. For instance, in His commentary on the 'Súriy-i-V'al-'Aṣr', one of the chapters of the *Qur'án*, He devoted no less than three thousand verses in explanation of the significance of the first letter 'V' of that Súrih. Bahá'u'lláh has also revealed wonderful Tablets in which He has dwelt on the interpretation of individual letters.

The Most Exalted Pen

Among the inestimable bounties of the Revelation of Bahá'u'lláh are the outpourings of His Most Exalted Pen, referred to as the Pen of the Most High, signifying, among other things, the Revealer of the Most Great Spirit. Never before in the history of religions, with the exception of the Bábí Dispensation, do we find that a Manifestation of God has left to posterity Tablets written in His own hand. But innumerable are the Tablets in the form of exhortations, prayers and meditations which

* The letter B in Arabic is ب.

Bahá'u'lláh has penned and which constitute the most precious part of Bahá'í Holy Writings.

The early believers often wrote to Bahá'u'lláh asking questions, seeking advice or sending information. Many of His Tablets are revealed in answer to such letters, and Siyyid Asadu'lláh-i-Qumí has described how Bahá'u'lláh revealed them. This believer attained the presence of Bahá'u'lláh around 1886 and was permitted by Him to reside permanently in 'Akká. He served the Cause for years, was one of those who accompanied 'Abdu'l-Bahá to Europe and America, and on these journeys often served the Master as cook. The following is an extract from his spoken chronicle:

> I recall that as Mírzá Áqá Ján was recording the words of Bahá'u'lláh at the time of revelation, the shrill sound of his pen could be heard from a distance of about twenty paces.* In the history of the Faith not a great deal has been recorded about the manner in which Tablets were revealed. For this reason . . . I shall describe it . . .
>
> Mírzá Áqá Ján had a large ink-pot the size of a small bowl. He also had available about ten to twelve pens and large sheets of paper in stacks. In those days all letters which arrived for Bahá'u'lláh were received by Mírzá Áqá Ján. He would bring these into the presence of Bahá'u'lláh and, having obtained permission, would read them. Afterwards the Blessed Beauty would direct him to take up his pen and record the Tablet which was revealed in reply . . .
>
> Such was the speed with which he used to write the

* The Persian and Arabic scripts are commonly written with reed pens. This type of pen often makes a shrieking sound when moved in a certain way. The calligrapher could control this sound to a certain extent. For instance, he could allow the sound to accompany the writing of a particular stroke or curve throughout. This sound not only revealed the extent to which a single letter had been drawn out, but also aroused feelings of excitement in the calligrapher and the onlookers. Bahá'u'lláh has, in many of His Tablets, referred to the Most Exalted Pen, signifying thereby the Manifestation of God and His Revelation. He has also referred to the shrill voice of that same Pen. This expression is symbolic of the proclamation of His Message among the peoples of the world.

revealed Word that the ink of the first word was scarcely yet dry when the whole page was finished. It seemed as if some one had dipped a lock of hair in the ink and applied it over the whole page. None of the words was written clearly and they were illegible to all except Mírzá Áqá Ján. There were occasions when even he could not decipher the words and had to seek the help of Bahá'u'lláh.* When revelation had ceased, then in accordance with Bahá'u'lláh's instruction Mírzá Áqá Ján would rewrite the Tablet in his best hand and dispatch it to its destination . . .[8]

A similar account has been given by Mírzá Ṭarázu'lláh Samandarí, who at the age of sixteen attained the presence of Bahá'u'lláh during the last year of His ministry. Mírzá Ṭarázu'lláh, a native of Qazvín, was born of a Bahá'í family. His grandfather was one of the followers of the Báb; his father, Shaykh Káẓim, surnamed Samandar by Bahá'u'lláh, was an outstanding Apostle of the Blessed Beauty. He himself served the Faith with great distinction and in 1951 was appointed Hand of the Cause of God † by Shoghi Effendi, the Guardian of the Cause.

During an interview in Ṭihrán, Mírzá Ṭarázu'lláh made the following remarks:

> In those days Mírzá Áqá Ján, as instructed by Bahá'u'lláh, would first read the letters to Him and then, as Bahá'u'lláh dictated, write the Tablets in answer to them. The verses of God were revealed with great rapidity and without prior contemplation or meditation. By reason of the speed with which these were written, the recorded words were mostly illegible. Some of them no one was able to read; even Mírzá Áqá Ján himself at times had difficulty in deciphering his own writing and had to seek the help of Bahá'u'lláh for clarification. Thus the Word of God was revealed. The greatest proof of the authenticity of the Manifestations of God is the revelation of the words of God. No one else is capable of doing this. The holy Word revealed from the heaven of the

* See a specimen of 'Revelation writing' by Mírzá Áqá Ján facing p. 110.

† See note, p. 241.

Will of the All-Merciful first descends upon the pure and radiant heart of the Manifestation of God and then is spoken by Him. In His Tablet to Náṣiri'd-Dín Sháh, Bahá'u'lláh confirms this in these words: 'This thing is not from Me, but from One Who is Almighty and All-Knowing'[9]. . . . I had the great privilege of being present on two occasions when Tablets were being revealed . . . The holy words were flowing from His lips as He paced up and down the room, and His amanuensis was recording them . . . It is not easy to describe the manner in which revelation came to Bahá'u'lláh.[10]

The early believers often received from Bahá'u'lláh Tablets revealed in their honour. These were their precious possessions. But the most treasured of all was a Tablet in His own handwriting. This special privilege, however, was not often bestowed, especially after the days in Adrianople when Bahá'u'lláh was poisoned by His half-brother Mírzá Yaḥyá. So grave was His condition from consuming this poison that the doctor deemed His case hopeless, and it was only through the power of the Almighty that His life was spared. As a result He was left with a shaking hand and would seldom take up the pen to write. Nevertheless, some special and important Tablets were written in His own hand, including His Will and Testament and many Tablets addressed to 'Abdu'l-Bahá. These Writings even at a glance demonstrate the shaking of His blessed hand.

One of the early believers, Ḥájí Muḥammad-Ṭáhir-i-Málmírí,* a historian and teacher of wide repute, has left to posterity an interesting account of receiving a Tablet in the handwriting of Bahá'u'lláh. Ḥájí Muḥammad-Ṭáhir was born into a family who had embraced the Bábí Faith in the early days of its inception. As a young man he went to 'Akká and was permitted to enter the presence of Bahá'u'lláh every second day. After spending nine months in this way, magnetized by the power of Bahá'u'lláh's utterances, he was sent back to his native town of Yazd with explicit instructions from Bahá'u'lláh as to how he should teach the Faith among the people.

* The author's father. See Appendix II for an account of his life.

In this way, for a period of nearly eighty years, he taught the Faith to hundreds. His soul was so galvanized by contact with Bahá'u'lláh that no calamity or tribulation ever dampened his zeal and enthusiasm and, until the end of his life, at the age of one hundred, he endured many sufferings and bitter persecutions in a spirit of joy and steadfastness. The following is a translation of an extract from his memoirs of Bahá'u'lláh:*

> ... One day I asked Mírzá Áqá Ján to mention my humble request to Bahá'u'lláh for a Tablet, or even a few words, in His own handwriting, because I had heard that one of the counsels of the Báb was that if any of His followers lived during the days of 'Him Whom God shall make manifest' [Bahá'u'lláh] he should try to obtain a Tablet, a line or even a word in His handwriting, for such a possession was immeasurably exalted above all other things. Mírzá Áqá Ján refused to convey this request on the grounds that since Bahá'u'lláh had been exiled to 'Akká He had seldom taken the pen into His hand. I felt disappointed and sad but did not pursue the subject any further. The next day when I entered the presence of Bahá'u'lláh, the first thing He told me was the glad-tidings that He had written a Tablet in His own handwriting for me and that I would receive this. It is not possible for me to describe the joy which encompassed my entire being on hearing of such an unexpected favour.
>
> Some time later I handed to Mírzá Áqá Ján, for presentation to Bahá'u'lláh, a list of the names of some of the Bahá'ís of Yazd, with a humble request that He might graciously reveal a Tablet † for each one of them. One day I was in His presence when He referred to the list of names and assured me that for each person a Tablet had been revealed, but for reasons of safety, I was not to take these with me; they would be dispatched later. On hearing this, I presumed that the

* The memoirs of Ḥájí Muḥammad Ṭáhir-i-Málmírí, written in Persian, are not as yet published. The original copy was presented in 1951 to Shoghi Effendi, Guardian of the Bahá'í Faith, who referred to it as an interesting storehouse of information for future historians.

† The request did not entail that these Tablets should be written in the hand of Bahá'u'lláh.

Tablet in His handwriting which was promised me would also be dispatched to Yazd with the others. But I was wrong. I received this Tablet years later . . .

After some time, permission was granted for my mother to go to the Holy Land and attain the presence of Bahá'u'lláh. She was given the great honour of residing in 'Akká permanently. On her journey she was accompanied by my cousin Siyyid Muḥammad, who stayed a short period in 'Akká and then returned to Yazd. On the occasion of the latter's departure from 'Akká, Bahá'u'lláh summoned him to His presence and, among other things, asked him to convey His greetings to this servant, with the assurance that a Tablet had been written in His own handwriting for me and that I would receive it in Yazd.[11]

Some years passed and Ḥájí Muḥammad-Ṭáhir in his teaching activities encountered great opposition from the Muslim divines, which culminated in his death-warrant being issued by the leading divine of Yazd, Shaykh Muḥammad-Ḥasan-i-Sabzavárí, who was denounced by Bahá'u'lláh as the 'Tyrant of the Land of Yá' (Yazd). In obedience to Bahá'u'lláh's command to protect his life so that he could be spared to teach the Faith, Ḥájí Muḥammad-Ṭáhir decided to leave Yazd temporarily for another province. He writes in his memoirs:

. . . Arrangements were made for me to leave the city in the middle of the night. As I was on the point of mounting the donkey which had been hired for me, a Bahá'í lady, Bíbí Ṣáḥib, one of the most devoted and sincere among the Bahá'í women of Yazd, arrived . . . She then gave me a Tablet in Bahá'u'lláh's own handwriting. I inquired from her as to the history of the Tablet. 'Twenty-four years ago,' she replied, 'when Raḍa'r-Rúḥ* returned from Baghdád,† he

* A notable divine from the village of Manshád, near Yazd, who embraced the Bábí Faith in the early days and went to Baghdád where he attained the presence of Bahá'u'lláh.

† At this time Ḥájí Muḥammad-Ṭáhir was only a child, which means that the Tablet was already written for him in Baghdád years before he requested to have one.

entrusted this Tablet to me on Bahá'u'lláh's instruction, saying that its owner would be found later. It is twelve years since Raḍa'r-Rúḥ was martyred and now intuitively I feel that you should have this Tablet.' I took the Tablet with great joy from her . . . Later on 'Abdu'l-Bahá . . . confirmed that this was the Tablet which Bahá'u'lláh had especially revealed for me.[12]

The Authenticity of the Word of God

Some of the Writings of Bahá'u'lláh which were revealed in answer to individuals are written in such a way that they appear to have been composed by Mírzá Áqá Ján. Sometimes, these Writings consisted of two different parts, each with its own distinctive style, one appearing to be the words of Mírzá Áqá Ján, and the other clearly the words of Bahá'u'lláh. It is an established fact, however, that every word of these Tablets, regardless of their style and content, was dictated by Bahá'u'lláh and that not a single word originated from Mírzá Áqá Ján. Bahá'u'lláh always dictated the answer to letters addressed to Mírzá Áqá Ján. In His inscrutable wisdom, however, He would dictate in such a way that one part of the Tablet appeared to have been composed by Mírzá Áqá Ján and the other by Himself. Some of the believers were under the false impression that Mírzá Áqá Ján had actually composed those parts which seemed to be in his words.

In order to appreciate the confusion which was created among the early believers in this respect, it is necessary to become more familiar with the life of Mírzá Áqá Ján. This man served Bahá'u'lláh for nearly forty years, not only as amanuensis but also as companion and attendant. He was with Bahá'u'lláh throughout His ministry with the exception of the two years which Bahá'u'lláh spent in retirement in Kurdistán. During this period he was for some time in the service of Mírzá Yaḥyá, who sent him to Ṭihrán on a secret mission to assassinate Náṣiri'd-Dín Sh̲áh. Soon after his arrival in Ṭihrán, he managed to obtain access to the court of the S͟háh in the guise of a labourer but, having failed to carry out his sinister intention, he returned to Bag͟hdád fully realizing the extent of his folly.

At length, Bahá'u'lláh returned to Bag͟hdád and Mírzá Yaḥyá's manipulations came to an end. The fire of love and devotion which had been ignited in Mírzá Áqá Ján's heart before Bahá'u'lláh's departure was kindled once again. With great zeal and enthusiasm he began to serve Bahá'u'lláh as amanuensis.

Towards the end of his service, however, Mírzá Áqá Ján grew proud and, shortly before the death of Bahá'u'lláh, he fell from grace. On several occasions, by his actions and attitude, he provoked feelings of sadness and displeasure in the heart of Bahá'u'lláh. At such times it was always 'Abdu'l-Bahá who rebuked Mírzá Áqá Ján for his conduct.

Shortly before the death of Bahá'u'lláh, a certain believer, Ḥájí Mírzá 'Abdu'lláh, the father-in-law of the martyred Varqá,* personally asked Bahá'u'lláh about those Tablets which appeared to have been composed by Mírzá Áqá Ján. He wanted to know who was the actual author. Bahá'u'lláh indicated that the answer to this question must come from Mírzá Áqá Ján himself. 'Abdu'l-Bahá, in one of the talks He gave in Haifa in 1919, refers to this episode. He mentions that when asked, Mírzá Áqá Ján's answer was not readily forthcoming, and for this reason some of the believers rose against him.

One day, during Bahá'u'lláh's illness prior to His ascension, 'Abdu'l-Bahá found the believers arguing and divided into two groups, one headed by Nabíl-i-A'ẓam, the other by Fúrúg͟híyyih, a daughter of Bahá'u'lláh and wife of Ḥájí Siyyid 'Alíy-i-Afnán. (Both husband and wife later became Covenant-breakers.) He immediately closed their argument and censured them severely for creating an unnecessary division at such a critical time.

It was then that He learned that Mírzá Áqá Ján had spoken to Bahá'u'lláh in an arrogant manner, causing Him extreme dis-

---

* A distinguished Apostle of Bahá'u'lláh to whom reference will be made in future volumes.

pleasure. At once, 'Abdu'l-Bahá confronted Mírzá Áqá Ján and rebuked him for his offensive behaviour. Nevertheless, 'Abdu'l-Bahá went three times into the presence of Bahá'u'lláh to intercede for him, each time prostrating Himself at Bahá'u'lláh's feet and begging forgiveness for Mírzá Áqá Ján.

The ascension of Bahá'u'lláh occurred soon after these events. Whereupon 'Abdu'l-Bahá asked Mírzá Áqá Ján to send his long-awaited reply to Ḥájí Mírzá 'Abdu'lláh. This he did. The letter which he wrote in his own hand, dated one month after the ascension of Bahá'u'lláh, is very clear indeed. In it he unequivocally stated that every word of the Tablets which seemed to have been composed by him had, in fact, been dictated by Bahá'u'lláh. Here is Mírzá Áqá Ján's testimony:

> Not one word has originated from this servant. Every word was revealed from the Kingdom of God—my Lord, yours, and the Lord of all who are in the heavens and on earth. Always, after obtaining permission, I would, in His most holy and exalted presence, read the letters which were addressed to this servant. He would then direct me to take my pen and write the answer which, from the beginning to end, was revealed by His blessed tongue. This practice was not limited to this servant alone. Many times has the Tongue of Grandeur* revealed in the words of His companions or those believers who came from abroad what amounts to a mighty book for all the world . . . I was only a servant recording His words in His presence . . .[13]

True Knowledge

In the *Súriy-i-Haykal* (Súrih of the Temple) revealed in 'Akká, Bahá'u'lláh states that in this Dispensation the verses of God have been revealed in nine different styles or categories. A well-known Bahá'í scholar, Jináb-i-Fáḍil-i-Mázindarání, after careful study of the Writings, has enumerated these styles as follows:[14]

* Bahá'u'lláh.

1. Tablets with the tone of command and authority.
2. Those with the tone of servitude, meekness and supplication.
3. Writings dealing with interpretation of the old Scriptures, religious beliefs and doctrines of the past.
4. Writings in which laws and ordinances have been enjoined for this age and laws of the past abrogated.
5. Mystical Writings.
6. Tablets concerning matters of government and world order, and those addressed to the kings.
7. Tablets dealing with subjects of learning and knowledge, divine philosophy, mysteries of creation, medicine, alchemy, etc.
8. Tablets exhorting men to education, goodly character and divine virtues.
9. Tablets dealing with social teachings.

The Writings of Bahá'u'lláh are extensive in their range and are revealed in various forms and styles, dealing with every aspect of human needs, both physical and spiritual, and opening before one's eyes great vistas of knowledge and wisdom. Yet His Writings are simple to understand, provided that the heart is pure and sanctified. The understanding of the Revelation of Bahá'u'lláh need not depend upon academic knowledge; the unsophisticated and the illiterate can recognize its divine origin and understand its teachings.

Indeed, some of the outstanding disciples of Bahá'u'lláh, whose lives shed great lustre on the annals of the Heroic Age of the Faith and whose names are immortalized as the spiritual giants of this Dispensation, were people with little or no education.

The Revelation of Bahá'u'lláh confers a new capacity on those whose hearts are touched by its light and enables them to acquire a knowledge which is not dependent on learning. This knowledge is referred to in Islám as 'a light which God casteth into the heart of whomsoever He willeth'. Bahá'u'lláh describes it in these words:

> It is this kind of knowledge which is and hath ever been praiseworthy, and not the limited knowledge that hath sprung forth from veiled and obscured minds. This limited knowledge they even stealthily borrow one from the other, and vainly pride themselves therein![15]

A deeper understanding of the verities of the Faith of Bahá'u'lláh and a sharper insight into its mysterious unfoldment do not depend necessarily on the degree of one's intellectual capacity or academic knowledge. Indeed, such knowledge has often become a barrier between man and God. Bahá'u'lláh, in one of His Tablets, displays a fascinating panorama of divine mysteries, recounting in wonderful language the appearance before Him of some of the attributes of God, each one relating in descriptive terms its own distinguishing features. When the attribute of knowledge presented itself, however, it wept aloud, saying that it was the greatest of God's attributes and the source of all knowledge in the world of humanity; yet, because of it, mankind failed to recognize His Manifestations.

This does not mean, however, that learning and knowledge are to be condemned. On the contrary, Bahá'u'lláh regarded knowledge as a great gift of God and ordained that religion and science go hand in hand. He enjoined on His followers the study of arts and sciences, advocated compulsory education and praised in glowing terms the exalted station of those truly learned men whose knowledge does not give rise to pride and vainglory. Their knowledge and learning are praiseworthy and meritorious if coupled with the knowledge of God. Such men are exalted by Bahá'u'lláh as the 'billows of the Most Mighty Ocean' and the 'stars of the firmament of Glory' to all that dwell on earth.[16]

4

The First Emanations of the Supreme Pen

The Poem of *Rashḥ-i-'Amá*

To our knowledge Bahá'u'lláh's first Tablet was a poem in Persian, *Rashḥ-i-'Amá*, revealed in the Síyáh-Chál of Ṭihrán soon after the descent of the Most Great Spirit upon His radiant soul. It is a song of victory and joy. Although its language is allusive, His divine experience is clearly proclaimed. In every line He extols the glory of God of which He had become the embodiment, and in every phrase He unveils the spiritual worlds which were then manifested within His soul.

Although consisting of only nineteen lines, this poem in itself constitutes a mighty book. Within it are contained the potentialities, the character, the power and the glory of forty years of Divine Revelation to come. It announces the glad-tidings of the release of spiritual energies which are described by Bahá'u'lláh in such terms as the wafting of the divine musk-laden Breeze, the appearance of the Ocean of the Cause of God, the sounding of the Trumpet Blast, the flow of the Living Waters, the warbling of the Nightingale of Paradise and the appearance of the Maid of Heaven. In language supremely beautiful and soul-stirring, He attributes these energies to Himself. His choice of words, and the beauty, power, depth and mystery of this poem and, indeed, of others which were revealed later, are such that they may well prove impossible to translate.

It is in this ode that Bahá'u'lláh disclosed for the first time one of the unique features of His Revelation, namely, the advent of the 'Day of God' which, at this early stage in His ministry,

He clearly associated with Himself. In this poem He also identified His Revelation with the Day foretold in Islám when the well-known saying 'I am He' would be fulfilled. 'I' signifies the person of the Manifestation of God, that is, Bahá'u'lláh, and 'He' is the designation of God Himself. This is an indication of the greatness of His Revelation. Speaking with the voice of God, Bahá'u'lláh indeed proclaimed in many of His Tablets, 'I am God'. This identity with God, however, is in the realm of God's attributes and not of His essence which is, according to Bahá'u'lláh:

> . . . immensely exalted beyond every human attribute, such as corporeal existence, ascent and descent, egress and regress. Far be it from His glory that human tongue should adequately recount His praise, or that human heart comprehend His fathomless mystery. He is and hath ever been veiled in the ancient eternity of His Essence, and will remain in His Reality everlastingly hidden from the sight of men.[1]

One of the traditions of Shí'ah Islám states that when the Promised One appears He will utter one word which will cause people to flee Him. Bahá'u'lláh has explained in a Tablet that this word is the changing of 'He' into 'I'; instead of saying 'He is God', the Manifestation of God in this day will say 'I am God', and people bereft of understanding and insight will turn away from Him.

The revelation of this joyful and wondrous poem in the Síyáh-Chál, at a time when He was still weighed down by so much suffering, is yet another proof of the vitality and vigour of Bahá'u'lláh's indomitable spirit. It is also noteworthy that only this one Tablet, as far as we can gather, was revealed in the land of His birth—a land to which He was devoted and which was the cradle of His Revelation.

The City of Ṭihrán

During His forty years of exile Bahá'u'lláh often turned His thoughts to Ṭihrán and recalled the momentous events

MÍRZÁ MÚSÁ, SURNAMED ÁQÁY-I-KALÍM

A most faithful brother of Bahá'u'lláh
and foremost among His Apostles

MÍRZÁ MUḤAMMAD-QULÍ

The youngest half-brother of Bahá'u'lláh
Devoted to Him and steadfast in His Cause

associated with the dawning-place of His Revelation. Many of His Tablets extol the city of Ṭihrán, calling it the 'Land of Ṭá' and referring to it as the 'mother of the world', the 'Day-spring of the Cause of God', the 'fountain of His Revelation', the 'holy and shining city', the 'Abode of supreme blissfulness', the 'land of resplendent glory' and the 'source of the joy of all mankind'.[2]

In the *Kitáb-i-Aqdas* Bahá'u'lláh has written these assuring words:

> Let nothing grieve thee, O Land of Ṭá (Ṭihrán), for God hath chosen thee to be the source of the joy of all mankind. He shall, if it be His Will, bless thy throne with one who will rule with justice, who will gather together the flock of God which the wolves have scattered. Such a ruler will, with joy and gladness, turn his face towards, and extend his favours unto, the people of Bahá. He indeed is accounted in the sight of God as a jewel among men. Upon him rest forever the glory of God, and the glory of all that dwell in the kingdom of His revelation.
>
> Rejoice with great joy, for God hath made thee 'the Day-spring of His light', inasmuch as within thee was born the Manifestation of His Glory. Be thou glad for this name that hath been conferred upon thee—a name through which the Day-star of grace hath shed its splendour, through which both earth and heaven have been illumined.
>
> Ere long will the state of affairs within thee be changed, and the reins of power fall into the hands of the people. Verily, thy Lord is the All-Knowing. His authority embraceth all things. Rest thou assured in the gracious favour of thy Lord. The eye of His loving-kindness shall everlastingly be directed towards thee. The day is approaching when thy agitation will have been transmuted into peace and quiet calm. Thus hath it been decreed in the wondrous Book.[3]

The significance of the verse, 'Be thou glad for this name that hath been conferred upon thee—a name through which the Day-star of grace hath shed its splendour, through which both earth and heaven have been illumined', is that, numerically, 'Ṭá' (the first letter of Ṭihrán) is equal to nine, which is the numerical value of Bahá, the greatest Name of God, and this in the sight of God is a great distinction. In fact Bahá'u'lláh in one of His Tablets has referred to the letter Ṭ as the king of letters. To appreciate this, however, some basic knowledge of Arabic is necessary. It is a language vast in its vocabulary and expressive in its terms, and because each letter of its alphabet has a numerical value, it is possible to express numbers in words and vice versa. Literature has been enriched by scholars and writers employing this technique. Although its origin is in the Arabic language, this art has also been used extensively in Persian. It is often considered more eloquent in these two languages to use words instead of numbers. For instance, Nabíl-i-A'ẓam, the famous chronicler and poet, on the occasion of the ascension of Bahá'u'lláh wrote a most moving elegy which he concluded with a verse signifying the year of His passing: 'The Lord has departed from this world'. By adding the numerical value of all the letters in this Arabic verse, the year 1309 A.H. (A.D. 1892) is obtained. This use of words is more expressive than merely giving a number. Bahá'u'lláh and the Báb have both used this art in Their Writings, not only to elucidate many prophecies of the *Qur'án* and the ḥadíth* which had hitherto remained obscure and undisclosed, but also to express some deeper meaning of a name, word or number.

To a follower who had attained His presence in 'Akká and was to visit Ṭihrán on his return, Bahá'u'lláh addressed a Tablet which reveals how much He cherished the city of His birth. In this Tablet He says:

> As soon as thine eyes behold from afar My native city (Ṭihrán), stand thou and say: 'I am come to thee out of the prison, O Land of Ṭá, with tidings from God, the Help in Peril, the Self-Subsisting. I announce unto thee, O mother of the world and fountain of light unto all its peoples, the tender mercies of thy Lord, and greet thee in the name of Him

* Ḥadíth or 'the traditions' are the sayings of Muḥammad or the Imáms (successors of Muḥammad), recorded by those who themselves claimed to have heard them either directly or indirectly.

Who is the Eternal Truth, the Knower of things unseen. I testify that within thee He Who is the Hidden Name was revealed, and the Unseen Treasure uncovered. Through thee the secret of all things, be they of the past or of the future, hath been unfolded . . .'[4]

In another Tablet the following words have been revealed in honour of the city:

Call thou to remembrance, O Land of Ṭá (Ṭihrán), the former days in which thy Lord had made thee the seat of His throne, and had enveloped thee with the effulgence of His glory. How vast the number of those sanctified beings, those symbols of certitude, who, in their great love for thee, have laid down their lives and sacrificed their all for thy sake! Joy be to thee, and blissfulness to them that inhabit thee. I testify that out of thee, as every discerning heart knoweth, proceedeth the living breath of Him Who is the Desire of the world. In thee the Unseen hath been revealed, and out of thee hath gone forth that which lay hid from the eyes of men. Which one of the multitude of thy sincere lovers shall We remember, whose blood hath been shed within thy gates, and whose dust is now concealed beneath thy soil? The sweet savours of God have unceasingly been wafted, and shall everlastingly continue to be wafted upon thee. Our Pen is moved to commemorate thee, and to extol the victims of tyranny, those men and women that sleep beneath thy dust.

Among them is Our own sister, whom We now call to mind as a token of Our fidelity, and as proof of Our loving-kindness, unto her. How piteous was her plight! In what a state of resignation she returned to her God! We, alone, in Our all-encompassing knowledge, have known it . . .[5]

The Sisters of Bahá'u'lláh

This Tablet refers to Bahá'u'lláh's full-sister Sárih Khánum, in whose honour many Tablets have been revealed. She was older than Bahá'u'lláh, a faithful follower and unswervingly steadfast in His Cause. She died in the year 1296 A.H. (about

A.D. 1879) in Ṭihrán, and is buried a short distance from the city. So great was the esteem in which Bahá'u'lláh held her that He mentions in one Tablet that there is as much reward in visiting her grave as in visiting Him. Bahá'u'lláh had five other sisters, but of them only one half-sister, Sakínih Khánum, known as Ṭallán Khánum,* was a true and faithful believer. She endured many sufferings in the path of God and Bahá'u'lláh cherished her with great love and affection. She is buried in the village of Tákúr in the province of Núr, and a special Tablet of visitation has been revealed in her honour by 'Abdu'l-Bahá.

Of the four remaining sisters two were not influenced by the Faith, and two became followers of Mírzá Yaḥyá. One in particular, Sháh Sulṭán Khánum, known as Khánum Buzurg, arose against Bahá'u'lláh and caused Him much suffering and pain. Bahá'u'lláh has referred to her in the following passage from *Epistle to the Son of the Wolf*:

> Ḥasan-i-Mázindarání† was the bearer of seventy Tablets. Upon his death, these were not delivered unto those for whom they were intended, but were entrusted to one of the sisters of this Wronged One, who, for no reason whatever, had turned aside from Me. God knoweth what befell His Tablets.‡ This sister had never lived with Us. I swear by the Sun of Truth that after these things had happened she never saw Mírzá Yaḥyá, and remained unaware of Our Cause, for in those days she had been estranged from Us . . . Later on, she threw in her lot with Mírzá Yaḥyá. Conflicting reports concerning her are now reaching Us, nor is it clear what she

* She was the daughter by a former marriage of Bahá'u'lláh's mother.

† Ḥasan-i-Mázindarání was a cousin and a devoted follower of Bahá'u'lláh. He visited Him several times in 'Akká and, on each of these occasions, carried some of His Tablets back to Persia where he delivered them to the friends.

‡ On the last of his journeys he died before being able to complete his mission, with the result that seventy Tablets found their way into the hands of Sháh Sulṭán Khánum, the half-sister of Bahá'u'lláh, mentioned in the above passage. These Tablets, as far as we know, have never been recovered.

is saying or doing. We beseech God—blessed and glorified be He—to cause her to turn unto Him, and aid her to repent before the door of His grace . . .[6]

A Prayer on Leaving Persia

The initial outpourings of the Pen of Bahá'u'lláh, which had begun in Ṭihrán with the revelation of *Rashḥ-i-'Amá*, continued in the course of His exile to 'Iráq. The following is an extract from one of the prayers revealed by Him as He journeyed through the west of Persia during the cold and arduous winter months; it portrays the sufferings and hardships which befell Him in the early days of His ministry.

My God, My Master, My Desire! . . . Thou hast created this atom of dust through the consummate power of Thy might, and nurtured Him with Thine hands which none can chain up . . . Thou hast destined for Him trials and tribulations which no tongue can describe, nor any of Thy Tablets adequately recount. The throat Thou didst accustom to the touch of silk Thou hast, in the end, clasped with strong chains, and the body Thou didst ease with brocades and velvets Thou hast at last subjected to the abasement of a dungeon. Thy decree hath shackled Me with unnumbered fetters, and cast about My neck chains that none can sunder. A number of years have passed during which afflictions have, like showers of mercy, rained upon Me . . . How many the nights during which the weight of chains and fetters allowed Me no rest, and how numerous the days during which peace and tranquillity were denied Me, by reason of that wherewith the hands and tongues of men have afflicted Me! Both bread and water which Thou hast, through Thy all-embracing mercy, allowed unto the beasts of the field, they have, for a time, forbidden unto this servant, and the things they refused to inflict upon such as have seceded from Thy Cause, the same have they suffered to be inflicted upon Me, until, finally, Thy decree was irrevocably fixed, and Thy behest summoned this servant to depart out of Persia, accompanied by a number of frail-bodied men and children of tender age, at this time when the cold is so intense that one cannot even speak, and ice and snow so abundant that it is impossible to move.[7]

5

The Early Tablets in 'Iráq

Circumstances of Their Revelation

In order to appreciate the Writings of Bahá'u'lláh which were revealed in 'Iráq we must first become acquainted with the circumstances and events associated with His person in that land. Bahá'u'lláh's sojourn in 'Iráq, which lasted for ten years, can be divided into three periods. The first witnessed the dawning of His Revelation and the crisis within the Bábí community brought about by the disloyalty of His half-brother Mírzá Yaḥyá.* The second was the period in which the orb of Bahá'u'lláh's Revelation suffered a momentary eclipse as a result of His voluntary retirement into the remote mountains of Kurdistán; and the third was the gradual rise of that same orb and the irradiation of its light, culminating in the declaration of His Message in the Garden of Riḍván outside Baghdád.

Mírzá Yaḥyá came into prominence not because he possessed any outstanding qualities, but rather through his close link with Bahá'u'lláh. In order to divert the attention of the enemies of the Faith from the person of Bahá'u'lláh, Who had emerged as a focal point among the early believers, the Báb wholeheartedly approved the suggestion of nominating the youthful and relatively unknown Mírzá Yaḥyá as the chief of the Bábí community. This suggestion had come from Bahá'u'lláh and only two others were aware of the plan, namely, Bahá'u'lláh's faithful brother Mírzá Músá (Áqáy-i-Kalím) and a certain Mullá 'Abdu'l-Karím-i-Qazvíní who had been entrusted by the Báb, shortly before His martyrdom, with the task of

* He was known as Ṣubḥ-i-Azal (Morning of Eternity).

delivering His pen-case, seals and writings to Bahá'u'lláh; he was subsequently martyred in Ṭihrán at the time of Bahá'u'lláh's imprisonment in the Síyáh-Chál.

The advantages of this nomination were obvious and, as this system operated for some time, those who were endowed with insight and wisdom were able to see that Mírzá Yaḥyá was only a figure-head, and that it was the guiding hand of Bahá'u'lláh alone that was unobtrusively directing the affairs of the Bábí community after the martyrdom of the Báb.

When the news of the martyrdom of the Báb reached Ṭihrán, Mírzá Yaḥyá, who was then nineteen years of age, was so shaken and frightened that he fled in disguise to the mountains of Mázindarán where he sought refuge. It was through his cowardly behaviour that many believers in that area lost their faith, some even joining the enemies of the Cause. After wandering for about two years in the north and west of Persia, Mírzá Yaḥyá eventually followed Bahá'u'lláh to 'Iráq, but he was so fearful of being recognized that he spent most of his time either in concealment or in disguise. Such was his state of panic that at one stage he threatened to excommunicate any Bábí who might introduce him in public as the chief of the Bábí community, or show signs of recognition towards him in the streets and bazaars of Baghdád.

Yet it was not so much his lack of courage or his unfaithfulness which harmed the Cause as his opposition to the One Who was the Supreme Manifestation of God in this age. Mírzá Yaḥyá became jealous of Bahá'u'lláh's rising prestige with both friends and enemies, as he witnessed the power and majesty of His person and the influence He was winning over the inhabitants of Baghdád, both high and low. Mírzá Yaḥyá was apprehensive of losing his own position, which was already being undermined by the disillusionment of many outstanding followers of the Báb who had recognized the shallowness of his knowledge, and were disheartened by his cowardice and deceit. So, aided by the notorious Siyyid Muḥammad-i-Iṣfahání, he began to sow seeds of doubt in the minds of those who were attracted to Bahá'u'lláh and sought, by various means, to discredit Him and to misrepresent His efforts to revive and resuscitate the fortunes of the fast-degenerating community of the followers of the Báb.

It was mostly through the machinations of Siyyid Muḥammad, the embodiment of wickedness and corruption, that Mírzá Yaḥyá, without any authority and in direct opposition to the explicit teachings of the Báb, claimed to be His successor —a position never contemplated by the Báb in His Writings. Mírzá Yaḥyá, in close association with the Siyyid, created much dissension and confusion among the believers. They were engaged, in a subtle way, in spreading false accusations against Bahá'u'lláh, Whom they introduced as the One destroying the Cause of the Báb and subverting His Laws.

As a result of such malicious and harmful designs, Bahá'u'lláh's trials and sufferings were extreme. He departed one day from Baghdád without informing even His family, and retired to the remote mountainous areas of Kurdistán where He remained for almost two years. 'The one object of Our retirement', writes Bahá'u'lláh in the *Kitáb-i-Íqán*, 'was to avoid becoming a subject of discord among the faithful, a source of disturbance unto Our companions, the means of injury to any soul, or the cause of sorrow to any heart.'[1]

The words of God which flowed from Bahá'u'lláh's lips during the first year of His sojourn in 'Iráq, prior to this retirement, remained for the most part unrecorded. Those, however, which were recorded in the form of Tablets and are left to posterity reveal the sorrow and anguish felt by Him on account of the unfaithfulness shown by Mírzá Yaḥyá and some of his ignoble companions.

Lawḥ-i-Kullu'ṭ-Ṭa'ám

Shortly before Bahá'u'lláh's departure for Kurdistán, the *Lawḥ-i-Kullu'ṭ-Ṭa'ám* (Tablet of All Food) was revealed by Him. This was addressed to Ḥájí Mírzá Kamálu'd-Dín of the town of Naráq whose great-grandfather, Ḥájí Mullá Mihdí, had written an account of the martyrdom of Imám Ḥusayn and had extolled, in moving language, his virtues and lamented his death. It was the recital of this book which provoked intense emotion in the heart of the Báb and moved Him to tears when He was imprisoned in the castle of Máh-Kú.

Ḥájí Mírzá Kamálu'd-Dín was a man of culture and knowledge, and had been converted to the Bábí Faith by a certain Mullá Ja'far, who had attained the presence of the Báb in Ká<u>sh</u>án. He travelled to Ba<u>gh</u>dád in order to meet and receive enlightenment from Mírzá Yaḥyá, the nominee of the Báb. Unable to trace him, he wrote a letter to Bahá'u'lláh requesting Him to ask Mírzá Yaḥyá for a commentary on the following verse of the *Qur'án* by which he had been puzzled: 'All food was allowed to the children of Israel except what Israel made unlawful for itself.'[2]

Bahá'u'lláh passed on this letter to Mírzá Yaḥyá whose inadequate and superficial answer caused Ḥájí Mírzá Kamálu'd-Dín to become completely disillusioned and to lose all faith in him. Ḥájí Mírzá Kamálu'd-Dín then turned to Bahá'u'lláh and requested Him to enlighten him on the subject. The Tablet of *Kullu'ṭ-Ṭa'ám* was revealed in Arabic in answer to his question.

Upon receiving and perusing the Tablet, Ḥájí Mírzá Kamálu'd-Dín was inspired and uplifted; his heart was filled with a new spirit and his soul became illumined by the light of the New Day. Through this Tablet he found the Source of all knowledge and recognized the station of Bahá'u'lláh as 'Him Whom God shall make manifest'. On attaining this state of recognition, he declared his belief and pledged his loyalty to Bahá'u'lláh, Who cautioned him not to divulge to anyone the truth he had found. He was directed to return to his native town of Naráq, and to share his Tablet with the friends there.

This he did, serving the Cause of Bahá'u'lláh with devotion and self-sacrifice until his death in Naráq about the year A.D. 1881.

Bahá'u'lláh in this Tablet, which was revealed shortly before

His retirement to the mountains of Kurdistán, alluded to His intention of leaving Baghdád and lamented the afflictions and sufferings heaped upon Him by those who claimed to be the promoters of the Cause of God.

> Oceans of sadness have surged over Me, a drop of which no soul could bear to drink. Such is My grief that My soul hath well nigh departed from My body . . . Give ear, O Kamál! to the voice of this lowly, this forsaken ant, that hath hid itself in its hole, and whose desire is to depart from your midst, and vanish from your sight, by reason of that which the hands of men have wrought. God, verily, hath been witness between Me and His servants . . . Woe is Me, woe is Me! . . . All that I have seen from the day on which I first drank the pure milk from the breast of My mother until this moment hath been effaced from My memory, in consequence of that which the hands of the people have committed.[3]

Because the Tablet of *Kullu'ṭ-Ṭa'ám* is not translated into English in its entirety, it is not possible adequately to convey its significance. The verse of the *Qur'án* concerning food and the children of Israel was apparently revealed in answer to the Jews' assertion that the laws of Islám on the prohibition of certain foods, contrary to the claims of the Muslims, did not conform to Jewish laws. Bahá'u'lláh explained that this verse in the spiritual worlds of God has infinite meanings, most of which are beyond the comprehension of man, and that He could, through His All-encompassing knowledge, continue to reveal them for many years. But He elucidated some of these, including the spiritual meaning of 'food', and in so doing unveiled in an infinitesimal measure the glory, the mystery and the vastness of the spiritual worlds of God which are without limit and far beyond the understanding of men.

Of these worlds He mentioned four in this Tablet. To gain some appreciation of their mysteries, let us turn our thoughts to God's creation on this earth, where different kingdoms exist together, each one fulfilling its particular purpose. And let us consider the human being who, in this life, functions on three different levels simultaneously. In relation to the lower kingdoms, such as the vegetable and animal, man is superior and dominant. Within his own kingdom, however, man is created to live in unity with his fellow men; whereas, in relation to the Manifestations of God, he is vastly inferior. In this example it can be seen that although man remains the same being, he manifests three degrees of qualities and attributes: those of unity, of inferiority and superiority.

Likewise, the spiritual worlds of God mentioned in this Tablet are of different degrees. The world of Háhút is described by Bahá'u'lláh as the Heaven of Oneness, the realm of the Divine Being, the imperishable Essence, a realm so exalted that even the Manifestations of God are unable to understand it. Bahá'u'lláh has written in one of His Tablets:

> From time immemorial, He, the Divine Being, hath been veiled in the ineffable sanctity of His exalted Self, and will everlastingly continue to be wrapt in the impenetrable mystery of His unknowable Essence . . . Ten thousand Prophets, each a Moses, are thunderstruck upon the Sinai of their search at God's forbidding voice, 'Thou shalt never behold Me!'; whilst a myriad Messengers, each as great as Jesus, stand dismayed upon their heavenly thrones by the interdiction 'Mine Essence thou shalt never apprehend!' [4]

The next is the world of Láhút which is the plane of Divinity, the Heavenly Court. In the Writings of Bahá'u'lláh it appears that the realm of Láhút is perhaps the world of God in relation to His Manifestations and Chosen Ones. Immersed in the ocean of His Presence, They claim no station for Themselves on this plane and are as utter nothingness in relation to Him. In this realm no one is identified with God and the designation 'He alone, and no one else beside Him, is God' becomes manifest here.

Yet another spiritual world which Bahá'u'lláh describes in this Tablet is that of Jabarút, the All-Highest Dominion. The station of those who abide therein is closely identified with God, insofar as they manifest all the attributes of God, speak with His voice and are united with Him. This world appears to be the realm in which God's Chosen Ones, in relation to created things, are invested with His authority.

In the Writings of Bahá'u'lláh there are many statements concerning the dual station of the Manifestations of God and His Chosen Ones. In relation to God, these Holy Souls appear as utter nothingness, but in relation to the world of creation They are endowed with all the attributes of God and are closely identified with Him. As Bahá'u'lláh has stated in one of His prayers:

> When I contemplate, O my God, the relationship that bindeth me to Thee, I am moved to proclaim to all created things 'verily I am God!'; and when I consider my own self, lo, I find it coarser than clay![5]

Similar statements have also been made in Islám. The following tradition attributed to Muḥammad, the Prophet of Islám, clearly indicates the dual nature of the Messengers of God. 'Manifold are Our relationships with God. At one time, We are He Himself, and He is We Ourself. At another He is that He is, and We are that We are.'[6]

Another plane in the spiritual worlds of God is that of Malakút, the Kingdom of God, often referred to by the Prophets of the past. In the Tablet of *Kullu'ṭ-Ṭa'ám*, Bahá'u'lláh has described it as the Heaven of Justice.

Apart from these four spiritual worlds, Bahá'u'lláh also refers in this Tablet to the realm of Násút—this mortal world—which He describes as the Heaven of Bounty. In many of His Tablets He has confirmed that both the human world and Divine Revelation have come into being through the bounty of God alone, and that if His bounty were to be replaced for one moment by the operation of His justice, the whole of creation would cease to exist.

In this Tablet of *Kullu'ṭ-Ṭa'ám*, Bahá'u'lláh describes other meanings of the word 'food' as used in the aforementioned verse of the *Qur'án*. In one instance 'food' is interpreted as all knowledge; in another, recognition of the Manifestation of God. He has also stated that the word 'food', in relation to the Islamic Dispensation, may be understood as the Guardianship of that Faith by the Imáms who succeeded the Prophet. And in relation to His own yet undisclosed Revelation, He has identified 'food' with the ocean of knowledge hidden within His Tablets.

In this Tablet, also, he gives many interpretations of the words 'Israel' and the 'children of Israel', and refers to Quddús, foremost among the Letters of the Living,* as the 'Last Point', a designation which closely identifies him with the Báb, the 'Primal Point', and alludes to the greatness of his station.

This Tablet of *Kullu'ṭ-Ṭa'ám*, which captured the imagination of Ḥájí Mírzá Kamálu'd-Dín and unravelled many mysteries, is characteristic of the Tablets which were revealed by Bahá'u'lláh in this period. The style of His Writings, especially those in Arabic during the early years of His ministry, somewhat resembles that of the Báb. As the sun of His Revelation mounted towards its zenith in the years following this period, the Writings of Bahá'u'lláh evolved a new style, reaching its consummation in the revelation of the *Kitáb-i-Aqdas*, the Most Holy Book, which with lucidity and eloquence manifests the power, the majesty and the beauty of Bahá'u'lláh's matchless utterance.

Some Tablets Revealed in Kurdistán

Bahá'u'lláh's retirement to the mountains of Kurdistán opened a new chapter in the history of His Revelation. Here He lived in utter seclusion for some time on a mountain named Sar-Galú, far away from the world; He left behind His loved ones and admirers, as well as those who had betrayed Him and

* The eighteen disciples who first accepted the Báb.

brought about, through their evil designs, the near extinction of the Cause of the Báb. He had with Him only one change of clothes which were made of coarse material of the type worn by the poor; His food was chiefly milk and occasionally a little rice; His dwelling-place was sometimes a cave and sometimes a rude structure made of stones; and His companions, as attested by Himself in a Tablet addressed to His cousin Maryam, were the 'birds of the air' and the 'beasts of the field'.[7] In the *Kitáb-i-Íqán*, He refers to those days in the following words:

> From Our eyes there rained tears of anguish, and in Our bleeding heart there surged an ocean of agonizing pain. Many a night We had no food for sustenance, and many a day Our body found no rest . . . Alone, We communed with Our spirit, oblivious of the world and all that is therein . . .[8]

Alone in the wilderness, He chanted aloud many prayers and odes extolling the attributes and glorifying the character of His Revelation. These outpourings could have revivified the souls of men and illumined the whole of humanity, but were instead confined to this remote land; and these words of God were, alas, for ever lost.

He also meditated on such things as the Cause of God which He would manifest, the fierce opposition His enemies would launch, the adversities which had already befallen Him and were still to come, and the perversity and unfaithfulness of the leaders of the Bábí community who had stained the good name of, and brought shame upon, the Cause of the Báb.

After Bahá'u'lláh had spent some time in that area, a certain Shaykh Ismá'íl, the leader of the Khálidíyyih Order, a sect of Sunní Islám, came in contact with Him and was intensely attracted to His person. In the end he succeeded in persuading Him to leave His abode for the town of Sulaymáníyyih. There, within a short period of time, Bahá'u'lláh's greatness became manifest not only to the leaders of religion and men of learning but also to all the inhabitants of the area.

His recognition as a man of outstanding qualities and knowledge occurred when His exquisite penmanship was first noticed, as well as His masterly composition and the beauty of His style in the letters He wrote acknowledging some messages He had received from a few religious leaders. It is interesting to note that some of these letters written by Bahá'u'lláh to eminent personalities such as Shaykh 'Abdu'r-Raḥmán, the leader of the Qádiríyyih Order, Mullá Ḥámid, a celebrated divine of Sulaymáníyyih, and to a few others, have been left to posterity and testify to His sorrow and anguish in those days. In a letter He wrote to Shaykh 'Abdu'r-Raḥmán He laments the loss of His trusted Muslim servant, Abu'l-Qásim-i-Hamadání, who accompanied Him from Baghdád and was attacked and killed by brigands.

Bahá'u'lláh's fame thus spread in Sulaymáníyyih and to neighbouring towns. He soon became the focal point for many who thirsted after true knowledge and enlightenment. Without disclosing His identity He appeared among them day after day, and with simplicity and eloquence answered their questions on various abstruse and perplexing features of their religious teachings. Soon the people of Kurdistán, as testified by 'Abdu'l-Bahá, were magnetized by His love. Some of His admirers even believed that His station was that of a Prophet.

One of the most outstanding events of Bahá'u'lláh's sojourn in Sulaymáníyyih, which captured the hearts of the people, was the revelation in public of a poem in Arabic known as *Qaṣídiy-i-Varqá'íyyih*. The divines of Sulaymáníyyih requested Bahá'u'lláh to undertake a task, which no one had previously accomplished, of writing a poem in the same rhyme as *Qaṣídiy-i-Tá'íyyih*, one of the works of the celebrated Arabic poet Ibn-i-Fáriḍ.

Accepting their request, Bahá'u'lláh dictated no less than two thousand verses as He sat in their midst. Amazed at such a revelation, those present were spellbound and lost in admiration at His performance. They acclaimed His verses as far superior in their beauty, lucidity and profundity to the original poem by Ibn-i-Fáriḍ. Knowing that the subject-matter was beyond the people's comprehension, He chose one hundred and twenty-seven verses and allowed them to be copied.

If we remember that Bahá'u'lláh was a Persian and that He had not attended a school where the intricacies of the Arabic language were studied, this poem, from the literary point of view alone, stands out as a great testimony to His genius which was born of the Divine Spirit. The words He has used in this poem are very rich in their meanings and as they blend together, they produce a divine orchestra of spiritual melodies. With the use of only one or two words Bahá'u'lláh often makes reference to a verse of the *Qur'án* or a certain tradition of Islám. In this way, within a line He alludes to and welds together a series of passages from the *Qur'án*, revealing thereby the mysteries of God's Revelation. Each one of these verses is like an ocean created from many rivers flowing together, and hidden in their depths are innumerable pearls of wisdom and knowledge.

After His return to Baghdád, Bahá'u'lláh wrote some footnotes to this poem; in these He gave the meanings in Persian of the difficult words and also interpreted some of its abstruse verses. In two or three instances He even pointed to His own apparent deviation from grammatical rules which, in the circumstances, He clearly justified.

The theme of the *Qaṣídiy-i-Varqá'íyyih* is the praise and glorification of the Most Great Spirit which had descended upon Him in the symbolic form of the 'Maid of Heaven'. There is a dialogue between Himself as the Bearer of God's Message and the Holy Spirit personified as the Maid of Heaven, whose attributes and splendours He glorifies. For His own part, He dwells on His past sufferings, recounts the cruel fashion in which His enemies had imprisoned Him with chains and fetters, speaks of His grief and loneliness and resolutely affirms His determination to arise and face, with steadfastness and joy, any calamity which might in the future descend upon Him in the path of God.

The poem demonstrates the relationship between the person of the Manifestation of God and the Holy Spirit which animates and sustains Him. It also throws light on the immensity of the spiritual domains of God from which all Revelations have been sent down.

Apart from this poem, some prayers and meditations were revealed by Bahá'u'lláh in Kurdistán, which are written in His own hand and have been preserved for posterity. Among them is another poem known as *Sáqí-Az-Ghayb-i-Baqá*. This is in Persian and again, like other odes of Bahá'u'lláh, is soul-stirring and very beautiful. It expresses His longing for the day when the glory of His Countenance will be unveiled to men and the splendours of His Revelation will shed their light upon them. It affirms that those who desire to attain the light of His Revelation must detach themselves from all earthly things, and warns them that they will be acceptable in His presence only when they are ready to offer up their lives in His path.

The Day of God

Bahá'u'lláh also alludes to the greatness of His Cause by stating that Sinai, the scene of the transcendent glory unveiled to Moses, was now revolving around His Revelation and that the Spirit of Christ longed to attain it. In many of His Tablets we find similar statements indicating that this is the Day of God Himself, a Day that all the Manifestations of the past had longed to attain:

> The purpose underlying all creation is the revelation of this most sublime, this most holy Day, the Day known as the Day of God, in His Books and Scriptures—the Day which all the Prophets, and the Chosen Ones, and the holy ones, have wished to witness.[9]

And in another passage He proclaims:

> Verily I say! No one hath apprehended the root of this Cause. It is incumbent upon every one, in this day, to perceive with the eye of God, and to hearken with His ear.

> Whoso beholdeth Me with an eye besides Mine own will never be able to know Me. None among the Manifestations of old, except to a prescribed degree, hath ever completely apprehended the nature of this Revelation.[10]

The statement that the Revelation of Bahá'u'lláh is incomparably greater than the Revelations of the post, and that the Prophets of old were not fully informed as to its character, appears to contradict the fact that all the Manifestations of God are one and the same in reality and, as testified by Bahá'u'lláh:

> . . . They all abide in the same tabernacle, soar in the same heaven, are seated upon the same throne, utter the same speech, and proclaim the same Faith . . .[11]

A careful study of the Writings, however, will make it clear that both these statements are valid. Just as mankind has progressively evolved from the stage of infancy into childhood and adolescence, and will eventually become mature, so Divine Revelations have unfolded in a progressive manner.

Let us consider the growth of a human being from infancy to manhood. As he grows his capacity and powers increase; yet at each stage he remains the same person and retains the same identity. When he is in the state of childhood, he manifests the characteristics of a child; and although he longs to reach maturity, he is incapable of understanding it at this stage. However, a few years later his attitude and interests will have so changed and his abilities so much increased that he will find it hard to think of himself as the same person. For him the child no longer exists and all that is left is a memory and perhaps a picture. But in essence he is the same person. Throughout his life the same principle applies, namely, oneness of identity with gradual increase of capacity.

In like manner, the Revealers of the Word of God are one and the same in essence; yet in each age the latest Manifestation of God manifests a greater measure of truth while containing within Himself and His Revelation the essence and reality of the former religions.

When a new Revelation is sent down by God, the preceding religion loses its spirit. Only its form remains. The power and efficacy with which its teachings were once endowed by the Almighty are withdrawn and the laws which were once the mainstay of its social institutions are abrogated. Its followers, if they are to remain faithful to their Prophet, will turn to the new Messenger of God who embodies the spirit of former Manifestations. If they fail to do this, not only will they be worshipping a form without spirit and turning to darkened horizons but, in denying God's latest Manifestation, they will be denying the essence of their own Prophet. In one of His Tablets Bahá'u'lláh has confirmed this in these words:

> Be thou assured in thyself that verily, he who turns away from this Beauty* hath also turned away from the Messengers of the past and showeth pride towards God from all eternity to all eternity.[12]

Bahá'u'lláh has appeared at the historic time of humanity's coming of age. All that His Revelation bestows upon mankind existed potentially in the Dispensations of the past, but to reveal it then would have been premature. The analogy of the human being will demonstrate this fact, for a child has all the limbs, organs and potential faculties of an adult, but not until he attains maturity can he use them fully.

Through Bahá'u'lláh, the glory of God's Revelation to mankind is unveiled, a glory which the Manifestations of the past foretold. Indeed, Their purpose throughout all ages was to herald the coming of Bahá'u'lláh and prepare mankind for His advent. Muḥammad was the last to do so, referring to Himself as the 'Seal of the Prophets', for His was the last Dispensation of the prophetic cycle of religion. With the appearance of the Báb, this cycle closed, and He announced Bahá'u'lláh, Whose Mission was not to foretell the Day of God, but to inaugurate it,

* Bahá'u'lláh.

as God's supreme Manifestation. These words gleaned from His Tablets illuminate the greatness of His Revelation:

> Be fair, ye peoples of the world; is it meet and seemly for you to question the authority of One Whose presence 'He Who conversed with God' [Moses] hath longed to attain, the beauty of Whose countenance 'God's Well-beloved' [Muḥammad] had yearned to behold, through the potency of Whose love the 'Spirit of God' [Jesus] ascended to heaven, for Whose sake the 'Primal Point' [the Báb] offered up His life?[13]

> Seize your chance, inasmuch as a fleeting moment in this Day excelleth centuries of a bygone age . . . Neither sun nor moon hath witnessed a day such as this . . . It is evident that every age in which a Manifestation of God hath lived is divinely ordained and may, in a sense, be characterized as God's appointed Day. This Day, however, is unique and is to be distinguished from those that have preceded it. The designation 'Seal of the Prophets' fully reveals and demonstrates its high station.[14]

Bahá'u'lláh's Return to Baghdád

The fame of 'Darvísh Muḥammad'* was now spreading beyond Kurdistán. When the reports of His innate greatness and knowledge reached Baghdád, His family and friends realized that He could be none other than Bahá'u'lláh Himself. This was confirmed when officials discovered the will of Abu'l-Qásim-i-Hamadání, Bahá'u'lláh's murdered servant, which bequeathed all his possessions to a Darvísh Muḥammad in the mountains of Kurdistán. On hearing of it, His family dispatched the venerable Shaykh Sulṭán † to Kurdistán to seek out Bahá'u'lláh. He and a servant travelled for two months before being led to Him in the neighbourhood of Sulaymáníyyih. After a

* The name which Bahá'u'lláh assumed during His two-years' absence from Baghdád.

† The father-in-law of Mírzá Músá, Bahá'u'lláh's faithful brother. (See *The Dawn-Breakers*, index references to Sulṭán-i-Karbilá'í, Shaykh.)

time, Bahá'u'lláh responded favourably to Shaykh Sulṭán's insistent pleading that He end His two-year retirement. He returned to Baghdád, leaving behind a host of admirers and supporters who bitterly lamented His departure.

With the arrival of Bahá'u'lláh in Baghdád in March 1856, a new day opened for the company of exiles in 'Iráq. During His absence it had become apparent to friend and foe alike that the Bábí community, left for so long to the leadership of unfaithful persons such as Mírzá Yaḥyá and Siyyid Muḥammad-i-Iṣfahání, had degenerated completely. Most of its members were now dispirited; unlike the early heroes and martyrs who only a decade before had demonstrated with their life-blood the staunchness of their faith, the loftiness of their character, and the depth of their love, they were now devoid of such virtues and were spiritually as dead. And they were divided among themselves. For instance, in the town of Qazvín, the home of Ṭáhirih, that immortal heroine of the Bábí Dispensation, they had created four sects, each bearing a name. Some followed Mírzá Yaḥyá, others identified their faith with Quddús or Ṭáhirih, and some considered themselves the followers of the *Bayán*, the Mother Book of the Bábí Revelation.

It was during this period also that no less than twenty-five people audaciously announced themselves as 'Him Whom God shall make manifest'—a designation by which the Báb had referred to Bahá'u'lláh, the Promised One of all ages, Whose Herald He was. To support their claims, some even went so far as to disseminate their own writings among the rank and file of the community. However, a number of them who attained the presence of Bahá'u'lláh in Baghdád, where they had gone with the purpose of converting Him, recognized His station, prostrated themselves at His feet and begged forgiveness for their presumption. Some, indeed, rose to such heights of servitude and faith as to rank foremost among His disciples.

Once again Bahá'u'lláh took the reins of the Cause into His hands. The clouds of uncertainty and misfortune which had hung over the members of the Bábí community during His absence were now beginning to lift. Through His exhortations and the encouragement which He gave, both verbally and in writing, He breathed a new life into the dying community and, in a short time, succeeded in transforming some of its members into the spiritual giants of His Dispensation.

Bahá'u'lláh Himself has testified:

> By the aid of God and His divine grace and mercy, We revealed, as a copious rain, Our verses, and sent them to various parts of the world. We exhorted all men, and particularly this people, through Our wise counsels and loving admonitions, and forbade them to engage in sedition, quarrels, disputes or conflict. As a result of this, and by the grace of God, waywardness and folly were changed into piety and understanding, and weapons of war converted into instruments of peace.[15]

After His return to Baghdád, the words of Bahá'u'lláh were revealed in great profusion. They were uttered in the presence of some of the believers but for the most part were not recorded. Nabíl-i-A'ẓam, the immortal chronicler of this Dispensation, has written that Bahá'u'lláh revealed the equivalent of the *Qur'án* within the space of a single day and night, and that He continued in this way for two whole years after His return from Kurdistán.

In addition, many Tablets were revealed which were either written in Bahá'u'lláh's own hand, or dictated to His amanuensis, Mírzá Áqá Ján. But a great portion of the papers on which they were inscribed, comprising hundreds of thousands of verses, were wiped clean with water and then thrown into the river at the direction of Bahá'u'lláh, Who asserted: 'None is to be found at this time worthy to hear these melodies'.[16]

The Tablets which were preserved, however, exerted such an influence upon the members of the Bábí community that within a short period of time they were revivified, their vision was broadened, their characters transformed and their minds enlightened. Through the revelation of these Tablets and by His personal contact with them, these companions of Bahá'u'lláh became a new creation and were endowed with great spiritual powers.

6

The Hidden Words

Among the Writings of Bahá'u'lláh in this period, *The Hidden Words* stands out as a mighty charter for the salvation of the human soul. It shines as a beacon of light to men lost in the world of darkness and materialism; it gives light to their eyes, enabling them to see the path to their Lord. It also warns them of the many pitfalls on their way and extends a helping hand at every turn.

The Hidden Words was revealed by Bahá'u'lláh about A.D. 1858 on the banks of the Tigris. In one of His Tablets, He states that certain of its passages were revealed on a single occasion and recorded in one Tablet. The rest, revealed at different times, were later added to these. In the early days of the Faith this compilation was known as the 'Hidden Book of Fáṭimih'.

Fáṭimih was the daughter of Muḥammad, the holiest and the most outstanding woman of the Islamic Dispensation. At a young age she was married to 'Alí, the successor to Muḥammad, and bore him several children, two of whom, Ḥasan and Ḥusayn, succeeded their father to become the second and third Imáms, respectively, of the Shí'ah sect of Islám. Fáṭimih was a true and faithful believer and was much devoted to her Father. His death plunged her into a state of bitter anguish and grief.

According to the traditions of Shí'ah Islám, the Holy Spirit personified as the Angel Gabriel descended upon her and addressed certain words to her. These were dictated to 'Alí, her husband, and were revealed to bring consolation to her soul in her bereavement. She died soon after the passing of her illustrious Father, the Prophet of Islám.

Bahá'u'lláh has identified *The Hidden Words* with the verses which were revealed to Fáṭimih. He characterizes it as the essence of '. . . that which hath descended from the realm of glory, uttered by the tongue of power and might, and revealed unto the Prophets of old . . .'[1]

This marvellous collection of heavenly counsels and admonitions can be described as a perfect guide-book for man on his journey to the spiritual worlds of God. The soul of man is not subject to the laws of nature as they operate in this physical world. Rather, it is animated, sustained and governed by the operation of the great, the eternal Covenant of God with man. *The Hidden Words* not only sets out the provisions of this universal and everlasting Covenant which binds man to his Creator, but also demonstrates the way in which he can be faithful to it.

To understand *The Hidden Words* one must appreciate the dual nature of man, namely, the association within him of two opposite forces, the spiritual and the physical, the soul and the body.

The soul originates from the spiritual worlds of God. It is exalted above matter and the physical kingdom. The individual comes into being when the soul, emanating from these spiritual worlds, becomes associated with the embryo before birth. But this association is far above material relationship such as egress or regress, entry or exit, since the soul does not belong to the world of matter. The relationship is like that of light to a mirror. The light which appears in the mirror is not *inside* it. The radiance comes from a source outside. Similarly, the soul is not *within* the body. It has a special relationship to the body and together they form the human being. But this relationship lasts only for the duration of mortal life. When that ceases, each returns to its origin, the body to the world of dust and the soul to the spiritual worlds of God. Having emanated from the spiritual realms to become an individual being created in the image and likeness of God, and capable of acquiring divine qualities and heavenly attributes, the soul will, after its separation from the body, progress for all eternity.

But the condition of the soul after death depends upon the

extent to which it has acquired divine virtues in this life. If a child is born without a limb, he will never acquire it after birth and will remain handicapped as long as he lives. Similarly, the soul, if it does not turn to God in this life to become illumined with His guidance, will, though progressing, remain relatively deprived and in darkness.

The soul can take with it only good qualities to the next world. It cannot take bad ones. For bad is only the absence of good, as poverty is the absence of riches. Therefore, an evil person is a soul poor in divine virtues. He carries with him only a small measure of heavenly qualities. But a man who has led a virtuous life in this world carries a much greater measure. Through the bounty of God, however, both these souls will progress, but each on its own level.

In the next life, according to the Teachings of Bahá'u'lláh, there are different degrees of existence and, as in this life, those on lower levels will not be able to comprehend the attributes and qualities of the souls which dwell in higher realms.

The highest station destined for man is to be illumined by the 'spirit of faith', which comes through recognition of the Manifestation of God for the age and through obedience to His commandments. To attain this station is the very purpose for which God created man.

The vision of man in mortal life is greatly restricted. Like a prisoner in his cell who cannot see the vastness, the beauty and the order of a boundless universe which surrounds him, man is limited in his understanding of the spiritual worlds of God. His learning and knowledge, however deep, his intellect, however brilliant, cannot assure his comprehension of spiritual realities. Only through the recognition of Bahá'u'lláh in this day and by turning to Him, as a plant does to the sun, can the heart—the dawning-place of the attributes of God—be illumined. It is then that man can understand the inner meanings of the utterances of Bahá'u'lláh and so be enlightened and drawn to God.

Turning to Bahá'u'lláh is the key to spiritual growth. In his relationship to Bahá'u'lláh, the believer assumes a female role, submitting himself entirely to the will of the Manifestation of God and opening his heart to the influences of His Revelation. Then, as a result of this mystical intercourse, the soul of man may conceive, and eventually give birth to a child which is the 'spirit of faith'. The 'spirit of faith'—the fruit yielded by the soul—is especially precious because it is brought into being through the influences of Bahá'u'lláh upon the believer. He imparts to the soul a measure of His own power, His beauty and His light.

Once the 'spirit of faith' is born within the soul, it needs nourishment if it is to grow and mature. Again the Revelation of Bahá'u'lláh and His Word provide this food. By reading His words and meditating upon them, and immersing himself in the ocean of His Revelation, a man can develop spiritual qualities and his spiritual perceptiveness will grow day by day. His mind will become illumined and even though he may be uneducated or illiterate, he is enabled to understand the inner spirit of the Revelation of Bahá'u'lláh and to unravel the mysteries enshrined within it.

When the soul attains the 'spirit of faith', it grows humble. Humility and self-effacement are the signs of spiritual growth, whereas pride in one's self and one's accomplishments is a deadly enemy.

Because of its attachment to this world, the soul is not always illumined with the 'spirit of faith'. In one of His Tablets, Bahá'u'lláh, addressing His followers, has likened the soul of man to a bird:

> Ye are even as the bird which soareth, with the full force of its mighty wings and with complete and joyous confidence, through the immensity of the heavens, until, impelled to satisfy its hunger, it turneth longingly to the water and clay of the earth below it, and, having been entrapped in the mesh of its desire, findeth itself impotent to resume its flight to the realms whence it came. Powerless to shake off the burden weighing on its sullied wings, that bird, hitherto an inmate

of the heavens, is now forced to seek a dwelling-place upon the dust . . .[2]

The chief aim of Bahá'u'lláh in *The Hidden Words* is to detach man from this mortal world and to protect his soul from its greatest enemy, himself. *The Hidden Words* provides a means by which, in the terms of the above analogy, the bird of the human heart can cleanse its wings from the defilement of this world and resume its flight into the realms of God.

Attachment to this world can be described as anything which prevents the soul from drawing nearer to God. Bahá'u'lláh has taught that this world and all that is therein is created for the benefit of man. He is entitled to possess all the good things he can earn, and enjoy all the legitimate pleasures that life bestows upon him. But at no time must he become attached to them. Bahá'u'lláh further teaches that man must take a great interest in this life, work for the betterment of this world and assist in the building of a new world order for mankind.

In one of His Tablets Bahá'u'lláh has made the following remarks:

> Should a man wish to adorn himself with the ornaments of the earth, to wear its apparels, or partake of the benefits it can bestow, no harm can befall him, if he alloweth nothing whatever to intervene between him and God, for God hath ordained every good thing, whether created in the heavens or in the earth, for such of His servants as truly believe in Him. Eat ye, O people, of the good things which God hath allowed you, and deprive not yourselves from His wondrous bounties. Render thanks and praise unto Him, and be of them that are truly thankful.[3]

On the other hand, Bahá'u'lláh has warned the rich in these words:

> O ye that pride yourselves on mortal riches!
> Know ye in truth that wealth is a mighty barrier between the seeker and his desire, the lover and his beloved. The rich,

> but for a few, shall in no wise attain the court of His presence nor enter the city of content and resignation. Well is it then with him, who, being rich, is not hindered by his riches from the eternal kingdom, nor deprived by them of imperishable dominion. By the Most Great Name! The splendour of such a wealthy man shall illuminate the dwellers of heaven even as the sun enlightens the people of the earth![4]

Whereas riches may become a mighty barrier between man and God, and rich people are often in great danger of attachment, yet people with small worldly possessions can also become attached to material things. The following Persian story of a king and a dervish* illustrates this. Once there was a king who had many spiritual qualities and whose deeds were based on justice and loving-kindness. He often envied the dervish who had renounced the world and appeared to be free from the cares of this material life, for he roamed the country, slept in any place when night fell and chanted the praises of his Lord during the day. He lived in poverty, yet thought he owned the whole world. His only possessions were his clothes and a basket in which he carried the food donated by his well-wishers. The king was attracted to this way of life.

Once he invited a well-known dervish to his palace, sat at his feet and begged him for some lessons about detachment. The dervish was delighted with the invitation. He stayed a few days in the palace and whenever the king was free preached the virtues of a mendicant's life to him. At last the king was converted. One day, dressed in the garb of a poor man, he left his palace in the company of the dervish. They had walked together some distance when the dervish realized that he had left his basket behind in the palace. This disturbed him greatly and, informing the king that he could not go without his basket, he begged permission to return for it. But the king admonished him, saying that he himself had left behind his palaces, his wealth and power, whereas the dervish, who had preached for

* A Muslim, often a mystic, who renounces the world and communes with God, subsisting on the charity of his fellow men.

a lifetime the virtues of detachment, had at last been tested and was found to be attached to this world—his small basket.

The possession of earthly goods is often misunderstood to be the only form of attachment. But this is not so. Man's pride in his accomplishments, his knowledge, his position, his popularity within society and, above all, his love for his own self are some of the barriers which come between him and God. To rid oneself of these attachments is not easy. It can be a painful process and may indeed prove to be a spiritual battle which lasts a lifetime.

The Hidden Words can exert a potent influence in freeing man from the fetters of materialism and enabling him to win the battle against his own self. In a Tablet to one of the teachers of the Cause—Mírzá 'Abbás known as Qábil, a native of Ábádih* —'Abdu'l-Bahá urged him to peruse the verses of *The Hidden Words* by day and night, and to supplicate God to enable him to carry out the exhortations of the Blessed Beauty.† In the same Tablet He makes it clear that *The Hidden Words* is not merely to be read. Rather, it was given to the believers by Bahá'u'lláh to enable them to put into practice His counsels and commandments.

Qábil's life of service and dedication is clearly indicative of a potent and transforming influence on his soul, partly derived from his chanting of some passages of *The Hidden Words* every day.

He was a zealous and enthusiastic man, a poet of remarkable talent, a teacher of wide repute and, above all, devoted to Bahá'u'lláh. He lived to old age, after suffering many persecutions and spending much of his life in travel and teaching. He used to stay at home with his family only a few months each year; the rest of the time he travelled long distances on a

* A town historic for its burial-place of over two hundred martyrs' heads. These were brought there, via Shíráz, carried aloft on bayonets, and accompanied mainly by the female next of kin who were forced to walk some of the way from the town of Nayríz (over two hundred miles).

† Bahá'u'lláh.

donkey, riding from village to village and town to town. His enthusiastic spirit, coupled with his deep love for Bahá'u'lláh, cheered and uplifted the believers whom he met on his way. They would gather to meet him and he would often request them, whenever circumstances permitted, to chant in unison certain Tablets or poems of Bahá'u'lláh which lent themselves to collective chanting, and would teach them to sing together some of his own beautiful, soul-stirring songs composed in praise and glorification of Bahá'u'lláh, 'Abdu'l-Bahá or Shoghi Effendi.*

In those days the playing of musical instruments was frowned upon by the Muslim clergy, and the Bahá'ís were careful not to upset a fanatical populace by playing them. But Qábil had a certain genius in clapping his hands to accompany their songs of love and praise. Where greater freedom prevailed, a home-made drum was a welcome accompaniment to his chant of love for Bahá'u'lláh. The believers, who were often oppressed and persecuted, always welcomed the few days that Qábil spent with them, for he created joy and enthusiasm wherever he went.

Bahá'u'lláh has referred to the revelation of *The Hidden Words* in these terms:

> The mystic and wondrous Bride, hidden ere this beneath the veiling of utterance, hath now, by the grace of God and His divine favour, been made manifest even as the resplendent light shed by the beauty of the Beloved. I bear witness, O friends! that the favour is complete, the argument fulfilled, the proof manifest and the evidence established. Let it now be seen what your endeavours in the path of detachment will reveal. In this wise hath the divine favour been fully vouchsafed unto you and unto them that are in heaven and on earth. All praise to God, the Lord of all Worlds.[5]

In this book, within the compass of a few pages, Bahá'u'lláh has given to humanity a prescription which safeguards its well-

* The eldest grandson of 'Abdu'l-Bahá, appointed by Him as His successor and 'Guardian of the Cause of God'.

THE SEALS OF BAHÁ'U'LLÁH

Displayed in an ornamental Persian design
(As reproduced in *The Bahá'í World*, vol. V, p. 4)

MULLÁ ZAYNU'L-'ÁBIDÍN

A noted scribe and Apostle of Bahá'u'lláh surnamed by Him Zaynu'l-Muqarrabín

being and happiness. Speaking with the voice of God, He addresses man and exhorts him to 'possess a pure, kindly and radiant heart'; He stresses the importance of cleansing his heart, which is the dawning-place of the Revelation of God, from the influences of the ungodly; calls on him to 'cast out . . . the stranger, that the Friend may enter His home'; advises him not to seek fellowship with the ungodly as this would turn 'the radiance of the heart into infernal fire'; and assures him of the immortality of the soul. He also affirms that God has placed within him 'the essence' of His 'light' which 'shall never be extinguished'; He confidently asserts that God has 'made death a messenger of joy' to man; establishes a Covenant with him to love God; enjoins on him to cling to justice, forbearance and love; reminds him that the 'healer' of all his ills is 'remembrance' of God; and describes the merits of turning to God in prayer at the hour of dawn. He counsels man to detach himself from this world, and not to abandon God's 'imperishable dominion' for a 'fleeting sovereignty'; rebukes him for his heedlessness, his indulgence of self and passion; directs him to avoid covetousness, envy, pride and vainglory; declares that the tongue is designed for the mention of God, that it should not be defiled with detraction and backbiting; mentions that the 'best of men are they that earn a livelihood by their calling and spend upon themselves and upon their kindred for the love of God'; denounces the 'idle and worthless souls' who 'yield no fruit on earth' as the 'basest of men'; speaks of the greatness of His Revelation; grieves that only a few souls have been found receptive to His Call and that of 'these few' only a 'handful hath been found with a pure heart and sanctified spirit'. He warns man to 'withdraw' his hand from 'tyranny'; pledges 'not to forgive any man's injustice' in this day; foreshadows 'an unforeseen calamity' and a 'grievous retribution' following man by reason of the deeds that he has committed; admonishes the rich to bestow their wealth upon the poor; states that 'wealth is a mighty barrier between the seeker and his desire, the lover and his beloved'; exalts the station of a rich man who is detached from his wealth to such a position that his 'splendour . . . shall illuminate the dwellers of heaven even as the sun enlightens the people of the earth'; urges everyone to 'show forth deeds that are pure and holy';[6] and describes the powers latent within man in these words:

> O Son of Spirit!
> I created thee rich, why dost thou bring thyself down to poverty? Noble I made thee, wherewith dost thou abase thyself? Out of the essence of knowledge I gave thee being, why seekest thou enlightenment from anyone beside Me? Out of the clay of love I moulded thee, how dost thou busy thyself with another? Turn thy sight unto thyself, that thou mayest find Me standing within thee, mighty, powerful and self-subsisting.[7]

There are a few passages in *The Hidden Words* which refer implicitly to the Covenant of Bahá'u'lláh—a Covenant which later became explicit with the revelation of the Will and Testament of Bahá'u'lláh, designated by Him the *Kitáb-i-'Ahdí* (The Book of My Covenant).

'Abdu'l-Bahá, Who is the Centre of that same Covenant and the appointed Interpreter of the words of Bahá'u'lláh, has explained the meaning of some of these passages. One instance is the following:

> O My Friends!
> Have ye forgotten that true and radiant morn, when in those hallowed and blessed surroundings ye were all gathered in My presence beneath the shade of the tree of life, which is planted in the all-glorious paradise? Awestruck ye listened as I gave utterance to these three most holy words: O friends! Prefer not your will to Mine, never desire that which I have not desired for you, and approach Me not with lifeless hearts, defiled with worldly desires and cravings. Would ye but sanctify your souls, ye would at this present hour recall that place and those surroundings, and the truth of My utterance should be made evident unto all of you.[8]

The 'true and radiant morn', 'Abdu'l-Bahá stated, refers to the Revelation of the Báb, the 'tree of life' to Bahá'u'lláh, and the 'hallowed and blessed surroundings' to the heart of the individual. He further explained that the gathering referred to in this verse was not a physical but a spiritual one. The call of God was raised within the sanctuary of their hearts; but they did not respond and were bewildered and awestruck.

In other Tablets, 'Abdu'l-Bahá interpreted the meaning of the gathering beneath the shade of the 'tree of life' as the establishment of the Covenant of Bahá'u'lláh. 'The Lord, the All-Glorified,' in the words of 'Abdu'l-Bahá, 'hath, beneath the shade of the Tree of Anísá [tree of life], made a new Covenant and established a great Testament . . .'[9] That this Covenant was established at so early a stage in the ministry of Bahá'u'lláh is one of the mysteries of Divine Revelation. Indeed, in a Tablet 'Abdu'l-Bahá stated that when the day-star of the Revelation of Bahá'u'lláh dawned upon humanity, the first ray which shed its light upon those gathered beneath the 'tree of life' was that of the Covenant of Bahá'u'lláh.

Another passage in *The Hidden Words* which refers to this Covenant is the following:

> O My Friends!
>
> Call ye to mind that covenant ye have entered into with Me upon Mount Párán, situate within the hallowed precincts of Zaman. I have taken to witness the concourse on high* and the dwellers in the city of eternity, yet now none do I find faithful unto the covenant. Of a certainty pride and rebellion have effaced it from the hearts, in such wise that no trace thereof remaineth. Yet knowing this, I waited and disclosed it not.[10]

'Abdu'l-Bahá has stated that the covenant upon Mount Párán refers to the Covenant of Bahá'u'lláh which was written by the Exalted Pen in the Holy Land and which was announced there after His ascension.

* The gathering of the holy souls in the next world.

Finally, the 'wings' and the 'comb' mentioned in the following verse are both interpreted by 'Abdu'l-Bahá as the Covenant of Bahá'u'lláh.

> O Son of Desire!
> How long wilt thou soar in the realms of desire? Wings have I bestowed upon thee, that thou mayest fly to the realms of mystic holiness and not the regions of satanic fancy. The comb, too, have I given thee that thou mayest dress My raven locks, and not lacerate My throat.[11]

In *The Hidden Words* Bahá'u'lláh has mentioned certain Tablets such as 'the fifth Tablet of Paradise', and the 'Ruby Tablet', together with certain lines from them.[12] 'Abdu'l-Bahá has clearly indicated that none of these Tablets or lines has been revealed in this world. They are preserved in the Kingdom of God and in the realms of heaven.

There is another passage in *The Hidden Words* which is of great significance inasmuch as it reveals the nature and intensity of the Revelation of Bahá'u'lláh and His exalted station. It is the following:

> O Son of Justice!
> In the night-season the beauty of the immortal Being hath repaired from the emerald height of fidelity unto the Sadratu'l-Muntahá, and wept with such a weeping that the concourse on high and the dwellers of the realms above wailed at His lamenting. Whereupon there was asked, Why the wailing and weeping? He made reply: As bidden I waited expectant upon the hill of faithfulness, yet inhaled not from them that dwell on earth the fragrance of fidelity. Then summoned to return I beheld, and lo! certain doves of holiness were sore tried within the claws of the dogs of earth. Thereupon the Maid of heaven hastened forth unveiled and resplendent from Her mystic mansion, and asked of their names, and all were told but one. And when urged, the first letter thereof was uttered, whereupon the dwellers of the celestial chambers rushed forth out of their habitation of glory. And whilst the second letter was pronounced they fell

down, one and all, upon the dust. At that moment a voice was heard from the inmost shrine: 'Thus far and no farther.' Verily we bear witness to that which they have done and now are doing.[13]

'Sadratu'l-Muntahá' in this passage literally means the tree beyond which there is no passing. The Arabs used to plant trees along certain roads and the last tree indicating the end of the road was known as 'Sadratu'l-Muntahá'. This term which has been used by Bahá'u'lláh in many of His Writings is, in one sense, the symbol of the station of the Manifestation of God, a station which is beyond the reach and understanding of men. The 'Maid of Heaven' in the Writings of Bahá'u'lláh is a symbolic term and assumes different meanings.*

The two letters mentioned in the above passage, according to 'Abdu'l-Bahá's interpretation, are B and H of the word 'Bahá'.[14] This means that only two letters out of three (B, H and A) have been revealed in this Dispensation, that the full significance and potency of the Revelation of Bahá'u'lláh which have been symbolically contained within the three letters of His name, have not been disclosed to mankind and that only a limited measure of His light and glory has been shed upon humanity in this age.† To this Bahá'u'lláh has testified in one of His Tablets:

> Know verily that the veil hiding Our countenance hath not been completely lifted. We have revealed Our Self to a degree corresponding to the capacity of the people of Our age. Should the Ancient Beauty be unveiled in the fullness of His glory mortal eyes would be blinded by the dazzling intensity of His revelation.[15]

* See p. 242.

† The word 'Bahá' in Arabic is composed of three letters. This statement should not be confused with a tradition of Islám that knowledge consists of twenty-seven letters, only two of which were revealed by the Prophets preceding the Báb. See p. 216.

7

Some Early Believers

It was not long after Bahá'u'lláh's return from Sulaymáníyyih that His Writings began to reach the Bábís in Persia. This gave them fresh hope and new vision. Some were inspired by these Writings; others were so moved and excited as to undertake, in some cases on foot and with extremely limited resources, the long and hazardous journey to Baghdád in the hope of attaining His presence and discovering in His person the mystery of God's Revelation which was to come; and a few who were endowed with spiritual insight, through the mere perusal of these Writings, recognized in Him the One designated by the Báb as 'Him Whom God shall make manifest'.

Mullá Riḍá of Muḥammad-Ábád

A notable example of a man of insight was Mullá Muḥammad-Riḍá, a native of Muḥammad-Ábád in the province of Yazd. He was a divine known for his piety, eloquence and courage. He had embraced the Bábí Faith in the early years of its inception and became a great light among the followers of the Báb in Yazd. The following is a brief account of how he recognized the station of Bahá'u'lláh.

Soon after the return of Bahá'u'lláh from Kurdistán, a well-known Bábí surnamed Raḍa'r-Rúḥ, noted for his knowledge and learning, travelled to Baghdád and attained His presence. Although he met Bahá'u'lláh face to face, he failed at that time to recognize the full glory of His station. On his return to Yazd, Raḍa'r-Rúḥ shared with Mullá Riḍá the *Qaṣídiy-i-Varqá'íyyih* revealed by the Pen of Bahá'u'lláh. Upon perusing this single

Tablet, Mullá Riḍá, through the purity of his heart and the clarity of his vision, recognized Bahá'u'lláh and exclaimed with great joy: 'I can see the Promised One of the *Bayán* made manifest and seated upon the throne of the words which have been revealed in this Tablet'.[1] Raḍa'r-Rúḥ, who had actually attained the presence of Bahá'u'lláh in Baghdád, became somewhat perturbed by the attitude and claims of Mullá Riḍá, and pointed out that Bahá'u'lláh Himself had not made such a claim. After some time, however, Raḍa'r-Rúḥ also accepted Bahá'u'lláh and His Faith, suffered much persecution in His path and, finally, about the year 1868 died a martyr's death in the village of Mihríz outside Yazd.

The story of Mullá Riḍá's life is a fascinating one. The following account is based on a biography of him:

> Mullá Riḍá belonged to a well-known family and had received his education as a Muslim clergyman. From the time he embraced the Cause till the very moment he passed away in Ṭihrán prison his whole life was dedicated to teaching work. He ought to be regarded as a great hero whom the Almighty had raised in the early days of the Cause to proclaim His Message and upon whom He had bestowed a sword-like power of utterance with which he tore asunder the veils of ignorance and superstition, and by doing so constantly exposed himself to intense pain and suffering. In fact, seldom a day passed without his being handed a cup of woeful trials which he would sip with abundant joy and satisfaction.
>
> Mullá Riḍá was an old man with a tall and shapely stature that enhanced his dignified bearing. His mode of behaviour was governed by a rare combination of frankness, humour, eloquence and exceptional courage, and dominated by his passionate love for Bahá'u'lláh. No one is known to have surpassed his unusual power of endurance. Of him it is authoritatively said by the friends that while he was detained in Yazd for Bahá'í activities and prior to his expulsion from the town, the Governor ordered that the bastinado* be

* The victim is made to lie on his back while his feet, inserted in a loop, are raised and the soles beaten with a cane or a whip.

inflicted on him in public at seven crossroads during a single day so as to dissuade the inhabitants from going over to the new creed. At each appointed spot, Mullá Riḍá would remove his abá [cloak], turban and socks and place them on a handkerchief which he would spread on the ground; then after lying down and inserting his feet into the loop, he would cover his face with the hem of his garment and ask his persecutors to proceed. At no time during these rounds of torture did he breathe a word, or make a sign or move that implied a painful feeling. At one point his unusual calm in the face of brutal lashings made the stupefied onlookers imagine that the victim had collapsed. However, when his face was uncovered, they found him cleaning his teeth in a quiet manner!

As a teacher, Mullá Riḍá was highly qualified, exceptionally well-informed and audacious. No one could rival him in speech or in the knowledge of the *Qur'án* and Islamic law and tradition. While in Ṭihrán prison, he was summoned on several occasions to answer questions about the Faith at gatherings of princes and notables of the realm. And at each session he prevailed over his distinguished opponents in argument and laid bare their ignorance and the absurdity of their notions.

Mullá Riḍá was a man of broad vision and great enterprise, though sometimes his imagination seemed to be bordering on the fantastic. For instance, he had a firm conviction that the organic unity of all substances will be established during the Bahá'í era and moreover he is quoted to have said that 'if I were guided to discover this transmuting alchemy, I would build a town and erect in it a Mashriq'ul-Adhkár* of crystal. Its central hall would be supported by ninety-five pillars and each of its 19 × 9-metre doors would be made of solid gold!'

Far from being cautious and calculating, Mullá Riḍá was extremely bold and frank in his manners, deeds and assertions. Always he spoke on the spur of the moment, unguardedly and effectively. He was not one to 'seek' opportunity for teaching; rather he would 'force' openings for himself in

* Literally, Dawning-Place of the Mention of God: a Bahá'í House of Worship.

order to speak about the Cause to almost everyone he met. The dungeon life, dismal and dreary as it was, failed to curb his heroic spirit or to prevent his bold adventure in teaching work. On the contrary, it brought him new opportunities and spiritual powers which he grasped and exploited to the full, always disregarding the fact that such an indiscreet manner of public teaching in the presence of fanatical prisoners and authorities would entail fresh dangers and sufferings not only for himself but also for the rest of the friends who shared his dire fate. 'His public discussions', Siyyid Asadu'lláh-i-Qumí, his companion in jail narrates, 'sometimes became highly controversial and the excited fanatics who looked for such opportunities would join in with their derisive and insulting words. We used to point out to him that these ignorant people who passed such abusive remarks about the Cause certainly were not seekers of truth, but only trouble-makers. But he contended that the Cause is great and therefore is bound to encounter great opposition and that those who try to defile its fair name through abuse and vituperation surely will never succeed in doing it any harm. What they actually do, he maintained, is to let everyone know how stupid they themselves are. Their foolish act resembles that of a man who tries vainly to spit on the sun.'

This same Siyyid Asadu'lláh further states that 'again and again we argued with Mullá Riḍá, begged and urged him to be moderate and sparing in his talks but nothing proved of any avail.* Then as the situation grew worse and new dangers loomed ahead, the sense of fear and anxiety in our hearts prompted us to take a step that soon brought in its wake a grievous trial for him and a world of sorrow for us all. As a precaution against incidents, we went to the jailer, Mas͟hhadí 'Alí, and asked him to tell Mullá Riḍá not to speak in public about the Cause, hoping that his words and authority would induce him to change his attitude. But alas, how little did we know then that no earthly power, no amount of pain and suffering could ever curb his uncompromising

* Although Bahá'u'lláh had counselled His followers to teach His Cause with wisdom, the character of Mullá Riḍá, his enthusiasm and devotion, perhaps led him to overlook this injunction.

spirit or dissuade this aged man of God from placing teaching work above safety and other personal considerations. So when he had refused to comply with the jailer's order, the latter grew angry and told his men to inflict corporal punishment on him. They took Mullá Riḍá into the prison yard and most brutally flogged his bare back. However, in spite of old age and the rigours of prison life, he remained steadfast as a rock throughout the ordeal. He neither budged nor did he raise the faintest cry, nor did his face bear the slightest expression of agony. It seemed as if he had momentarily lost his sense of feeling. All the friends were profoundly shocked and shaken at the sight of his suffering and soon after the torturing, I hurriedly went over to offer my sympathy and to dress his wounds. Mullá Riḍá, greatly surprised at my behaviour, shouted triumphantly: "O, Siyyid Asadu'lláh! Do you really think I am hurt? At the time of flogging I felt like a drunken elephant and never felt the slightest pain. I was in the presence of Bahá'u'lláh, talking to him." '

Among the non-Bahá'í prisoners who witnessed this harrowing scene there was a distinguished man by the name of Ghulám-Riḍá Khán, whose heart was deeply touched and transformed at the sight of the superhuman endurance manifested by the victim, and the interest and surprise thus aroused led him to investigate. His search for truth was soon rewarded by confirmation and he eventually became a devoted believer. When released from prison, this same man was asked how he happened to become a Bahá'í. 'I received my light from the floggings,' he said and added, 'If instead hundreds of verses from the *Qur'án* had been recited to me or a thousand reasons adduced to convince me of the truth of this Message, none would have influenced me as did the unruffled calm which the old, stout-hearted Mullá Riḍá evinced under torture.'

Another story told by Siyyid Asadu'lláh is the following. 'There was a poor prisoner of Jewish persuasion in our midst. One day Mullá Riḍá called me and said: "Do you see this Jew, how miserable and lonely he is? None of the Muslims ever speak to or associate with him, nor do they let him enter the public bath because they regard him as unclean. And look what dirty, ragged clothing he wears. Now would you not help me to bathe this poor Jew by the side of the prison pool?" He insisted so much that at last I consented to assist him in this odious task. We made the Jew sit beside the pool and removed the untidy clothing which barely covered his squalid figure. Then I kept pouring water over him while Mullá Riḍá scrubbed and sponged his foul body. Having washed him clean, Mullá Riḍá brought some clean clothing for him to wear. Throughout the whole time the Jew was lost in bewilderment. "Are you people angels or human beings?" muttered the Jew. "Why, surely you are not of the Jewish fold, yet so very kind and generous!" he added. "O, you wretched fellow!" exclaimed Mullá Riḍá, "it is none but the word of your Father that prompted me to wash and clothe you. But alas! You don't know your Father, do you? Nor have you heard this word of His: '*Consort ye with the peoples of all religions in a spirit of love and fellowship*'." '

Mullá Riḍá was a man of peculiar conduct and of a trend of thought unusual by our standards. He had attained a station from which he saw in every object a sign or a reflection of the glory of Bahá'u'lláh, and the love he cherished for Him dominated his whole being and to it he subordinated every other impulse. Mírzá Ḥusayn-i-Zanjání, another Bahá'í prisoner, gives the following account concerning Mullá Riḍá: 'For sixteen months I was his close companion during which I dedicated myself to his service. I prepared his food, washed his clothing, did everything in my power to make him comfortable. However, he seldom thanked me; instead he would say, "I thank the Blessed Beauty for the comfort and help He has provided for me." Whenever I brought him food he used to say: "I render Thee thanks, O Bahá'u'lláh!" Or when he happened to give away something as charity or do a service to others he would say: "I give this to Bahá'u'lláh . . ." One day they brought in a prisoner who had no shirt on. Mullá Riḍá on seeing him turned to me and said: "This poor young man is a servant of Bahá'u'lláh, though he does not know his Lord. As he is half-naked we would better let him have the spare shirt we have between ourselves. We do not need to have a spare shirt in prison; it is a sort of luxury and surely we can do without it." I said "Very well, you put on this spare shirt which I have just washed and give this boy the one you are now wearing." On hearing my suggestion, Mullá Riḍá lost his temper and shouted at me indignantly: "Do you mean to say that I put on the clean shirt and place my used one in the hands of the Blessed Beauty? How dare you make such a cruel suggestion? Aren't you a Bahá'í? Bahá'u'lláh says it is not charity unless you give away the things you hold dear. I wonder how long it will take you to attain and understand." '

Mírzá Ḥusayn further states: 'Early during the reign of Muẓaffari'd-Dín Sháh [1896–1907], the friends in Ṭihrán petitioned the Sháh on several occasions and succeeded in obtaining a decree for our release. On the day of liberation we were paraded in chains along the thickly crowded route to the house of the Farrásh-Báshí,* where we were taken into custody, awaiting necessary formalities to be over. Throughout that anxious time we begged and cautioned Mullá Riḍá to keep calm and silent, lest a heedless word to the authorities create fresh troubles and suffering for us. Yet, notwithstanding our constant warnings and against our advice, he went to an adjoining room to talk to a group of theological students headed by a fanatical evil-minded Siyyid. We could hear their conversation, as it developed into a heated dispute. Mullá Riḍá was hitting hard with the solid weapon of proofs, accompanied by a flood of verses from the *Qur'án*. The hostile group were utterly confounded and, as none could challenge him in argument, they grew hysterical and abusive, inflicted blows on Mullá Riḍá and ejected him from their midst. This tragic incident, however, did not end there. It led to grievous consequences. The same day through mischievous machinations on the part of the malicious Siyyid, Mullá Riḍá was ordered to go back to jail, while the rest of us were released.

'This new development brought immense grief and anxiety to our hearts but failed to disturb Mullá Riḍá in the least. He remained bold, happy, imperturbable and as jovial as ever. However, as there was no one to look after him in

* Chief police officer.

prison, the dire privations and hardships there made themselves strongly felt on his frail and aged frame and served to hasten his journey to the shores of eternity. His days of suffering were now numbered and his illustrious soul, only ten days after this last confinement, took its flight to the abode of the Beloved.'

The two wonderful Tablets revealed by 'Abdu'l-Bahá to his imperishable memory show how glorious is his rank as a teacher as well as a martyr, and how heroic an example he set in serving the Cause of God.[2]

Whereas Mullá Riḍá recognized the station of Bahá'u'lláh through a mere perusal of one of His Tablets, there were others who, though sincere in their search for truth, were deprived of this vision and because of their learning and knowledge took time to acknowledge the authenticity of the Message of Bahá'u'lláh.

Nabíl-i-Akbar

Of those who travelled to Baghdád and attained the presence of Bahá'u'lláh, unquestionably the most learned and erudite was Mullá Muḥammad-i-Qá'iní, later surnamed Nabíl-i-Akbar* by Bahá'u'lláh. This great man was endowed with extraordinary qualities and intellectual powers. Some considered him a prodigy among scholars and learned men. His eminence may be judged from the fact that, after several years' study at home, he spent about six years in 'Iráq studying theology and various other subjects associated with Islamic jurisprudence. His teacher was the renowned Mujtahid† of Karbilá, Shaykh Murtiḍáy-i-Anṣárí, the head of the Shí'ah community, who was well disposed towards the Faith. He was a divine whose standards were so exacting that he reputedly gave the title of mujtahid to only three people during his entire life. One of

* Not to be mistaken for Nabíl-i-A'ẓam, the famous Bahá'í historian, author of *The Dawn-Breakers*.

† Doctor of Islamic Law.

these three was Nabíl-i-Akbar. In His writings Bahá'u'lláh has extolled Shaykh Murtiḍá and numbered him among 'those doctors who have indeed drunk of the cup of renunciation'. 'Abdu'l-Bahá has also described him as 'the illustrious and erudite doctor, the noble and celebrated scholar, the seal of seekers after truth.'[3]

Nabíl-i-Akbar was acknowledged as one of the most outstanding men of learning in Persia. His fame had spread throughout the country to such an extent that once, when he spoke incognito to a number of divines in far-off Kirmán, his listeners were lost in admiration of his superb discourse and some were heard to say that the only person in the whole country who could rival such a man in the field of learning and knowledge would be the famous Mullá Muḥammad-i-Qá'iní (that is, Nabíl-i-Akbar himself).

He embraced the Bábí Faith about the year 1853. Some six years later, while in Baghdád, he went to visit Bahá'u'lláh. There he was warmly received by Him, and was accorded the honour of staying in the outer apartments of His house, normally reserved for the reception of visitors. Mírzá Áqá Ján was instructed by Bahá'u'lláh to act as host to him. The following is an extract from the spoken chronicle of Nabíl-i-Akbar relating the events of those few days that he spent in the house of Bahá'u'lláh:

> One afternoon I was seated in the room talking with Mullá Muḥammad-Ṣádiq-i-Khurásání, known as Muqaddas.[4] He was a learned man of great dignity and stature. As we were talking together, Bahá'u'lláh, Who had just returned from the town, arrived in the outer apartment accompanied by Prince Mulk-Ārá whose hand He was holding. Mullá Ṣádiq, who was the embodiment of dignity and solemnity, immediately rose to his feet and prostrated himself at the feet of Bahá'u'lláh. This action did not please Bahá'u'lláh Who angrily rebuked Mullá Ṣádiq and ordered him to rise immediately, after which He went out of the room followed by the Prince.

I was amazed and bewildered at such behaviour on the part of Mullá Ṣádiq as I had never expected such an important person to act in this manner. Having witnessed Bahá'u'lláh's reaction also, I expressed my disapproval of Mullá Ṣádiq's behaviour and admonished him for it, saying: 'You are a man who occupies an exalted position in the realm of knowledge and learning and, above all else, you had the honour of attaining the presence of the Báb Himself. Your rank is next to the Letters of the Living and you are one of the Witnesses* of the Dispensation of the Báb. It is true that Bahá'u'lláh is an eminent person Who belongs to the nobility and His ancestors have occupied high positions in the government. It is also true that He has suffered persecution and imprisonment as a result of embracing the Cause of God, that all His possessions have been confiscated and that He has finally been exiled to this land. Yet, your behaviour towards Him this afternoon was like that of an unworthy servant towards his glorious Lord.'

Mullá Ṣádiq refrained from answering me. He was in a state of spiritual intoxication, his face beaming with joy; he merely said to me, 'I beseech God to tear asunder the veil for thee and shower His bounties upon thy person through His abundant grace.'

After this incident, I decided in my heart to investigate and began to observe the person of Bahá'u'lláh and His actions very carefully. The more I observed the less I discovered any sign which could point to His claiming a station. On the contrary, I observed in Him nothing, either in word or deed, except humility, self-effacement, servitude and utter nothingness. As a result, I was led into grievous error, believing that I was in every way superior to Bahá'u'lláh, and preferred my own self to Him.

It was through my vain imagining that in the gatherings of the friends I always used to occupy the seat of honour, assume

* Certain believers were nominated as 'Witnesses' to the *Bayán*—the Mother Book of the Bábí Dispensation—to testify to its validity and authenticity as the Word of God, until the appearance of 'Him Whom God shall make manifest' (i.e., Bahá'u'lláh) when their function as 'Witnesses' would come to an end.

the function of the speaker and would not give an opportunity to Bahá'u'lláh or anyone else to say anything. One afternoon, Bahá'u'lláh arranged a meeting in His house and a number of friends had gathered, as usual, in the same large room, a room around which, according to the Pen of the Most High, circle in adoration the people of Bahá. Again, I occupied the seat of honour. Bahá'u'lláh sat in the midst of the friends and was serving tea with His own hands.

In the course of the meeting, a certain question was asked. Having satisfied myself that no one in the room was capable of tackling the problem, I began to speak. All the friends were attentively listening and were absolutely silent, except Bahá'u'lláh Who occasionally, while agreeing with my exposition, made a few comments on the subject. Gradually He took over and I became silent. His explanations were so profound and the ocean of His utterance surged with such a power that my whole being was overtaken with awe and fear. Spellbound by His words, I was plunged into a state of dazed bewilderment. After a few minutes of listening to His words —words of unparalleled wonder and majesty—I became dumbfounded. I could no longer hear His voice. Only by the movement of His lips did I know that He was still speaking. I felt deeply ashamed and troubled that I was occupying the seat of honour in that meeting. I waited impatiently until I saw that His lips were no longer moving when I knew that He had finished talking. Like a helpless bird which is freed from the claws of a mighty falcon I rose to my feet and went out. There three times I hit my head hard against the wall and rebuked myself for my spiritual blindness.[5]

The eyes of Nabíl-i-Akbar were at last opened. He attended another meeting, this time in Káẓimayn in the house of a certain Ḥájí 'Abdu'l-Majíd-i-S̲h̲írází. Bahá'u'lláh was present at this meeting. He spoke about the mysteries and origin of creation. Here a new world, full of fresh significances, dawned upon Nabíl-i-Akbar who considered every word of Bahá'u'lláh's to be like a priceless gem. All that Nabíl-i-Akbar had heard and studied during his life appeared to him to be but the talk of children.

At this point he decided to find out directly from Bahá'u'lláh Himself what His station was and wrote a letter to Him which he begged 'Abdu'l-Bahá to deliver. The next day he received a Tablet in which Bahá'u'lláh alluded to His lofty station. This was the end of Nabíl-i-Akbar's search for truth, for he wrote a second letter to Bahá'u'lláh, this time humbly acknowledging Him as the Supreme Manifestation of God and begging Him to guide his steps in His service. Bahá'u'lláh instructed him to return to Persia and teach the Cause of God there.

Nabíl-i-Akbar dedicated his whole life to the service of the Cause, suffering much persecution from the enemies of the Faith. He rose to such heights of service and dedication that few among the Apostles of Bahá'u'lláh have been able to rival his attainments.

He died in 1892 soon after the ascension of Bahá'u'lláh and was buried in the city of Bukhárá. 'Abdu'l-Bahá asked that a delegation of nine believers visit his grave on His behalf and there chant a Tablet of visitation which He had written especially for him. A few years later He instructed the nephew of Nabíl-i-Akbar to transfer his remains from Bukhárá to 'Ishqábád—a move which proved providential as the graveyard was demolished soon after by the authorities.

In the same way that Nabíl-i-Akbar came to Bahá'u'lláh and saw the light of Divine Revelation, many of the followers of the Báb did likewise. Some were learned and some were uneducated. They all sat at His feet and received, according to their varying capacities, a measure of the spiritual outpourings from His person. Most of the Tablets of Bahá'u'lláh which were revealed in that period were written in honour of these men.

8

The Seven Valleys

One of the Writings of Bahá'u'lláh which was revealed after His return from Sulaymáníyyih is *The Seven Valleys*. This work stands out as a masterpiece of mystical composition. It was written in response to the questions of Shaykh Muḥyi'd-Dín, the judge of the town of Kháníqayn, who was a Ṣúfí.* Although not a Bábí, he was an admirer of Bahá'u'lláh and had written a letter to Him, expressing certain thoughts and posing some questions in mystical terms.

The theme of *The Seven Valleys* is the journey of the soul from its abode in this world to the realms of nearness to God. The seven stages in the journey were already familiar to the Ṣúfís, having been described by Farídu'd-Dín-i-'Aṭṭár, an outstanding exponent of Ṣúfism in its early stages. Bahá'u'lláh elucidates the profound meaning and significance of these seven stages.

First comes 'The Valley of Search', wherein is described the path which a true seeker must take to attain his object, which is the recognition of the Manifestation of God for the age in which he lives. Before everything else he must 'cleanse the heart—which is the well-spring of divine treasures—from every marking', must turn away from following 'the traces of . . . forefathers and sires' and must 'shut the door of friendliness and enmity upon all the people of the earth'.[1] He must sacrifice 'whatever he hath seen, and heard, and understood . . .'[2] Ardour, zeal and patience are the necessary qualities for him on this plane.

Next is 'The Valley of Love'. Here the wayfarer is like a moth which has found a flame and, longing to reach it, circles

* A member of a Muslim mystical cult.

around, coming closer and closer until finally it is burnt in a blaze of sacrifice.

This is a stage in which the heart of man is touched by the glory of the Manifestation of God Whom he has sought and found. Here, the believer understands neither reasons nor proofs. His heart is attracted, for he has fallen in love with his Beloved. Indeed, the story of every religion is written in the language of love. In the early days of the Faith of Bahá'u'lláh, for instance, of the thousands who came in contact with the Manifestation of God and were attracted to Him, some, knowing little of the history, teachings, proofs or laws of His Cause, adored the Báb and Bahá'u'lláh. They were so intoxicated with the wine of Their utterances that, when occasion demanded it, they willingly gave their lives. So intense was their love that some believers who attained Bahá'u'lláh's presence begged Him to accept them as martyrs. Others were so magnetized by His supreme power that they could not bear the thought of separation from Him.

For example, when the news of Bahá'u'lláh's approaching departure for Constantinople reached His companions in Ba<u>gh</u>dád, they were plunged, one and all, into sorrow and consternation. On the first night none of them would eat or sleep, and many decided to take their own lives if deprived of accompanying Him on His journey. Without a shadow of doubt these companions who were the lovers of His beauty would have carried out their intention, had it not been for the words of counsel and exhortation which Bahá'u'lláh addressed to them, words which consoled them and enabled them to resign themselves to the will of God.

No greater story can be found to demonstrate this consuming love for Bahá'u'lláh than that of Ḥájí Muḥammad-Ja'far-i-Tabrízí. He was a devoted believer who first attained the presence of Bahá'u'lláh in Ba<u>gh</u>dád, recognized His station and devoted his life to the service of his Lord. When Bahá'u'lláh established His residence in Adrianople, Ḥájí Ja'far travelled with his brother (who was also a believer) to that city and resided there. He was so magnetized by Bahá'u'lláh that when he discovered that the authorities had not included his name among those who were to accompany Bahá'u'lláh to 'Akká, he attempted to cut his own throat. Some friends arrived just in time to save him.

As a result of this the authorities, who were at first adamant in not allowing any of Bahá'u'lláh's followers to accompany Him to 'Akká, changed their minds and permitted most of His companions to travel with Him. Ḥájí Ja'far's condition, however, was serious. His throat was bleeding profusely and he was taken to hospital for treatment. The authorities promised him that when his wounds healed, he would be allowed to proceed to 'Akká with his brother. Two months later they both arrived there and joined Bahá'u'lláh in the Most Great Prison.

The third stage of the journey is 'The Valley of Knowledge'. The word 'knowledge', however, can be misleading as it does not convey the full meaning of the original word 'Ma'rifat' used by Bahá'u'lláh. It is difficult to find a single word in English which can faithfully impart its full significance, a combination of true understanding, recognition and knowledge.

The knowledge referred to in this valley is not primarily based on learning. The knowledge of God dawns upon man through his heart. Pride in one's learning and accomplishments often deprives the heart of the light of true understanding. The soul in this valley recognizes the truth and reaches the stage of certitude. 'His inner eyes will open and he will privily converse with his Beloved.'[3] He acquires a new vision and begins to understand the mysteries of God's Revelation and creation. He will not be despondent when faced with pain and calamities. Rather, he will approach them with understanding and resignation, for he will 'see the end in the beginning'[4] and will discover that suffering and tribulations are eventually realized to be God's mercy and blessing. In everything he finds a wisdom. 'He in this station is content with the decree of God, and seeth war as peace, and findeth in death the secrets of everlasting life . . . In the ocean he findeth a drop, in a drop he beholdeth the secrets of the sea.'[5]

The next stage is 'The Valley of Unity' where the wayfarer is uplifted from the plane of limitation into that of the absolute. Here he no longer sees the world of creation subjectively, restricted by the limitations of his own eyes, but sees it objectively through the eyes of God. He discovers that each created thing manifests, according to its capacity, some of the attributes of God, and that the degree of such manifestation differs in each kingdom of creation.

Like a man who soars into outer space and looks down upon the earth with an all-encompassing vision, the wayfarer, freed from the cage of self and passion and released from the bondage of limitations, enters upon the plane of universality. His vision has widened to such an extent that no longer is he concerned with his own self or attached to this world. He sees in everything the signs and tokens of God. 'He looketh on all things with the eye of oneness, and seeth the brilliant rays of the divine sun shining . . . alike on all created things, and the lights of singleness reflected over all creation.' In this valley there is no place for ego; here the soul 'steppeth into the sanctuary of the Friend, and shareth as an intimate the pavilion of the Loved One . . . He seeth in himself neither name nor fame nor rank, but findeth his own praise in praising God.'[6]

Having attained to this lofty station of detachment from the world, the wayfarer becomes independent of all created things and enters 'The Valley of Contentment'. Although outwardly he may be poor, inwardly he is endowed with wealth and power from the world of spirit.

The history of the Faith has recorded many moving episodes in the lives of early believers who held high positions and enjoyed riches and luxury. On embracing the Faith, however, they were stripped of their rank and earthly possessions by the enemies of the Cause. Yet many of them, who had not focused their affection on the things of this world and had ascended to the 'plane of contentment', remained unaffected by poverty and destitution, persecution and suffering. The changes and chances of this world were powerless to weaken their faith or disturb their serenity and peace of mind.

Happiness is one of the attributes of the true believer, but this cannot be achieved by a life founded on the delights and pleasures of this world. For such happiness is only transitory and can indeed be sorrow in disguise. Only those who have entered the valley of contentment have experienced true joy, even though their lives be subjected to affliction and suffering. Bahá'u'lláh states that the wayfarer in the valley of contentment burns away the 'veils of want . . . From sorrow he turneth to bliss, from anguish to joy. His grief and mourning yield to delight and rapture.'[7]

The life of 'Abdu'l-Bahá, the Exemplar of the teachings of Bahá'u'lláh, stands out as a shining example of what real happiness is. From the age of nine He shared the sufferings and persecutions inflicted upon His Father, spending forty years in 'Akká as a prisoner of two Turkish despots. Yet during those dark years, He remained the most cheerful of the companions of Bahá'u'lláh, and poured out His love on all whom He met. A few years after His release, He said:

> Freedom is not a matter of place, but of condition. I was happy in that prison, for those days were passed in the path of service.
>
> To me prison was freedom.
>
> Troubles are a rest to me.
>
> Death is life.
>
> To be despised is honour.
>
> Therefore was I full of happiness all through that prison time.
>
> When one is released from the prison of self, that is indeed freedom! For self is the greatest prison.
>
> When this release takes place, one can never be imprisoned. Unless one accepts dire vicissitudes, not with dull resignation, but with radiant acquiescence, one cannot attain this freedom.[8]

Having attained contentment, the traveller comes to 'The Valley of Wonderment' and 'is . . . struck dumb with the beauty of the All-Glorious . . .'[9] Like a person who, diving into the ocean, suddenly becomes conscious of its enormous size and fathomless depth, the wayfarer in this valley beholds the vastness of creation and its infinite range. With unclouded vision and clear insight he now discovers the inner mysteries of God's Revelation, and is led from one mystery to a thousand more. 'At every moment he beholdeth a wondrous world, a new creation, and goeth from astonishment to astonishment, and is lost in awe at the works of the Lord of Oneness.'[10]

The last valley towards which the wayfarer can strive is 'The Valley of True Poverty and Absolute Nothingness'—'the furthermost state of mystic knowers, and the farthest homeland of the lovers'.[11] 'This station', Bahá'u'lláh affirms,

> is the dying from self and the living in God, the being poor in self and rich in the Desired One. Poverty as here referred to signifieth being poor in the things of the created world, rich in the things of God's world. For when the true lover and devoted friend reacheth to the presence of the Beloved, the sparkling beauty of the Loved One and the fire of the lover's heart will kindle a blaze and burn away all veils and wrappings. Yea, all he hath, from heart to skin, will be set aflame, so that nothing will remain save the Friend.[12]

Siyyid Ismá'íl of Zavárih (Dhabíḥ)

Some believers who attained the presence of Bahá'u'lláh had reached this lofty station. They saw a glimpse of that inner light which was concealed within His person. They were dazzled by it and could no longer bear to stand in the darkness of this world.

One such was Siyyid Ismá'íl of Zavárih surnamed Dhabíḥ (Sacrifice) by Bahá'u'lláh.* He was a devout man highly es-

* He should not be confused with Ḥájí Muḥammad-Ismá'íl of Káshán, also entitled Dhabíḥ, to whom reference will be made in the next volume.

teemed for his piety and rectitude of conduct, his learning and knowledge. He was converted to the Faith in the early days of the Báb's ministry, attained His presence in the house of the Imám-Jum'ih of Iṣfahán, and was present when the Báb revealed a commentary on the *Súrih of V'al-'Aṣr*. The rapidity with which the Báb penned that lengthy epistle and the power of His utterance as He chanted some of its passages, in the presence of a number of distinguished divines, captured the imagination of Dhabíḥ who became one of His devoted followers. Over a decade later, Dhabíḥ came to Baghdád and attained the presence of Bahá'u'lláh. In that city he stayed with a believer whose home was in the same neighbourhood as Bahá'u'lláh's house. This man, Áqá Muḥammad-Riḍá, had invited Bahá'u'lláh to his home, begging Him for the inestimable privilege of acting as His host. Bahá'u'lláh accepted his invitation and a few days later, in the afternoon, honoured Áqá Muḥammad-Riḍá by going to his house.

In the *Kitáb-i-Badí'*, revealed a few years later in Adrianople, Bahá'u'lláh Himself has described His meeting with Dhabíḥ on that occasion. As was customary at that time of day, their host had provided several trays of various fruits and sweetmeats. Dhabíḥ was invited by Bahá'u'lláh to partake of the food but he begged most humbly and earnestly to receive instead, through Bahá'u'lláh's bounty, a portion of spiritual food from the unseen treasury of His divine knowledge. Favourable to his plea, Bahá'u'lláh summoned Dhabíḥ to sit before Him and hearken to His words—words of incomparable power and awe which were filled with spiritual significance and which, according to Bahá'u'lláh's testimony, no one is capable of describing.

By hearing the utterances of Bahá'u'lláh on that day, Dhabíḥ was transformed and worlds of spirit were opened before his eyes. After this meeting he remained in a state of spiritual intoxication, wholly devoted to Bahá'u'lláh, his love for Him intensifying with the passing of each day.

In order to pay homage to his Lord and to express his inner feelings of humility and self-effacement towards Him, Dhabíḥ took upon himself the task of sweeping the approaches to the house of Bahá'u'lláh at the hour of dawn. In those days one of the duties of a servant in any household was to sweep a small portion of the path leading to the entrance of the house. As a token of humility and lowliness, however, Dhabíḥ would, instead of using a brush, unwind his green turban, the ensign of his holy lineage, and with it would sweep the approaches of the house of Bahá'u'lláh. He would then place in the fold of his cloak the dust on which the feet of his Beloved had trodden and, unwilling that others should tread on it, would carry it all the way to the river to throw it into its waters.

The story of Dhabíḥ is that of a passionate lover. The object of his adoration was Bahá'u'lláh, Who had ignited within his breast the fire of the love of God, a fire so intense that it began to consume his whole being. Eventually he reached a state where he would neither eat nor drink. For forty days he abstained from food. Unable, at last, to check the crushing force of love which pressed upon his soul, he came one day, at the hour of dawn, to the house of Bahá'u'lláh and for the last time swept its approaches with his turban. After performing this task, he paid a visit to the home of Áqá Muḥammad-Riḍá where he met some of the friends for the last time. Later he obtained a razor, went to the bank of the Tigris and there turning his face towards the house of Bahá'u'lláh, took his life by cutting his throat.

Bahá'u'lláh has extolled Dhabíḥ as the 'King and Beloved of Martyrs'. He is reported to have said that 'No blood has, till now, been poured upon the earth as pure as the blood he shed'.[13]*

* Dhabíḥ should not be confused with the brothers Mírzá Muḥammad-Ḥasan and Mírzá Muḥammad-Ḥusayn, who were designated by Bahá'u'lláh the 'King of the Martyrs' and the 'Beloved of the Martyrs', respectively. Dhabíḥ took his own life because he was intoxicated by the wine of the presence of Bahá'u'lláh, Who had enabled him to witness the glory of the spiritual worlds of God. This cannot be compared with ordinary suicide, nor can this episode be taken to mean that Bahá'í belief condones the taking of one's own life. On the contrary, suicide is strongly condemned in the Faith of Bahá'u'lláh and is clearly against His Teachings.

The Four Valleys

Another one of Bahá'u'lláh's mystical Writings which was revealed in Baghdád is *The Four Valleys*. This, too, is an epistle in which Bahá'u'lláh describes the journey of the wayfarer to his ultimate goal. He has divided wayfarers into four groups.

The highest station, the fourth valley, is for 'those who have reached to the beauty of the Beloved One . . .' 'This is the realm of full awareness, of utter self-effacement . . . Here love becometh an obstruction and a barrier, and all else save Him is but a curtain . . . The exalted dwellers in this mansion do wield divine authority . . . On the high seats of justice, they issue their commands . . .' They 'abide in the high bowers of splendour above the Throne of the Ancient of Days, and they sit in the Empyrean of Might within the Lofty Pavilion . . .'[14]

Although Bahá'u'lláh's approach in this epistle is somewhat different from *The Seven Valleys*, basically it conveys the same truth. *The Four Valleys* was written for Shaykh 'Abdu'r-Raḥmán-i-Karkúkí, a learned man and the leader of the Qádiríyyih Order,* who came in contact with Bahá'u'lláh in Kurdistán. He was a devoted admirer of Bahá'u'lláh, who used to sit at His feet in Sulaymáníyyih and hear His discourses. He also corresponded with Bahá'u'lláh in Kurdistán and, later, in Baghdád.

* A sect of Sunní Islám.

9

Some Outstanding Tablets

Ṣaḥífiy-i-Sh͟aṭṭíyyih

Among the Writings of Bahá'u'lláh revealed in Bag͟hdád is the *Ṣaḥífiy-i-Sh͟aṭṭíyyih* (Book of the River). This Tablet is mainly in Persian. In it Bahá'u'lláh speaks about the irresistible power of the Cause of God and its sovereignty. Alluding to the Tigris which runs through Bag͟hdád, He likens the onward march of the Faith to the flow of that river. Just as no obstacle, whether a fortified building or a mighty wall, can withstand the onrushing force of the water, or hold back its progress, so none of the enemies of the Cause, however fierce their onslaught or determined their opposition, can halt the advance of this resistless Faith of God. It will, in spite of all opposition, press onward, tear down every obstacle and ultimately establish its ascendancy over its adversaries. Similarly, the Cause of God will break up old and time-honoured institutions and will not allow any man, regardless of his rank or position, to stand in its way.

A cursory review of the history of the Faith will demonstrate the irresistible power of the Cause of Bahá'u'lláh. From the time of its inception this Faith had been oppressed by the civil and ecclesiastical authorities in the land of its birth. Its youthful Herald, the Báb, Who ushered in the dawn of a New Day and gave the glad-tidings of the coming of 'Him Whom God shall make manifest' (Bahá'u'lláh), was publicly martyred. Its Founder, Bahá'u'lláh, was imprisoned and exiled to far-off lands. For almost half a century He and His family were subjected to inhuman cruelties and hardships. No less than twenty thousand of its heroes were put to death in tragic circumstances and the remainder of its followers were persecuted all their lives.

Yet, the Faith of Bahá'u'lláh, supported by the unseen hosts of the Kingdom, triumphed over its adversaries and penetrated into every part of the world. Today its light has been diffused to every corner of the earth, its healing Message has reached almost every stratum of human society and people are responding to it in ever increasing numbers. Its adherents, enrolled from all the nations of the world, representing every race, colour and class, are actively engaged in the erection of the framework of Bahá'u'lláh's New World Order for mankind. Such achievements bear ample testimony to the fulfilment of the words of Bahá'u'lláh revealed in this Tablet over a century ago.

Bahá'u'lláh has also used the analogy of the river to demonstrate another point. He mentions that the outpourings of God's bounty are vouchsafed to all creation equally, but that every created thing receives them in accordance with its capacity.

Bahá'u'lláh also speaks in this Tablet about miracles which are attributed to the Prophets. He states that one should not deny the performance of miracles by these Holy Souls, but emphasizes that miracles are not a conclusive proof of the authenticity of Their Messages. The greatest and the most evident sign of Prophethood has always been the Revelation of the Word of God. Everything created in this world is a miracle in itself if we look at it with the eye of discernment. For example, the outpouring of energy from the sun is a miracle indeed, for the mind of man could never have believed in such a phenomenon if he had not actually seen the radiance of the sun with his own eyes.

In the Writings of Bahá'u'lláh there are many references to miracles. In all of these the Word revealed by the Prophet is regarded as the most potent force in the world. The creativeness of the Word is a miracle which is everlasting and cannot be obliterated by the passage of time. Other miracles, if performed, convince only those who witness them and are not accepted as conclusive proof by those who have not.

The followers of all religions have attributed many miracles to their Prophets, miracles which traditionally are passed on from generation to generation although their inner significances have not been fully understood. Upon these miracles have been built, over the centuries, many doctrines and dogmas which have become mighty barriers between God and man.

In the East, at the time of Bahá'u'lláh, when the light of religion was still burning brightly within the hearts of men, the followers of these religions adhered strictly, indeed often fanatically, to their beliefs. Bahá'í teachers had to lead them from blind belief in miracles to a rational recognition of the divine qualities and spiritual powers possessed by the Manifestations of God. Their principal task was to demonstrate to the followers of each religion the reality and truth of their own Prophet before explaining to them the station of Bahá'u'lláh and the validity of His claim. Once the seeker could understand the spiritual attributes of his own Prophet, he had no difficulty in recognizing Bahá'u'lláh. Christ confirmed this when He said to the Jews, 'For had ye believed Moses, ye would have believed me . . .' (John v. 46).

To the recipient of this Tablet Bahá'u'lláh offers one counsel, namely to 'possess a pure, kindly and radiant heart, that thine may be a sovereignty ancient, imperishable and everlasting'.* He affirms that He could find no better counsel than this for his spiritual growth and the attainment of eternal life.

This Tablet must have been revealed by Bahá'u'lláh at a time when His heart was full of anguish and grief. A few unfaithful companions such as Mírzá Yaḥyá and his notorious associate, Siyyid Muḥammad-i-Iṣfahání, had shown such envy and malice towards Him that, as stated in this Tablet, He had been most reluctant to write. Apprehensive of the reaction which His words might produce, and knowing full well what animosity and envy they might kindle if He were to elucidate further

* Bahá'u'lláh uses these same words in *The Hidden Words*. (Arabic, no. 1.)

these truths of the spirit or reveal the pearls of knowledge hidden within His own heart, He decided to withhold His Pen from disclosing words of deeper significance and wisdom.

Madínatu'r-Riḍá

Another Tablet revealed in Baghdád, in Arabic, was the *Madínatu'r-Riḍá* (City of Radiant Acquiescence). In it Bahá'u'lláh describes the attributes of 'contentment and radiant acquiescence' and reveals their manifold aspects. He explains that the prime requisite for those who wish to tread the path of contentment is to be resigned to the Will of God, to accept radiantly whatever He has destined for them and to acknowledge joyfully all that has been revealed by the Pen of the Báb.*

Another aspect is to be content with one's own self. Bahá'u'lláh states that man will never achieve this as long as he commits even a single sin, however insignificant it may be. It is, therefore, impossible for him to become content with his own self as long as he remains attached to this world, nor can he experience contentment if he resents the sufferings and hardships which are meted out to him in this life. For how can he claim to love God when he is unhappy at what his Beloved has ordained for him? The true state of resignation is to accept with radiant acquiescence the trials and tribulations which are sent by the Almighty.

Yet another aspect of contentment is to be pleased with the believers and to be humble before them. To show pride towards them is to show pride to God; for man cannot attain the good-pleasure of his Creator unless he obtains the good-pleasure of His loved ones.

Although this Tablet was revealed before His Declaration, Bahá'u'lláh alludes to Himself as the Nightingale warbling its

* Until Bahá'u'lláh had officially declared His Mission, the laws and teachings revealed by the Báb were operative and Bahá'u'lláh, in His Tablets, enjoined the Bábís to follow them.

melodies and the Light that shines within the lamp of holiness. Referring to the Cause as the Ark of God, He calls on the people of the *Bayán* to enter this Ark, rebukes them for sleeping while the Sun of Truth* is shining in its meridian splendour, and gives them the glad-tidings that soon the Trumpet † will be blown, the doors of the Riḍván ‡ will be opened, and God will manifest Himself with a new Revelation.

Further, He reminds the believers that this world and everything in it are vain and fleeting, exhorts them to be patient under ills and hardships and assures them of God's reward for those who endure patiently.

He also addresses the peoples of the world, admonishing them for rejecting their Creator, while putting their trust in themselves and in this world, and He counsels them to ponder the transitory nature of this world, in which human life is but the short journey of a traveller, and invites them to return to their God.

Madínatu't-Tawḥíd

The Tablet of *Madínatu't-Tawḥíd* (The City of Unity) was revealed by Bahá'u'lláh for Shaykh Salmán, one of His staunch and faithful disciples. He was from the village of Hindíyán in south-west Persia. He was originally called Shaykh Khanjar, but Bahá'u'lláh conferred upon him the name of Salmán, reminiscent of Rúz-bih, the Persian disciple of Muḥammad whom the Prophet loved so much and whose name He had changed to Salmán.

Bahá'u'lláh spent forty years of His ministry in exile away from His homeland where the great majority of His followers

* Bahá'u'lláh.

† The Trumpet-blast mentioned in the *Qur'án* signifies the proclamation of the Message of Bahá'u'lláh.

‡ Literally, Paradise. It is also significant to note here that Bahá'u'lláh declared His Mission in 1863 in a garden outside Baghdád which was designated the 'Garden of Riḍván'.

resided. It was most important, therefore, to establish a channel of communication through which His Tablets and Messages could reach the friends. Often, believers who had attained His presence were entrusted by Him with the task of taking back some of His Tablets to deliver them to their destinations. But this was not always an easy mission to accomplish, for the enemies of the Cause were vigilant both in Persia and in the neighbouring countries. They kept a careful watch not only along the borders of Persia but also within the country itself, and confiscated any material connected with the Faith.

Shaykh Salmán played a major part in the dissemination of Bahá'u'lláh's Writings among the believers in Persia, became renowned among the friends, and is immortalized in the annals of the Faith by the designation 'Messenger of the Merciful' conferred upon him by Bahá'u'lláh. He was the first messenger to arrive in 'Iráq shortly after Bahá'u'lláh's arrival in that country. From that time until the end of Bahá'u'lláh's ministry, for a period of forty years, he carried the Tablets of Bahá'u'lláh to the believers in Persia and brought back their letters and messages to Him. Each year he visited Bahá'u'lláh, travelling thousands of miles, often on foot. During these years he never remained in one place, but travelled continuously from one town to another, where he would meet the friends, give them news of Bahá'u'lláh and deliver His Tablets and Messages to them. And after the ascension of Bahá'u'lláh, he continued these journeys for many years in the service of 'Abdu'l-Bahá. In all his travels he acted with such prudence and wisdom that none of the Tablets in his care ever fell into the hands of enemies.

Shaykh Salmán had great physical stamina. Many times in the course of his journeys he was subjected to bitter persecution, but through the power of faith he endured such hardships with fortitude and resignation. He lived in poverty. His daily food was simple and often consisted of a loaf of bread and raw onions. He was illiterate, but the knowledge of God was bestowed upon him by Bahá'u'lláh. Through this bounty he

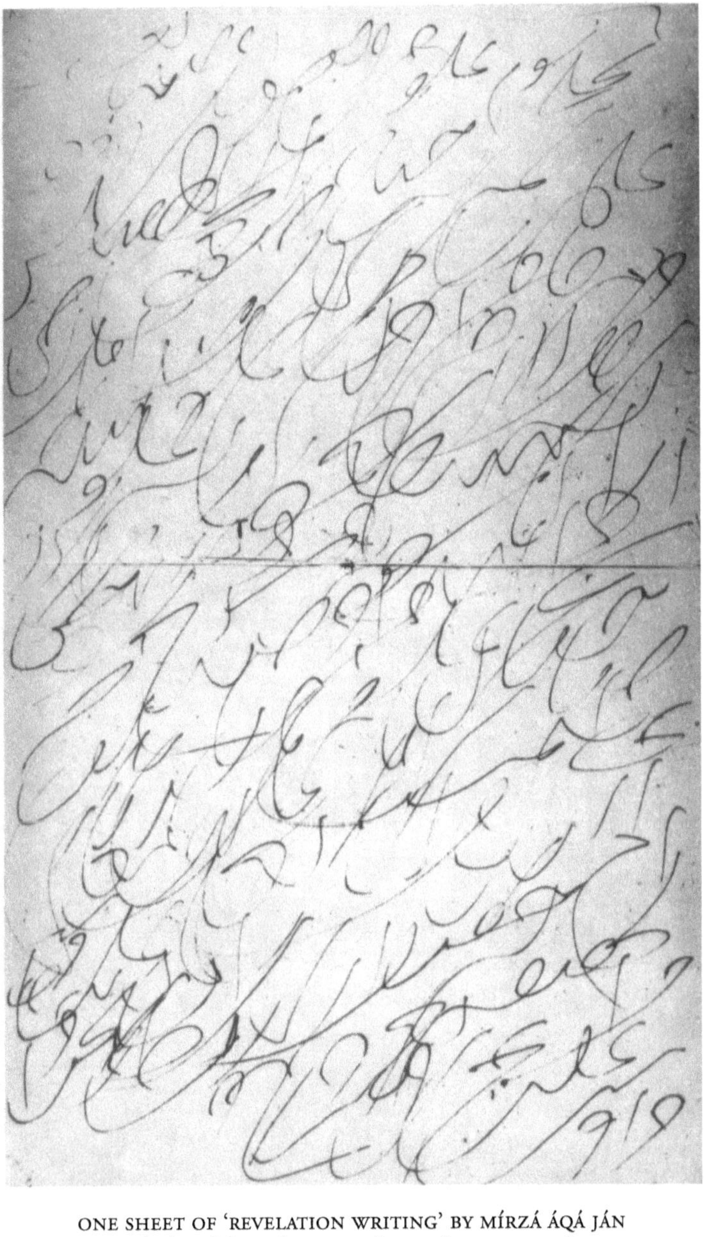

ONE SHEET OF 'REVELATION WRITING' BY MÍRZÁ ÁQÁ JÁN
(reduced from the original size of 35 x 22 cms)

Only the first few words are sufficiently legible to identify the passage as the third Tajallí of the Tablet of Tajallíyát

A FEW LINES OF THE 'REVELATION WRITING'

From the Tablet illustrated on the previous page *(actual size)*

MÍRZÁ ḤUSAYN-I-IṢFAHÁNÍ

Entitled Mis͟hkín-Qalam
An Apostle of Bahá'u'lláh and distinguished calligrapher

had acquired a deep understanding of the verities of the Cause of God and a clear vision of the worlds of spirit.

Believers who wished to attain the presence of Bahá'u'lláh would seek permission from Him to do so, and in this matter Bahá'u'lláh relied so much on Shaykh Salmán's judgement that at one stage He delegated to him the authority to give permission, on His behalf, to those upon whom this great privilege was to be conferred.

There are many anecdotes connected with the life of Shaykh Salmán. His simple and unsophisticated nature, his clear insight, his wisdom and tact when confronted with dangerous or difficult situations, above all his faith in Bahá'u'lláh are all vividly portrayed in these narratives. An interesting incident is recorded in the memoirs of Ḥájí Muḥammad-Ṭáhir-i-Málmírí which demonstrates Shaykh Salmán's sound judgement and understanding.

Ḥájí Muḥammad-Ṭáhir, to whom reference was made in a previous chapter, attained the presence of Bahá'u'lláh in 'Akká about 1878 and returned to Persia in company with Shaykh Salmán. The following is a translation of an extract from his memoirs describing their journey together to Shíráz.

> Before our arrival in Shíráz, in the village of Zarqán, Shaykh Salmán sent a letter to Ḥájí Siyyid Ismá'íl-i-Azghandí [a Bahá'í] requesting him to come and meet us outside the city. The reason for this was that Shaykh Salmán had a number of Tablets and other Bahá'í relics with him and as a precaution he wanted this man to take them to Shíráz, because each passenger travelling with the caravan* would be searched by officials before entering the city.
>
> In response to this letter, Ḥájí Siyyid Ismá'íl came on his donkey to Zarqán and took the Tablets and other articles with him to Shíráz. We ourselves followed him in due course and after being searched at the check-point went straight to his house in Shíráz. Our host used to spend much of his time

* A number of camels or donkeys travelling together carrying passengers from one place to another.

in the company of Mushíru'l-Mulk.* The latter had recently retired from his government post and his nephew had succeeded him in this high office. Since his retirement Mushíru'l-Mulk used to spend most of his time in his country home. It was through his gardener there . . . , a Bahá'í, that he was attracted to the Faith.

Soon after his conversion, Mushíru'l-Mulk deputized his friend Ḥájí Siyyid Ismá'íl to attain the presence of Bahá'u'lláh and present to Him, on his behalf, the sum of one thousand túmáns and an exquisite pen-case.† Bahá'u'lláh graciously accepted the pen-case but declined the money which He gave to the bearer. He revealed a Tablet for Mushíru'l-Mulk which was brought to Shíráz by Shaykh Salmán and delivered to him through his friend Ḥájí Siyyid Ismá'íl.

On hearing that Shaykh Salmán was in Shíráz, Mushíru'l-Mulk intimated his desire to meet him and asked his friend to bring Shaykh Salmán to his house the next day. But Shaykh Salmán did not wish to meet Mushíru'l-Mulk. He declined the invitation, giving the excuse that he had no time as he was in a hurry to leave Shíráz. Mushíru'l-Mulk, however, was very eager for this meeting and responded to this message by saying: 'Now that Shaykh Salmán is in such a hurry to go, I shall come instead to his place of residence in the morning.'

When this message was conveyed to Shaykh Salmán he turned to me and said, 'Let us collect our belongings and leave this place.' We left the home of Ḥájí Siyyid Ismá'íl and took residence in a caravanserai in the town.

Ḥájí Siyyid Ismá'íl could not understand Shaykh Salmán's reason for refusing to meet Mushíru'l-Mulk and begged him to change his mind. But he refused, saying: 'If Mushíru'l-Mulk meets me he will lose his faith and will leave the Cause.' When pressed to give his reasons Shaykh Salmán replied, 'Mushíru'l-Mulk has heard many traditions and stories about

* A civil dignitary of the city of Shíráz who held a high position in government circles. In those days such people had immense prestige in the community and were honoured by all.

† It appears that Mushíru'l-Mulk had not been strong in the Faith and because of his position had been careful not to become known publicly as a Bahá'í.

Salmán, the disciple of Muḥammad. For instance, he has heard the fantastic story that fire had no effect upon the feet of Salmán, and that he used to put his own feet instead of wood into a fireplace and heat the pots up with them. No doubt, Mushíru'l-Mulk expects to see similar things from me or he thinks that I have a face radiant and beautiful as an angel's. When he sees my ugly face and rough appearance he will leave the Faith.' Later on this story was mentioned to Bahá'u'lláh, Who confirmed that Shaykh Salmán had been right and that Mushíru'l-Mulk would have left the Faith had that meeting taken place.[1]

Shaykh Salmán, through his long association with the friends and his intimate knowledge of the spirit of the Faith, had acquired an unusual insight into the Writings of Bahá'u'lláh. For instance, the same Ḥájí Muḥammad-Ṭáhir is reported to have said that on their journey together Shaykh Salmán was carrying many Tablets for distribution among the believers in Persia. But none of those Tablets carried the name or address of the one for whom it was destined. This was possibly for the protection of the friends. When, in the course of this journey, Shaykh Salmán reached a place of safety he would take out these Tablets and, being himself illiterate, would ask Ḥájí Muḥammad-Ṭáhir to read them for him. From the contents and the tone of Bahá'u'lláh's words Shaykh Salmán knew for whom the Tablets were intended. He would then ask Ḥájí Muḥammad-Ṭáhir to inscribe their names upon them.

These and many other instances in the life of Shaykh Salmán illustrate the purity of his heart and the clarity of his vision. Although unlettered, he had been endowed with a deep understanding of spiritual verities and divine mysteries and stands out as one of the spiritual giants of this Dispensation.

Bahá'u'lláh has revealed many Tablets for Shaykh Salmán, which often deal with weighty and profound subjects. The Tablet of *Madínatu't-Tawḥíd* is an example. It is in Arabic and its theme is the oneness of God—a subject which Shaykh Salmán had requested Bahá'u'lláh to elucidate for him. He asserts that the unity of God has innumerable features, most of which are beyond the comprehension of man.

With the exception of a short passage which appears in *Gleanings from the Writings of Bahá'u'lláh*,* this Tablet has not so far been translated into English. But Bahá'u'lláh's description of a personal God, incomparable, inaccessible, unknowable, omnipotent, self-subsistent, is similar to that found in other Tablets, some of which are available in English. For example, the following are words of Bahá'u'lláh as He communes with God and extols the Supreme Being:

> Exalted, immeasurably exalted art Thou, O my Beloved, above the strivings of any of Thy creatures, however learned, to know Thee; exalted, immensely exalted art Thou above every human attempt, no matter how searching, to describe Thee! For the highest thought of men, however deep their contemplation, can never hope to outsoar the limitations imposed upon Thy creation, nor ascend beyond the state of the contingent world, nor break the bounds irrevocably set for it by Thee. How can, then, a thing that hath been created by Thy will that overruleth the whole of creation, a thing that is itself a part of the contingent world, have the power to soar into the holy atmosphere of Thy knowledge, or reach unto the seat of Thy transcendent power?
>
> High, immeasurably high art Thou above the endeavours of the evanescent creature to soar unto the throne of Thine eternity, or of the poor and wretched to attain the summit of Thine all-sufficing glory! From eternity Thou didst Thyself describe Thine own Self unto Thy Self, and extol, in Thine own Essence, Thine Essence unto Thine Essence. I swear by Thy glory, O my Best-Beloved! Who is there besides Thee that can claim to know Thee, and who save Thyself can make fitting mention of Thee? Thou art He Who, from eternity, abode in His realm, in the glory of His transcendent unity, and the splendours of His holy grandeur. Were any one except Thee to be deemed worthy of mention, in all the kingdoms of Thy creation, from the highest realms of immortality

* Section XXIV.

down to the level of this nether world, how could it, then, be demonstrated that Thou art established upon the throne of Thy unity, and how could the wondrous virtues of Thy oneness and Thy singleness be glorified?

I bear witness, this very moment, to what Thou hast testified for Thine own Self, ere Thou hadst created the heavens and the earth, that Thou art God, and that there is none other God besides Thee. Thou hast from everlasting been potent, through the Manifestations of Thy might, to reveal the signs of Thy power, and Thou hast ever known, through the Day-Springs of Thy knowledge, the words of Thy wisdom. No one besides Thee hath ever been found worthy to be mentioned before the Tabernacle of Thy unity, and none except Thyself hath proved himself capable of being praised within the hallowed court of Thy oneness.[2]

And again:

Lauded be Thy name, O my God! I testify that no thought of Thee, howsoever wondrous, can ever ascend into the heaven of Thy knowledge, and no praise of Thee, no matter how transcendent, can soar up to the atmosphere of Thy wisdom. From eternity Thou hast been removed far above the reach and the ken of the comprehension of Thy servants, and immeasurably exalted above the strivings of Thy bondslaves to express Thy mystery. What power can the shadowy creature claim to possess when face to face with Him Who is the Uncreated?

I bear witness that the highest thoughts of all such as adore Thy unity, and the profoundest contemplations of all them that have recognized Thee, are but the product of what hath been generated through the movement of the Pen of Thy behest, and hath been begotten by Thy will. I swear by Thy glory, O Thou Who art the Beloved of my soul and the Fountain of my life! I am persuaded of my powerlessness to describe and extol Thee in a manner that becometh the greatness of Thy glory and the excellence of Thy majesty. Aware as I am of this, I beseech Thee, by Thy mercy that hath surpassed all created things, and Thy grace that hath embraced the entire creation, to accept from Thy servants what they are capable of showing forth in Thy path. Aid them, then, by Thy strengthening grace, to exalt Thy word and to blazon Thy praise.

Powerful art Thou to do what pleaseth Thee. Thou, truly, art the All-Glorious, the All-Wise.[3]

In innumerable Tablets and prayers Bahá'u'lláh has proclaimed the existence of God, described His manifold attributes, and glorified His Essence. Indeed, one of the greatest contributions which Bahá'u'lláh has made to religious knowledge is that He has revealed, to the extent of man's understanding in this age, the true nature of God, unravelled some of the mysteries of His creation and removed many misunderstandings and man-made theories concerning Him.

In the Tablet of *Madínatu't-Tawḥíd* Bahá'u'lláh speaks about the Manifestation of God. He explains that since man can never know God's essence, He has, through His grace and bounty, sent His Messengers and Chosen Ones and has, through Them, manifested all His attributes. To know Them is to know God and to obey Them is to obey God. The nearest that man can approach to God is to recognize His Manifestations.

In one of His Tablets Bahá'u'lláh describes the Manifestation as the mirror reflecting the sun. Physically the mirror is made of matter but the light which it reflects comes from the sun. Similarly, the Manifestation, although a human being, manifests all the attributes of God to man. In the Writings of Bahá'u'lláh and the Báb and in other Holy Books there are many references to God's names and attributes which are manifested in this creation.

There is a beautiful prayer in Shí'ah Islám, usually said during the period of fasting in the month of Ramaḍán, which invokes God through His names. There are nineteen invocations in this prayer and each revolves around one of His names, the first being Bahá (Glory). The Báb has taken these names in the same order and given them to the nineteen months of His calendar, each month having nineteen days. This calendar is the basis of the Badí' Calendar, which is the one in use in this Dispensation.*

It is one of the traditions of Islám that the 'Greatest Name of God' is among these nineteen names. Many Islamic scholars failed to solve this mystery. However, in the late sixteenth century a scholar of renown claimed that the 'Greatest Name of God' was Bahá and, in consequence, himself adopted the name of Shaykh Bahá'í. He was born in Lebanon in the year 953 A.H. and travelled as a young boy to Persia. There he received his education, proceeding later to the court of Sháh 'Abbás where he attained unsurpassed eminence on account of his achievements in the arts, sciences and theology.

Bahá'u'lláh has confirmed that the 'Greatest Name' is Bahá. The various derivatives of this word in Arabic are also regarded as the 'Greatest Name'. The Báb, recognizing the station of Bahá'u'lláh as the Supreme Manifestation of God, has lauded His name in His Writings and has made many wonderful references to the name 'Bahá'. For example, before His martyrdom, He wrote on a scroll, in the form of a pentacle, three hundred and sixty derivatives of the word 'Bahá' which He sent to Bahá'u'lláh, together with some documents, His seals and other Writings.

In the Tablet of *Madínatu't-Tawḥíd* Bahá'u'lláh mentions that although God's attributes are numerous, yet in His own realm He is sanctified above all attributes and exalted above all names. To apply any attribute to Him would indeed be tantamount to a limitation. In God's dominion there can be no multiplicity. His Essence and attributes remain one and the same and are indivisible. It is within the realms of the Manifestations that multiplicity of attributes occurs. Here we see many attributes

* Bahá'u'lláh specified that this calendar should begin in A.D. 1844 (the year of the Declaration of the Báb), and He also determined the position of the intercalary days. Nabíl-i-A'ẓam was asked by Bahá'u'lláh, about A.D. 1871, to transcribe the text of the Badí' Calendar and instruct the believers in its details.

such as love, knowledge, power and sovereignty revealed by these Holy Souls.

In this Tablet Bahá'u'lláh affirms that God, through His bounty, sends His Manifestations to the world of humanity so that They may reveal His teachings and exhort men to follow the right way. But man in this life has been given freedom of choice. He can choose the path of truth or tarry in the wilderness of self and passion. Whichever path he selects, God will assist him through His justice. For it would be unjust if the Almighty forced His servants to change their ways. This statement throws light on the relationship of the two attributes of God, His bounty and His justice.

In explaining the Unity of God, Bahá'u'lláh in this Tablet states that there is but one God Whose worshippers may come from various backgrounds and may worship Him in different ways. Nevertheless, their words, if pure, will ascend to His exalted threshold and will be acceptable in His sight.

Speaking of the Manifestations of God, Bahá'u'lláh affirms that since They reveal the same attributes there can be no difference between Them. Here are words of Bahá'u'lláh revealed in the Tablet of *Madínatu't-Tawḥíd*:

> Beware, O believers in the Unity of God, lest ye be tempted to make any distinction between any of the Manifestations of His Cause, or to discriminate against the signs that have accompanied and proclaimed their Revelation. This indeed is the true meaning of Divine Unity, if ye be of them that apprehend and believe this truth. Be ye assured, moreover, that the works and acts of each and every one of these Manifestations of God, nay whatever pertaineth unto them, and whatsoever they may manifest in the future, are all ordained by God, and are a reflection of His Will and Purpose. Whoso maketh the slightest possible difference between their persons, their words, their messages, their acts and manners, hath indeed disbelieved in God, hath repudiated His signs, and betrayed the Cause of His Messengers.[4]

Bahá'u'lláh further explains in this Tablet that although there is no basic difference between the Manifestations, yet They differ in the intensity of Their Revelations and because of this Some are exalted above Others. He speaks of the loftiness of the station of the Báb and refers to Him as the Point around Whom the souls of all the Messengers of God revolve. Although Bahá'u'lláh had not yet declared His Mission, He alludes to His own Revelation as the advent of the Day of God when the doors of Paradise will be opened to all mankind, a Day that shall not be followed by night, a Day in which man can behold the Face of God Himself.*

Súriy-i-Qadír

Another of Bahá'u'lláh's Writings revealed in Baghdád is the *Súriy-i-Qadír* (Súrih of the Omnipotent). Here Bahá'u'lláh reveals the potentialities of this single divine attribute, declaring that the Day-star of the name of God 'The Mighty' has, through the revelation of this Tablet, shed its splendours upon the whole of creation. He calls the peoples of the world to turn their hearts towards its effulgent rays, to be illumined by them and to witness the manifestation of this name, the Mighty, the Omnipotent, within themselves.

He whose heart is enlightened by its radiance, Bahá'u'lláh unequivocally declares, will be filled with power to accomplish whatever he wishes. Should all the world arise against him, through the power of God he will alone withstand its onslaught and establish his ascendancy. But he who deprives himself of this Source of power will never be able to realize God's Omnipotence.

Stories of the heroism demonstrated by Bahá'u'lláh's disciples and companions fill the pages of the Faith's history. Though outwardly weak and helpless, they received such power from on

* In the *Qur'án* and the ḥadíth there are many references to the Day in which man will be able to attain the presence of God. Bahá'u'lláh has clearly proclaimed that, since God is inaccessible, the object of these prophecies is none other than Bahá'u'lláh Himself.

high that their extraordinary courage and spirit made them appear as giants and they were enabled to overcome insurmountable obstacles. Indeed, they performed the miracles of which Christ speaks: '. . . If ye have faith as a grain of mustard seed, ye shall say unto this mountain, Remove hence to yonder place; and it shall remove; and nothing shall be impossible unto you.' (Matt. xvii. 20.)

But Bahá'u'lláh warns those who attain this attribute and reach the summit of authority and power to guard against pride and vainglory. He alludes to Mírzá Yaḥyá, who grew proud of the loftiness and grandeur of his position, showed arrogance towards his Lord and repudiated the Cause of God.

This Tablet, Bahá'u'lláh states, has released a power in the world which each being can manifest in accordance with its capacity. 'This is a new cycle of human power' are the words with which 'Abdu'l-Bahá chose to address His first audience of the Western world, in City Temple, London, in the year 1911.

> All the horizons of the world are luminous, and the world will become indeed as a garden and a paradise. It is the hour of unity of the sons of men and of the drawing together of all races and all classes.[5]

The history of mankind demonstrates that for thousands of years man's progress in every field was slow and unspectacular. But since the coming of the Báb and Bahá'u'lláh, the rate of progress has accelerated astonishingly. Today, man is possessed of such power that he can travel in space and may soon reach other planets. On the other hand, such achievements if not coupled with spiritual progress will bring in their wake man's destruction upon this earth.

The Revelation of Bahá'u'lláh is designed to create a balance between the spiritual and material so that this power can work within proper channels to introduce the most wonderful age in human history. Bahá'u'lláh has made ample provision in His Teachings for the establishment of a divine civilization. He has delineated the basic features of a New World Order for mankind, and Bahá'ís throughout the world are actively engaged in the building of its embryonic institutions. They are convinced that only through this divinely-ordained, world-encircling system can the Kingdom of God, promised by the Prophets of the past, be established upon the earth.

The release of power into the world of humanity by Bahá'u'lláh is a continuing process. No one can as yet see its noble fruits, nor visualize the glory and wonder of the Golden Age of His Faith which is destined to emerge after the establishment of His World Order.

To the emergence of this day Bahá'u'lláh has testified in these words:

> The heights which, through the most gracious favour of God, mortal man can attain in this Day are as yet unrevealed to his sight. The world of being hath never had, nor doth it yet possess, the capacity for such a revelation. The day, however, is approaching when the potentialities of so great a favour will, by virtue of His behest, be manifested unto men.[6]

And again:

> The whole earth is now in a state of pregnancy. The day is approaching when it will have yielded its noblest fruits, when from it will have sprung forth the loftiest trees, the most enchanting blossoms, the most heavenly blessings. Immeasurably exalted is the breeze that wafteth from the garment of thy Lord, the Glorified! For lo, it hath breathed its fragrance and made all things new! Well is it with them that comprehend.[7]

And, finally, in the *Súriy-i-Haykal* (Súrih of the Temple), one of His mighty Tablets revealed in 'Akká, He proclaims:

> The onrushing winds of the grace of God have passed over all things. Every creature hath been endowed with all the potentialities it can carry. And yet the peoples of the world have denied this grace! Every tree hath been endowed with

the choicest fruits, every ocean enriched with the most luminous gems. Man, himself, hath been invested with the gifts of understanding and knowledge. The whole creation hath been made the recipient of the revelation of the All-Merciful, and the earth the repository of things inscrutable to all except God, the Truth, the Knower of things unseen. The time is approaching when every created thing will have cast its burden. Glorified be God Who hath vouchsafed this grace that encompasseth all things, whether seen or unseen![8]

The revelation of the *Súrih of Qadír*, through which Bahá'u'lláh has breathed the spirit of might and power upon the world, is an example of the creativeness of His utterances. Through the agency of His words He has similarly caused other divine attributes to be manifested to men. Bahá'u'lláh testifies in one of His Tablets:

> Know thou of a certainty that the Revelation of every other Name is accompanied by a similar manifestation of Divine power. Every single letter proceeding out of the mouth of God is indeed a mother letter, and every word uttered by Him Who is the Well-Spring of Divine Revelation is a mother word, and His Tablet a Mother Tablet. Well is it with them that apprehend this truth.[9]

Ḥurúfát-i-'Állín

*Ḥurúfát-i-'Állín** (The Exalted Letters) is a Tablet in eight parts revealed by Bahá'u'lláh and dedicated to the memory of Mírzá Muḥammad-i-Vazír, a cousin who died in the province of Núr. He sent it at the hour of their loneliness and grief to Maryam, the sister of Mírzá Muḥammad, and Ḥavvá, his wife, to comfort and console them. Maryam and Ḥavvá were also cousins of Bahá'u'lláh.

Reference has already been made to Maryam in a previous chapter. She was devoted to Bahá'u'lláh and His Faith and was very dear to Him. Mírzá Muḥammad-i-Vazír was also a

* Also titled Muṣíbát-i-Ḥurúfát-i-'Álíyát.

believer, reputed to be the very first among the family of Bahá'u'lláh to have been converted by Him to the Bábí Faith in the province of Núr in 1844.

Ḥurúfát-i-'Állín was revealed originally in Arabic. At the request of some friends Bahá'u'lláh Himself translated it into Persian of a particularly beautiful style. The Tablet speaks of death and the life hereafter, and is often chanted when commemorating the death of a believer.

In it, Bahá'u'lláh portrays creation in vivid terms but refers mainly to the individual life of the believer. For example, He describes his coming into being and recalls the various stages of his creation: first, his seed existing potentially within his forefathers, then its transference from one to another, and finally his appearance as an embryo within the womb of his mother.

This Tablet recounts the bounties of God which have been showered upon the believer's soul from the moment of creation: how, with the invisible hands of love and care He has endowed him with a soul eternal and imperishable, imprinted on him His own image, caused him to be born into this world, fashioned him into a noble creation, enabled him to grow under the shadow of His providence, bestowed upon him His gifts and bounties, opening his eyes to behold the grandeur, the beauty and vastness of His creation and enabling him to recognize His Manifestation and thus gain eternal life.

Bahá'u'lláh states that the believer, having obtained the spirit of faith, reaches the stage of certitude, endures suffering and persecutions in the path of God, renounces the world, becomes wholly devoted to Him and manifests the power, the glory and all the other virtues with which his soul had been invested.

Having glorified, in detail and with much eloquence, the station of the soul and described its immortality, Bahá'u'lláh then directs His attention to physical death and dwells on the afflictions which befall the human temple. At this point the vehicle of so precious an entity as the soul becomes useless, is discarded and buried under the dust. The being who once pulsated with life, whose thoughts, words and actions affected others, whose feelings of love, compassion and generosity imparted joy to his fellow-men is gone from this world. The hands and feet which moved for many years in the service of God are now stilled. The eyes that beheld His glory are now closed. The ears which heard the melodies of the Kingdom are shut. The perfect union which for a lifetime brought the soul and the body together is now ended, as one is elevated to great heights and the other abased and condemned to perish.

In this Tablet Bahá'u'lláh refers to death as an affliction for the body and confirms that since the spiritual worlds of God are hidden from the eyes of men, it is difficult for those who are bereaved by the death of their loved ones not to feel the anguish of separation in their hearts. He therefore counsels them to fix their attention on the spiritual realms of God and the immortality of the soul.

Elsewhere in His Writings Bahá'u'lláh has referred to the habits and customs of various peoples when mourning the departed. Some celebrate the occasion, play music and make merry, while others cry unceasingly, scream and beat upon their heads. Bahá'u'lláh has disapproved of both extremes. Instead He has enjoined His followers to take the path of moderation. He asks them, while their hearts are filled with grief in their bereavement, to meditate upon their own fate, to take heed that one day they too will have to depart in the same way, and to prepare themselves for the next life. In the *Kitáb-i-Aqdas* He counsels His followers in these words:

> Lament not in your hours of trial, neither rejoice therein; seek ye the Middle Way which is the remembrance of Me in your afflictions and reflection over that which may befall you in future. Thus informeth you, He Who is the Omniscient, He Who is Aware.[10]

The last part of this Tablet was revealed particularly for Maryam and Ḥavvá. In it Bahá'u'lláh has poured His love and sympathy upon them both, and consoled them with tenderness and affection.

Lawḥ-i-Ḥúríyyih

A beautiful Tablet in Arabic known as the *Lawḥ-i-Ḥúríyyih* (Tablet of the Maiden) was revealed in Baghdád. Its perusal moves the heart and evokes feelings of excitement and wonder within the soul. For Bahá'u'lláh has portrayed in this Tablet a marvellous picture of Divine Revelation. He has clothed with the garment of words a noble spiritual experience which is at once inexpressible, mysterious and soul-stirring. With His Pen He has depicted, as if in a sublime drama, a vision of divine attributes. The two figures of this drama are Bahá'u'lláh, the Supreme Manifestation of God, and a Maid of Heaven symbolic of some of God's glorious attributes hitherto veiled to mankind.

The dialogue between the two is fascinating. It reveals, on the one hand, the unique station of Bahá'u'lláh and, on the other, the afflictions which had befallen Him through the misdeeds of a perverse generation.

It is not an easy task to describe this Tablet, bearing in mind that it was revealed by Bahá'u'lláh in allusive language which has not been translated into English.

Lawḥ-i-Áyiy-i-Núr

Another Tablet whose significance cannot easily be conveyed is the *Lawḥ-i-Áyiy-i-Núr* (Tablet of the Verse of Light), otherwise known as *Tafsír-i-Ḥurúfát-i-Muqaṭṭa'ih* (Interpretation of the Isolated Letters). It was revealed in Arabic, in honour of Mírzá Áqáy-i-Rikáb-Sáz, a native of Shíráz who laid down his life in the path of Bahá'u'lláh and is one of the martyrs of the Faith.

He requested Bahá'u'lláh to interpret for him a certain verse of the *Qur'án* and to explain the significance and the inner meanings of the isolated letters which appear in the beginning of certain chapters of that Book—letters which had puzzled many of the divines and students of the *Qur'án*.

It should be borne in mind that the fifth Imám of Shí'ah Islám (Imám Muḥammad-Báqir) had already given an interpretation of these letters. For instance, he had indicated that the date of the appearance of the Qá'im* would be equal to the numerical value of certain specified isolated letters of the *Qur'án*, that is, 1260 A.H. (A.D. 1844), which is the year in which the Báb declared His Mission as the Promised One of Islám.

Bahá'u'lláh in this lengthy Tablet deals with both questions which Mírzá Áqá had asked. In His elucidation of the significance of the isolated letters, He throws further light on the subject and reveals certain hidden verities enshrined in these letters. His explanations are so profound as to overwhelm the imagination.

Although Bahá'u'lláh has expounded some of the mysteries which are contained within the isolated letters of the *Qur'án*, yet it is not possible to convey them to those who are not well versed in Islám nor familiar with the Arabic language.

Islám has made a great contribution to religious knowledge and provided a sound foundation for the comprehension of spiritual verities. The *Qur'án* is the repository of the Word of God revealed to Muḥammad. But belief in, and knowledge of, the *Qur'án* does not necessarily help the individual fully to understand the spirit of Islám. The reason for this is that although Divine Revelation had ceased with the death of Muḥammad, for over two hundred years God's guidance was vouchsafed to the Muslim community through the Holy Imáms. Those who turned to them received the spirit of faith and became filled with the knowledge of God, and those who rejected their authority and relied on their own understanding of the *Qur'án* were deprived of the inner significances of that Book.

The first Imám who was appointed by Muḥammad to succeed Him was 'Alí, His cousin and son-in-law, and the first to be His

* Literally, He Who arises: the Promised One of Islám.

disciple. He was to be regarded as the Guardian of the Faith of Islám and its spiritual head. This appointment, however, was not in writing and there is no mention of it in the *Qur'án*. It was made verbally to a great number of His followers assembled at a place called the Pool of Khumm, with the result that divisions arose within the Muslim community immediately after the Prophet's death, and an upheaval which was to have dire consequences engulfed the followers of Islám.

Because the appointment of 'Alí was not considered conclusive or binding by the majority of the followers of Muḥammad, they disregarded the wishes of their Prophet and acted against His counsels. The arch-opponent of this appointment was 'Umar, who became the second Caliph of Islám. He campaigned against 'Alí, usurped his right of succession and rallied the people instead around the old and venerable person of Abú-Bakr who was installed as the first Caliph.

'Umar repudiated 'Alí and his position as the 'Interpreter of the *Qur'án*', saying: 'The Book of God is sufficient for us.' 'Abdu'l-Bahá has explained that these few words, embodying the forces of negation, were so potent that they became the prime factor in precipitating all the discord and bloodshed in the Islamic Dispensation. They caused the martyrdom of Imám 'Alí and His illustrious son, Imám Ḥusayn. They gave rise to untold sufferings and death for countless devoted souls within the Islamic fold. The effect of these words, according to 'Abdu'l-Bahá's testimony, was so far-reaching that a thousand years later it brought about the martyrdom of the Báb and all the sufferings of Bahá'u'lláh.*

When man opposes the plan of God, the course of history changes. Who knows what further blessings would have been vouchsafed to mankind in general, and to Islám in particular, if the followers of Muḥammad had remained faithful to 'Alí. For it was he who was endowed with divine guidance and

* These statements were made by 'Abdu'l-Bahá in a Tablet known as *Lawḥ-i-Hizár-Baytí* (Tablet of One Thousand Verses), one of His most important Tablets concerning the Covenant.

through his unopposed leadership Islám could have exerted a far greater influence upon the peoples of the world.

As a result of man's rebelliousness Islám was divided into two major sects. The Sunnís who constitute the majority followed the Caliphs and built up the temporal power of Islám. The Shí'ahs, followers of 'Alí and eleven other Imáms* who were descended from him, concentrated on spiritual attainments, and are regarded by the Báb and Bahá'u'lláh as followers of the true sect of Islám.

The Imáms, extolled by Bahá'u'lláh as 'those unquenchable lights of Divine guidance', were the lawful successors of Muḥammad. Through their elucidation and interpretation of the *Qur'án* they shed a great lustre upon the Faith of Islám, enriched its literature and disclosed many abstruse mysteries contained within its Scriptures.

Lawḥ-i-Fitnih

The *Lawḥ-i-Fitnih* (Tablet of the Test) is another of Bahá'u'lláh's Arabic Tablets revealed in Baghdád, in honour of Princess Shams-i-Jihán.† She was a granddaughter of Fatḥ-'Alí Sháh, and was known by the designation Fitnih. Her interest in the Faith began when she came in contact with, and became a close friend of Ṭáhirih.‡

Shams-i-Jihán came to Baghdád, attained the presence of Bahá'u'lláh, recognized His station and became a devoted believer. The Pen of the Most High § has revealed several

* It is believed by a major sect of Shí'ah Islám that the Qá'im (the Promised One of Islám) will be the return of the Twelfth Imám. (See *The Dawn-Breakers*, Introduction, xxvii–ix (British ed.); li–iv (U.S. ed.).)

† Some Bahá'í scholars have stated that this Tablet was revealed in Adrianople; they may well be right.

‡ One of the 'Letters of the Living', the great heroine and the most outstanding woman among the apostles of the Báb.

§ A designation by which Bahá'u'lláh has referred to Himself as the Revealer of the Word of God.

Tablets for her and bestowed upon her the title of Varaqatu'r-Riḍván (The Leaf of Paradise).

The *Lawḥ-i-Fitnih*, as its title indicates, is all about tests and trials which are associated with the Day of God. In it Bahá'u'lláh alludes to His own Revelation and states that through His advent the whole creation will be tried; no soul will be exempt. All those who are the embodiments of piety and wisdom, of knowledge and virtue, and even the realities of the Prophets and Messengers of God, will be tested.

In many of His Tablets Bahá'u'lláh has warned His followers about trials and tribulations which will come upon them when they enter the Faith. In every age the heart of man has been proved with the coming of the Manifestation of God. This is the law of God, eternal in the past and eternal in the future. However, this is the Day of God Himself and Bahá'u'lláh has released to humanity enormous spiritual energies. Therefore, the tests which accompany such a mighty Revelation are also great.

The Cause of God is exalted above the world of humanity. In order to embrace it, man must acquire divine qualities. Here, self and worldly ambitions become great barriers. The test of man, therefore, is to subdue his own self. Without this he cannot recognize the Prophet. For the Manifestation of God has two natures, the divine and the human. The former is always hidden by the latter. Only those who have spiritual eyes can penetrate through the veil of human limitations and behold the reality of the Manifestation. Those who are spiritually blind are tested by the personality of the Prophet. They can see only the human qualities and often seek to find fault with these Holy Souls.

After recognition of the Manifestation, the believer will be tested by God in many ways. Each time he passes a test, he will acquire greater spiritual insight and will grow stronger in faith. The closer he gets to the person of the Manifestation the more difficult become his tests. It is then that any trace of ambition or ego may imperil his spiritual life.

There is a tradition in Islám which sets forth the difficulties and perils encountered by man on his journey to God. It describes how all men will perish and die except the believers; all the believers will perish and die except those who are tested; all who are tested will perish and die except those who are sincere, and those who are sincere will be in great danger.

The history of the Faith amply demonstrates this. There were some disciples of Bahá'u'lláh whose faith and devotion had carried them to great heights. They were very close to His person and had become renowned among the believers. Yet, when the winds of test blew, the flame of faith was extinguished within their hearts because of their pride and ambition. As a result, they fell from grace and died spiritually. Among them were some of Bahá'u'lláh's own family. His half-brother, Mírzá Yaḥyá, rebelled against Him, and after His ascension three of His sons and two daughters, together with several relatives and a number of outstanding teachers of the Cause who all hitherto had served the Faith assiduously, broke His Covenant, opposed its appointed Centre 'Abdu'l-Bahá and arose unitedly to extinguish His Cause.

Some people are puzzled by the betrayals and opposition which took place from within the community, especially by those who were closest to Him. But the reason they turned away from Him was because they lacked sufficient faith and qualities of spirit, the essential prerequisites for recognition of the Manifestation of God and submission to His commandments.

One might by way of analogy compare such persons to those who, with no knowledge of mathematics, go to hear an eminent scientist expounding his theories in complicated mathematical terms. Obviously, they are not able to understand him or appreciate his brilliant work. They can see him in no other light than as an ordinary human being whose words are incomprehensible to them. So they begin to judge the scientist by their own standards and will consequently remain unmoved by his intellectual powers. The closer they are to him the better they can see his personal nature, which acts as a veil and hides his greatness from them. Only those who understand mathematics can appreciate the real genius of the scientist. In their view, his scientific knowledge outweighs his human qualities and, therefore, they do not focus their attention on his outward appearance.

Most of those who opposed Bahá'u'lláh or broke His Covenant after having embraced His Faith were ambitious men lacking in spiritual qualities, whose overriding purpose was to enhance their prestige and gain eminence within the Bahá'í community.

One such was Mírzá Muḥammad-'Alí, Bahá'u'lláh's son. He was proud and craved leadership and power. Many of the disciples of Bahá'u'lláh who had spiritual eyes were able to detect in him an air of superiority and self-glorification. They felt his insincerity even before his violation of the Covenant of Bahá'u'lláh.

For instance, Ḥájí Muḥammad-Ṭáhir-i-Málmírí has described in his memoirs his arrival in 'Akká around 1878 and his first meeting with Mírzá Muḥammad-'Alí:

> When we* arrived in Haifa . . . we were taken to the home of Áqá Muḥammad-Ibráhím-i-Ká<u>sh</u>ání. He was directed by Bahá'u'lláh to make his residence in Haifa, to handle the distribution of letters and to give assistance and hospitality to Bahá'í pilgrims. When Bahá'u'lláh was informed that the three of us had arrived, He advised, through Mírzá Áqá Ján . . . that in 'Akká I should stay with my brother Ḥájí 'Alí.† We were driven from Haifa to 'Akká in 'Abdu'l-Bahá's carriage. I was taken to Ḥájí 'Alí's residence, which was situated in the <u>Kh</u>án-i-Súq-i-Abiyaḍ (White Market), in close proximity to the residence of Mírzá Músá, Bahá'u'lláh's brother, and several other Bahá'ís such as Nabíl-i-A'ẓam . . . That day I was most happy. Joy and ecstasy filled my soul. The next day, Mírzá Muḥammad-'Alí accompanied by his two brothers, Mírzá Ḍíyá'u'lláh and Mírzá Badí'u'lláh, came

* Ḥájí Muḥammad-Ṭáhir and two of his fellow pilgrims.
† See *The Bahá'í World*, vol. IX, pp. 624–5, article on Ḥájí 'Alí Yazdí.

to Nabíl-i-A'ẓam's quarters to meet me. Very eagerly my brother and I went there to meet them. But no sooner had I met Mírzá Muḥammad-'Alí and Badí'u'lláh than I became depressed and all the joy in my heart was transformed into sadness and grief. I was distressed . . . and bitterly disappointed with myself. I was wondering what had happened so suddenly that, in spite of all the eagerness and excitement which had filled my being on arrival in 'Akká, I had become so utterly gloomy and dispirited. I was convinced at that time that I had been rejected by God . . .

I was plunged into such a state of distress and anguish that I wanted to leave that gathering forthwith, but did not dare to do so. In my heart I was communing with God . . . anxiously waiting for the visitors to leave so that I could go out and try to find a solution for my sad condition. I noticed that whereas my brother and Nabíl-i-A'ẓam were enjoying themselves talking most happily with these sons of Bahá'u'lláh, I was in a state of mental turmoil and agony throughout the meeting . . . After about an hour, when the visitors were leaving, my brother thanked them most warmly and joyfully.

In the evening he informed me that we were to go and attain the presence of the Master in His reception room. Although depressed and grief-stricken as a result of meeting Mírzá Muḥammad-'Alí, I went with him. As soon as I came into the presence of the Most Great Branch,* a new life was breathed into me. My whole being was filled with such joy and felicity that all the agonies and disturbances of the past vanished in an instant.

A few days later my brother invited me to go with him to meet Mírzá Muḥammad-'Alí again, but in spite of much persuasion on his part I refused to go . . . During the period that I stayed in 'Akká, Mírzá Muḥammad-'Alí came several times to the residence of Nabíl-i-A'ẓam, but I always found some excuse not to go there.[11]

After the ascension of his Father, Mírzá Muḥammad-'Alí opposed 'Abdu'l-Bahá, the appointed Centre of the Cause, and

* 'Abdu'l-Bahá, known as the Master.

precipitated a crisis within the community no less severe than that which shook the Cause to its foundations with the rebellion of Mírzá Yaḥyá. Even in the days of Bahá'u'lláh, Mírzá Muḥammad-'Alí had conducted himself in such a way as to cause, on several occasions, great pain and anguish to Bahá'u'lláh. Once he was sent to India by his Father to publish a compilation of certain Tablets and on this occasion, as stated by Shoghi Effendi in *God Passes By*, he 'tampered with the text of the holy Writings entrusted to his care . . .' He also succeeded, 'by an exceedingly adroit and simple forgery of a word recurring in some of the denunciatory passages addressed by the Supreme Pen [Bahá'u'lláh] to Mírzá Yaḥyá, and by other devices such as mutilation and interpolation, . . . in making them directly applicable' to 'Abdu'l-Bahá. He even went so far as to advance 'openly and shamelessly . . . in a written statement, signed and sealed by him, the very claim' which, after Bahá'u'lláh's ascension, he imputed to 'Abdu'l-Bahá, namely, 'to inaugurate a new Dispensation, and to share with Him [Bahá'u'lláh] the Most Great Infallibility, the exclusive prerogative of the holders of the prophetic office'.[12] Such an impious action evoked the wrath of Bahá'u'lláh. In a Tablet He warned that should Mírzá Muḥammad-'Alí deviate for one moment from the Cause of God he would become as a dead branch. He emphasized in the same Tablet that no one can ever enter into partnership with the Manifestation of God and claim infallibility for himself.

One of the remarkable features of the Cause of God is that it does not harbour egotistical personalities. Its watchword is servitude, a servitude which is real and complete and which manifests itself in the form of humility and self-effacement.

In His Teachings Bahá'u'lláh has made it clear that there are only three stations in this world of existence. First, the station of God which is beyond our comprehension, then the station of the Manifestation of God which is exalted above the world of humanity, and lastly, the station of man which is that of servitude. In the service of the Cause of God the greatest protection for the individual is meekness and humility. It is the most acceptable gift that man can offer to God. For, by virtue of His sovereignty and dominion, humility is not one of God's attributes.

'Abdu'l-Bahá, the true Exemplar of the Teachings of Bahá'u'lláh, has established the pattern of servitude for all to follow. He descended to the lowest plane of servitude which is the highest station for man to attain.

Bahá'u'lláh's position was that of sovereignty and lordship. The position of His Son, 'Abdu'l-Bahá, was that of servitude. When water flows from the summit of a mountain and falls to the valley, it creates energy. Similarly, the flow of spiritual forces from Bahá'u'lláh to 'Abdu'l-Bahá has produced a great power which is released to mankind. When Bahá'u'lláh appeared there was no one worthy or capable of receiving His Revelation. 'Abdu'l-Bahá on behalf of humanity became its perfect recipient and, although not a Manifestation of God, He was invested with divine authority and power by Bahá'u'lláh.

In His *Will and Testament*, written by His own hand, Bahá'u'lláh has appointed 'Abdu'l-Bahá as the One to whom all the believers should turn after His ascension. In this momentous document Bahá'u'lláh writes:

> It is incumbent upon the Aghṣán,* the Afnán† and My kindred to turn, one and all, their faces towards the Most Mighty Branch. Consider that which We have revealed in Our Most Holy Book: 'When the ocean of My presence hath ebbed and the Book of My Revelation is ended, turn your faces towards Him Whom God hath purposed, Who hath branched from this Ancient Root.' The object of this sacred verse is none other except the Most Mighty Branch ['Abdu'l-Bahá]. Thus have We graciously revealed unto you our potent Will, and I am verily the Gracious, the All-Powerful.[13]

* The male descendants of Bahá'u'lláh.

† 'Twigs', a designation used by Bahá'u'lláh to indicate the Báb's kinsmen, who are the descendants of the three maternal uncles of the Báb, and of the two brothers of His wife.

In other Tablets Bahá'u'lláh has paid glowing tribute to the Most Mighty Branch and extolled His station. For instance, in the *Súriy-i-Ghuṣn* (Tablet of the Branch) Bahá'u'lláh has revealed the following words:

> There hath branched from the Sadratu'l-Muntahá* this sacred and glorious Being, this Branch of Holiness; well is it with him that hath sought His shelter and abideth beneath His shadow. Verily the Limb of the Law of God hath sprung forth from this Root† which God hath firmly implanted in the Ground of His Will, and Whose Branch hath been so uplifted as to encompass the whole of creation. Magnified be He, therefore, for this sublime, this blessed, this mighty, this exalted Handiwork! . . . A Word hath, as a token of Our grace, gone forth from the Most Great Tablet—a Word which God hath adorned with the ornament of His own Self, and made it sovereign over the earth and all that is therein, and a sign of His greatness and power among its people . . . Render thanks unto God, O people, for His appearance; for verily He is the most great Favour unto you, the most perfect bounty upon you; and through Him every mouldering bone is quickened. Whoso turneth towards Him hath turned towards God, and whoso turneth away from Him hath turned away from My Beauty, hath repudiated My Proof, and transgressed against Me. He is the Trust of God amongst you, His charge within you, His manifestation unto you and His appearance among His favoured servants . . . We have sent Him down in the form of a human temple. Blest and sanctified be God Who createth whatsoever He willeth through His inviolable, His infallible decree. They who deprive themselves of the shadow of the Branch, are lost in the wilderness of error, are consumed by the heat of worldly desires, and are of those who will assuredly perish.[14]

In the *Lawḥ-i-Fitnih* Bahá'u'lláh states that the tests and trials accompanying His Revelation are so severe that a great many

* A title of Bahá'u'lláh. See p. 83.

† Bahá'u'lláh.

people who believe in God and are well-informed of the mysteries of His Cause will be deprived and left in darkness. Alluding to religious leaders, He foreshadows that these stars of the heaven of knowledge will fall. He affirms that through these tests all that is hidden within men's hearts will be disclosed, that mankind will be separated, some elevated to the heights of faithfulness, others cast down upon the dust. He mentions that the winds of this mighty test of God have already begun to blow and that the full force of their impact would be felt in the year of Shidád* (Stress). This is a reference to the rebellion of Mírzá Yaḥyá in Adrianople which shook the Faith to its foundations and temporarily breached the ranks of its followers. It is also an allusion to the ascension of Bahá'u'lláh which brought in its wake the rebellion of Mírzá Muḥammad-'Alí and the breaking of the Covenant of Bahá'u'lláh.

A careful study of the lives and teachings of the Founders of great religions will demonstrate that one of the functions of the Manifestation of God has always been to explain the meaning and purpose of His Revelation and to solve any difficult problem which perplexes the minds of His followers. Bahá'u'lláh and 'Abdu'l-Bahá were always ready to answer questions asked by the believers. These ranged from weighty subjects down to various minor details dealing with every aspect of the Revelation of Bahá'u'lláh. Indeed, great portions of the Writings of Bahá'u'lláh and 'Abdu'l-Bahá were written in response to these questions. They interpreted the Scriptures of the past, explained many of their abstruse passages and statements, elucidated divine mysteries, expounded the Teachings of God for this age, delineated the features of a New World Order and gave the details of the application of the laws and ordinances of Bahá'u'lláh.

However, on the subject of succession They remained silent and only at the end of Their lives did They disclose the identity of Their successors. There are many wisdoms in this. Such an

* The numerical value of Shidád is 309, meaning 1309 A.H. (A.D. 1892), the year of the ascension of Bahá'u'lláh.

action may be likened to that of a teacher who is always ready to answer questions and help his pupils solve their problems. Only on one occasion does he remain silent and refrain from helping them, namely, on the day of examination. On that day the students alone will have to find the answers. It is their test and it is also the day of separation. Those who pass are elevated to a higher class and those who fail are not.

The history of the Faith demonstrates that the Covenant has always provided the testing-ground for the believers. The Báb gave the glad-tidings of the appearance of 'Him Whom God shall make manifest' but did not explicitly disclose the identity of Bahá'u'lláh. Bahá'u'lláh established a mighty Covenant appointing 'Abdu'l-Bahá as the Centre of that same Covenant but kept this appointment a well-guarded secret until, shortly before His ascension, He handed the *Kitáb-i-'Ahdí* (Book of My Covenant) to 'Abdu'l-Bahá. This document, in the terms of the above analogy, became the examination paper for the entire body of Bahá'u'lláh's followers. Some passed and others failed the test. Similarly, the *Will and Testament* of 'Abdu'l-Bahá in which Shoghi Effendi was appointed as the Guardian of the Faith was kept a secret. It was after His passing that this document was read. Again, this produced tests for the believers. Some who had ambitious ideas and a lust for leadership opposed Shoghi Effendi as the Guardian of the Faith. These men tried very hard to create divisions within the Cause. But one of the distinguishing features of the Faith is that although many outstanding followers of Bahá'u'lláh broke the Covenant and arose, with every means at their disposal, to create schism in the Faith, they failed to bring this about. The Covenant of Bahá'u'lláh triumphed and those who opposed it perished and were brought to naught.

Súriy-i-Nuṣḥ

The *Súriy-i-Nuṣḥ* in Arabic was revealed in Baghdád in honour of Siyyid Ja'far-i-Yazdí, a distinguished divine and a man highly esteemed by the inhabitants of Yazd.* It was on the occasion of Vaḥíd's † visit to that city for the purpose of teaching the Cause that he embraced the Bábí Faith. Soon afterwards a wave of persecutions compelled Vaḥíd and Siyyid Ja'far, together with some other believers, to leave Yazd and go to Nayríz in the province of Fárs.

Having enjoyed great prestige as a divine and being endowed with a wonderful power of exposition, Siyyid Ja'far, under the direction of Vaḥíd, began to teach the Cause publicly in Nayríz. It was not long before a great multitude joined the Faith. This in turn provoked bitter opposition from government authorities and ecclesiastics. A great upheaval followed resulting in the martyrdom of many, including Vaḥíd himself.

The chief instigator of these dire happenings, Zaynu'l-'Ábidín Khán, the Governor of Nayríz, captured a few survivors whom he proposed to torture to death for various specific reasons. Among these was Siyyid Ja'far, who, because of his knowledge and power of utterance, was regarded by the Governor as one of those sharing the major responsibility for converting people to the new Faith. Nabíl, the famous Bahá'í chronicler, has recorded the following about Siyyid Ja'far's arrest:

> Among them [survivors of the Nayríz upheaval] was a certain Siyyid Ja'far-i-Yazdí, who in former days had exercised immense influence and had been greatly honoured by the people. So great was the respect they owed him that Zaynu'l-'Ábidín Khán gave him precedence over himself and treated him with extreme deference and courtesy. He gave orders that the turban of that same man be befouled and flung into the fire. Shorn of the emblem of his lineage, he was exposed to the eyes of the public, who marched before him and overwhelmed him with abuse and ridicule.[15]

* The author's great-great-grandfather.

† An outstanding divine who became a follower of the Báb. His first contact with the Faith came about when as an envoy of Muḥammad Sháh he met the Báb for the purpose of investigating His Message. As a result, Vaḥíd became an ardent believer. See Appendix III.

The Nayríz upheaval which lasted for many months brought widespread poverty and famine in its wake. The troops who were engaged in this conflict had drawn too heavily upon the meagre resources of the local community and at long last, after the departure of the troops, food had become almost unobtainable and many poor people were starving. In the meantime, the Governor had hoarded a large stock of corn to sell to the public at an inflated price. When, however, the situation became desperate, he consented to distribute the corn among the people at a nominal sum.

When the ration was given out, Siyyid Ja'far would be brought from the dungeon and posted at the entrance to the barn. The Governor's orders were that all those who wished to obtain corn must first spit upon Siyyid Ja'far's face. Failure to do this would deprive them of their ration.

The following extract from a biography of Siyyid Ja'far reveals something of this ordeal and other indignities which were heaped upon him and his fellow-prisoner, Ḥájí Muḥammad-Taqí, an eminent personage of Nayríz and an ardent follower of the Báb.*

> For hours this champion of the Cause of God [Siyyid Ja'far], this once revered man of learning, stood by the door of the barn while hundreds of men and women spat upon his blessed face as they filed through that door, looking at him with bitter hate and prejudice.
>
> In the face of this dire humiliation, Áqá Siyyid Ja'far's feelings were not those of disgust, intolerance or indignation. On the contrary, he remained calm and resigned throughout his ordeal and manifested a spirit of sublime joy and love and thankfulness towards those who offended him.
>
> Once during the ordeal, it is authoritatively stated, he noticed several people who hesitated to come forward for their share. Apparently the ghastly deed of spitting upon his face kept them away. With a face beaming with heavenly joy he beckoned them and said: 'You had better come and get

* See p. 263.

your share before it is too late; it won't matter if you spit upon my face; I'll wipe it off with my handkerchief . . .'

A deed such as this, so rare, so Christ-like, constitutes a shining proof of the transmuting power which is latent in the words of the Manifestations of God.

Very probably, as he stood by the door of the barn that day, his thoughts went back to those glamorous days in Yazd, where each Friday at the close of his sermon, standing on the steps of the pulpit, he would receive the homage and the tumultuous ovation of the vast audience. Now how striking was the contrast! Although the object of the vilest indignity, he was extremely happy, because his beloved Lord had revealed to his eyes the glorious vista of a new life and bestowed upon him the crown of eternal glory. Little wonder, therefore, that those bitter persecutions could not becloud the radiance of his heavenly joy . . .

This monstrous treatment meted out to Áqá Siyyid Ja'far was but a prelude to a period of agonizing tortures for himself as well as for his illustrious companion. Among other things, the ruthless Governor ordered that the bastinado be inflicted on Áqá Siyyid Ja'far in public. Each day he was conducted from the dungeon to the gate of the house of a well-to-do-citizen where this heart-rending scene was staged. There he was beaten until, as was the fashion, the occupants of the house as well as passers-by would secure the victim's temporary release by offering money to the torturers as a ransom. Then, next day, the scene would be shifted to another point along the street. After a while, as a result of this daily torture, Áqá Siyyid Ja'far's legs and feet became so horribly sore and swollen that they could no longer support his body.

The fate of his companion, Ḥájí Muḥammad-Taqí, was even more cruel and appalling. Daily, he was conducted to the Governor's mansion where, stripped of his clothes, he was flung into the pool. A number of men, placed around and armed with long sticks, would administer severe blows upon his body. The standing order was that the beating should be continued until the water around him turned reddish with blood.

However, the mighty Hand that had raised up and reared these wondrous beings was now to stay the tide of suffering which was about to engulf them. They were destined to live to receive the greatest privilege of all, having their eyes illumined by gazing upon the heavenly countenance of Bahá'u'lláh.

It was the Governor's wife who, as the result of a dream, was prompted to secure their freedom. She approached her husband with an earnest appeal to release these unfortunate victims, but her intercession proved of no avail. Moreover, she was rebuked for being too soft and sentimental. Undismayed by her husband's ruthless attitude, she decided to work secretly towards that end.

With the goodwill and support of a few trusted persons at her disposal she worked out a plan and made the necessary arrangements with utmost caution. Then, late one evening the prison door was opened and the pitiable figures of Ḥájí Muḥammad-Taqí and Áqá Siyyid Ja'far were taken out, propped up on donkeys and entrusted to a muleteer with the express order to carry them at full speed to Harát—a small town beyond the area of jurisdiction of the Governor of Nayríz.

Eventually, when these oppressed souls reached Harát they were utterly exhausted. The sight of their appalling condition presented a study in grief and aroused the sympathy of the headman of the village who received and treated them with the utmost kindness.

They remained in Harát for a number of months to recuperate and heal their terrible wounds. Afterwards they travelled to Yazd. When the friends came to know about the banishment of Bahá'u'lláh to 'Iráq, Ḥájí Muḥammad-Taqí set out on foot on a journey of no less than 1,500 kilometres to Baghdád, where he attained the presence of Bahá'u'lláh and received His abundant blessings. The momentous *Súrih of Ṣabr** was revealed to his imperishable memory.

Later Áqá Siyyid Ja'far followed the example of his old companion. Those feet that had received such beastly tortures for months did not fail to carry him all the long way to

* This Tablet is also known as *Lawḥ-i-Ayyúb*.

the abode of his Lord where the Hands of Glory showered heavenly bounties upon him . . .[16]

Although the *Súriy-i-Nuṣḥ* was revealed before His declaration, nevertheless Bahá'u'lláh has left no doubt as to His own station. For throughout this Tablet He identifies Himself with God and speaks as His mouthpiece. He describes the appearance of the Prophets from Adam to the Báb, proclaims Their divine origin, depicts the life, character and mission of Each, demonstrates that in every age They were denounced and fiercely opposed by the priests and religious leaders, portrays Their suffering and persecution at the hands of the people and speaks of Their ultimate victory over Their adversaries.

Anticipating His own declaration, Bahá'u'lláh in this Tablet counsels the learned men of the Bábí community not to rely on their knowledge. He urges them to cleanse their hearts so that when the appointed hour comes and the beauty of the Promised One is unveiled they may be enabled to recognize Him and embrace His Cause.

It is in this Tablet that Bahá'u'lláh makes reference to one of His bitterest enemies, Shaykh 'Abdu'l-Ḥusayn-i-Ṭihrání, a crafty and deceitful mujtahid who was sent to 'Iráq by order of the Sháh to carry out the repair of the Muslim holy sites in Karbilá. This man was notorious in royal circles for his mischief-making and this post was devised in order to remove him from Ṭihrán.

Soon after his arrival in 'Iráq, Shaykh 'Abdu'l-Ḥusayn became alarmed at the rising prestige and ascendancy of Bahá'u'lláh. The outpourings of His divine Pen which had inspired many to sacrifice their lives in His path, the extraordinary love and devotion which His companions had for Him, the manner in which they expressed, both in public and private, their loyalty and reverence, the high esteem in which the inhabitants of Baghdád held Him—all aroused the animosity of the Shaykh and ignited the fire of jealousy and hatred within his breast.

HÁJÍ MUḤAMMAD-ṬÁHIR-I-MÁLMÍRÍ

Historian and teacher of the Faith, father of the author.
Some of his memoirs concerning Bahá'u'lláh are quoted in this book

TABLET OF BAHÁ’U’LLÁH

In His own handwriting

Intended for Hájí Muḥammad-Ṭáhir-i-Málmírí

(*see page* 39)

With all the evil forces he could muster, he arose to oppose Bahá'u'lláh and His companions.

The proud and hateful Mírzá Buzurg Khán, the Persian Consul-General in Baghdád, soon after his arrival in the year 1276 A.H. (A.D. 1860), allied himself with the Shaykh to uproot the Cause and destroy its Author.

The first move was to discredit Bahá'u'lláh by spreading false accusations against Him, demanding from the authorities in Baghdád His extradition from 'Iráq. But when the Shaykh realized the futility of these efforts, he turned his attention to arousing public animosity against Him. The following are the words of Shoghi Effendi as he describes some of the activities of Mírzá Buzurg Khán:

> Mírzá Buzurg Khán, on his part, used his influence in order to arouse the animosity of the lower elements of the population against the common Adversary, by inciting them to affront Him in public, in the hope of provoking some rash retaliatory act that could be used as a ground for false charges through which the desired order for Bahá'u'lláh's extradition might be procured. This attempt too proved abortive, as the presence of Bahá'u'lláh, Who, despite the warnings and pleadings of His friends, continued to walk unescorted, both by day and by night, through the streets of the city, was enough to plunge His would-be molesters into consternation and shame. Well aware of their motives, He would approach them, rally them on their intentions, joke with them, and leave them covered with confusion and firmly resolved to abandon whatever schemes they had in mind. The consul-general had even gone so far as to hire a ruffian, a Turk, named Riḍá, for the sum of one hundred túmáns, provide him with a horse and with two pistols, and order him to seek out and kill Bahá'u'lláh, promising him that his own protection would be fully assured. Riḍá, learning one day that his would-be victim was attending the public bath, eluded the vigilance of the Bábís in attendance, entered the bath with a pistol concealed in his cloak, and confronted Bahá'u'lláh in the inner chamber, only to discover that he

lacked the courage to accomplish his task. He himself, years later, related that on another occasion he was lying in wait for Bahá'u'lláh, pistol in hand, when, on Bahá'u'lláh's approach, he was so overcome with fear that the pistol dropped from his hand; whereupon Bahá'u'lláh bade Áqáy-i-Kalím, who accompanied Him, to hand it back to him, and show him the way to his home.[17]

But all these plans failed miserably and Shaykh 'Abdu'l-Ḥusayn began to dispatch a series of alarming letters to the court of the Sháh in Ṭihrán telling of Bahá'u'lláh's rising power. At last he managed to obtain full authority from the Sháh to take necessary measures against the Bábís with assistance from the Persian divines residing in 'Iráq.

Immediately upon receipt of this mandate the Shaykh invited all ranks of clergy to a conference held at his home. There he forcefully condemned Bahá'u'lláh's activities, accused Him of destroying the Faith of Islám, and demanded that holy war should be proclaimed against the Bábís of 'Iráq. The body of the divines approved. However, Shaykh Murtiḍáy-i-Anṣárí, the leading mujtahid of the Shí'ah community, a man of justice and piety to whom reference has been made in a previous chapter,* refused to sanction their evil plans and arose and abruptly left the meeting.

Some time before, Bahá'u'lláh had invited Shaykh 'Abdu'l-Ḥusayn to meet Him face to face so that the truth of His Cause might be established. But the Shaykh, who had accepted the invitation at first, was afraid to meet the challenge and did not appear at the appointed place. This time, however, the conference of the divines decided to send the devout and high-minded Ḥájí Mullá Ḥasan-i-'Ammú as an emissary to Bahá'u'lláh to put certain questions to Him, designed to establish the truth of His Mission. Ḥájí Mullá Ḥasan asked Prince Zaynu'l-'Ábidín Khán, the Fakhru'd-Dawlih, a friend and admirer of Bahá'u'lláh who often visited His home, to arrange an interview with Him.

* See p. 91.

When the appointed day came, the prince took him personally to the house of Bahá'u'lláh.*

No sooner had Ḥájí Mullá Ḥasan presented himself to Bahá'u'lláh than he discovered the ocean of His utterance surging before him and saw himself as a mere drop compared to the vastness of Bahá'u'lláh's knowledge. Having had his questions answered with brilliance and simplicity, he then ventured to inform Bahá'u'lláh that the divines regarded the performance of a miracle to be the final and conclusive evidence of the authenticity of His mission. These are the words of Bahá'u'lláh in answer to him:

> Although you have no right to ask this, for God should test His creatures, and they should not test God, still I allow and accept this request ... The 'ulamás† must assemble, and, with one accord, choose one miracle, and write that, after the performance of this miracle they will no longer entertain doubts about Me, and that all will acknowledge and confess the truth of My Cause. Let them seal this paper, and bring it to Me. This must be the accepted criterion: if the miracle is performed, no doubt will remain for them; and if not, We shall be convicted of imposture.[18]

Ḥájí Mullá Ḥasan found this answer to be satisfactory. He arose, reverently kissed the knee of Bahá'u'lláh and promised to convey His words to the divines. But the assemblage of the divines decided not to respond to Bahá'u'lláh's challenge and did not pursue the matter. Ḥájí Mullá Ḥasan conveyed this decision to Bahá'u'lláh through Prince Zaynu'l-'Ábidín Khán. Upon hearing this news, Bahá'u'lláh is reported to have said:

* When Ḥájí Mullá Ḥasan arrived in Bahá'u'lláh's reception room, to his amazement he found the celebrated mujtahid, Mullá Muḥammad-i-Qá'iní surnamed Nabíl-i-Akbar (one of the Apostles of Bahá'u'lláh) seated there with reverence and humility. Quietly he asked Nabíl-i-Akbar, 'What are you doing here, sir?' The reply came, 'I am here for the same reason that you are.' (See pp. 91–5.)

† Divines and learned men of Islám.

> We have, through this all-satisfying, all-embracing message which We sent, revealed and vindicated the miracles of all the Prophets, inasmuch as We left the choice to the 'ulamás themselves, undertaking to reveal whatever they would decide upon.[19]

Shaykh 'Abdu'l-Ḥusayn, who had so ignominiously failed to carry out his designs, decided to put further pressure on the Persian government. Assisted by his scheming accomplice Mírzá Buzurg Khán, he dispatched a series of false and grossly exaggerated reports to the authorities in Ṭihrán, urging them to take steps to remove Bahá'u'lláh from 'Iráq.

No wonder that the Shaykh, who had so relentlessly sought to extinguish the light of the Cause and destroy its Leader, was stigmatized by Bahá'u'lláh in the *Súriy-i-Nuṣḥ* as the 'scoundrel', the 'schemer', the 'wicked one', he who 'drew the sword of his self against the face of God', 'in whose soul Satan hath whispered' and 'from whose impiety Satan flies', the 'depraved one', 'from whom originated and to whom will return all infidelity, cruelty and crime'.[20]

In a passage in the *Súriy-i-Mulúk* (Súrih of the Kings), addressing the Persian Ambassador in Constantinople, Bahá'u'lláh alludes to Mírzá Buzurg Khán, the Persian Consul-General in Baghdád:

> For eleven years We dwelt in that land, until the Minister representing thy government arrived, whose name Our pen is loth to mention, who was given to wine, who followed his lusts, and committed wickedness, and was corrupt and corrupted 'Iráq. To this will bear witness most of the inhabitants of Baghdád, wert thou to inquire of them, and be of such as seek the truth. He it was who wrongfully seized the substance of his fellow men, who forsook all the commandments of God, and perpetrated whatever God had forbidden. Eventually, he, following his desires, rose up against Us, and walked in the ways of the unjust. He accused Us, in his letter to thee, and thou didst believe him and followed in his way, without seeking any proof or trustworthy evidence from

him. Thou didst ask for no explanation, nor didst thou attempt either to investigate or ascertain the matter, that the truth might be distinguished from falsehood in thy sight, and that thou mightest be clear in thy discernment. Find out for thyself the sort of man he was by asking those Ministers who were, at that time, in 'Iráq, as well as the Governor of the City* and its high Counsellor, that the truth may be revealed to thee, and that thou mayest be of the well-informed.[21]

In the end, the intrigues and machinations of the Shaykh and the efforts of the Consul-General so influenced the Sháh that he instructed Mírzá Sa'íd Khán, the Persian Foreign Minister, to send a request to the Ottoman government for the transfer of Bahá'u'lláh from Baghdád. In the meantime, the enemy was becoming increasingly hostile towards Bahá'u'lláh. Siyyid Mírzá Ḥusayn-i-Mutavallí, a notorious Bábí, suggested in a letter to Him that He remain at home for the sake of His own safety. In reply to this, Bahá'u'lláh revealed a Tablet in Persian known as *Shikkar-Shikan-Shavand.*

Shikkar-Shikan-Shavand

This soul-stirring Tablet, notable for the beauty and lucidity of its composition, inspires a believer with faith and assurance. In it Bahá'u'lláh agrees that great dangers are ahead, that a relentless enemy is poised to launch a fierce onslaught against Him and that in people's opinion the right course would be to flee and retire to a place of safety. Nevertheless, He unequivocally proclaims, the Chosen Ones of God are not fearful of calamities and tribulations. Having renounced the world and placed their trust and confidence in God, they brave every danger and welcome sufferings in His path.

Likewise, no calamity can quench His ardour in the path of God. He will never flee from His enemies, neither will He resist them. For they are powerless to destroy the foundation of the Cause of God. Should they bury Him beneath the earth, the

* Baghdád.

hand of Divine Power would assuredly raise Him up again, resplendent and victorious. Despite all opposition to Him in Baghdád, He is seated on the throne of glory, serene, majestic and manifest as the sun. For those who have spiritual eyes, His very appearance in public at a time when the enemy is intent upon taking His life is but an evidence of His divine authority.

In this Tablet Bahá'u'lláh calls on Siyyid Ḥusayn to meditate on the sufferings which were inflicted upon Muḥammad, the Prophet of God. So grievously was He persecuted that the Holy Spirit appeared to Him and spoke these words:

> But if their opposition be grievous to Thee—if Thou canst, seek out an opening into the earth or a ladder into heaven.[23]

This verse implies that the Prophet had no other course to take but that of enduring hardships and tribulations in the path of God. Bahá'u'lláh urges Siyyid Ḥusayn to consider it and similar verses of the *Qur'án*, that he may discover their mysteries and realize that in every age the Manifestations of God suffer at the hands of the ungodly.

In the Tablet of *Shikkar-Shikan* Bahá'u'lláh alludes to Shaykh 'Abdu'l-Ḥusayn, condemns his actions and confidently asserts that he will fail miserably in his evil designs to harm His person.

Bahá'u'lláh states in many of His Tablets that suffering and tribulation in the path of God will ultimately lead the Cause to victory. He welcomed adversities in order that mankind may be freed and united. In one of His Tablets He thus proclaims:

> The Ancient Beauty hath consented to be bound with chains that mankind may be released from its bondage, and hath accepted to be made a prisoner within this most mighty Stronghold that the whole world may attain unto true liberty. He hath drained to its dregs the cup of sorrow, that all the peoples of the earth may attain unto abiding joy, and be filled with gladness. This is of the mercy of your Lord, the Compassionate, the Most Merciful. We have accepted to be abased, O believers in the Unity of God, that ye may be exalted, and have suffered manifold afflictions, that ye might prosper and flourish.[23]

In *The Hidden Words* Bahá'u'lláh states:

> My calamity is My providence, outwardly it is fire and vengeance, but inwardly it is light and mercy.[24]

Speaking of man's impotence to quench the Cause of God He has revealed:

> As My tribulations multiplied, so did My love for God and for His Cause increase, in such wise that all that befell Me from the hosts of the wayward was powerless to deter Me from My purpose. Should they hide Me away in the depths of the earth, yet would they find Me riding aloft on the clouds, and calling out unto God, the Lord of strength and of might. I have offered Myself up in the way of God, and I yearn after tribulations in My love for Him, and for the sake of His good-pleasure. Unto this bear witness the woes which now afflict Me, the like of which no other man hath suffered.[25]

And again:

> By God! Troubles have failed to unnerve Me, and the repudiation of the divines hath been powerless to weaken Me. I have spoken and still speak forth before the face of men: 'The door of grace hath been unlocked and He Who is the Dayspring of Justice is come with perspicuous signs and evident testimonies, from God, the Lord of strength and of might!'[26]

After the Tablet of *S͟hikkar-S͟hikan* was revealed, Bahá'u'lláh instructed that copies be sent to several dignitaries both civil and ecclesiastic. All those who received it were astounded by Bahá'u'lláh's faith and courage. Siyyid Ḥusayn, for whom Bahá'u'lláh revealed this challenging Tablet, was a native of Qum. He became a Bábí in the early days of the Faith and joined the defenders of the fort of S͟hayk͟h Ṭabarsí, where over three hundred Bábís under the leadership of Quddús were besieged by the army of the S͟háh. For several months they had to endure starvation and fierce attack. The acts of heroism and self-sacrifice demonstrated by these men of God are unparalleled in the history of religion.

However, Siyyid Ḥusayn was no hero. Towards the end when tests and trials were at their peak, he betrayed his friends. This happened after Quddús had warned his companions that days of intense suffering and devastating affliction were at hand. The very night this warning was uttered, the Siyyid despatched a message to the retreating commander of the army, informed him of the death of Mullá Ḥusayn whom the enemy dreaded so much, revealed some facts concerning the fewness of the defenders of the fort, and urged him to make a final onslaught, assuring him of victory.

Emboldened by these revelations, the army launched several attacks. But each time they were ignominiously defeated. At last, finding the situation unbearable and alarmed at the prospect of losing his life, Siyyid Ḥusayn deserted the fort and went straight to the enemy camp. There he recanted his Faith and gained his freedom.

Bahá'u'lláh's amanuensis*, in a Tablet apparently written in Adrianople, has condemned Siyyid Ḥusayn for his unfaithfulness and treachery. In it he states that his disgraceful treatment of Quddús was so heinous that he is ashamed to mention it. This refers to the day that Quddús was being conducted to the scene of his martyrdom, chained, surrounded by a howling mob, and assailed from every direction. During such tragic circumstances, in order to demonstrate his withdrawal from the Faith, Siyyid Ḥusayn went forward and smote Quddús in the face.

In spite of his unfaithfulness and treachery, the Siyyid managed, soon after this shameful act, to enter into the fold again. Indeed, in 1852, when Bahá'u'lláh was taken to the Síyáh-Chál, he too was imprisoned there as a Bábí.† Later he went to Baghdád and joined the community there. He was never faithful to the Cause of God. When Bahá'u'lláh was in Adrianople, he

* Mírzá Áqá Ján. See p. 40.

† Some have reached the conclusion that Siyyid Ḥusayn was not a genuine Bábí, had adopted the Faith as a convenient cover for his activities, and was planted as a spy both at Shaykh Ṭabarsí and the Síyáh-Chál.

openly showed opposition to Him and became a follower of Mírzá Yaḥyá.

Javáhiru'l-Asrár

The *Javáhiru'l-Asrár* (The Essence of Mysteries) was revealed in Arabic by Bahá'u'lláh in Baghdád in honour of Siyyid Yúsuf-i-Sidihí, a resident of Karbilá, who had compiled some questions concerning the coming of the Promised One of Islám, claiming that anyone who could answer them would be the possessor of Truth. As soon as his questions reached Bahá'u'lláh, He revealed this Tablet and despatched it to Siyyid Yúsuf the same day.

The *Javáhiru'l-Asrár* must have been revealed while Bahá'u'lláh's enemies were actively plotting against His life. For in it He speaks briefly of the sufferings which were inflicted upon Him and mentions the machinations of those who were intent upon banishing or assassinating Him. Another clue pointing to the period of its revelation is to be found in the *Kitáb-i-Íqán*. There Bahá'u'lláh alludes to the Tablet of *Javáhiru'l-Asrár* when He says:

> Similarly, in the three other Gospels, according to Luke, Mark, and John, the same statements are recorded. As We have referred at length to these in Our Tablets revealed in the Arabic tongue, We have made no mention of them in these pages, and have confined Ourselves to but one reference.[27]

This outstanding Tablet deals with many subjects, unravels many mysteries, reveals the meanings of several passages in the Holy Books of older religions and gives some of the noblest counsels for man's spiritual advancement. In part it resembles—though not on a mystical level—some of the features of *The Seven Valleys*.

One such similarity is Bahá'u'lláh's explanation of the seven stages in man's journey to his ultimate spiritual goal. These stages he calls 'cities' of 'search', 'love', 'unity', 'wonderment', 'utter nothingness', 'immortality', followed by a 'city' known only to God and His Manifestations, so exalted that man cannot comprehend its nature, for which there can be no name or definition. Of the 'city of unity' Bahá'u'lláh states that therein man will see in all things the signs of God, will become humble, never exalting himself above others, and at all times will regard himself as being in the presence of his Lord. In the 'city of immortality', he will find himself independent of all things but God, having access to God's inexhaustible treasures although living in poverty. On this plane all the attributes of God will be manifested within him and his life will become divine.

Bahá'u'lláh testifies that the essential prerequisites for man in all these journeys are humility and self-effacement before the believers. Any trace of pride or self will debar the wayfarer from entering any of these 'cities' and will cause him to return to the first stage. The importance of this Tablet becomes apparent when we note that its themes are similar to those of the *Kitáb-i-Íqán*. Although less in compass, its subjects are those which Bahá'u'lláh has more fully elaborated in that book. For example, He enumerates in this Tablet a number of causes which have prevented the followers of all religions from recognizing the next Manifestation of God; stipulates some of the qualities which the seeker must possess in order to find the truth; affirms that God is unknowable in His Essence; asserts the unity of all His Messengers; explains the meaning of such terms as the Day of Judgement, resurrection, life, death and similar terminologies mentioned in the Holy Books of the past; interprets certain prophecies from the Old and New Testaments, and elucidates passages from the *Qur'án* and traditions of Islám which anticipate the coming of the Qá'im* and the advent of the Day of God, identified by Bahá'u'lláh with the appearance of 'Him Whom God shall make manifest'.

* The Promised One of Islám Whose advent the Báb fulfilled. See p. 126.

10

The Kitáb-i-Íqán

Circumstances of Its Revelation

In the whole range of Bahá'u'lláh's Writings, the *Kitáb-i-Íqán* (The Book of Certitude) has most importance, with the exception of the *Kitáb-i-Aqdas* (The Most Holy Book). It was revealed in Baghdád about two years before His Declaration, in honour of Ḥájí Mírzá Siyyid Muḥammad, the Báb's maternal uncle.

The Báb had three maternal uncles. The first to embrace His Faith was Ḥájí Mírzá Siyyid 'Alí, known as Khál-i-A'ẓam (the Greatest Uncle). It was he who cared for the Báb and, after the passing of His father, was responsible for bringing Him up.

Ḥájí Mírzá Siyyid 'Alí became aware of the spiritual qualities and superhuman powers which his Nephew manifested from an early age. He readily recognized the station of the Báb and became an ardent believer as soon as he became acquainted with His claims. Indeed, next to the Letters of the Living, he was the first person in Shíráz to acknowledge the divine origin of the Message of the Báb. From then on he devoted his life entirely to the promotion of the newly-born Faith and the protection of its youthful Founder. A few months before the martyrdom of the Báb, he was arrested and, upon refusing to recant his faith, was publicly martyred. He is one of the Seven Martyrs of Ṭihrán.

The eldest uncle, Ḥájí Mírzá Siyyid Muḥammad, although fully aware of the outstanding qualities of his Nephew, was not converted to His Faith until he met Bahá'u'lláh in Baghdád and received the *Kitáb-i-Íqán* in answer to his questions. The third uncle was Ḥájí Mírzá Ḥasan-'Alí.

For some years Ḥájí Mírzá Siyyid Muḥammad carried out his business as a merchant away from home, in Búshihr (Bushire), in association with his brother Ḥájí Mírzá Siyyid 'Alí and his Nephew the Báb. When these two left for Shíráz he continued to work on his own and was still in Búshihr when the Báb declared His Mission to His first disciples. Later, when the Báb made His pilgrimage to Mecca, He travelled by way of Búshihr where He stayed at the home of Ḥájí Mírzá Siyyid Muḥammad. He returned there some months later while journeying back to Shíráz. It was during these visits that Ḥájí Mírzá Siyyid Muḥammad witnessed a transformation of spirit in the Báb and wrote about it to his own mother and sister (the mother of the Báb) in these words:

> . . . His eminence Jináb-i-Ḥájí* has safely arrived and I am pleased to spend my time in His presence. It seems advisable that He should stay in Búshihr for a short while; but please rest assured that soon He will depart for home . . . Truly, His bountiful soul is the source of felicity for the people of this world, and the next. He brings honour to us all . . .[1]

Yet in spite of these remarks and of his unfailing admiration and respect for the Báb, Ḥájí Mírzá Siyyid Muḥammad did not recognize His station for many years and remained uncommitted to His Cause.

In the meantime, the martyrdoms of the Báb and His illustrious uncle in 1850 brought immense grief and shock to all the members of the family. The Báb's mother, Fáṭimih-Bagum, could no longer bear to live in her home in Shíráz and took up residence in far-off 'Iráq, in the city of Karbilá, to be near the Shrine of Imám Ḥusayn. Until the time Bahá'u'lláh arrived in 'Iráq after His imprisonment in the Síyáh-Chál, and established contact with her, she remained unaware of the significance of the Message of the Báb. It was Bahá'u'lláh Who arranged for

* The Báb was referred to as Ḥájí because of His pilgrimage to Mecca.

Ḥájí Siyyid Javád-i-Karbilá'í,* one of the distinguished early disciples of the Báb, accompanied by a devoted believer, the wife of a certain Shaykh 'Abdu'l-Majíd-i-Shírází, to meet with the mother of the Báb and demonstrate to her the truth of the Mission of her illustrious Son. This contact established by Bahá'u'lláh brought forth a wonderful response. Her soul was quickened and the glory of the new Faith of God founded by the Báb was unveiled before her eyes. Later she recognized the station of Bahá'u'lláh, embraced His Faith and remained steadfast till the end of her life.

Although several of the Báb's kinsmen, including His wife, had accepted the Faith during the early days of His ministry, and thousands of His followers had laid down their lives in His path, nevertheless Ḥájí Mírzá Siyyid Muḥammad was not absolutely convinced that the Báb, his Nephew, could be the Promised One of Islám. Several believers tried to dispel his doubts but their efforts did not win him over. Ḥájí Mírzá Ḥabíbu'lláh, an Afnán who was one of the custodians of the House of the Báb in Shíráz, has recorded the following account by his father, Áqá Mírzá Núru'd-Dín, a follower of the Báb, of a series of discussions which he held with Ḥájí Mírzá Siyyid Muḥammad. These discussions appear to have been the turning-point in the spiritual life of the Báb's uncle.

> . . . During the initial stages of our discussions Ḥájí Mírzá Siyyid Muḥammad maintained a negative attitude and would repudiate any proof or argument that I put forward. These discussions lasted for several meetings. Once when I was talking with great fervour and conviction about the Faith, he turned to me in astonishment and exclaimed: 'Are you really saying that my nephew is the promised Qá'im?' When I reaffirmed my belief that He was, Ḥájí Mírzá Siyyid Muḥammad became perplexed and expressed his view that this was all

* An eminent divine of great learning who became a devoted follower of the Báb in the first year of His Declaration, and later recognized the station of Bahá'u'lláh and embraced His Faith. (See pp. 221–4, and Nabíl-i-A'ẓam, *The Dawn-Breakers,* index reference.)

very strange. He then began to meditate and was lost in thought. Seeing him in this reflective mood, I could not prevent myself from laughing. He asked my reason for laughing, but as it would reflect badly upon him I was reluctant to tell. However, he insisted, so I told him: 'Your view that your nephew cannot be the promised Qá'im is similar to the objection which Abú-Lahab* had. He also said "how could it be possible for my nephew to become a prophet?" But Muḥammad was the true Prophet of God. Now it is up to you to investigate this Cause. You must be very proud that this Sun of Truth has dawned from your family and its Light shone forth from your home. Do not hold back from it and be not surprised. For God is able to make of your nephew the Promised One of Islám. Be assured that the hands of God are never tied.'

Ḥájí Mírzá Siyyid Muḥammad was moved by these words. He said: 'This is an irrefutable answer. Now what shall I do?' I suggested to him that he might go as a pilgrim to the holy Shrines† in 'Iráq, where he could also visit his sister (the mother of the Báb) who had been living there since the martyrdom of her son, then go to Baghdád, attain the presence of Bahá'u'lláh, ask his questions of Him and put forward his difficulties. I urged him to persevere in his search and to rely upon God. I expressed the hope that the veils which now prevented him from seeing the truth might be lifted from his eyes and that he might attain to the true Faith of God . . . He agreed to my suggestion and said that he felt in his heart that this was the right course to take.

Ḥájí Mírzá Siyyid Muḥammad thereupon wrote a letter to his youngest brother Ḥájí Mírzá Ḥasan-'Alí, who was a merchant in Yazd, acquainted him with his plans to visit the Shrines and their sister, and invited him to join him in the journey. Ḥájí Mírzá Ḥasan-'Alí accepted and asked his brother to wait until he joined him in Shíráz . . . They both travelled to 'Iráq via Búshihr. Ḥájí Mírzá Siyyid Muḥammad,

* An uncle of Muḥammad who refused to acknowledge His Prophethood and was hostile to Him.

† Some of the Imáms of Shí'ah Islám, including Imám Ḥusayn, are buried in Karbilá, Najaf, Káẓimayn and Sámarrá.

however, did not intimate the real purpose of his journey to his brother until they arrived in Baghdád. There he informed him that his primary object in travelling to 'Iráq was to investigate the authenticity of the Faith and then to visit the Shrines and the mother of the Báb. He invited his brother to remain in Baghdád for a short period so that they both could attain the presence of Bahá'u'lláh and afterwards proceed to visit the Shrines.

On hearing this Ḥájí Mírzá Ḥasan-'Alí became angry and, although his junior in age, he spoke harshly to his brother. He warned that under no circumstances would he become a partner in these matters and that he did not wish to hear about the Faith. On that day he left Baghdád.[2]

When this happened, Ḥájí Mírzá Siyyid Muḥammad decided to accompany his brother to the Shrines. It was on his return to Baghdád that he was taken to the house of Bahá'u'lláh where he attained His presence alone. This was in the year 1278 A.H. (A.D. 1862).

Bahá'u'lláh's amanuensis, Mírzá Áqá Ján, has described the circumstances which led to the revelation of the *Kitáb-i-Íqán*, in a Tablet* addressed to Shaykh 'Abdu'l-Majíd-i-Shírází. He says that one day Ḥájí Siyyid Javád-i-Karbilá'í went to Bahá'u'lláh and informed Him that the two uncles of the Báb, having visited the holy Shrines in Najaf and Karbilá, were now in Baghdád and would be returning home soon. Having ascertained from Ḥájí Siyyid Javád that he had not discussed the Faith with them, Bahá'u'lláh lovingly admonished him for not being engaged in the teaching of the Cause. He then instructed him to invite the two brothers to come to His presence.

The next day Ḥájí Siyyid Javád arrived with the uncle of the Báb, Ḥájí Mírzá Siyyid Muḥammad. The youngest brother did not come. The utterances of Bahá'u'lláh uplifted and overwhelmed the Báb's uncle as he sat in His presence. At the end he begged Bahá'u'lláh to clarify the truth of the Báb's Message, bearing in mind that, in his view, some of the traditions of

* See pp. 40–42 regarding the Tablets recorded by Mírzá Áqá Ján.

Islám concerning the promised Qá'im were apparently not fulfilled by his Nephew. To this Bahá'u'lláh readily consented. He bade him go home and, after careful consideration, make a list of all the questions which had puzzled him and all the traditions which had bred doubts in his mind, and to bring these to Him.

The following day Ḥájí Mírzá Siyyid Muḥammad arrived with his questions. Within the span of two days and two nights the *Kitáb-i-Íqán*, a lengthy epistle (of over two hundred pages) dealing with all his questions, was revealed by Bahá'u'lláh. In the early days this book was known as *Risáliy-i-Khál* (Epistle to the Uncle) but later Bahá'u'lláh designated it as the *Kitáb-i-Íqán*.

Among the papers which are preserved in the family of the Afnán are the questions which Ḥájí Mírzá Siyyid Muḥammad presented to Bahá'u'lláh. They are written on two sheets in his own hand and are under four headings, all dealing with the coming of the promised Qá'im. The sincerity of the uncle of the Báb in seeking the truth is evident in his questions. Repeatedly he begs Bahá'u'lláh to dispel his doubts so that his heart may be assured and he may acquire absolute faith and certitude in the Cause of the Báb.

Ḥájí Mírzá Siyyid Muḥammad was so affected by meeting Bahá'u'lláh that he immediately wrote a letter to His son, Ḥájí Mírzá Muḥammad-Taqí, in which he said:

> . . . I attained the presence of His Honour Bahá (may peace be upon Him) and I wish you could have been present! He treated me with the utmost affection and favour and graciously asked me to stay for the night. It is an absolute truth that deprivation from His bounteous presence is a grievous loss. May God bestow upon me the privilege of attaining His presence perpetually . . .[3]

The *Kitáb-i-Íqán* dispelled every doubt that Ḥájí Mírzá Siyyid Muḥammad had harboured in his mind. As a result of reading this book he reached the stage of certitude and recognized the station of the Báb. In his will, written some years later, he declared his faith, acknowledged the authenticity of the Messages of the Báb and Bahá'u'lláh and identified himself as a follower of these twin Manifestations of God.

As to Ḥájí Mírzá Siyyid Ḥasan-'Alí, the youngest uncle of the Báb, he returned to Yazd without meeting Bahá'u'lláh. Some years later, however, through the devoted efforts of his wife's brother, he too accepted the Faith and remained steadfast throughout his life.

Indeed, all the family of the Báb including His mother, His wife, His uncles and their children (designated as Afnán) embraced the Faith. This was actually prophesied by the Báb Himself, for He had said that God through His bounty would guide all His family to recognize the truth of His Cause.

The original copy of the *Kitáb-i-Íqán*, which Ḥájí Mírzá Siyyid Muḥammad received, was transcribed by 'Abdu'l-Bahá Who was then eighteen years of age. In the margins of a few pages Bahá'u'lláh has, in His own hand, made some corrections and towards the end of the book has written this passage:

> Amidst them all, We stand, life in hand, wholly resigned to His will; that perchance, through God's loving kindness and His grace, this revealed and manifest Letter* may lay down His life as a sacrifice in the path of the Primal Point,† the most exalted Word. By Him at Whose bidding the Spirit hath spoken, but for this yearning of Our soul, We would not, for one moment, have tarried any longer in this city. 'Sufficient Witness is God unto Us.'[4]

For many years this original copy of the *Kitáb-i-Íqán* remained with the family of Ḥájí Mírzá Siyyid Muḥammad, until in 1948 his great-granddaughter Fáṭimih K͟hánum-i-Afnán presented it to Shoghi Effendi, the Guardian of the Faith. It reached him a few years later and was placed in the Bahá'í International Archives Building on Mount Carmel, Haifa.‡

* Bahá'u'lláh.

† The Báb.

‡ See Giachery, *Shoghi Effendi—Recollections*, p. 149, for a description of this happy event.

The Importance of the *Kitáb-i-Íqán*

Perhaps it can be said that the *Kitáb-i-Íqán* was more widely disseminated among the early believers in Persia than any other Writing of Bahá'u'lláh. In those days the only way of making the Holy Writings available to the friends was by transcribing them. As new Tablets would arrive, the believers were most anxious to make copies for themselves. Copies of several of these Tablets were often assembled and bound as a book. There are many such volumes of handwritten compilations of the Tablets of the Báb, Bahá'u'lláh and 'Abdu'l-Bahá in the possession of Bahá'í families, who have inherited them from their forbears and to whom they are very precious.

There were also some individuals in Persia whose full-time occupation was the transcription of the Writings, and the believers used to obtain their copies from them. The *Kitáb-i-Íqán* was one of the items which kept these men transcribing for many years in order to cope with the demand.

From the literary point of view the *Kitáb-i-Íqán* can be regarded as an outstanding work in Persian literature. Shoghi Effendi, the Guardian of the Faith, who translated this book superbly into English has described it in these words:

> Foremost among the priceless treasures cast forth from the billowing ocean of Bahá'u'lláh's Revelation ranks the Kitáb-i-Íqán . . . A model of Persian prose, of a style at once original, chaste and vigorous, and remarkably lucid, both cogent in argument and matchless in its irresistible eloquence, this Book, setting forth in outline the Grand Redemptive Scheme of God, occupies a position unequalled by any work in the entire range of Bahá'í literature, except the Kitáb-i-Aqdas, Bahá'u'lláh's Most Holy Book.[5]

Until the *Kitáb-i-Íqán* was revealed, the significance of the Missions of all the Prophets of God, the purpose of Their Revelations and the true meaning of Their words had remained undisclosed. With the revelation of this book, the significance of the 'words' which according to Daniel were 'closed up and sealed till the time of the end'[6] became apparent. The 'seal' which Providence for thousands of years had placed upon the Holy Books of all religions was removed.

The *Kitáb-i-Íqán* is the best example of how to teach the Cause of God. Instead of explaining at once the proofs of the authenticity of the Message of the Báb, Bahá'u'lláh first speaks about other Prophets, portrays Their lives and Their sufferings, demonstrates the truth of Their Missions and describes the common features of Their Faiths. In this way He brings to the understanding of the reader the truth of his own religion and enables him to recognize the reality of his own Prophet. Having built this strong foundation He then, towards the end of the book, speaks of the Báb and His Message and applies to this new Revelation the standards He has applied in verifying the truth of other Prophets.

Since all the Manifestations of God derive Their authority from the same Source, it is therefore possible to know the latest Manifestation if one knows the qualities and attributes of One Who appeared in a former age.

The great majority of the followers of the world's religions, however, are taught to believe only in one Messenger of God. While sincere in their belief that their religion is true and divine in origin, they often have not recognized the reality of their own Prophet. There is a great deal of difference between having knowledge of a religion and knowing the reality of the Founder of one's Faith. For example, a man may possess a piece of gold and may know that it is precious, yet be unable to distinguish gold from brass. Such a man will fail to recognize a new piece of gold when he sees it.

Such is mankind's condition today. But should anyone recognize the reality of the Founder of his own religion, he will have no difficulty in accepting Bahá'u'lláh as the Manifestation of God for this age.

The *Kitáb-i-Íqán* has enabled a vast number of people from various backgrounds to understand the truth of their own religions, the first step towards believing in Bahá'u'lláh. This book has shed great lustre upon the Holy Books of past Dispensations. It has unfolded the pattern and disclosed the meaning of progressive revelation. It has laid down an enduring foundation for the ultimate unity of all past religions. It has served as a key with which the followers of Bahá'u'lláh have opened doors of knowledge hitherto unknown to man. It has become a fountain-head of inspiration for Bahá'í scholars and teachers who have since written volumes proving the authenticity of the Message of Bahá'u'lláh by rational and intellectual proofs or by interpretation of past Holy Scriptures. Indeed, this book has given a new vision to the Bahá'ís enabling them to unravel the mysteries of religion and teach their Faith with greater insight and knowledge.

Major Themes of the *Kitáb-i-Íqán* (Part One)

The first thing to bear in mind when studying the *Kitáb-i-Íqán* is the fact that Bahá'u'lláh wrote this book for a man whose background was Muslim; the passages He quoted are often from the *Qur'án* or the traditions of Islám.

In the opening paragraphs Bahá'u'lláh has made the recognition of truth conditional upon man's detachment from this world, a point which He stresses throughout the book. These are His words:

> No man shall attain the shores of the ocean of true understanding except he be detached from all that is in heaven and on earth . . .
>
> The essence of these words is this: they that tread the path of faith, they that thirst for the wine of certitude, must cleanse themselves of all that is earthly—their ears from idle talk, their minds from vain imaginings, their hearts from worldly affections, their eyes from that which perisheth. They should put their trust in God, and, holding fast unto Him, follow in His way. Then will they be made worthy of the effulgent glories of the sun of divine knowledge and

understanding, and become the recipients of a grace that is infinite and unseen . . .[7]

The reasons for man's opposition to the Prophets of God

In the first section of the *Kitáb-i-Íqán* Bahá'u'lláh dwells on the history of the Prophets of the past and explains the main reasons for man's opposition to Them. By understanding these reasons, one can be guided to recognize the truth of the Cause of God in this day. He attaches such importance to this theme that He devotes a considerable portion of the book to it.

After describing some of the cruelties and indignities which were heaped upon certain Prophets of old, Bahá'u'lláh remarks:

> And now, ponder upon these things. What could have caused such contention and conflict? Why is it that the advent of every true Manifestation of God hath been accompanied by such strife and tumult, by such tyranny and upheaval? This notwithstanding the fact that all the Prophets of God, whenever made manifest unto the peoples of the world, have invariably foretold the coming of yet another Prophet after them, and have established such signs as would herald the advent of the future Dispensation. To this the records of all sacred books bear witness. Why then is it that despite the expectation of men in their quest of the Manifestations of Holiness, and in spite of the signs recorded in the sacred books, should such acts of violence, of oppression and cruelty, have been perpetrated in every age and cycle against all the Prophets and chosen Ones of God?[8]

Bahá'u'lláh then enumerates several causes for man's rejection of the Manifestations of God. First among these is the fact that the masses in every age have blindly followed their clergy who have, for the most part, opposed the new Prophet of God. Concerning the religious leaders, Bahá'u'lláh writes:

> Leaders of religion, in every age, have hindered their people from attaining the shores of eternal salvation, inasmuch as they held the reins of authority in their mighty grasp.

> Some for the lust of leadership, others through want of knowledge and understanding, have been the cause of the deprivation of the people. By their sanction and authority, every Prophet of God hath drunk from the chalice of sacrifice, and winged His flight unto the heights of glory. What unspeakable cruelties they that have occupied the seats of authority and learning have inflicted upon the true Monarchs of the world, those Gems of divine virtue! Content with a transitory dominion, they have deprived themselves of an everlasting sovereignty.[9]

Later in the book Bahá'u'lláh condemns the divines for their ignorance and lack of insight:

> Among these . . . are the divines and doctors living in the days of the Manifestation of God, who, because of their want of discernment and their love and eagerness for leadership, have failed to submit to the Cause of God, nay, have even refused to incline their ears unto the divine Melody. 'They have thrust their fingers into their ears.'* And the people also, utterly ignoring God and taking them for their masters, have placed themselves unreservedly under the authority of these pompous and hypocritical leaders, for they have no sight, no hearing, no heart, of their own to distinguish truth from falsehood.[10]

Another cause of man's refusal to accept the new Messenger is that He brings new teachings, abrogates the laws of the past and establishes a new order. This radical change upsets religious leaders, for they see the new Message as a challenge to their authority and arise to oppose Him with all their power.

Another reason for rejecting the new Prophet is that in every religion certain signs are given for the advent of the next Manifestation of God. Because man has expected a literal fulfilment of these signs and has failed to understand their true meaning, he has been unable to recognize the new Message from God.

* *Qur'án* ii. 19. (The verse number is that of the Arabic text.)

The signs of the return of Christ

To elucidate this point, Bahá'u'lláh devotes no less than seventy pages to the interpretation of one passage from the Gospels which gives the signs of the return of Christ.* In doing so He also touches upon several other subjects.

Concerning the signs of the coming of Christ, He reveals:

> Afterwards, the companions and disciples of Jesus asked Him concerning those signs that must needs signalize the return of His manifestation. When, they asked, shall these things be? Several times they questioned that peerless Beauty, and, every time He made reply, He set forth a special sign that should herald the advent of the promised Dispensation. To this testify the records of the four Gospels.
>
> This wronged One will cite but one of these instances, thus conferring upon mankind, for the sake of God, such bounties as are yet concealed within the treasury of the hidden and sacred Tree, that haply mortal men may not remain deprived of their share of the immortal fruit, and attain to a dewdrop of the waters of everlasting life which, from Baghdád, the 'Abode of Peace', are being vouchsafed unto all mankind . . .
>
> These are the melodies, sung by Jesus, Son of Mary, in accents of majestic power in the Riḍván of the Gospel, revealing those signs that must needs herald the advent of the Manifestation after Him. In the first Gospel according to Matthew it is recorded: And when they asked Jesus concerning the signs of His coming, He said unto them: 'Immediately after the oppression of those days shall the sun be darkened, and the moon shall not give her light, and the stars shall fall from heaven, and the powers of the earth shall be shaken: and then shall appear the sign of the Son of man in heaven: and then shall all the tribes of the earth mourn, and they shall see the Son of man coming in the clouds of heaven with power and great glory. And he shall send his angel with a great sound of a trumpet'† . . .

* Matt. xxiv. 29–31.

† *ibid.*, as quoted in *Kitáb-i-Íqán.*

Inasmuch as the Christian divines have failed to apprehend the meaning of these words, and did not recognize their object and purpose, and have clung to the literal interpretation of the words of Jesus, they therefore became deprived of the streaming grace of the Muḥammadan Revelation and its showering bounties.[11]

Interpretation of symbolic terms

Bahá'u'lláh then explains at some length the meaning of these words:

> ... by 'oppression' is meant the want of capacity to acquire spiritual knowledge and apprehend the Word of God. By it is meant that when the Day-star of Truth hath set, and the mirrors that reflect His light have departed, mankind will become afflicted with 'oppression' and hardship, knowing not whither to turn for guidance ... Such a condition as this is witnessed in this day when the reins of every community have fallen into the grasp of foolish leaders, who lead after their own whims and desire. On their tongue the mention of God hath become an empty name; in their midst His holy Word a dead letter ... Though they recognize in their hearts the Law of God to be one and the same, yet from every direction they issue a new command, and in every season proclaim a fresh decree. No two are found to agree on one and the same law, for they seek no God but their own desire, and tread no path but the path of error ... With all their power and strength they strive to secure themselves in their petty pursuits, fearful lest the least discredit undermine their authority or blemish the display of their magnificence. Were the eye to be anointed and illumined with the collyrium of the knowledge of God, it would surely discover that a number of voracious beasts have gathered and preyed upon the carrion of the souls of men.
>
> What 'oppression' is greater than that which hath been recounted? What 'oppression' is more grievous than that a soul seeking the truth, and wishing to attain unto the knowledge of God, should know not where to go for it and from whom to seek it? For opinions have sorely differed, and the ways

unto the attainment of God have multiplied. This 'oppression' is the essential feature of every Revelation. Unless it cometh to pass, the Sun of Truth will not be made manifest. For the break of the morn of divine guidance must needs follow the darkness of the night of error . . .[12]

Concerning the words 'sun' and 'moon', Bahá'u'lláh states:

By the terms 'sun' and 'moon', mentioned in the writings of the Prophets of God, is not meant solely the sun and moon of the visible universe. Nay rather, manifold are the meanings they have intended for these terms. In every instance they have attached to them a particular significance. Thus, by the 'sun' in one sense is meant those Suns of Truth Who rise from the dayspring of ancient glory, and fill the world with a liberal effusion of grace from on high. These Suns of Truth are the universal Manifestations of God in the worlds of His attributes and names; even as the visible sun that assisteth, as decreed by God, the true One, the Adored, in the development of all earthly things, such as the trees, the fruits, and colours thereof, the minerals of the earth, and all that may be witnessed in the world of creation, so do the divine Luminaries, by their loving care and educative influence, cause the trees of divine unity, the fruits of His oneness, the leaves of detachment, the blossoms of knowledge and certitude, and the myrtles of wisdom and utterance, to exist and be made manifest . . . It is the warmth that these Luminaries of God generate, and the undying fires they kindle, which cause the light of the love of God to burn fiercely in the heart of humanity . . .

In another sense, by these terms is intended the divines of the former Dispensation, who live in the days of the subsequent Revelations, and who hold the reins of religion in their grasp. If these divines be illumined by the light of the latter Revelation they will be acceptable unto God, and will shine with a light everlasting. Otherwise, they will be declared as darkened, even though to outward seeming they be leaders of men, inasmuch as belief and unbelief, guidance and error, felicity and misery, light and darkness, are all dependent upon the sanction of Him Who is the Day-star of Truth. Whosoever among the divines of every age receiveth, in the Day of Reckoning, the testimony of faith from the Source of true knowledge, he verily becometh the recipient of learning, of divine favour, and of the light of true understanding. Otherwise, he is branded as guilty of folly, denial, blasphemy, and oppression.

It is evident and manifest unto every discerning observer that even as the light of the star fadeth before the effulgent splendour of the sun, so doth the luminary of earthly knowledge, of wisdom, and understanding vanish into nothingness when brought face to face with the resplendent glories of the Sun of Truth, the Day-star of divine enlightenment...

In another sense, by the terms 'sun', 'moon', and 'stars' are meant such laws and teachings as have been established and proclaimed in every Dispensation, such as the laws of prayer and fasting . . .

. . . Hence, it is clear and manifest that by the words 'the sun shall be darkened, and the moon shall not give her light, and the stars shall fall from heaven' is intended the waywardness of the divines, and the annulment of laws firmly established by divine Revelation, all of which, in symbolic language, have been foreshadowed by the Manifestation of God . . .

It is unquestionable that in every succeeding Revelation the 'sun' and 'moon' of the teachings, laws, commandments, and prohibitions which have been established in the preceding Dispensation, and which have overshadowed the people of that age, become darkened, that is, are exhausted, and cease to exert their influence.[13]

Concerning the 'sign of the Son of man in heaven', Bahá'u'lláh affirms that this sign is manifest both in the visible and invisible heavens. Before the coming of each Prophet, not only has a star appeared in the skies indicating the birth of a new Revelation, but a herald has also announced these glad-tidings to the people of that age. For example, the soothsayers in the time of Moses warned Pharaoh:

'A star hath risen in the heaven, and lo! it foreshadoweth the conception of a Child Who holdeth your fate and the fate of your people in His hand.' In like manner, there appeared a sage who, in the darkness of the night, brought tidings of joy unto the people of Israel, imparting consolation to their souls, and assurance to their hearts.[14]

Before the days of the Revelation of Christ a few of the Magi went to Herod and said: 'Where is he that is born King of the Jews? for we have seen his star in the east, and are come to worship him.'* This was the sign appearing in the visible heaven. However, it was John the Baptist who was the spiritual star. He foretold the coming of Christ and prepared people for His Revelation.

Before the advent of Muḥammad, also, similar events took place. The following are the words of Bahá'u'lláh concerning those who heralded the Prophet of Islám:

> As to the signs of the invisible heaven, there appeared four men who successively announced unto the people the joyful tidings of the rise of that divine Luminary. Rúz-bih, later named Salmán, was honoured by being in their service. As the end of one of these approached, he would send Rúz-bih unto the other, until the fourth who, feeling his death to be nigh, addressed Rúz-bih saying: 'O Rúz-bih! when thou hast taken up my body and buried it, go to Ḥijáz for there the Day-star of Muḥammad will arise. Happy art thou, for thou shalt behold His face!'[15]

And in this Revelation, before the Declaration of the Báb, this twofold sign appeared. Bahá'u'lláh states:

> Know thou verily that many an astronomer hath announced the appearance of its star in the visible heaven. Likewise, there appeared on earth Aḥmad and Káẓim,† those twin resplendent lights . . .[16]

* Matt. ii. 2.

† S͟hay͟kh Aḥmad-i-Aḥsá'í was the founder of the S͟hay͟khí school of Islám. He was followed by Siyyid Káẓim-i-Ras͟htí. Both taught their followers that the coming of the Promised One of Islám was at hand and prepared them for His advent. Most of the early Bábís were from the S͟hay͟khí sect.

Concerning the mourning of the 'tribes of the earth' and the coming of the Son of Man in the 'clouds of heaven', Bahá'u'lláh writes:

> These words signify that in those days men will lament the loss of the Sun of the divine beauty, of the Moon of knowledge, and of the Stars of divine wisdom. Thereupon, they will behold the countenance of the promised One, the adored Beauty, descending from heaven and riding upon the clouds. By this is meant that the divine Beauty will be made manifest from the heaven of the will of God, and will appear in the form of the human temple. The term 'heaven' denoteth loftiness and exaltation, inasmuch as it is the seat of the revelation of those Manifestations of Holiness, the Day-springs of ancient glory. These ancient Beings, though delivered from the womb of their mother, have in reality descended from the heaven of the will of God. Though they be dwelling on this earth, yet their true habitations are the retreats of glory in the realms above. Whilst walking amongst mortals, they soar in the heaven of the divine presence. Without feet they tread the path of the spirit, and without wings they rise unto the exalted heights of divine unity. With every fleeting breath they cover the immensity of space, and at every moment traverse the kingdoms of the visible and the invisible.[17]

As to the meaning of the 'clouds', Bahá'u'lláh asserts:

> These 'clouds' signify, in one sense, the annulment of laws, the abrogation of former Dispensations, the repeal of rituals and customs current amongst men, the exalting of the illiterate faithful above the learned opposers of the Faith. In another sense, they mean the appearance of that immortal Beauty in the image of mortal man, with such human limitations as eating and drinking, poverty and riches, glory and abasement, sleeping and waking, and such other things as cast doubt in the minds of men, and cause them to turn away. All such veils are symbolically referred to as 'clouds'.[18]

Regarding the sending of 'angels', Bahá'u'lláh explains that these are holy souls who

> . . . have sanctified themselves from every human limitation, have become endowed with the attributes of the spiritual, and have been adorned with the noble traits of the blessed, [and] they therefore have been designated as 'angels'.[19]

In the course of interpreting the aforementioned passage from the Gospel, Bahá'u'lláh elucidates several other points, throws light on some obscure and hidden words of the Prophets, quotes extensively from the *Qur'án* and traditions of Islám, and reveals a vast range of new verities which had remained unknown and concealed within all former religions. He explains the meaning of such terms as the 'changing of the earth', the 'cleaving of heaven' expected by Islám to happen at the Last Hour, the Day of Resurrection, the day 'when the heaven shall give out a palpable smoke, which shall enshroud mankind' . . .*

He further asserts:

> . . . were the signs of the Manifestation of God in every age to appear in the visible realm in accordance with the text of established traditions, none could possibly deny or turn away, nor would the blessed be distinguished from the miserable, and the transgressor from the God-fearing. Judge fairly: Were the prophecies recorded in the Gospel to be literally fulfilled; were Jesus, Son of Mary, accompanied by angels, to descend from the visible heaven upon the clouds; who would dare to disbelieve, who would dare to reject the truth, and wax disdainful? Nay, such consternation would immediately seize all the dwellers of the earth that no soul would feel able to utter a word, much less to reject or accept the truth.[20]

Further reasons for man's rejection of the Prophets

The reason that people have not understood the meaning of the signs given in the Holy Books is that they have blindly

* *Qur'án* xliv. 10. (The verse number is that of the Arabic text.)

followed their religious leaders. Bahá'u'lláh confirms this in the *Kitáb-i-Íqán* in these words:

> Such objections and differences have persisted in every age and century. The people have always busied themselves with such specious discourses, vainly protesting: 'Wherefore hath not this or that sign appeared?' Such ills befell them only because they have clung to the ways of the divines of the age in which they lived, and blindly imitated them in accepting or denying these Essences of Detachment, these holy and divine Beings. These leaders, owing to their immersion in selfish desires, and their pursuit of transitory and sordid things, have regarded these divine Luminaries as being opposed to the standards of their knowledge and understanding, and the opponents of their ways and judgments. As they have literally interpreted the Word of God, and the sayings and traditions of the Letters of Unity, and expounded them according to their own deficient understanding, they have therefore deprived themselves and all their people of the bountiful showers of the grace and mercies of God.[21]

To understand the mysteries enshrined in God's religion, Bahá'u'lláh repeatedly states, man must cleanse his heart from all earthly things. Here is one passage:

> Wert thou to cleanse the mirror of thy heart from the dust of malice, thou wouldst apprehend the meaning of the symbolic terms revealed by the all-embracing Word of God made manifest in every Dispensation, and wouldst discover the mysteries of divine knowledge. Not, however, until thou consumest with the flame of utter detachment those veils of idle learning, that are current amongst men, canst thou behold the resplendent morn of true knowledge.
>
> Know verily that Knowledge is of two kinds: Divine and Satanic. The one welleth out from the fountain of divine inspiration; the other is but a reflection of vain and obscure thoughts. The source of the former is God Himself; the motive-force of the latter the whisperings of selfish desire. The one is guided by the principle: 'Fear ye God; God will

teach you;' the other is but a confirmation of the truth: 'Knowledge is the most grievous veil between man and his Creator.' The former bringeth forth the fruit of patience, of longing desire, of true understanding, and love; whilst the latter can yield naught but arrogance, vainglory and conceit. From the sayings of those Masters of holy utterance, Who have expounded the meaning of true knowledge, the odour of these dark teachings, which have obscured the world, can in no wise be detected. The tree of such teachings can yield no result except iniquity and rebellion, and beareth no fruit but hatred and envy. Its fruit is deadly poison; its shadow a consuming fire.[22]

Another important factor which has hindered recognition of the Manifestations of God is the tests which are associated with Their Revelations. In each case certain events in the life of the Manifestation have acted as stumbling-blocks to people, preventing them from recognizing the truth. Concerning this Bahá'u'lláh has revealed these words:

Know verily that the purpose underlying all these symbolic terms and abstruse allusions, which emanate from the Revealers of God's holy Cause, hath been to test and prove the peoples of the world; that thereby the earth of the pure and illuminated hearts may be known from the perishable and barren soil. From time immemorial such hath been the way of God amidst His creatures, and to this testify the records of the sacred books.[23]

He demonstrates this important principle by giving a few examples. Speaking of Muḥammad, Who used to face Jerusalem while leading His followers in prayer, Bahá'u'lláh recounts this story of His sudden turning towards the Holy Mosque (Mecca):

. . . when the Prophet, together with His companions, was offering the noontide prayer . . . the Voice of Gabriel* was heard . . . : 'Turn Thou Thy face towards the sacred Mosque.'

* The angel who embodied the Holy Spirit for Muḥammad.

> In the midst of that same prayer, Muḥammad suddenly turned His face away from Jerusalem and faced the Ka'bih.* Whereupon, a profound dismay seized suddenly the companions of the Prophet. Their faith was shaken severely. So great was their alarm, that many of them, discontinuing their prayer, apostatized their faith. Verily, God caused not this turmoil, but to test and prove His servants . . . Yea, such things as throw consternation into the hearts of all men come to pass only that each soul may be tested by the touchstone of God, that the true may be known and distinguished from the false.[24]

Yet another story mentioned by Bahá'u'lláh in illustration of this theme concerns Moses:

> For instance, consider Moses . . . Whilst passing, one day . . . ere His ministry was proclaimed, He saw two men engaged in fighting. One of them asked the help of Moses against his opponent. Whereupon, Moses intervened and slew him . . .
>
> And now ponder in thy heart the commotion which God stirreth up. Reflect upon the strange and manifold trials with which He doth test His servants. Consider how He hath suddenly chosen from among His servants, and entrusted with the exalted mission of divine guidance Him Who was known as guilty of homicide, Who, Himself, had acknowledged His cruelty, and Who for well-nigh thirty years had, in the eyes of the world, been reared in the home of Pharaoh and been nourished at his table. Was not God, the omnipotent King, able to withhold the hand of Moses from murder, so that manslaughter should not be attributed unto Him, causing bewilderment and aversion among the people?[25]

Mankind was similarly tested when Christ appeared. But on that occasion, the circumstances of His birth were the test, as Bahá'u'lláh explains:

> Likewise, reflect upon the state and condition of Mary. So

* The ancient shrine at Mecca, now the holiest place in Islám.

MULLÁ MUḤAMMAD-RIḌÁ OF MUḤAMMAD-ÁBÁD

An outstanding and heroic exponent of the Faith

MULLÁ MUḤAMMAD-I-QÁ'INÍ

An erudite teacher and Apostle of Bahá'u'lláh
Surnamed by Him Nabíl-i-Akbar

deep was the perplexity of that most beauteous countenance, so grievous her case, that she bitterly regretted she had ever been born. . . . Reflect, what answer could Mary have given to the people around her? How could she claim that a Babe Whose father was unknown had been conceived of the Holy Ghost? Therefore did Mary, that veiled and immortal Countenance, take up her Child and return unto her home . . .

And now, meditate upon this most great convulsion, this grievous test. Notwithstanding all these things, God conferred upon that essence of the Spirit, Who was known amongst the people as fatherless, the glory of Prophethood, and made Him His testimony unto all that are in heaven and on earth.[26]

Major Themes (Part Two)

The nature of God and His Manifestations

Having clearly demonstrated some of the causes which have prevented men from recognizing the Messengers of God, Bahá'u'lláh begins the second part of the *Kitáb-i-Íqán* with one of the most illuminating passages revealed by Him concerning the nature of the Manifestation and His relationship to God and man. In the following words He states most eloquently that man shall never of himself be able to know his Creator, but by His bounty God reveals Himself through a Prophet in each age:

To every discerning and illumined heart it is evident that God, the unknowable Essence, the divine Being, is immensely exalted beyond every human attribute, such as corporeal existence, ascent and descent, egress and regress. Far be it from His glory that human tongue should adequately recount His praise, or that human heart comprehend His fathomless mystery. He is and hath ever been veiled in the ancient eternity of His Essence, and will remain in His Reality everlastingly hidden from the sight of men . . . He standeth exalted beyond and above all separation and union, all proximity and remoteness. No sign can indicate His presence or His absence; inasmuch as by a word of His command all that are in heaven and on earth have come to exist, and by His wish, which is the Primal Will itself, all have stepped out of utter nothingness into the realm of being, the world of the visible.

... All the Prophets of God and their chosen Ones, all the divines, the sages, and the wise of every generation, unanimously recognize their inability to attain unto the comprehension of that Quintessence of all truth, and confess their incapacity to grasp Him, Who is the inmost Reality of all things.[27]

The station and nature of the Manifestation of God are exalted above the world of humanity. He is in truth the embodiment of God's attributes revealed to man. He is the source of all the spiritual energies which are released from age to age. Just as the sun is the source of life and energy to this earth, so the Manifestation of God is the Sun to mankind. The life, growth and progress of humanity are due to, and depend upon, the appearance of these heavenly Souls. Bahá'u'lláh extols the station of the Manifestations of God and reveals a measure of Their glory in these words:

The door of the knowledge of the Ancient of Days being thus closed in the face of all beings, the Source of infinite grace, according to His saying: 'His grace hath transcended all things; My grace hath encompassed them all' hath caused those luminous Gems of Holiness to appear out of the realm of the spirit, in the noble form of the human temple, and be made manifest unto all men, that they may impart unto the world the mysteries of the unchangeable Being, and tell of the subtleties of His imperishable Essence. These sanctified Mirrors, these Day-springs of ancient glory are one and all the Exponents on earth of Him Who is the central Orb of the universe, its Essence and ultimate Purpose. From Him proceed their knowledge and power; from Him is derived their sovereignty. The beauty of their countenance is but a reflection of His image, and their revelation a sign of His deathless glory. They are the Treasuries of divine knowledge, and the Repositories of celestial wisdom. Through them is transmitted a grace that is infinite, and by them is revealed the light that can never fade. Even as He hath said: 'There is no distinction whatsoever between Thee and Them; except that they are Thy servants, and are created of Thee.' This is the significance of the tradition: 'I am He, Himself, and He is I, myself.'[28]

And again He reveals the following:

. . . And of all men, the most accomplished, the most distinguished and the most excellent are the Manifestations of the Sun of Truth. Nay, all else besides these Manifestations, live by the operation of their Will, and move and have their being through the outpourings of their grace. 'But for Thee, I would have not created the heavens.' Nay, all in their holy presence fade into utter nothingness, and are a thing forgotten. Human tongue can never befittingly sing their praise, and human speech can never unfold their mystery. These Tabernacles of holiness, these primal Mirrors which reflect the light of unfading glory, are but expressions of Him Who is the Invisible of the Invisibles. By the revelation of these gems of divine virtue all the names and attributes of God, such as knowledge and power, sovereignty and dominion, mercy and wisdom, glory, bounty and grace, are made manifest.[29]

There are two passages in the *Qur'án* which appear to be contradictory. One speaks of the unity of the Messengers of God, the other exalts Some above Others. Bahá'u'lláh quotes these and explains the oneness of the Manifestations of God, on the one hand, and their differences on the other. Of their unity He states:

Furthermore, it is evident to thee that the Bearers of the trust of God are made manifest unto the peoples of the earth as the Exponents of a new Cause and the Bearers of a new Message. Inasmuch as these Birds of the Celestial Throne are all sent down from the heaven of the Will of God, and as they all arise to proclaim His irresistible Faith, they therefore are regarded as one soul and the same person . . . These Manifestations of God have each a twofold station. One is the station of pure abstraction and essential unity. In this respect, if thou callest them all by one name, and dost ascribe to them the same attribute, thou hast not erred from the truth. Even as He hath revealed: 'No distinction do We make between any of His Messengers!'* For they one and all summon the people of the earth to acknowledge the Unity of God, and herald unto them the Kawthar of an infinite grace and bounty. They are all invested with the robe of Prophethood, and honoured with the mantle of glory . . .

It is clear and evident to thee that all the Prophets are the Temples of the Cause of God, Who have appeared clothed in divers attire. If thou wilt observe with discriminating eyes, thou wilt behold them all abiding in the same tabernacle, soaring in the same heaven, seated upon the same throne, uttering the same speech, and proclaiming the same Faith. Such is the unity of those Essences of being, those Luminaries of infinite and immeasurable splendour. Wherefore, should one of these Manifestations of Holiness proclaim saying: 'I am the return of all the Prophets,' He verily speaketh the truth. In like manner, in every subsequent Revelation, the return of the former Revelation is a fact, the truth of which is firmly established.[30]

Then, speaking of the differences which distinguish the Manifestations of God, Bahá'u'lláh explains:

. . . In this respect, each Manifestation of God hath a distinct individuality, a definitely prescribed mission, a predestined Revelation, and specially designated limitations. Each one of them is known by a different name, is characterized by a special attribute, fulfils a definite Mission, and is entrusted with a particular Revelation. Even as He saith: 'Some of the Apostles We have caused to excel the others. To some God hath spoken, some He hath raised and exalted. And to Jesus,

* *Qur'án* ii. 285.

Son of Mary, We gave manifest signs, and We strengthened Him with the Holy Spirit.'*

It is because of this difference in their station and mission that the words and utterances flowing from these Well-springs of divine knowledge appear to diverge and differ. Otherwise, in the eyes of them that are initiated into the mysteries of divine wisdom, all their utterances are in reality but the expressions of one Truth.[31]

Just as the reality of each Manifestation of God is the same as that of former Manifestations, so Their followers are likewise the return of the essence of the followers of former Dispensations. In this connection Bahá'u'lláh uses the following analogy:

> . . . Consider the rose: whether it blossometh in the East or in the West, it is none the less a rose. For what mattereth in this respect is not the outward shape and form of the rose, but rather the smell and fragrance which it doth impart.[32]

As already indicated, the Manifestation of God has a dual nature, divine and human. Bahá'u'lláh's explanation is illuminating:

> Thus, viewed from the standpoint of their oneness and sublime detachment, the attributes of Godhead, Divinity, Supreme Singleness, and Inmost Essence, have been and are applicable to those Essences of being, inasmuch as they all abide on the throne of divine Revelation, and are established upon the seat of divine Concealment. Through their appearance the Revelation of God is made manifest, and by their countenance the Beauty of God is revealed. Thus it is that the accents of God Himself have been heard uttered by these Manifestations of the divine Being.
>
> Viewed in the light of their second station—the station of distinction, differentiation, temporal limitations, characteristics and standards—they manifest absolute servitude, utter destitution and complete self-effacement. Even as He

* *Qur'án* ii. 253. (The verse number is that of the Arabic text.)

saith: 'I am the servant of God. I am but a man like you' . . . Were any of the all-embracing Manifestations of God to declare: 'I am God!' He verily speaketh the truth, and no doubt attacheth thereto. For it hath been repeatedly demonstrated that through their Revelation, their attributes and names, the Revelation of God, His name and His attributes, are made manifest in the world . . . And were they to say: 'We are the servants of God,' this also is a manifest and indisputable fact. For they have been made manifest in the uttermost state of servitude, a servitude the like of which no man can possibly attain.[33]

The sovereignty of the Prophets

One of the questions which Ḥájí Mírzá Siyyid Muḥammad asked Bahá'u'lláh to resolve for him concerned the circumstances of the appearance of the Qá'im. According to the traditions of Islám, He is to come with great sovereignty and rule over the people. These conditions were not literally fulfilled by the Báb. Bahá'u'lláh devotes a considerable part of the *Kitáb-i-Íqán* to His reply, demonstrating that all the Prophets of God have appeared with majesty and power, but that these were spiritual conditions rather than physical. Their sovereignty was heavenly, and through it they established their ascendancy and lordship over mankind. Speaking of the sovereignty of the Qá'im, He writes:

This sovereignty, however, is not the sovereignty which the minds of men have falsely imagined. Moreover, the Prophets of old, each and every one, whenever announcing to the people of their day the advent of the coming Revelation, have invariably and specifically referred to that sovereignty with which the promised Manifestation must needs be invested. This is attested by the records of the scriptures of the past. This sovereignty hath not been solely and exclusively attributed to the Qá'im. Nay rather, the attribute of sovereignty and all other names and attributes of God have been and will ever be vouchsafed unto all the Manifestations of God, before and after Him, inasmuch as these Manifestations, as it hath already been explained, are the Embodiments of the attributes of God, the Invisible, and the Revealers of the divine mysteries.

Furthermore, by sovereignty is meant the all-encompassing, all-pervading power which is inherently exercised by the Qá'im whether or not He appear to the world clothed in the majesty of earthly dominion. This is solely dependent upon the will and pleasure of the Qá'im Himself. You will readily recognize that the terms sovereignty, wealth, life, death, judgment and resurrection, spoken of by the scriptures of old, are not what this generation hath conceived and vainly imagined. Nay, by sovereignty is meant that sovereignty which in every dispensation resideth within, and is exercised by, the person of the Manifestation, the Day-star of Truth. That sovereignty is the spiritual ascendancy which He exerciseth to the fullest degree over all that is in heaven and on earth, and which in due time revealeth itself to the world in direct proportion to its capacity and spiritual receptiveness.[34]

Comparing the ascendancy and creative power of the Manifestations of God with the fleeting sovereignty of earthly kings, Bahá'u'lláh states:

Be fair: Is this sovereignty which, through the utterance of one Word, hath manifested such pervading influence, ascendancy, and awful majesty, is this sovereignty superior, or is the worldly dominion of these kings of the earth who, despite their solicitude for their subjects and their help of the poor, are assured only of an outward and fleeting allegiance, while in the hearts of men they inspire neither affection nor respect? Hath not that sovereignty, through the potency of one word, subdued, quickened, and revitalized the whole world? What! Can the lowly dust compare with Him Who is the Lord of Lords? What tongue dare utter the immensity of difference that lieth between them? Nay, all comparison falleth short in attaining the hallowed sanctuary of His sovereignty. Were man to reflect, he would surely perceive that even the servant of His threshold ruleth over all created things! This hath already been witnessed, and will in future be made manifest.[35]

Among other stories which Bahá'u'lláh recounts, to demonstrate the meaning of the sovereignty and dominion attributed to the Prophets of God, is that of Jesus during His captivity in the hands of the Jews:

> Similarly, call thou to mind the day when the Jews, who had surrounded Jesus, Son of Mary, were pressing Him to confess His claim of being the Messiah and Prophet of God, so that they might declare Him an infidel and sentence Him to death. Then, they led Him away, He Who was the Day-star of the heaven of divine Revelation, unto Pilate and Caiaphas, who was the leading divine of that age. The chief priests were all assembled in the palace, also a multitude of people who had gathered to witness His sufferings, to deride and injure Him. Though they repeatedly questioned Him, hoping that He would confess His claim, yet Jesus held His peace and spake not. Finally, an accursed of God arose and, approaching Jesus, adjured Him saying: 'Didst thou not claim to be the Divine Messiah? Didst thou not say, "I am the King of Kings, My word is the Word of God, and I am the breaker of the Sabbath day?" ' Thereupon Jesus lifted up His head and said: 'Beholdest thou not the Son of Man sitting on the right hand of power and might?' These were His words, and yet consider how to outward seeming He was devoid of all power except that inner power which was of God and which had encompassed all that is in heaven and on earth.[36]

In the course of His exposition of sovereignty, Bahá'u'lláh dwells on the sufferings which were heaped upon the Prophets of God and His Chosen Ones. He describes the martyrdom of Imám Ḥusayn which shed a glorious lustre upon the Faith of Islám. He also portrays the sufferings and tribulations which were inflicted upon Muḥammad during the earlier years of His ministry. In this connection, Bahá'u'lláh demonstrates that the Word spoken by the Manifestation transports the human soul from a state of wretchedness and ignorance into the glorious realm of divine virtues and perfections. Through the potency of His Revelation He welds the hearts of contending peoples and kindreds and makes of them a single nation. And He shows the relevance of a well-known Biblical prophecy:

> . . . Furthermore, how numerous are those peoples of divers beliefs, of conflicting creeds, and opposing temperaments, who, through the reviving fragrance of the Divine springtime,* breathing from the Riḍván of God, have been arrayed with the new robe of divine Unity, and have drunk from the cup of His singleness!
>
> This is the significance of the well-known words: 'The wolf and the lamb shall feed together.' † Behold the ignorance and folly of those who, like the nations of old, are still expecting to witness the time when these beasts will feed together in one pasture! Such is their low estate. Methinks, never have their lips touched the cup of understanding, neither have their feet trodden the path of justice. Besides, of what profit would it be to the world were such a thing to take place? How well hath He spoken concerning them: 'Hearts have they, with which they understand not, and eyes have they with which they see not!' ‡[37]

The meaning of 'life', 'death' and 'resurrection'

Once again,§ Bahá'u'lláh reveals the meaning of terms used in the Holy Books of former religions, such terms as 'life', 'death', 'resurrection', the 'trumpet blast', 'paradise', and 'hell'. He states:

> . . . By the terms 'life' and 'death', spoken of in the scriptures, is intended the life of faith and the death of unbelief. The generality of the people, owing to their failure to grasp the meaning of these words, rejected and despised the person of

* Associated with the appearance of the Manifestation of God.

† Isaiah lxv. 25.

‡ *Qur'án* vii. 178.

§ See pp. 166–71.

the Manifestation, deprived themselves of the light of His divine guidance, and refused to follow the example of that immortal Beauty.[38]

The 'Day of Resurrection', Bahá'u'lláh affirms, is ushered in through the advent of each Manifestation of God; by His Revelation the faithful arise from the sepulchres of unbelief and acquire spiritual life. These are some of His words:

> Such things have come to pass in the days of every Manifestation of God. Even as Jesus said: 'Ye must be born again.'* Again He saith: 'Except a man be born of water and of the Spirit, he cannot enter into the Kingdom of God. That which is born of the flesh is flesh; and that which is born of the Spirit is spirit.'† The purport of these words is that whosoever in every dispensation is born of the Spirit and is quickened by the breath of the Manifestation of Holiness, he verily is of those that have attained unto 'life' and 'resurrection' and have entered into the 'paradise' of the love of God. And whosoever is not of them, is condemned to 'death' and 'deprivation', to the 'fire' of unbelief, and to the 'wrath' of God. In all the scriptures, the books and chronicles, the sentence of death, of fire, of blindness, of want of understanding and hearing, hath been pronounced against those whose lips have tasted not the ethereal cup of true knowledge, and whose hearts have been deprived of the grace of the holy Spirit in their day. Even as it hath been previously recorded: 'Hearts have they with which they understand not.'‡
>
> In another passage of the Gospel it is written: 'And it came to pass that on a certain day the father of one of the disciples of Jesus had died. That disciple reporting the death of his father unto Jesus, asked for leave to go and bury him. Whereupon, Jesus, that Essence of Detachment, answered and said: '"Let the dead bury their dead."'§[39]

* John iii. 7.
† *ibid.*, vv. 5–6.
‡ *Qur'án* vii. 178.
§ Luke ix. 60, as cited in the *Kitáb-i-Íqán*.

In the *Qur'án* there are many references to the Day when man will attain to the presence of God. This, Bahá'u'lláh affirms, can only be interpreted as attaining to the presence of the Manifestation of God:

> Attainment unto such presence is possible only in the Day of Resurrection, which is the Day of the rise of God Himself through His all-embracing Revelation.
>
> This is the meaning of the 'Day of Resurrection', spoken of in all the scriptures, and announced unto all people. Reflect, can a more precious, a mightier, and more glorious day than this be conceived, so that man should willingly forego its grace, and deprive himself of its bounties, which like unto vernal showers are raining from the heaven of mercy upon all mankind? Having thus conclusively demonstrated that no day is greater than this Day, and no revelation more glorious than this Revelation, and having set forth all these weighty and infallible proofs which no understanding mind can question, and no man of learning overlook, how can man possibly, through the idle contention of the people of doubt and fancy, deprive himself of such a bountiful grace? Have they not heard the well-known tradition: 'When the Qá'im riseth, that day is the Day of Resurrection?' In like manner, the Imáms, those unquenchable lights of divine guidance, have interpreted the verse: 'What can such expect but that God should come down to them overshadowed with clouds,'*—a sign which they have unquestionably regarded as one of the features of the Day of Resurrection—as referring to Qá'im and His manifestation.[40]

The veil of knowledge

There are several references in the second part of the *Kitáb-i-Íqán* to the divines and religious leaders who through their 'so-called learning' have hindered the people from turning to the Manifestations of God. These statements are similar to those made in the first part of the book, but now are mainly directed to

* *Qur'án* ii. 210. (Verse number is in accordance with the Arabic text.)

the divines of Islám.* For acquired knowledge can become a veil between man and God. Referring to this veil, Bahá'u'lláh states:

> We have consumed this densest of all veils, with the fire of the love of the Beloved—the veil referred to in the saying: 'The most grievous of all veils is the veil of knowledge.' Upon its ashes, We have reared the tabernacle of divine knowledge . . . We have driven from the human heart all else but Him Who is the Desire of the world, and glory therein. We cleave to no knowledge but His Knowledge, and set our hearts on naught save the effulgent glories of His light.[41]

Recognition of the Manifestation of God is not dependent upon acquired knowledge:

> The understanding of His words and the comprehension of the utterances of the Birds of Heaven† are in no wise dependent upon human learning. They depend solely upon purity of heart, chastity of soul, and freedom of spirit. This is evidenced by those who, today, though without a single letter of the accepted standards of learning, are occupying the loftiest seats of knowledge; and the garden of their hearts is adorned, through the showers of divine grace, with the roses of wisdom and the tulips of understanding. Well is it with the sincere in heart for their share of the light of a mighty Day![42]

The true seeker

One of the most illuminating of Bahá'u'lláh's utterances in the *Kitáb-i-Íqán* is to be found in those passages concerning the qualities and attributes of a true seeker. These are His words as He addresses Ḥájí Mírzá Siyyid Muḥammad, the uncle of the Báb:

* See Appendix IV for an account of Ḥájí Mírzá Karím Khán, one of those divines to whom Bahá'u'lláh refers in the *Kitáb-i-Íqán*.

† The Manifestations of God.

But, O my brother, when a true seeker determines to take the step of search in the path leading to the knowledge of the Ancient of Days, he must, before all else, cleanse and purify his heart, which is the seat of the revelation of the inner mysteries of God, from the obscuring dust of all acquired knowledge, and the allusions of the embodiments of satanic fancy. He must purge his breast, which is the sanctuary of the abiding love of the Beloved, of every defilement, and sanctify his soul from all that pertaineth to water and clay, from all shadowy and ephemeral attachments. He must so cleanse his heart that no remnant of either love or hate may linger therein, lest that love blindly incline him to error, or that hate repel him away from the truth. Even as thou dost witness in this day how most of the people, because of such love and hate, are bereft of the immortal Face, have strayed far from the Embodiments of the divine mysteries, and, shepherdless, are roaming through the wilderness of oblivion and error. That seeker must at all times put his trust in God, must renounce the peoples of the earth, detach himself from the world of dust, and cleave unto Him Who is the Lord of Lords. He must never seek to exalt himself above any one, must wash away from the tablet of his heart every trace of pride and vainglory, must cling unto patience and resignation, observe silence, and refrain from idle talk. For the tongue is a smouldering fire, and excess of speech a deadly poison. Material fire consumeth the body, whereas the fire of the tongue devoureth both heart and soul. The force of the former lasteth but for a time, whilst the effects of the latter endure a century.

That seeker should also regard backbiting as grievous error, and keep himself aloof from its dominion, inasmuch as backbiting quencheth the light of the heart, and extinguisheth the life of the soul. He should be content with little, and be freed from all inordinate desire. He should treasure the companionship of those that have renounced the world, and regard avoidance of boastful and worldly people a precious benefit. At the dawn of every day he should commune with God, and with all his soul persevere in the quest of his Beloved. He should consume every wayward thought with the flame of

His loving mention, and, with the swiftness of lightning, pass by all else save Him. He should succour the dispossessed, and never withhold his favour from the destitute. He should show kindness to animals, how much more unto his fellow-man, to him who is endowed with the power of utterance. He should not hesitate to offer up his life for his Beloved, nor allow the censure of the people to turn him away from the Truth. He should not wish for others that which he doth not wish for himself, nor promise that which he doth not fulfil. With all his heart should the seeker avoid fellowship with evil doers, and pray for the remission of their sins. He should forgive the sinful, and never despise his low estate, for none knoweth what his own end shall be. How often hath a sinner, at the hour of death, attained to the essence of faith, and, quaffing the immortal draught, hath taken his flight unto the celestial Concourse. And how often hath a devout believer, at the hour of his soul's ascension, been so changed as to fall into the nethermost fire. Our purpose in revealing these convincing and weighty utterances is to impress upon the seeker that he should regard all else beside God as transient, and count all things save Him, Who is the Object of all adoration, as utter nothingness.

These are among the attributes of the exalted, and constitute the hallmark of the spiritually-minded. They have already been mentioned in connection with the requirements of the wayfarers that tread the Path of Positive Knowledge. When the detached wayfarer and sincere seeker hath fulfilled these essential conditions, then and only then can he be called a true seeker. Whensoever he hath fulfilled the conditions implied in the verse: 'Whoso maketh efforts for Us,'* he shall enjoy the blessing conferred by the words: 'In Our ways shall We assuredly guide him.'†

Only when the lamp of search, of earnest striving, of longing desire, of passionate devotion, of fervid love, of rapture, and ecstasy, is kindled within the seeker's heart, and the breeze of His loving-kindness is wafted upon his soul, will the darkness of error be dispelled, the mists of doubts and

* *Qur'án* xxix: 69.
† *ibid.*

misgivings be dissipated, and the lights of knowledge and certitude envelop his being. At that hour will the mystic Herald, bearing the joyful tidings of the Spirit, shine forth from the City of God resplendent as the morn, and, through the trumpet-blast of knowledge, will awaken the heart, the soul, and the spirit from the slumber of negligence. Then will the manifold favours and outpouring grace of the holy and everlasting Spirit confer such new life upon the seeker that he will find himself endowed with a new eye, a new ear, a new heart, and a new mind. He will contemplate the manifest signs of the universe, and will penetrate the hidden mysteries of the soul. Gazing with the eye of God, he will perceive within every atom a door that leadeth him to the stations of absolute certitude. He will discover in all things the mysteries of divine Revelation and the evidences of an everlasting manifestation.[43]

Proofs of the Báb's Revelation

Having clarified these basic points for Ḥájí Mírzá Siyyid Muḥammad, Bahá'u'lláh then introduces proofs of the authenticity of the Message of the Báb. Once again He prepares the way by speaking generally about the Manifestations of God, devoting several pages to clarify that the greatest proof of a Prophet is His own self, just as the proof of the sun is the sun itself.

Next in importance as a proof of the Manifestation of God is the revelation of the Word of God. Bahá'u'lláh shows how Muḥammad, on more than one occasion, pointed to the *Qur'án* as a proof of His mission:

> In the beginning of His Book He saith: '. . . No doubt is there about this Book: It is a guidance unto the God-fearing . . .'* He, the divine Being, and unknowable Essence, hath, Himself, testified that this Book is, beyond all doubt and uncertainty, the guide of all mankind until the Day of Resurrection . . .

* *Qur'án* ii. 1.

In another passage He likewise saith: 'And if ye be in doubt as to that which We have sent down to Our Servant, then produce a Súrah like it, and summon your witnesses, beside God, if ye are men of truth.'* Behold, how lofty is the station, and how consummate the virtue, of these verses which He hath declared to be His surest testimony, His infallible proof, the evidence of His all-subduing power, and a revelation of the potency of His will.[44]

The study of the lives of the Founders of all religions demonstrates that the Word of God is the most effective instrument by which the Prophet creates a new civilization. It penetrates into the hearts of people and becomes the spirit of the age. When a seeker recognizes the Source of the revealed Word he enters the City of Certitude, Bahá'u'lláh affirms, and He describes that city as

> . . . none other than the Word of God revealed in every age and dispensation. In the days of Moses it was the Pentateuch; in the days of Jesus the Gospel; in the days of Muḥammad the Messenger of God the Qur'án; in this day the Bayán;† and in the dispensation of Him Whom God will make manifest His own Book—the Book unto which all the Books of former Dispensations must needs be referred, the Book which standeth amongst them all transcendent and supreme.[45]

Concerning the Revelation of the Báb, He writes as follows:

> Such bounty and revelation have been made manifest, that the revealed verses seemed as vernal showers raining from the clouds of the mercy of the All-Bountiful. The Prophets 'endowed with constancy', whose loftiness and glory shine as the sun, were each honoured with a Book which all have seen, and the verses of which have been duly ascertained. Whereas the verses which have rained from this Cloud of divine mercy have been so abundant that none hath yet been

* *Qur'án* ii. 23. (Verse number is according to the Arabic text.)

† See footnote, p. 23.

able to estimate their number. A score of volumes are now available. How many still remain beyond our reach! How many have been plundered and have fallen into the hands of the enemy, the fate of which none knoweth.[46]

Because in the beginning of former Dispensations certain obscure souls embraced the Faith of God, the learned belittled it and scorned its followers. Bahá'u'lláh points out how different was the situation when the Báb appeared:

In this most resplendent Dispensation, however, this most mighty Sovereignty, a number of illumined divines, of men of consummate learning, of doctors of mature wisdom, have attained unto His Court, drunk the cup of His divine Presence, and been invested with the honour of His most excellent favour. They have renounced, for the sake of the Beloved, the world and all that is therein. We will mention the names of some of them, that perchance it may strengthen the faint-hearted, and encourage the timorous.

Among them was Mullá Ḥusayn,* who became the recipient of the effulgent glory of the Sun of divine Revelation. But for him, God would not have been established upon the seat of His mercy, nor ascended the throne of eternal glory. Among them also was Siyyid Yaḥyá,† that unique and peerless figure of his age . . . and others, well nigh four hundred in number, whose names are all inscribed upon the 'Guarded Tablet' of God.

All these were guided by the light of that Sun of divine Revelation, confessed and acknowledged His truth. Such was their faith, that most of them renounced their substance and kindred, and cleaved to the good-pleasure of the All-Glorious. They laid down their lives for their Well-Beloved, and surrendered their all in His path.[47]

Then follow passages of tribute by Bahá'u'lláh to the Báb, as

* A distinguished man of learning, foremost among the disciples of Siyyid Káẓim. He was the first to believe in the Báb and is the great hero of the Bábí Dispensation.

† Known as Vaḥíd. See Appendix III.

He describes His steadfastness in proclaiming His Cause, in the face of bitter opposition. Such steadfastness has characterized all the Prophets of God and is yet another of Their proofs. These are some of Bahá'u'lláh's statements about the Báb:

> Another proof and evidence of the truth of this Revelation, which amongst all other proofs shineth as the sun, is the constancy of the eternal Beauty in proclaiming the Faith of God. Though young and tender of age, and though the Cause He revealed was contrary to the desire of all the peoples of earth, both high and low, rich and poor, exalted and abased, king and subject, yet He arose and steadfastly proclaimed it. All have known and heard this. He was afraid of no one; He was regardless of consequences. Could such a thing be made manifest except through the power of a divine Revelation, and the potency of God's invincible Will? By the righteousness of God! Were any one to entertain so great a Revelation in his heart, the thought of such a declaration would alone confound him! Were the hearts of all men to be crowded into his heart, he would still hesitate to venture upon so awful an enterprise. He could achieve it only by the permission of God, only if the channel of his heart were to be linked with the Source of divine grace, and his soul be assured of the unfailing sustenance of the Almighty.[48]

> Steadfastness in the Faith is a sure testimony, and a glorious evidence of the truth . . .
>
> And now consider how this Sadrih of the Riḍván of God hath, in the prime of youth, risen to proclaim the Cause of God. Behold what steadfastness that Beauty of God hath revealed. The whole world rose to hinder Him, yet it utterly failed. The more severe the persecution they inflicted on that Sadrih of Blessedness, the more His fervour increased, and the brighter burned the flame of His love. All this is evident, and none disputeth its truth. Finally, He surrendered His soul, and winged His flight unto the realms above.[49]

As to the effect of the Revelation of the Báb upon His followers, Bahá'u'lláh writes:

And among the evidences of the truth of His manifestation were the ascendancy, the transcendent power, and supremacy which He, the Revealer of being and Manifestation of the Adored, hath, unaided and alone, revealed throughout the world. No sooner had that eternal Beauty revealed Himself in Shíráz, in the year sixty,* and rent asunder the veil of concealment, than the signs of the ascendancy, the might, the sovereignty, and power, emanating from that Essence of Essences and Sea of Seas, were manifest in every land. So much so, that from every city there appeared the signs, the evidences, the tokens, the testimonies of that divine Luminary. How many were those pure and kindly hearts which faithfully reflected the light of that eternal Sun, and how manifold the emanations of knowledge from that Ocean of divine wisdom which encompassed all beings! In every city, all the divines and dignitaries rose to hinder and repress them, and girded up the loins of malice, of envy, and tyranny for their suppression. How great the number of those holy souls, those essences of justice, who, accused of tyranny, were put to death! And how many embodiments of purity, who showed forth naught but true knowledge and stainless deeds, suffered an agonizing death! Notwithstanding all this, each of these holy beings, up to his last moment, breathed the Name of God, and soared in the realm of submission and resignation. Such was the potency and transmuting influence which He exercised over them, that they ceased to cherish any desire but His will, and wedded their soul to His remembrance.[50]

It is important to realize that the Báb fulfilled prophecies recorded in the Scriptures, particularly those of Islám. The Revelation of the Báb had a special link with Islám. Not only was He Himself descended from Muḥammad, but His advent was also most eagerly anticipated by Muslims, both Shí'ah and Sunní, and was considered the climax and the fruit of the Faith of Islám. Muḥammad and the Holy Imáms have left behind innumerable prophecies concerning the coming of the Promised

* 1260 A.H. (A.D. 1844); the year of the Báb's Declaration.

One. All the circumstances of His Revelation, the time, the place and many other aspects of His Cause are mentioned in the traditions of Islám either explicitly or by allusion.

Mírzá Aḥmad-i-Azghandí, who became an ardent believer, was one of the most outstanding divines of Khurásán. Prior to the Declaration of the Báb, he had felt the urge to compile all the prophecies and traditions of Islám connected with the advent of the Promised One. So vast is the scope of these prophecies that his compilation consisted of almost twelve thousand traditions!

The fulfilment of prophecies concerning the appearance of the Qá'im is of the utmost importance to Shí'ah Islám. For over a thousand years its adherents had discussed these in their mosques, schools and homes. It is perhaps for this reason that Bahá'u'lláh has devoted a few pages of the *Kitáb-i-Íqán* to explaining some of these traditions. In doing so He has demonstrated how the Báb has clearly fulfilled these prophecies.

Bahá'u'lláh anticipates His own Revelation

In anticipation of His own Revelation, while alluding to Himself as the 'Quintessence of truth', 'the inmost Reality', 'the Source of all light' and 'the King of divine might', Bahá'u'lláh addresses the leaders of the Bábí community and their learned men in these words:

> And now, We beseech the people of the Bayán, all the learned, the sages, the divines, and witnesses amongst them, not to forget the wishes and admonitions revealed in their Book. Let them, at all times, fix their gaze upon the essentials of His Cause, lest when He, Who is the Quintessence of truth, the inmost Reality of all things, the Source of all light, is made manifest, they cling unto certain passages of the Book, and inflict upon Him that which was inflicted in the Dispensation of the Qur'án. For, verily, powerful is He, the King of divine might,* to extinguish with one letter of His

* This is a reference to 'Him Whom God shall make manifest'.

wondrous words, the breath of life in the whole of the Bayán and the people thereof, and with one letter bestow upon them a new and everlasting life, and cause them to arise and speed out of the sepulchres of their vain and selfish desires. Take heed, and be watchful; and remember that all things have their consummation in belief in Him, in attainment unto His day, and in the realization of His divine presence.[51]

In another passage, alluding to Himself as the 'Bird of Heaven', He asserts:

By God! This Bird of Heaven, now dwelling upon the dust, can, besides these melodies, utter a myriad songs, and is able, apart from these utterances, to unfold innumerable mysteries. Every single note of its unpronounced utterances is immeasurably exalted above all that hath already been revealed, and immensely glorified beyond that which hath streamed from this Pen. Let the future disclose the hour when the Brides of inner meaning, will, as decreed by the Will of God, hasten forth, unveiled, out of their mystic mansions, and manifest themselves in the ancient realm of being.[52]

Yet Bahá'u'lláh anticipates, in some passages of the *Kitáb-i-Íqán*, the opposition He would meet and the sufferings He would endure at the hands of enemies from within the Bábí community. Alluding to Mírzá Yaḥyá and those around him, Bahá'u'lláh writes:

In these days, however, such odours of jealousy are diffused, that—I swear by the Educator of all beings, visible and invisible—from the beginning of the foundation of the world —though it hath no beginning—until the present day, such malice, envy, and hate have in no wise appeared, nor will they ever be witnessed in the future. For a number of people who have never inhaled the fragrance of justice, have raised the standard of sedition, and have leagued themselves against Us. On every side We witness the menace of their spears, and in all directions We recognize the shafts of their arrows. This, although We have never gloried in any thing, nor did We seek preference over any soul. To everyone We have been a most kindly companion, a most forbearing and affectionate friend. In the company of the poor We have sought their fellowship, and amidst the exalted and learned We have been submissive and resigned.[53]

Bahá'u'lláh refers to His sufferings in many of His Writings and makes clear that the greatest suffering inflicted upon the Manifestation of God comes from those who profess His Faith but are unfaithful to Him. The pain which Bahá'u'lláh endured as a result of the unfaithfulness of Mírzá Yaḥyá, his insincerity and dishonourable behaviour, was not physical. He felt this grief and anguish deep within His soul and states in the *Kitáb-i-Íqán*:

I swear by God, the one true God! grievous as have been the woes and sufferings which the hand of the enemy and the people of the Book* inflicted upon Us, yet all these fade into utter nothingness when compared with that which hath befallen Us at the hand of those who profess to be Our friends.[54]

The authority with which Bahá'u'lláh speaks in the *Kitáb-i-Íqán*, the tone of many of His remarks and the allusions He makes to Himself are all indicative of His divine station and His impending Declaration. In one passage He states:

The universe is pregnant with these manifold bounties, awaiting the hour when the effects of Its unseen gifts will be made manifest in this world, when the languishing and sore athirst will attain the living Kawthar† of their Well-Beloved, and the erring wanderer, lost in the wilds of remoteness and nothingness, will enter the tabernacle of life, and attain reunion with his heart's desire.[55]

* In this instance, the followers of Islám.

† Literally, a river in Paradise; symbolically, the life-giving waters of the Revelation of God.

The *Kitáb-i-Íqán* is like an ocean. It contains the innermost reality of religion and its depths are unfathomable. One may read it many times, yet each time new truths and new visions manifest themselves before the eye.

11

Other Early Believers

Ḥájí Mírzá Muḥammad-Taqíy-i-Afnán

It is little wonder that soon after its revelation the *Kitáb-i-Íqán* became the source of divine knowledge for all the believers and the cause of converting countless souls to the Faith. Several of the Báb's kinsmen acknowledged the truth of the Message of the Báb by studying this book.

One such was Ḥájí Mírzá Muḥammad-Taqí,* entitled the Vakílu'd-Dawlih, one of the most eminent believers among the Afnán. As soon as he read the *Kitáb-i-Íqán*, which was revealed in honour of his father, he recognized the truth of the Cause and hastened to Ba<u>gh</u>dád to attain the presence of Bahá'u'lláh. He was accompanied on this journey by his elder brother Ḥájí Mírzá Muḥammad-'Alí, who also embraced the Faith and became a most outstanding believer.

This meeting with Bahá'u'lláh exerted a tremendous influence upon Ḥájí Mírzá Muḥammad-Taqí. His whole being was magnetized by love for Bahá'u'lláh and he became filled with a new spirit which enabled him to realize the station of Bahá'u'lláh before His Declaration and to arise in His service. His devotion and enthusiasm in the Cause of God were exemplary and, as he walked in the streets of Ba<u>gh</u>dád, he radiated such heavenly joy that the believers in that city used to refer to him as the 'delightful Afnán'. It seemed as if the flame of divine love kindled by the hand of Bahá'u'lláh had completely burned away all his attachments to this world.

* A cousin of the Báb, the son of Ḥájí Mírzá Siyyid Muḥammad for whom Bahá'u'lláh revealed the *Kitáb-i-Íqán*.

In this state he returned to Yazd, where he continued his work as a merchant and was highly esteemed by its citizens.

Although from the beginning of this Dispensation the people of Yazd have been fanatical enemies of the new-born Faith and have ruthlessly persecuted its followers in that city, yet the family of the Afnán were not involved in this. Government officials and other dignitaries treated them with consideration and respect. In particular, they had a high regard for Ḥájí Mírzá Muḥammad-Taqí whose deeds and personality endeared him to the authorities.

Towards the close of Bahá'u'lláh's ministry, the nucleus of a Bahá'í community began to grow rapidly in 'Ishqábád, in the province of Turkistán. Several Bahá'í families from Persia migrated to this city where they enjoyed a measure of freedom in their Bahá'í activities.

At one stage, Ḥájí Mírzá Muḥammad-Taqí arranged for the purchase of some properties in 'Ishqábád and, upon informing Bahá'u'lláh of this, he was instructed to use a certain portion of these properties for the building of a Mashriqu'l-Adhkár. After the ascension of Bahá'u'lláh, Ḥájí Mírzá Muḥammad-Taqí, as directed by 'Abdu'l-Bahá, travelled to 'Ishqábád and undertook the task of supervising the construction of this House of Worship. He dedicated all his efforts towards, and expended all his financial resources in, the execution of this vast undertaking. With the help of other Bahá'ís, he erected this noble edifice, the first Mashriqu'l-Adhkár in the Bahá'í world.*

When the building of the Mashriqu'l-Adhkár was completed and the interior ornamentation was well on the way, 'Abdu'l-Bahá summoned Ḥájí Mírzá Muḥammad-Taqí to the Holy Land. He left 'Ishqábád in 1325 A.H. (A.D. 1907), committing all his affairs and those of the House of Worship to his eldest son, Ḥájí Mírzá Maḥmúd, and spent his last days in the presence of the Master.

He passed away in the Holy Land and is buried on the slopes

* As a result of an earthquake in the area this building became dangerous and had to be demolished in 1963.

of Mount Carmel, in the shadow of the Shrine of the Báb and in the vicinity of the Cave of Elijah.

No account of Ḥájí Mírzá Muḥammad-Taqí would be complete without referring to his early days when, as a youth of fifteen, he would sit in the presence of the Báb listening to His melodious voice as He revealed prayers and the verses of God. In his brief memoirs, which he wrote in 'Ishqábád, Ḥájí Mírzá Muḥammad-Taqí speaks of those days:

> I remember that every Sunday I used to go to the house of my illustrious aunt, the mother of the Báb, where I had the great privilege of attaining His presence . . . I remember especially on one occasion He permitted me to sit in His presence, and graciously cut a slice of melon which He gave to me. He was busy writing some prayers and verses. He then handed me one of the prayers He had revealed during the week and asked me to chant it in His presence . . . The Báb left Shíráz for Mecca via Búshihr that same week or the week after . . . Two or three months later I went to Búshihr to join my father . . . On His return from Mecca the Báb came to our house in Búshihr where I spent several days in His presence. During those days every moment of His time was spent in revealing the verses of God and writing prayers . . . One evening with tearful eyes I begged Him in all sincerity to pray for me so that I might spend my days in the service of God and in the end attain to His good pleasure. He assured me that it would be so.[1]

Ḥájí Mírzá Muḥammad-Taqí was an embodiment of detachment, humility and servitude. His only aim in life was to serve the Cause he loved so much. He often communed with Bahá'u'lláh in spirit and through prayer. Of him it is reported that every day at home he would put on his best clothes, sit for a few hours in a room by himself and with the utmost devotion and sincerity turn his heart and soul to Bahá'u'lláh, regarding himself as being in the very presence of the Blessed Beauty.

'Abdu'l-Bahá has said that whenever He was overtaken by grief, His meeting with Ḥájí Mírzá Muḥammad-Taqí would cause His sadness to disappear and His heart to be filled with joy.

During His darkest hours of incarceration in 'Akká, when the Covenant-breakers were working hand-in-hand with the Turkish authorities to threaten His life, 'Abdu'l-Bahá wrote a Tablet to Hájí Mírzá Muḥammad-Taqí and instructed him to arrange for the election of the Universal House of Justice,* should the threats against Him be carried out.

In the same Tablet 'Abdu'l-Bahá speaks of the greatness of the Cause of God and foreshadows the future attacks which will be made against it. These are His prophetic and ominous words, written at a time when the Message of Bahá'u'lláh had reached only a small number of people in the Western world:

> How great, how very great is the Cause! How very fierce the onslaught of all the peoples and kindreds of the earth. Ere long shall the clamour of the multitude throughout Africa, throughout America, the cry of the European and of the Turk, the groaning of India and China, be heard from far and near. One and all, they shall arise with all their power to resist His Cause. Then shall the knights of the Lord, assisted by His grace from on high, strengthened by faith, aided by the power of understanding, and reinforced by the legions of the Covenant, arise and make manifest the truth of the verse: 'Behold the confusion that hath befallen the tribes of the defeated!'[2]

In his devoted services Ḥájí Mírzá Muḥammad-Taqí brought victory and honour to the Cause of God. 'Abdu'l-Bahá has designated him as one of the '. . . four and twenty elders which sat before God on their seats . . .', mentioned in the Revelation of S. John the Divine.†

* Bahá'u'lláh ordained the Universal House of Justice as the supreme body of the Faith. It was first elected in 1963 and has its seat in Haifa.

† Of the other twenty-three 'elders', only nineteen have been named, i.e., the Báb and eighteen Letters of the Living.

Nabíl-i-A'ẓam

No account of the Revelation of Bahá'u'lláh would be complete without referring to Mullá Muḥammad-i-Zarandí, surnamed Nabíl-i-A'ẓam, one of His outstanding Apostles who played a great role in the propagation of His Message and the dissemination of His words. He is immortalized by his detailed narratives, a part of which, *The Dawn-Breakers*, mainly dealing with the story of the Báb, has been translated into English by Shoghi Effendi, the Guardian of the Faith. The other part dealing with the ministry of Bahá'u'lláh remains to be published.

In his early days Nabíl was a shepherd. He had a great love of nature and would often spend the night lying on the ground in contemplation of the stars and in solitary communion with his Creator. While following his flock over the fields he would chant the verses of the *Qur'án* and pray to God that He might enable him to find the truth during this life.

One day in 1847 he overheard two men telling the story of the Báb. His heart was immediately attracted to the new Message and soon afterwards he came in contact with a believer who taught him the Faith. He became an ardent follower of the Báb and, in spite of many obstacles which were placed in his path, remained active in the promotion of His Message.

His first meeting with Bahá'u'lláh was in Ṭihrán around the year 1850. At that stage, however, Nabíl did not appreciate the loftiness of His station. Later, when the Bábí community seemed leaderless and the believers dispirited and confused, Nabíl in his delusion claimed to be 'Him Whom God shall make manifest', and disseminated some of his own writings among the Bábís. Then he came to Baghdád and attained the presence of Bahá'u'lláh. This time his inner eyes beheld the glory of His Revelation and his soul was quickened by His mighty Spirit. He prostrated himself at His feet and begged forgiveness for his presumption. As an act of repentance and in order to demonstrate the measure of his humility towards Bahá'u'lláh, he cut his beard, which in those days was the symbol of a man's dignity, made a brush and with it swept the approaches to the house of Bahá'u'lláh.

Animated by an ardent desire to serve Bahá'u'lláh and fortified by His unfailing grace, Nabíl was enabled to render notable services to His Cause. His loyalty and devotion to Him were exemplary. He stands out among all the companions of Bahá'u'lláh as one who was dominated by a passionate love for Him. So intense was this love that those who came in contact with him could not fail to detect its fire burning within his soul.

Nabíl was a gifted poet, an inspired genius who wrote most fluently. Some of his narratives are actually composed in verse. These poems reveal the intensity of his faith, and the ardour of his love.

Bahá'u'lláh sent him on many important missions to Persia. In these travels, wherever he went he imparted the news of Bahá'u'lláh and inspired the believers to arise and serve Him. When Bahá'u'lláh left Baghdád for Constantinople, Nabíl could not stay behind. He dressed in the garb of a dervish and followed the route to Constantinople on foot and incognito, joining Bahá'u'lláh's party on the way. From Constantinople Bahá'u'lláh directed him to Persia, to teach and to spread the news of the Cause there. From Persia he proceeded to Adrianople, the scene of the proclamation of Bahá'u'lláh's Message. Again Bahá'u'lláh sent him to Persia to disseminate His Writings and help the believers to appreciate the significance of His Revelation. With great zeal and enthusiasm he travelled far and wide and assisted in establishing the basis of a growing Bahá'í community, distinct from the very small number who in their blindness followed Mírzá Yaḥyá. The latter community, known as the Azalís, in future years declined into insignificance and oblivion. It was during this period, also, that the word Bahá'í denoting the followers of Bahá'u'lláh came to replace the term Bábí.

Another mission with which Nabíl was entrusted by Bahá'u'lláh after this journey was to proceed to Egypt to appeal to the Khedive on behalf of seven fellow-believers who had been committed to prison at the instigation of one of the enemies of the Faith, the Persian Consul-General in that country. Soon after his arrival, however, Nabíl himself was cast into a prison in Alexandria. There he came in contact with Fáris Effendi, a Christian physician and clergyman who was also a prisoner. Nabíl taught him the Faith and Fáris Effendi became a deep and devoted believer, probably the first Christian to do so.

When Bahá'u'lláh was exiled to 'Akká, the ship that carried Him anchored in Alexandria close to the prison. By a strange coincidence Nabíl was informed of this. He and Fáris Effendi sent a letter to Bahá'u'lláh on the ship informing Him of their fate. Bahá'u'lláh sent a Tablet in reply, expressing His pleasure at receiving their letter and assuring them of His loving-kindness. He especially wrote words of encouragement to Fáris Effendi, who, addressing Bahá'u'lláh as his glorious Lord, begged that he might be accepted as one of His devoted servants.

Some time later Nabíl was able to leave Egypt. He travelled to the Holy Land and came to the gate of 'Akká in disguise, but the enemies of Bahá'u'lláh recognized him and reported him to the authorities, who expelled him from the city. After that he lived in various parts of the Holy Land and for some time in a cave on Mount Carmel. He spent his days in prayer and supplication, longing for the time when he could enter the presence of his Lord again. At last his prayers were answered, the doors of the prison were flung open to the believers, and Nabíl entered the presence of Bahá'u'lláh with tremendous joy. That was the moment of victory for him. He spent the rest of his life in 'Akká and often had the privilege of attaining His presence. It was in 1887 that he began the important task of writing his narratives which he begins with these words as a preface:

> It is my intention, by the aid and assistance of God, to devote the introductory pages of this narrative to such accounts as I have been able to obtain regarding those twin great lights, Shaykh Aḥmad-i-Aḥsá'í and Siyyid Káẓim-i-

Rashtí, after which it is my hope to recount, in their chronological order, the chief events that have happened since the year '60,* the year that witnessed the declaration of the Faith by the Báb, until the present time, the year 1305 A.H.†

In certain instances I shall go into some detail, in others I shall content myself with a brief summary of events. I shall place on record a description of the episodes I myself have witnessed, as well as those that have been reported to me by trustworthy and recognised informants, specifying in every case their names and standing. Those to whom I am primarily indebted are the following: Mírzá Aḥmad-i-Qazvíní, the Báb's amanuensis; Siyyid Ismá'íl-i-Dhabíḥ; Shaykh Ḥasan-i-Zunúzí; Shaykh Abú-Turáb-i-Qazvíní; and, last but not least, Mírzá Músá, Áqáy-i-Kalím, brother of Bahá'u'lláh.

I render thanks to God for having assisted me in the writing of these preliminary pages, and for having blessed and honoured them with the approval of Bahá'u'lláh, who has graciously deigned to consider them and who signified, through His amanuensis Mírzá Áqá Ján, who read them to Him, His pleasure and acceptance. I pray that the Almighty may sustain and guide me lest I err and falter in the task I have set myself to accomplish.[3]

When Bahá'u'lláh passed away, Nabíl was inconsolable. He could not live without his Beloved. The fire of love, which had burned within him so fiercely and so long, had now engulfed him and was about to set him aflame with the blaze of sacrifice. For some time, he tried very hard to adjust but this became increasingly difficult and, at last, unable to contain the ocean of love which surged within his soul, he took his life by drowning in the sea. He was truly a lover of the Blessed Beauty. He left behind a note paying homage to 'Abdu'l-Bahá, writing the date of his death in a single Arabic word 'Gharíq' (drowned). The numerical value of this word is 1310 A.H. (A.D. 1892–3).

One of his last contributions was to write an account of the passing of Bahá'u'lláh which stirs the heart. He was, moreover,

* 1260 A.H. (A.D. 1844).

† A.D. 1887–8.

chosen by 'Abdu'l-Bahá to select from the Writings of Bahá'u'lláh those passages which now constitute the text of the *Tablet of Visitation.** This Tablet is recited in the Most Holy Tomb† and the Shrine of the Báb, and for the commemoration of the ascension of Bahá'u'lláh and the martyrdom of the Báb. It is a unique Tablet, which is used by Bahá'ís throughout the world on these and other appropriate occasions.

Nabíl's contribution to Bábí and Bahá'í history is enormous in its scope. The believers find his already published narratives not only informative, but also a source of inspiration and deepening in the Faith. He has left behind a treasure-house which the passage of time shall never destroy, and from which generations yet unborn will reap their own harvest of knowledge and inspiration.

Companions of Bahá'u'lláh

By the time the *Kitáb-i-Íqán* was revealed, a considerable number of Bábís had come to Baghdád for the sole purpose of attaining Bahá'u'lláh's presence. Many had recognized His station and had become His ardent followers years before the Declaration of His Mission. Of these, He permitted a few to remain in Baghdád, while the rest He directed to return to their homes and spread the Cause of God in their native lands.

In this way, a small community of dedicated souls who were magnetized by His power came into being in Baghdád. These God-intoxicated companions of Bahá'u'lláh, the spiritual giants of this Dispensation, were the lovers of His beauty, the embodiments of detachment, a new race of men who had completely

* The first four paragraphs of this Tablet (no. 180, *Prayers and Meditations by Bahá'u'lláh*) are extracted from a Tablet of Bahá'u'lláh to one of His followers, Áqá Bábá; paragraphs five and six come from another Tablet revealed for an individual Bahá'í whom I have not been able to identify, and the last paragraph from a Tablet of Bahá'u'lláh to Khadíjih-Bagum, the wife of the Báb.

† The Shrine of Bahá'u'lláh at Bahjí.

SHAYKH SALMÁN

The indefatigable special messenger of Bahá'u'lláh

ḤÁJÍ MÍRZÁ MUḤAMMAD-TAQÍY-I-AFNÁN

A cousin of the Báb
And a renowned follower of Bahá'u'lláh

submitted themselves to His will and longed to sacrifice everything, even their lives, in His path. No earthly power was able to deflect their thoughts from His glory, nor any human agency to separate them from His person. They circled around Him as the moth does around a candle, and were unaware of their own selves in their adoration of Him. Their greatest joy was to attain His presence and the first thought that must have occurred to them after leaving Him was how they might enter His presence again. They lived in a state of perpetual expectation, hoping that through His bounty Bahá'u'lláh might summon them to His house or bestow upon them the great honour of visiting their gatherings and feasts.

History has not seen such a degree of love, of dedication and utter self-abnegation manifested by men, and never in the history of religion have so many devoted followers gathered around a Figure Whom they knew to be their Lord, years before His Declaration. Indeed, the Báb had indicated in His Writings that the station of 'Him Whom God shall make manifest' was so exalted that, before the unveiling of His glory, holy souls would recognize Him and with absolute devotion would long to lay down their lives in His path.

Not only did this happen before His Declaration, but there were some who became assured of His exalted station even during the ministry of the Báb. Although it was in the Síyáh-Chál of Ṭihrán that Bahá'u'lláh received the first intimations of His Revelation, yet, prior to this, several of the early Bábís recognized Him as the One foretold by the Báb.

One of these was Ṭáhirih, that immortal heroine of the Bábí Dispensation. Long before Bahá'u'lláh's imprisonment in the Síyáh-Chál, she became fully aware of His station, and wrote some of her most beautiful poetry extolling Him as her Lord and the object of her adoration. Shaykh Ḥasan-i-Zunúzí, a most zealous Bábí, was another who realized in advance the station of Bahá'u'lláh. The Báb had assured him that he would meet 'Him Whom God shall make manifest' in the city of Karbilá. In that very city, a year before Bahá'u'lláh's imprisonment in the

Síyáh-Chál, by chance he met Bahá'u'lláh in the street, Who confided to him the secret of His station which would be revealed at a later time in Baghdád. Several others, who were endowed with insight and spiritual vision, were likewise guided to behold the Glory of God shining behind a myriad veils of concealment.

Many are puzzled by this. For how could a Manifestation of God be recognized before He Himself had received the first intimation of His Mission? 'Abdu'l-Bahá has explained this. He states that a Manifestation of God is always a Manifestation. He has within Him all the divine attributes long before He receives the call of Prophethood. He is like a man asleep, or like a lamp placed under a cover, its light concealed from the eyes of men. The Prophet does not reveal His powers and attributes until the hour strikes for the birth of His mission. That hour marks His appearance as a Manifestation of God, although the declaration of His mission may come later when He publicly announces it. The birth of Bahá'u'lláh's Revelation took place in Ṭihrán, whereas He did not declare this until ten years later outside Baghdád.

No wonder that the companions of Bahá'u'lláh in Baghdád, who had spiritual eyes to behold the glory of their Lord prior to the Declaration of His Mission, were filled with the spirit of ecstasy and joy. They lived in a state of complete detachment, oblivious of this world and all its peoples. Of their fervour and love for Bahá'u'lláh, Shoghi Effendi writes:

> The joyous feasts which these companions, despite their extremely modest earnings, continually offered in honour of their Beloved; the gatherings, lasting far into the night, in which they loudly celebrated, with prayers, poetry and song, the praises of the Báb, of Quddús and of Bahá'u'lláh; the fasts they observed; the vigils they kept; the dreams and visions which fired their souls, and which they recounted to each other with feelings of unbounded enthusiasm; the eagerness with which those who served Bahá'u'lláh performed His errands, waited upon His needs, and carried

heavy skins of water for His ablutions and other domestic purposes; the acts of imprudence which, in moments of rapture, they occasionally committed; the expressions of wonder and admiration which their words and acts evoked in a populace that had seldom witnessed such demonstrations of religious transport and personal devotion—these, and many others, will forever remain associated with the history of that immortal period, intervening between the birth hour of Bahá'u'lláh's Revelation and its announcement on the eve of His departure from 'Iráq.[4]

Speaking of these companions, Nabíl has recorded the following:

So intoxicated were those who had quaffed from the cup of Bahá'u'lláh's presence, that in their eyes the palaces of kings appeared more ephemeral than a spider's web . . . The celebrations and festivities that were theirs were such as the kings of the earth had never dreamt of . . .

Many a night, no less than ten persons subsisted on no more than a pennyworth of dates. No one knew to whom actually belonged the shoes, the cloaks, or the robes that were to be found in their houses. Whoever went to the bazaar could claim that the shoes upon his feet were his own, and each one who entered the presence of Bahá'u'lláh could affirm that the cloak and robe he then wore belonged to him. Their own names they had forgotten, their hearts were emptied of aught else except adoration for their Beloved . . . O, for the joy of those days, and the gladness and wonder of those hours![5]

12

Bahá'u'lláh's Approaching Declaration

As the year 1863 drew closer, the signs of the Declaration of Bahá'u'lláh's Mission became increasingly manifest from the tone of the Tablets which streamed from His pen and the allusions He made both in public and private. Every day a new Tablet would be revealed and these were clearly indicative of the approaching hour when His sublime station would be unveiled.

It was a period of joy and ecstasy for those around Him, who were enraptured when they read these soul-stirring Tablets and festive odes. They would gather at night in a small room, light numerous camphorated candles and chant aloud these joyous odes. Oblivious of this world and wholly immersed in the realms of the spirit, they would suddenly discover that night had become day. Apart from the chanting of Tablets, the conversations which these heroes of Bahá'u'lláh held during these historic nights revolved entirely around His blessed person. The stories they told each other of Him; the sharing of joyous feelings which they had experienced through meeting Him either at His home or in the streets and bazaars of Ba<u>gh</u>dád; the profound discussions which they held to unravel the mysteries enshrined in His Tablets; the speculations they made on the timing and nature of the Declaration of His Mission, all these created an atmosphere of excitement and rapture far beyond the experience of any man today.

By virtue of their unique style and wording and their soul-entrancing power, the odes and Tablets which were revealed by Bahá'u'lláh in this period are very difficult to describe and may well prove impossible to translate. Among them are the following: *Subḥána-Rabbíya'l-A'lá*, *Ghulámu'l-Khuld*, *Ḥúr-i-'Ujáb*, *Az-Bágh-i-Iláhí* and *Halih-Halih-Yá-Bishárat*.

Subḥána-Rabbíya'l-A'lá

This Tablet in Arabic is revealed in honour of Ḥájí Mírzá Músáy-i-Javáhirí, entitled by Bahá'u'lláh the Ḥarf-i-Baqá (Letter of Eternity). His father, Ḥájí Mírzá Hádí, formerly a Persian vizir, was a remarkable person who was held in high repute among the notables of Persia and 'Iráq. He had migrated to Baghdád where he had established his residence and, being a man of great wealth and influence, was highly esteemed by the inhabitants of that city. Towards the end of his life, Ḥájí Mírzá Hádí became attracted to Bahá'u'lláh and was devoted to Him. He would often enter His presence and sit at His feet in humility and self-effacement.

After his death great difficulties arose over his estate. When everything was settled, his son, Ḥájí Mírzá Músá, who was a loyal and steadfast follower of Bahá'u'lláh, inherited a portion of the estate. He owned the house of Bahá'u'lláh in Baghdád and was eager to present it to Him, along with other properties. But Bahá'u'lláh refused to accept this gift. Ḥájí Mírzá Músá continued to plead with Him, however, until at last Bahá'u'lláh gave instructions that the house be purchased from him at a fair price. This was accomplished and the house became a property of the Faith.

Bahá'u'lláh has designated this house as the 'House of God', the 'Most Great House', and ordained it to be a centre of pilgrimage. Within its walls innumerable Tablets were revealed and the verses of God were sent down in great profusion for many years. From this sacred spot Bahá'u'lláh shed the splendour of His name upon the peoples of the world and breathed the spirit of life into the body of mankind. This House and the House of the Báb in Shíráz are, next to the Holy Shrines in 'Akká and Haifa where the earthly remains of Bahá'u'lláh and the Báb are interred, regarded by Bahá'ís as the holiest places on earth.

Pilgrimage to the House of Bahá'u'lláh in Baghdád and that of the Báb in Shíráz is one of the holy observances of the Faith ordained in the *Kitáb-i-Aqdas*. When Bahá'u'lláh was in Adrianople He revealed the two *Súrihs of Ḥajj* (Pilgrimage). He then directed Nabíl-i-A'ẓam to proceed to Baghdád and Shíráz on pilgrimage. He is the first, and so far the only one, who has performed all the rites of pilgrimage prescribed in these Tablets.

Towards the end of 'Abdu'l-Bahá's life, in accordance with His directives, certain constructional work was done on the House of Bahá'u'lláh in Baghdád. Its foundations were reinforced and the building was restored to its original form. Soon after this, however, the enemies of the Faith seized it unlawfully and this led eventually to the submission of a petition to the Council of the League of Nations. In 1929 this body upheld the claims of the Bahá'ís to the House, but for a variety of reasons, their verdict was not enforced by the authorities and the House is still unliberated.

In some of His Tablets Bahá'u'lláh has extolled the holiness and glory of this sacred spot, has foretold its fate and the abasement to which it would be subjected, and has prophesied its ultimate exaltation and grandeur in days to come. In one Tablet Bahá'u'lláh has revealed the following:

> Grieve not, O House of God, if the veil of thy sanctity be rent asunder by the infidels. God hath, in the world of creation, adorned thee with the jewel of His remembrance. Such an ornament no man can, at any time, profane. Towards thee the eyes of thy Lord shall, under all conditions, remain directed . . . In the fullness of time the Lord shall, by the power of truth, exalt it in the eyes of all men. He shall cause it to become the Standard of His Kingdom, the Shrine round which will circle the concourse of the faithful.[1]

Bahá'u'lláh opens the Tablet of *Subḥána-Rabbíya'l-A'lá* with words of encouragement to Mírzá Músá, the Ḥarf-i-Baqá, calling on him to detach himself from this world and everything in it, to enable him to soar in the realms of spirit and partake of the melodies of the Kingdom.

He portrays in dramatic terms the appearance before Him of the 'Maid of Heaven', personifying the 'Most Great Spirit',* and alludes to His own Revelation in such terms as no pen can describe. The whole Tablet conveys in symbolic language the joyous tidings of the advent of the Day of God, at the same time warning the faithful to beware of tests which will befall them, causing many to be deprived of attaining to His glory and grace.

This Tablet is written in allusive language. To understand it the believer must turn to Bahá'u'lláh and meditate upon His words. Only in this way can his heart receive Bahá'u'lláh's unfailing grace and realize the significance of His utterances.

Lawḥ-i-Ghulámu'l-Khuld

Another Tablet of the same nature, but written partly in Arabic and partly in Persian, is the Tablet of *Ghulámu'l-Khuld* (The Youth of Paradise). It is a very beautiful Tablet, and was revealed by Bahá'u'lláh to celebrate the anniversary of the Declaration of the Báb. Filled with imagery and allegorical language, it conveys clearly the glad tidings of the coming of Bahá'u'lláh. Alluding to Himself in symbolic terms, He announces the unveiling of His Beauty, glorifies His own Revelation, identifies Himself as the Word upon which depended the souls of all the Prophets of God and His chosen ones, declares to all His companions that He Who was hidden from the eyes of men has now come, asserts that through His coming a breath of life has been wafted over all created things, invites His true lovers to come forward and become united with their Beloved, exhorts them to purify their hearts so that they may be acceptable in His presence, and counsels them to rid themselves of every attachment to this world and to cast away their vain imaginings and superstitions.

* See note, p. 10.

Also in this Tablet Bahá'u'lláh testifies to the loftiness of the station of the Báb and affirms that He is the Point from which all knowledge has been generated. That the Báb is the source of all knowledge is one of the verities of the Cause of Bahá'u'lláh. Indeed, every Prophet of God has been the source of knowledge for His people. This is amply demonstrated by history.

For example, the children of Israel were captive in the hands of Pharaoh, deprived of their rights of freedom and justice. But through the influence of Moses, they were relieved of this bondage. Under His guidance, born of God, they attained importance and became renowned throughout the world for having built a great civilization. 'Abdu'l-Bahá states that some of the Greek philosophers went to the Holy Land, especially to acquire knowledge from the Jewish people. There they learned about the unity of God and the immortality of the soul, and took these teachings back to Greece.*

The Christian Faith likewise brought forth a civilization which spread throughout the Western world, swept aside the standards of Rome and put in their place a new way of life. It enlightened the minds of millions and established a new basis for learning and knowledge.

Islám, however, offers the best example in this respect. Although it originated among the warlike tribes of Arabia, the civilization which it reared gave, on the one hand, spiritual life to millions and, on the other, created seats of learning and knowledge all over the Muslim world. Its scholars and scientists laid the foundations of many arts and sciences which later reached the people of the Christian world and revolutionized their lives.

Describing the Arabs under the influence of Islám, George Townshend, the great Irish scholar, writes in *Christ and Bahá'u'lláh*:

Because of the central position of the Qur'án, revered as a

* See *Some Answered Questions*, ch. v.

literary miracle, and because of Arabian pride in their language, which they held to be the one perfect tongue spoken by man and which is indeed regarded by scholars today as one of the greatest intellectual achievements of the race, literature in all its uses and forms was given a place of eminence. Schools and universities were founded and thronged by students of many nations. Great works were produced on all manner of subjects; great libraries were collected containing hundreds of thousands of volumes. The Caliphs ransacked the earth for knowledge, sending out expeditions of inquiry and making foreign lands and distant ages give up their lore. An army of translators was employed, rendering Greek, Egyptian, Indian and Jewish works into Arabic. Grammar and its laws were studied with great elaboration. Dictionaries, lexicons and encyclopaedias on a vast scale were prepared. Paper was introduced from China; a new system of numerals (usually known as Arabic) from India. Arabic became the universal language. Caliphs would invite literary men of international repute to the court. Scholars, philosophers, poets, grammarians from diverse lands would find a meeting place in the great bookshops of the capital.

The pursuit of science, practical as well as abstract, kept pace with that of letters. In experimental science, in medicine and surgery, in chemistry and physics, in geography as well as in mathematics and astronomy, the Arabs led the world of that day. They invented a new and exquisite form of architecture, distinguished by its combination of airy grace with solid strength, and by its use of light. The influence of this style can be traced through India as far as Java, to China, to the Sudan and to the whole of Russia. They developed many branches of industry and improved methods of agriculture and horticulture. Introducing the use of the mariner's compass their ships traversed the seas while caravans maintained a trade between all provinces of the empire, carrying produce from India and China, Turkistan and Russia, from Africa and the Malayan Archipelago.

The glory of Baghdád with its mosques and palaces, its temples of learning, its fragrant gardens, was reproduced in

> the lesser centres of the world of Islám: in Basra, in Bokhara, in Granada and Córdoba. It is written of the last-named city that at the height of its prosperity it contained more than 200,000 houses and more than a million inhabitants and that a man after sunset might walk in a straight line for ten miles along paved and illuminated streets—yet in Europe centuries later there was not a paved street in Paris nor a public lamp in London.
>
> Córdoba was the first University founded in Europe, and in its halls multitudes of Christian scholars received instruction, among them being Gerbert who afterwards became Sylvester II, the brilliant Pope of Rome.
>
> Inevitably, and in spite of the antagonism between Christendom and Islám, this advanced civilization influenced the course of life and thought in Europe. Through the Muslim outpost in Sicily and the scintillating brilliance of Muslim Spain, through the intelligence of scholars and the resources of the Muslim universities, through traders, through diplomats and travellers, through soldiers, sailors and reconquered peasants, new ideas, techniques and attitudes passed from Islám to Western Europe.[2]

In this Dispensation, which is the consummation of past ages and centuries, humanity has been endowed with enormous capacity to grow and develop in every field of human knowledge. Up to the time of the manifestation of the Báb, human progress had been very slow and limited in extent. With the coming of the Báb, however, a new era of knowledge unprecedented in its scope opened before mankind.

In one of the traditions of Islám it is clearly stated that 'Knowledge is twenty and seven letters. All that the Prophets have revealed are two letters thereof. No man thus far hath known more than these two letters. But when the Qá'im shall arise, He will cause the remaining twenty and five letters to be made manifest.'[3]

Since the appearance of the Báb, man's advances in both material and spiritual civilization have been prodigious. The unprecedented increase in scientific discoveries has, within a short period of time, established a marvellous system of communication throughout the world, which is of the utmost significance if we are to evaluate correctly the plan of God for mankind.

The diffusion of the light of the Faith of Bahá'u'lláh throughout the entire planet and the proclamation of its Message on a global scale could be realized only at a time when the peoples of the world are able to communicate easily with one another. Without a world-wide system of communication linking all humanity together, the Faith of Bahá'u'lláh would have been impractical and ineffective. For this is a Faith whose basic teachings revolve around the principle of the oneness of mankind. Its message is universal and its aim is to establish a spiritual world order for all who dwell on earth.

In the early days of the Faith in Persia, many believers could not visualize the manner in which the Cause of Bahá'u'lláh would reach the remote corners of the earth. The only way of travelling known to them was by walking or riding a donkey or a mule. The question which puzzled them most was how they could cover such long distances to teach the Cause. At that time no one could have offered a solution except to say that God would create the means. But the Báb had stated that mankind should establish a system of swift communications so that the news of the coming of 'Him Whom God shall make manifest' could reach the whole world.

Now this has happened, and within such a short period a miraculous scientific revolution has taken place. Today the world has become one world. Man can communicate with the speed of light and travel faster than sound. The Báb had indeed ushered in a new era in human knowledge, paving the way for the coming of Bahá'u'lláh. Today the Cause of Bahá'u'lláh has reached all humanity and the rising institutions of its World Order are firmly established in every land.

The outpouring of knowledge in this Dispensation has occurred in both the spiritual and material fields. These two must go hand in hand in order that a divine civilization may come into being. One without the other will create such an imbalance in the life of man as to impair completely his advancement. Scientific knowledge alone will lead to materialism, whereas spiritual knowledge by itself would result in superstition.

The Revelation of Bahá'u'lláh aims at creating this balance within human society. When this is achieved on a world-wide scale, the Bahá'í civilization will come into being. Then the knowledge of God will so dominate the human soul that nobility of character and divine virtues will become the distinguishing features of the human race. Then scientific progress matched with spiritual attainments will usher in a new era of human accomplishments. Within such a society Bahá'í arts, literature, music and other outpourings of the human spirit will be born and develop, and the tree of humanity will blossom and grow to maturity.

Ḥúr-i-'Ujáb

Another Tablet of Bahá'u'lláh's which was revealed in the same period is the *Ḥúr-i-'Ujáb* (The Wondrous Maiden). It is in Arabic and is similar to the two preceding Tablets, in that it conveys the same glad-tidings, is written in allegorical language and contains the symbolism of the 'Maid of Heaven'.

In it Bahá'u'lláh alludes to the unveiling of His glorious station, asserts that the light of His countenance has been lifted upon men, and states that the outpouring of His Revelation has been so stupendous as to cause the pure in heart to be dumbfounded. He also denounces the perversity and blindness of the unfaithful among His companions. This is an allusion to Mírzá Yaḥyá and his associates, who betrayed the Faith of God and caused Bahá'u'lláh much sorrow and pain.

Az-Bágh-i-Iláhí

Az-Bágh-i-Iláhí is an ode revealed not long before the Declaration of Bahá'u'lláh. It is one of His most joyous odes, composed in an exalted style. Each Persian verse is followed by one in Arabic, and the combination of the two creates a rich melody of unsurpassed beauty and enchantment. Its theme is the advent of the Promised Day of God, but to describe its contents is not an easy task, especially in the absence of an English translation.

In each and every line Bahá'u'lláh alludes to Himself and extols His own attributes. He unveils the splendours of His exalted station and, among other designations, refers to Himself as the Lord of all mankind, the Day-star of Truth, the Promise of all ages, the Youth of Paradise, the Quickener of men and the Essence of the Spirit of Truth. This poem is an eloquent description of Bahá'u'lláh's stupendous station, the character of His Mission and the outpourings of His Revelation.

The chanting of this beautiful ode creates an atmosphere of ecstasy and joy. It moves the heart and evokes a feeling of awe and excitement within the soul. No wonder that the companions of Bahá'u'lláh in Baghdád, who chanted it in their gatherings, were carried away into the realms of spirit, completely oblivious of this world and all its peoples.

Halih-Halih-Yá-Bishárat

Another ode in Persian revealed during this period is known as *Halih-Halih-Yá-Bishárat*, which is very similar in its contents to *Az-Bágh-i-Iláhí*.

Nabíl has recounted in his as yet unpublished narratives the story of a gathering held one evening in the house of Bahá'u'lláh in Baghdád, sometime before His Declaration. He considered that gathering to have been one of the most memorable of his life.

That night a wonderful feast had been arranged and 'Abdu'l-Bahá, then eighteen years of age, was acting as host. His youthful and radiant personality added distinction to the assembly. A number of believers from Baghdád and Karbilá were present, among them some eminent personalities such as Ḥájí Siyyid Javád-i-Karbilá'í, Shaykh Sulṭán, and Sayyáḥ.

After partaking of food they began to chant the Tablets of Bahá'u'lláh, and soon the atmosphere became deeply spiritual. Hearts were filled with divine love and souls were illumined by the light of the New Day; so when the poem of *Az Bágh-i-Iláhí* was chanted, its mysteries became apparent to them, revealing thereby the approaching hour of the unveiling of Bahá'u'lláh's divine station. Every sincere soul in that company experienced ecstasy and joy, and the atmosphere became alive with excitement and rapture.

An interesting incident occurred during the chanting of this ode. In one verse Bahá'u'lláh condemns the unfaithful among His companions. When this particular verse was chanted the believers all turned to look at Siyyid Muḥammad-i-Iṣfahání. Although embarrassed, he arose, and to the amusement of some and the amazement of others, performed a dance of rapture in an attempt to dispel their suspicion.

Then without warning the door opened and Bahá'u'lláh entered majestically, holding in His hand a small glass vessel of rose-water. He greeted them with the salutation 'Alláh'u'-Akbar',* and bade them not to arise or disrupt their meeting. He had felt the spirituality of that gathering, He said, and so had come to anoint them with rose-water.† This He graciously did, going to every person in the room, after which He left.

It was a mighty climax and the highlight of the evening. No one was able to sleep that night, so intoxicated were they with the wine of His presence. 'The like of that night', Nabíl writes, 'the eye of creation had not seen.'

* Literally, 'God is the Greatest'. With these words the followers of the Báb greeted each other.

† In those days it was considered a gracious act for the host to anoint his guests with rose-water.

13

Friends and Foes

Ḥájí Siyyid Javád-i-Karbilá'í

Notable among the companions of Bahá'u'lláh in 'Iráq, one who rendered memorable services to the Faith and was especially mentioned by Nabíl in the aforementioned story, is Ḥájí Siyyid Javád-i-Karbilá'í to whom reference has been made in previous chapters.

He was one of the outstanding disciples of Siyyid Káẓim-i-Ras̲h̲tí, and in his early youth had met the renowned S̲h̲ayk̲h̲ Aḥmad-i-Aḥsá'í, who was the founder of the S̲h̲ayk̲h̲í sect of Islám. He was distinguished by his learning and knowledge, his piety and uprightness. He was reserved in his speech and very gentle in his manners, and had a dignified bearing which endeared him to people.

Ḥájí Siyyid Javád was one of the early believers of the Bábí Dispensation. He had known the Báb from the days of His childhood, years before His Declaration, and was fascinated by the remarkable qualities which were so strikingly apparent in Him. Some years later, he went to Bús̲h̲ihr and for almost six months lived in the building where the Báb and His uncle had their business premises. There he became attracted to the Báb and attained His presence many times, but never did it cross his mind that the Promised One of Islám could be any other than one of the divines or men of learning.

In a spoken chronicle recorded by Mírzá Abu'l-Faḍl, the outstanding scholar of the Faith, Ḥájí Siyyid Javád recalls with excitement the circumstances which led him to embrace the Faith of the Báb in Karbilá:

... It was in 1844 that Mullá 'Alíy-i-Basṭámí returned to Karbilá from S͟híráz, bringing the news of the appearance of the Báb* and announcing that he himself together with other disciples had already attained His presence. This news, which spread rapidly, created a great excitement among the divines who trusted Mullá 'Alí and had regard for his dignity and pious life.

Mullá 'Alí only mentioned the title of the Báb, however, and refused to disclose His identity. He used to say: 'The Báb has appeared and some of us have attained His presence, but He has forbidden us to mention His name or disclose His identity or that of His family at the present time. Soon however His Message will be noised abroad and His name will be disclosed to all.'

This news brought about an amazing sensation in 'Iráq. In all the gatherings the appearance of the Báb was the topic of discussion. Many people speculated as to His identity, but no one ever suspected that Mírzá 'Alí-Muḥammad could be the Báb. The possibility never crossed anyone's mind, owing to the fact that He was only a youth and a merchant by profession. The people without exception thought that the Báb, the Gate of the knowledge of God, would appear from among the learned and not from the trading and professional classes. The S͟hayk͟hís, in particular, thought that He would be one of the leading disciples of Siyyid Káẓim.

One day I invited Mullá 'Alí to my home ... We talked about this wonderful event, but in spite of the strong bonds of love and friendship which existed between us, I could not extract from him any clues by which I could recognize the person of the Báb. In the end I became desperate. Jokingly I gripped his arms and pushed him hard against the wall ... There I held him, demanding that he disclose the name of that wondrous Being. But Mullá 'Alí calmly reminded me that he was forbidden to do so ... In the midst of all this, Mullá 'Alí quite inadvertently mentioned that the Báb had re-

* Literally, 'Gate': One Who is regarded as an intermediary between the faithful and the Promised One. This is a designation well known to the followers of S͟hí'ah Islám.

quested him to collect any letters He had written to people in Karbilá and send them back to Shíráz.

On hearing this, the thought of Mírzá 'Alí-Muḥammad suddenly flashed through my mind. Although it seemed very unlikely, I wondered whether it could be He. So I rushed to my room and fetched some of His letters which were addressed to me. As soon as Mullá 'Alí's eyes fell upon the seal of the Báb, he burst into tears. I was so filled with emotion that I too wept. Between his sobs Mullá 'Alí's constant plea to me was: 'I did not mention His name. Please do not disclose it to anyone . . .'

It was not long after this that the Báb declared His station in Mecca and the news of this was widely spread throughout the Muslim world and His identity disclosed.[1]

Soon after this interview, Ḥájí Siyyid Javád travelled to Shíráz and attained the presence of the Báb, this time as an ardent believer. He dedicated his life to the service of the Cause in Karbilá. It was in this city in the year 1851 that he met Bahá'u'lláh for the first time. He immediately recognized the greatness of Bahá'u'lláh, but did not appreciate His glorious station until some time later.

The following is a translation of his spoken chronicle as he describes his first meeting with Bahá'u'lláh:

. . . I was in Karbilá when the news of the arrival of Bahá'u'lláh in that city reached me. The first person who gave me this information was Ḥájí Siyyid Muḥammad-i-Iṣfahání.*

Before I attained His presence I expected to find Him a youth of noble lineage, the son of a vizir, but not one endowed with immense knowledge or wisdom. Together with some friends I went to meet Bahá'u'lláh. As was their custom, my friends would not enter the room before me; so I went in first and occupied the seat of honour in that gathering.

After we had exchanged greetings Bahá'u'lláh turned to those present and asked them what subjects they, the disciples of the late Siyyid,† usually discussed when they

* The 'Antichrist of the Bahá'í Revelation'.

† Siyyid Káẓim-i-Rashtí.

gathered in a meeting. Did they discuss the topics of religion as current among men? What would they do if God manifested Himself to man, rolled up the old doctrines and philosophies, revealed a new set of teachings and opened up a new page in divine knowledge? What then would be their position?

Bahá'u'lláh spoke for some time in this vein. It was not long before I realized that we, known to be men of learning and knowledge, dwelt in the depths of ignorance, whereas He, whom we considered to be only a youth, the son of a vizir, stood upon the highest pinnacle of understanding and wisdom.

After this experience, whenever I entered His presence, I would sit at His feet in absolute humility and refrain from speaking. I always listened attentively to Him in order to benefit from His knowledge and understanding. This attitude of mine, however, used to annoy my friend Ḥájí Siyyid Muḥammad. Once he rebuked me, saying: 'Assuming that all agree that Jináb-i-Bahá is of the same calibre as ourselves, why do you sit in silence and show so much humility towards Him?'

I pleaded with my friend not to be angry with me. I told him that I could neither specify a station for Him nor, God forbid, consider Him as one of us. I regarded Him as incomparable and unique.[2]

Early in 1852 Bahá'u'lláh returned from Karbilá to His native city and was imprisoned a few months later in the Síyáh-Chál of Ṭihrán. Ḥájí Siyyid Javád was in Karbilá when Bahá'u'lláh was exiled to 'Iráq after His release from that dungeon. During the ten years of Bahá'u'lláh's sojourn in 'Iráq, he was a faithful companion, one who truly recognized the station of Bahá'u'lláh before His Declaration.

When Bahá'u'lláh was exiled to Adrianople, Ḥájí Siyyid Javád travelled to Persia and lived in various parts of the country, serving the Faith with great distinction. He remained a loyal and steadfast believer until his death in Kirmán about 1882.

Some Powerful Enemies

At the time that the companions of Bahá'u'lláh in Baghdád were basking in the sunshine of His presence and the fortunes of the Faith had begun to rise, a campaign of opposition and enmity towards its Author was mounting. The machinations of a number of the 'ulamá, headed by the crafty and evil-minded Shaykh 'Abdu'l-Ḥusayn, and ably assisted by the scheming Mírzá Buzurg Khán, the Persian Consul-General in Baghdád to whom reference has been made in a previous chapter, were now beginning to have effect.

Their letters of calumny and accusation against Bahá'u'lláh, in which they grossly misrepresented His Cause, were influencing the tyrannical Náṣiri'd-Dín Sháh. The Persian Foreign Minister, Mírzá Sa'íd Khán, was greatly surprised by Bahá'u'lláh's steadfastness and courage in the face of mounting opposition from His powerful enemies. He did not take any steps, however, to allay the Sháh's fears and suspicions, but instead unquestioningly carried out his orders. These were to instruct the Persian Ambassador in Constantinople, Ḥájí Mírzá Ḥusayn Khán, the Mushíru'd-Dawlih, to persuade the Ottoman government to remove Bahá'u'lláh from Baghdád, mainly on the grounds that His presence in a city so close to the borders of Persia would exert a harmful influence upon its people. A special dispatch was sent from Ṭihrán to Constantinople, urging the Ambassador to meet 'Álí Páshá, the Grand Vizir of the Sulṭán, and Fu'ád Páshá, the Foreign Minister, to discuss the whole situation with them and obtain an order from the Sulṭán for the transfer of Bahá'u'lláh from Baghdád.

In this communication, Mírzá Sa'íd Khán condemns the Bábí community as a misguided and detestable sect whose foundation, he affirms, had been uprooted through the concerted efforts of the government and the sovereign himself. He points out the necessity of exterminating each and every one of its members and deplores the release of Bahá'u'lláh from the Síyáh-Chál, which he attributes to lack of prudence on the part of the government of the time. He accuses Bahá'u'lláh of being the source of mischief, of secretly corrupting and misleading ignorant men and weaklings, and expresses concern at Bahá'u'lláh's rising prestige in Baghdád and at the increasing number of His followers who would willingly give their lives in His path. In order to imbue his correspondent with his own fears, he quotes the following celebrated Arabic verse: 'I see beneath the ashes the glow of fire, and it wants but little to burst into flames.'

In this communication he further speaks about the cordial relationship and good intentions which bind the two Islamic nations together on a basis of equality regarding all matters vital to their common interests. He then states that the Sháh has ordered him to send this communication by special messenger to Constantinople, and to instruct the Ambassador to proceed without delay in presenting the case to the Sulṭán's Grand Vizir and his Foreign Minister, putting before them two possible solutions. The one which the Persian government favoured was an extradition order, instructing Námiq Páshá, the Governor of Baghdád, to hand over Bahá'u'lláh and some of His followers to the Persian authorities in Kirmánsháh. In this way the Persian government could keep them in custody in a suitable place and prevent them from spreading their Cause. Should this suggestion prove to be unacceptable to the Sulṭán's government, Mírzá Sa'íd Khán proposed an alternative, which was to transfer Bahá'u'lláh from Baghdád to a remote part of the Ottoman territory where He could be confined far from the borders of Persia.

In order to strengthen his case, Mírzá Sa'íd Khán enclosed in this dispatch the original letter which Mírzá Buzurg Khán, the Consul-General in Baghdád, had sent through the Governor of Kirmánsháh to the Sháh, and which contained alarming reports, lies and misrepresentations concerning Bahá'u'lláh. But reports of Bahá'u'lláh's outstanding qualities and attributes had from time to time reached the Sulṭán, who had been so impressed by these accounts that he resolutely refused to accede to the demands of the Persian government for the extradition of Bahá'u'lláh from his territory. Instead, through 'Álí Páshá he issued orders that Bahá'u'lláh proceed to Constantinople as a guest of the Ottoman government. A mounted escort was ordered to accompany Him for His protection.

In the meantime the believers in Baghdád, unaware of such moves, were happy in their enjoyment of nearness to Bahá'u'lláh.

14

Tablet of the Holy Mariner

On the occasion of Naw-Rúz* 1863, Bahá'u'lláh had pitched His tent in a field on the outskirts of Baghdád, known as the Mazra'iy-i-Vashshásh—a place rented by His faithful brother Mírzá Músá. Bahá'u'lláh was celebrating this festival with a number of His companions, who were likewise living in tents in the open countryside. Outings at this time of year when the spring season had just begun and the weather was mild were extremely pleasant, and Bahá'u'lláh always enjoyed nature and beautiful scenery and loved to be in the country.

On the fifth day of Naw-Rúz, the *Lawḥ-i-Malláḥu'l-Quds* (Tablet of the Holy Mariner) was revealed. Mírzá Áqá Ján, Bahá'u'lláh's amanuensis, emerged from the tent of Bahá'u'lláh, gathered the believers around him and chanted that mournful Tablet to them. Although during the last year of His sojourn in 'Iráq He had, on several occasions, alluded to trials and tribulations which were to come, His companions had not felt previously such sadness as they did on that day.

Nabíl, who was present, has recorded the following:

> Oceans of sorrow surged in the hearts of the listeners when the Tablet of the Holy Mariner was read aloud to them . . . It was evident to every one that the chapter of Baghdád was about to be closed, and a new one opened, in its stead. No sooner had that Tablet been chanted than Bahá'u'lláh ordered

* An ancient festival when the Persians celebrate their New Year on the day of the vernal equinox, usually on the 21st March. The Bahá'í calendar also begins with Naw-Rúz which is one of the Bahá'í Holy Days. In 1863, Naw-Rúz was celebrated on the 22nd March as the vernal equinox took place after sunset on the 21st.

that the tents which had been pitched should be folded up, and that all His companions should return to the city. While the tents were being removed He observed: '*These tents may be likened to the trappings of this world, which no sooner are they spread out than the time cometh for them to be rolled up.*' From these words of His they who heard them perceived that these tents would never again be pitched on that spot.[1]

He further mentions that the tents had not yet been taken away when an emissary of Námiq Pá<u>sh</u>á, the Governor of Ba<u>gh</u>dád, arrived and handed to Bahá'u'lláh a communication inviting Him to come for interview with the Governor at his headquarters. Bahá'u'lláh accepted the invitation, but not wishing to visit the authorities in government headquarters, He suggested that the meeting take place instead in a certain mosque in the city on the following day.

Námiq Pá<u>sh</u>á, like his predecessors, admired Bahá'u'lláh and was deeply conscious of His innate knowledge and exalted position. He held Bahá'u'lláh in such high esteem that for three months he could not bring himself to tell Him of the decision of the Ottoman government that He should proceed to Constantinople. After being ordered for the fifth time by the Prime Minister to arrange the transfer of Bahá'u'lláh to the capital, Námiq Pá<u>sh</u>á reluctantly took the necessary step of informing Bahá'u'lláh of this. Feeling ashamed to meet Him face to face on that fateful occasion, the Governor sent his deputy, Amín Effendi, to the mosque to deliver the message. A few weeks later, when Bahá'u'lláh was in the Garden of Riḍván, Námiq Pá<u>sh</u>á went there, attained His presence and paid his respects to the One Whom he regarded as one of the lights of the age.

The *Tablet of the Holy Mariner* is in two parts, one in Arabic and the other in Persian. So far only the Arabic Tablet has been rendered into English and is published.

The theme of this Tablet is the story of the Covenant and man's unfaithfulness to it. Its message is applicable not only to the days of Bahá'u'lláh, but also to the ministries of 'Abdu'l-Bahá and Shoghi Effendi, and indeed to the present time. Concerning this Tablet 'Abdu'l-Bahá said: 'Study the *Tablet of the Holy Mariner* that ye may know the truth, and consider that the Blessed Beauty* hath fully foretold future events. Let them who perceive, take warning!'[2]

Not only did 'Abdu'l-Bahá ask the believers to study this Tablet during His own ministry, when the Covenant of Bahá'u'lláh was being violated by the Covenant-breakers, but He urged them shortly before His passing to study it again. For He knew too well that there were a few among His followers who would violate the Covenant and rise up against Shoghi Effendi, the Guardian of the Cause of God.

The *Tablet of the Holy Mariner* is revealed in symbolic language. To appreciate it one must acquire for himself a knowledge of the spiritual verities enshrined within Bahá'u'lláh's Writings and meditate upon His words. Although the allegorical terms Bahá'u'lláh has used in this Tablet assume various meanings, He has nonetheless manifestly foreshadowed coming events and conveyed some aspects of the Covenant.

The following is a translation of the *Tablet of the Holy Mariner* from the original Arabic.†

He is the Gracious, the Well-Beloved!

O Holy Mariner!

Bid thine ark of eternity appear before the Celestial Concourse,

Launch it upon the ancient sea, in His Name, the Most Wondrous,

And let the angelic spirits enter, in the Name of God, the Most High.

* Bahá'u'lláh.

† After each verse, except the last three, is the refrain: 'Glorified be my Lord, the All-Glorious!'

Unmoor it, then, that it may sail upon the ocean of glory,

Haply the dwellers therein may attain the retreats of nearness in the everlasting realm.

Having reached the sacred strand, the shore of the crimson seas,

Bid them issue forth and attain this ethereal invisible station,

A station wherein the Lord hath in the Flame of His Beauty appeared within the deathless tree;

Wherein the embodiments of His Cause cleansed themselves of self and passion;

Around which the Glory of Moses doth circle with the everlasting hosts;

Wherein the Hand of God was drawn forth from His bosom of Grandeur;

Wherein the ark of the Cause remaineth motionless even though to its dwellers be declared all divine attributes.

O Mariner! Teach them that are within the ark that which we have taught thee behind the mystic veil,

Perchance they may not tarry in the sacred snow-white spot,

But may soar upon the wings of the spirit unto that station which the Lord hath exalted above all mention in the worlds below,

May wing through space even as the favoured birds in the realm of eternal reunion;

May know the mysteries hidden in the Seas of light.

They passed the grades of worldly limitations and reached that of the divine unity, the centre of heavenly guidance.

They have desired to ascend unto that state which the Lord hath ordained to be above their stations.

Whereupon the burning meteor cast them out from them that abide in the Kingdom of His Presence,

And they heard the Voice of Grandeur raised from behind the unseen pavilion upon the Height of Glory:

'O guardian angels! Return them to their abode in the world below,

'Inasmuch as they have purposed to rise to that sphere which the wings of the celestial dove have never attained;

'Whereupon the ship of fancy standeth still which the minds of them that comprehend cannot grasp.'

Whereupon the maid of heaven looked out from her exalted chamber,

And with her brow signed to the Celestial Concourse,

Flooding with the light of her countenance the heaven and the earth,

And as the radiance of her beauty shone upon the people of dust,

All beings were shaken in their mortal graves.

She then raised the call which no ear through all eternity hath ever heard,

And thus proclaimed: 'By the Lord! He whose heart hath not the fragrance of the love of the exalted and glorious Arabian Youth,

'Can in no wise ascend unto the glory of the highest heaven.'

Thereupon she summoned unto herself one maiden from her handmaidens,

And commanded her: 'Descend into space from the mansions of eternity,

'And turn thou unto that which they have concealed in the inmost of their hearts.

'Shouldst thou inhale the perfume of the robe from the Youth that hath been hidden within the tabernacle of light by reason of that which the hands of the wicked have wrought,

'Raise a cry within thyself, that all the inmates of the chambers of Paradise, that are the embodiments of the eternal wealth, may understand and hearken;

'That they may all come down from their everlasting chambers and tremble,

'And kiss their hands and feet for having soared to the heights of faithfulness;

'Perchance they may find from their robes the fragrance of the Beloved One.'

Thereupon the countenance of the favoured damsel beamed above the celestial chambers even as the light that shineth from the face of the Youth above His mortal temple;

She then descended with such an adorning as to illumine the heavens and all that is therein.

She bestirred herself and perfumed all things in the lands of holiness and grandeur.

When she reached that place she rose to her full height in the midmost heart of creation,

And sought to inhale their fragrance at a time that knoweth neither beginning nor end.

She found not in them that which she did desire, and this, verily, is but one of His wondrous tales.

She then cried aloud, wailed and repaired to her own station within her most lofty mansion,

And then gave utterance to one mystic word, whispered privily by her honeyed tongue,

And raised the call amidst the Celestial Concourse and the immortal maids of heaven:

'By the Lord! I found not from these idle claimants the breeze of Faithfulness!

'By the Lord! The Youth hath remained lone and forlorn in the land of exile in the hands of the ungodly.'

She then uttered within herself such a cry that the Celestial Concourse did shriek and tremble,

And she fell upon the dust and gave up the spirit. It seemeth she was called and hearkened unto Him that summoned her unto the Realm on High.

Glorified be He that created her out of the essence of love in the midmost heart of His exalted paradise!

Thereupon the maids of heaven hastened forth from their chambers, upon whose countenances the eye of no dweller in the highest paradise had ever gazed.

Glorified be our Lord, the Most High!

They all gathered around her, and lo! they found her body fallen upon the dust;

Glorified be our Lord, the Most High!

And as they beheld her state and comprehended a word of the tale told by the Youth, they bared their heads, rent their garments asunder, beat upon their faces, forgot their joy, shed tears and smote with their hands upon their cheeks, and this is verily one of the mysterious grievous afflictions—

Glorified be our Lord, the Most High![3]

Bahá'u'lláh refers to Himself in this Tablet as the 'Holy Mariner', and to the believers as the 'dwellers' in the 'ark'. In His Writings the term 'ark' often symbolizes the Cause of God and the Covenant. Those who enter it are safe and secure; they sail towards the shores of salvation and acquire divine light.

In the opening passages of the Tablet, Bahá'u'lláh alludes to the inconceivable greatness of His Revelation, in which 'the flame of His Beauty [hath] appeared within the deathless tree', around which 'the Glory of Moses doth circle with the everlasting hosts'. He testifies that He Who conversed with Moses on Sinai is now, in this Day, manifested to men, that the believers—'them that are within the ark' and the 'angelic spirits'—can, if they but purify their hearts, 'attain the retreats of nearness in the everlasting realm'.

To grasp the significance of this Tablet we must remember that with the coming of Bahá'u'lláh, the Day of God Himself has been ushered in, and that mankind has been given the most precious gift of His Faith.

Throughout His Writings there are many references to the greatness of His Revelation. The following are only a few passages gleaned from His Tablets:*

> 'The purpose underlying all creation is the revelation of this most sublime, this most holy Day, the Day known as the Day of God, in His Books and Scriptures—the Day which all the Prophets, and the Chosen Ones, and the holy ones, have wished to witness.' 'The highest essence and most perfect expression of whatsoever the peoples of old have either said or written hath, through this most potent Revelation, been sent down from the heaven of the Will of the All-Possessing, the Ever-Abiding God.' (p. 65.)

> 'By the righteousness of God! These are the days in which God hath proved the hearts of the entire company of His Messengers and Prophets, and beyond them those that

* These passages are quoted in *The Advent of Divine Justice* by Shoghi Effendi; page nos. refer to this text.

stand guard over His sacred and inviolable Sanctuary, the inmates of the celestial Pavilion and dwellers of the Tabernacle of Glory.' 'Should the greatness of this Day be revealed in its fullness, every man would forsake a myriad lives in his longing to partake, though it be for one moment, of its great glory—how much more this world and its corruptible treasures!' (p. 67.)

'By the righteousness of Mine own Self! Great, immeasurably great is this Cause! Mighty, inconceivably mighty is this Day!' 'Every Prophet hath announced the coming of this Day, and every Messenger hath groaned in His yearning for this Revelation—a revelation which, no sooner had it been revealed than all created things cried out saying, "The earth is God's, the Most Exalted, the Most Great!" ' (p. 65.)

'Verily I say! No one hath apprehended the root of this Cause. It is incumbent upon every one, in this day, to perceive with the eye of God, and to hearken with His ear. Whoso beholdeth Me with an eye besides Mine own will never be able to know Me. None among the Manifestations of old, except to a prescribed degree, hath ever completely apprehended the nature of this Revelation.' (p. 64.)

'Great indeed is this Day! The allusions made to it in all the sacred Scriptures as the Day of God attest its greatness. The soul of every Prophet of God, of every Divine Messenger, hath thirsted for this wondrous Day. All the divers kindreds of the earth have, likewise, yearned to attain it.' (p. 65.)

'This is the Day whereon human ears have been privileged to hear what He Who conversed with God [Moses] heard upon Sinai, what He Who is the Friend of God [Muḥammad] heard when lifted up towards Him, what He Who is the Spirit of God [Jesus] heard as He ascended unto Him, the Help in Peril, the Self-Subsisting.' (p. 66.)

To be born in this Day and to be the recipient of such favours is the greatest of God's bounties to man. But this privilege carries with it great responsibilities, too. For once the believer has recognized the Manifestation of God, his function is to obey His commandments faithfully. If such loyalty and devotion are not whole-hearted and unqualified, he cannot be called steadfast in the Covenant of God. The destiny of the true believer and the heights to which he can attain are dependent upon his sincerity and faithfulness in the Cause of God.

When the individual recognizes Bahá'u'lláh and is assured of His divine station, he then enters the 'ark'. The spiritual energies released by Bahá'u'lláh, as well as His Teachings, will assist him to advance and deepen in the Cause, but at the same time his tests will correspondingly multiply. For the faith of a believer is tested in various ways. Some are afflicted with suffering and persecution, others have spiritual battles which may last a lifetime. But if one has faith and is ready at all times to surrender his will fully to that of Bahá'u'lláh, he can win through. Otherwise, any trace of self or passion, of desire for and attachment to earthly things, will bar his spiritual advancement, and may in the end kill the spark of his faith altogether.

The station to which a true believer can attain in this day is extremely high. This is because Bahá'u'lláh has ushered in the Day of God and has shed His glory upon mankind. The world of being has become filled with the ocean of His Revelation and mankind has been given a new capacity. The following are the words of Bahá'u'lláh concerning the station of the true believer:

> 'O people of Bahá! The river that is Life indeed hath flowed for your sakes. Quaff ye in My name, despite them that have disbelieved in God, the Lord of Revelation. We have made you to be the hands of Our Cause. Render ye victorious this Wronged One, Who hath been sore-tried in the hands of the workers of iniquity. He, verily, will aid every one that aideth Him, and will remember every one that remembereth Him. To this beareth witness this Tablet that hath shed the splendour of the loving-kindness of your Lord, the All-Glorious, the All-Compelling.' 'Blessed are the

MULLÁ MUḤAMMAD-I-ZARANDÍ

Historian, Apostle of Bahá'u'lláh and His poet-laureate
Surnamed by Him Nabíl-i-A'ẓam

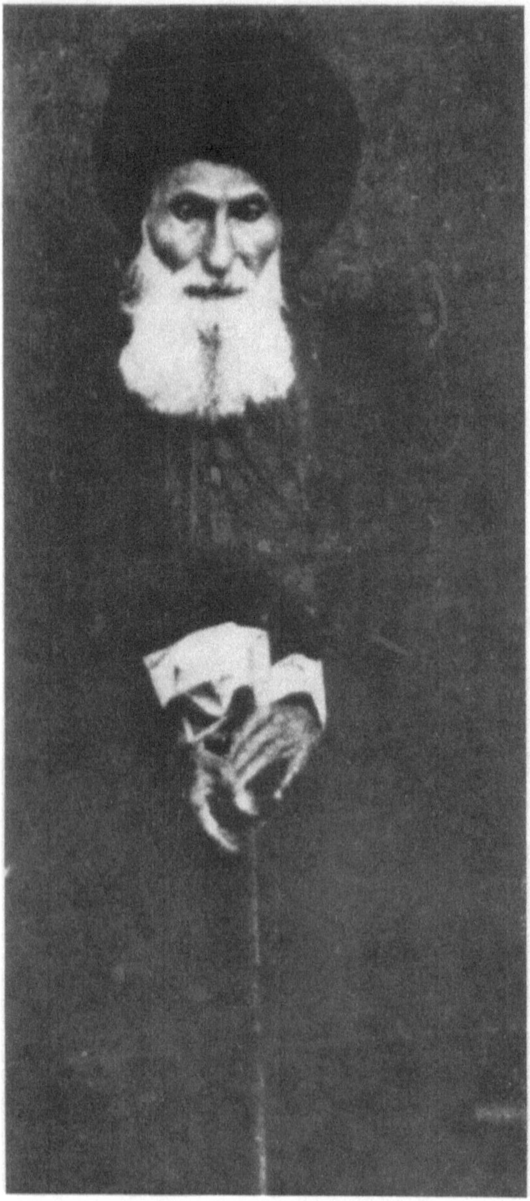

ḤAJÍ SIYYID JAVÁD-I-KARBILÁ'Í

One of the 'Mirrors' of the Bábí Dispensation
And an outstanding follower of Bahá'u'lláh

people of Bahá! God beareth Me witness! They are the solace of the eye of creation. Through them the universes have been adorned, and the Preserved Tablet embellished. They are the ones who have sailed on the ark of complete independence, with their faces set towards the Day-Spring of Beauty. How great is their blessedness that they have attained unto what their Lord, the Omniscient, the All-Wise, hath willed. Through their light the heavens have been adorned, and the faces of those that have drawn nigh unto Him made to shine.' 'By the sorrows which afflict the beauty of the All-Glorious! Such is the station ordained for the true believer that if to an extent smaller than a needle's eye the glory of that station were to be unveiled to mankind, every beholder would be consumed away in his longing to attain it. For this reason it hath been decreed that in this earthly life the full measure of the glory of his own station should remain concealed from the eyes of such a believer.' 'If the veil be lifted, and the full glory of the station of those who have turned wholly towards God, and in their love for Him renounced the world, be made manifest, the entire creation would be dumbfounded.'[4]

And 'Abdu'l-Bahá has written these words:

> The station which he who hath truly recognized this Revelation will attain is the same as the one ordained for such prophets of the house of Israel as are not regarded as Manifestations 'endowed with constancy'.[5]

Whoever achieves this station will become the embodiment of selflessness, humility and servitude, will die to himself and live in God. Such a believer is indeed worthy, as Bahá'u'lláh mentions in the *Tablet of the Holy Mariner*, to 'soar upon the wings of the spirit unto that station which the Lord hath exalted above all mention in the worlds below', to 'wing through space even as the favoured birds in the realm of eternal reunion', and to 'know the mysteries hidden in the Seas of light'.

Among His companions there were some who had reached this lofty station. These souls manifested such a degree of faith and devotion, such humility and detachment as had rarely been experienced by mankind in former Dispensations.

Others would enter the presence of Bahá'u'lláh and partake of His divine knowledge, yet, because of their ego and ambition, be unable to attain the necessary qualities of lowliness, humility and submissiveness before the Manifestation of God. They were blind to Bahá'u'lláh's divine station, were filled with jealousy at His rising prestige and power, and aspired to occupy the same position as He.

Man is created to love and worship God, to recognize His Manifestation and to obey Him. His greatest attainment is to abide in the realm of servitude and to develop spiritual qualities. But there have ever been those who, having recognized the Manifestation of God, rise up to oppose Him and consciously try to elevate themselves to His station. Such an act invokes the wrath of God and brings destruction upon man. For instance, those who broke the Covenant of the Báb and opposed Bahá'u'lláh were of this kind, as were those who broke the Covenant of Bahá'u'lláh and opposed the Centre of His Covenant, 'Abdu'l-Bahá.

It is concerning such individuals that Bahá'u'lláh in the *Tablet of the Holy Mariner* writes:

> They have desired to ascend unto that state which the Lord hath ordained to be above their stations.
>
> Whereupon the burning meteor cast them out from them that abide in the Kingdom of His Presence,
>
> And they heard the Voice of Grandeur raised from behind the unseen pavilion upon the Height of Glory,
>
> 'O guardian angels! Return them to their abode in the world below,

'Inasmuch as they have purposed to rise to that
sphere which the wings of the celestial dove
have never attained . . .'

In these words Bahá'u'lláh has, for the first time, clearly indicated that those who oppose the Centre of the Cause and break His Covenant will be cast out from the people of Bahá.

The 'burning meteor' may be regarded as symbolic of a mighty instrument that Bahá'u'lláh has instituted for the protection of His Cause, namely, His Covenant. In the days of Bahá'u'lláh the authority to expel Covenant-breakers was vested in Himself alone; later it devolved upon 'Abdu'l-Bahá, as the Centre of the Covenant, and then upon Shoghi Effendi, as the Guardian of the Cause, to exercise this authority. In this day, should anyone break the Covenant his expulsion would be by decision of the Hands of the Cause of God residing in the Holy Land,* subject to the approval of the Universal House of Justice.

Never before in religious history has a Manifestation of God created the means whereby the breakers of His Covenant, and those from within the community who oppose the Centre of the Cause, are cast out. This is one of the unique features of the Revelation of Bahá'u'lláh. By this process the Cause of God is purged from the impurities which enter it from time to time. Just as the physical body of man has a special organ for removing poisonous substances from the blood-stream and discharging them at intervals, so the Cause of God has been endowed with institutions designed to purge the community of unwholesome elements within its ranks.

At the time that the *Tablet of the Holy Mariner* was revealed, Bahá'u'lláh's unfaithful half-brother Mírzá Yaḥyá, Siyyid Muḥammad-i-Iṣfahání and a few others were still mingling with the believers. In spite of all their misdeeds they were still

* The functions of the Hands of the Cause, as defined in the *Will and Testament* of 'Abdu'l-Bahá, are mainly protection and propagation of the Faith. Those now living were appointed by the Guardian, Shoghi Effendi.

considered part of the Bábí community. Bahá'u'lláh foreshadowed their fate in this Tablet. A few years later, as we shall see in more detail in the next volume, these men were cast out of the community of the Most Great Name and God's infant Faith, cleansed of this pollution, continued to grow with greater vitality and vigour.

In every Dispensation some men have violated the Covenant of God and been unfaithful to His Manifestation. In former religions they have succeeded in dividing the Faith of God and creating schism. But in this Dispensation, which is the consummation of all past religions and cycles, although many from within the community have risen against the Centre of the Cause, they have never succeeded in dividing it. Bahá'u'lláh, in one of His Tablets, states that as the Cause in this day is very great so also are the forces of negation which oppose it; the onslaught of the unfaithful against it is formidable. The violators of the Covenant of the Báb and Bahá'u'lláh did everything in their power to undermine the edifice of the Cause of God; yet in spite of their concerted efforts they were unable to break its unity. This is one of the unique features of the Cause and is due to the Covenant of Bahá'u'lláh through which the unity of His Faith is permanently safeguarded.

Every violator of Bahá'u'lláh's Covenant has been expelled from His community. A diseased branch cut from the tree at first appears full of life, but eventually it will die in isolation. This is true of the breakers of the Covenant in this day who, by reason of their attacks on the Faith, might, at first, have seemed to be creating havoc within its ranks. But cut off from the Tree of the Cause of God, they eventually perished. Today only their names are recorded; their influence has long ceased to exist.

The appearance of the 'Maid of Heaven' mentioned in the *Tablet of the Holy Mariner* is allegorical. In the Writings of Bahá'u'lláh, He has used the 'Maid of Heaven' to refer to Himself or to one of the attributes of God, and sometimes as the personification of the 'Most Great Spirit'. He has also referred to Himself in this Tablet as the 'exalted and glorious' Youth 'that hath been hidden within the tabernacle of light', and Who 'hath remained lone and forlorn in the land of exile in the hands of the ungodly'.

The Tablet contains many precious gems of knowledge, and many verities of His Cause are hidden therein. These can be discovered only through deepening in the Faith and meditation upon His words.

The *Tablet of the Holy Mariner* in Persian is, for the most part, similar in content to the Arabic Tablet. In addition, it contains some of Bahá'u'lláh's choicest exhortations and counsels to His followers. For example, He urges the believers not to barter the bounty of His presence for all that is in earth and heaven and not to seek nearness to anyone but Him. He reminds them that the heart is the seat of the Best-Beloved and warns them not to allow a stranger to enter it. He calls on them to arise and emerge from the sepulchre of self and passion, and exhorts them to be faithful; even if they are unable to reach the lofty summits of detachment and sanctity they should at least try to become sincere, should strive earnestly that their conduct may faithfully reflect the secrets of their hearts.

Sincerity and faithfulness are the attributes of a true believer. The most painful affliction of the Manifestation of God is unfaithfulness shown by those who profess to be His followers. No other suffering, even physical torture and martyrdom, can ever hurt Him as much as this.

It was the realization that Bahá'u'lláh would be afflicted by such suffering, foreshadowed in the *Tablet of the Holy Mariner*, that brought deepest anxiety to His companions when first they heard it. Indeed, on the day following its revelation, the grievous news of the Sulṭán's decision to call Bahá'u'lláh to Constantinople reached Him; it was news which dealt a crippling blow to every man, woman and child among His lovers in 'Iráq. That night, His stricken companions, without exception, could neither eat nor sleep. Some vowed that they would take their own lives should they be prevented from accompanying Him in His exile. In the end, however, through the power of His words and the warmth of His love, Bahá'u'lláh succeeded in calming their emotions so that they were content to resign their wills to His.

Other Tablets of This Period

The authorities in Baghdád were surprised that Bahá'u'lláh had not objected to the government's decision to invite Him to Constantinople. In fact, 'Álí Páshá's letter which was handed to Bahá'u'lláh in the mosque was couched in courteous language, and the Governor of Baghdád expressed his readiness to communicate any message He might wish to send to the Prime Minister, including that of declining the invitation. But Bahá'u'lláh accepted, requiring only that His family and a number of His companions accompany Him and that they be allowed a month to prepare for the journey.

During this period, Bahá'u'lláh showered His love especially upon those of His followers who were to stay behind and prepared them for the day when they would be left alone. He desired them to testify in their lives to their integrity and loftiness of purpose, their faith and radiance of spirit. Also, at this time He revealed in His own hand a Tablet for each one of them, including the children. In these Tablets He often alludes to Mírzá Yaḥyá's future rebellion, anticipates the most severe crisis to appear within the Cause, and urges the believers to be steadfast in the days of test and trial.

Of the numerous Tablets He revealed during this short period in Baghdád we mention only two, the *Lawḥ-i-Bulbulu'l-Firáq* (Tablet of the Nightingale of Bereavement) and *Súratu'-lláh* (Súrih of God).

The *Lawḥ-i-Bulbulu'l-Firáq* is one of His Tablets addressed to the believers collectively. In it, Bahá'u'lláh reminds His loved ones that the period of union has come to an end, that the Nightingale of Paradise has taken its flight from one branch and is now about to establish its nest on another. He rebukes the people of sedition for turning to the 'birds of night'* when the Sun of Truth is shining in its meridian splendour. The words of Bahá'u'lláh in this Tablet are written with such tenderness that, when the believers chanted it, their hearts were stirred and they were filled with grief at the thought of separation from Him.

The *Súratu'lláh* was revealed for a believer named Muḥammad-'Alí. In it Bahá'u'lláh addresses the people of the *Bayán*† and rebukes those who have been blind or shown malice towards Him. Referring to their attitude, He reminds them that if they regard it as a crime for Him to reveal the Word of God, He is not the first to have done so. For it was the Báb Who revealed the Word of God before Him and, earlier, Muḥammad, Jesus and Moses. Each One of these Holy Souls was animated and sustained by the Holy Spirit.

This Tablet discloses the greatness of Bahá'u'lláh's station to the people of the *Bayán*, for He affirms that He is incomparable in the entire creation and is its omnipotent Ruler. He who turns away from Him, He asserts, has in fact turned away from God, and he who denies His Cause has denied all the Prophets of the past.

Bahá'u'lláh counsels the recipient of this Tablet to turn away from the people of doubt, to renounce the world and to fix his gaze upon the splendours of His Revelation. Such an act, He assures him, will enable him to soar into the atmosphere of nearness to God and will endow him with such knowledge, such understanding and wisdom as no learned man, however great, will ever rival. And in this Tablet, once again, Bahá'u'lláh dwells upon the enmity of the unfaithful among the Bábís and speaks of their opposition to Him.

* This alludes to Mírzá Yaḥyá and his associates.

† The Bábís.

15

Mírzá Yaḥyá and Siyyid Muḥammad-i-Iṣfahání

In many of His Tablets revealed in Baghdád and Sulaymáníyyih, Bahá'u'lláh alludes to the unfaithfulness of Mírzá Yaḥyá and to the instigator of his wickedness, Siyyid Muḥammad. The crisis which Mírzá Yaḥyá created within the ranks of the believers was to reach its climax in Adrianople, with a complete break between the followers of Bahá'u'lláh and those of Mírzá Yaḥyá. Before this period, however, through the all-pervasive power which Bahá'u'lláh exerted upon the community in Baghdád, Mírzá Yaḥyá was unable to raise the standard of rebellion. His sojourn in 'Iráq was spent mostly in hiding and seclusion. He arrived in Baghdád in disguise and left it in the same fashion a decade later.

At the time of Bahá'u'lláh's release from the Síyáh-Chál, Mírzá Yaḥyá, who for almost two years had lived in disguise in various parts of Mázindarán and Gílán, moved to Kirmánsháh. So that no one might identify him there, he took work with a certain 'Abdu'lláh-i-Qazvíní, a maker of shrouds, and was engaged in selling his goods.

Bahá'u'lláh, on His way to 'Iráq, passed through various towns before He arrived in Kirmánsháh in the early winter months of 1853. In contrast to Mírzá Yaḥyá, Bahá'u'lláh, although despised by the Sháh and afflicted by poverty, manifested such greatness that *en route* several people of rank and position came to visit Him and pay their respects. In Kirmánsháh a certain prince, 'Imádu'd-Dawlih, sent Him a message and was disappointed that Bahá'u'lláh did not receive him.

But Mírzá Yaḥyá was afraid to make contact with Bahá'u'lláh in Kirmánsháh. Such was his state that when his half-brother, Mírzá Músá, went to see him, he was apprehensive lest someone should discover his identity. At last he mustered enough courage to come and meet Bahá'u'lláh, and expressed his desire to go to Baghdád, engage in a trade there, and live incognito and alone in a house close to Bahá'u'lláh's. With a small sum of money that Bahá'u'lláh gave him, he bought a few bales of cotton, disguised himself in the garb of an Arab and made his way to Baghdád.

Soon after his arrival he appeared outside the house of Bahá'u'lláh. Mírzá Músá, who answered the door, did not recognize him at first for he was dressed as a dervish, with a kashkúl (alms box) hanging from his shoulder. He stayed there for a few days but asked that his arrival and identity should not be divulged to anyone in Baghdád. Thereafter he found accommodation in the Arab quarter of the city where no Persians lived, and moved there. During the day-time he refused to meet anybody. In the evenings after dark he often used to go to the house of Bahá'u'lláh and meet with Mírzá Músá, returning to his quarters in the dead of night.

In the meantime, he employed a Persian merchant named Abu'l-Qásim and used him as a link between himself and the believers in Baghdád. Being nominally the leader of the Bábí community he now began to disseminate his misguided ideas to them, using Abu'l-Qásim as his intermediary.

It was during his early days in Baghdád that Siyyid Muḥammad-i-Iṣfahání came into contact with him. Siyyid Muḥammad, who was to become the 'Antichrist of the Bahá'í Revelation', had embraced the Bábí Faith soon after the Declaration of the Báb. He was residing in Karbilá when Bahá'u'lláh paid a visit to that city, about one year after the martyrdom of the Báb. On that occasion some of the followers of the Báb, as well as some Shaykhís who were all men of learning and knowledge in Karbilá, recognized the extraordinary qualities of greatness in Bahá'u'lláh, and demonstrated by their words and attitude their unbounded love and admiration for Him. But Siyyid Muḥammad, from the start, was filled with envy. The marks of veneration and esteem shown to Bahá'u'lláh by others only served to fan the fire of animosity and jealousy which had begun to burn within him.

When Bahá'u'lláh arrived in 'Iráq for the second time, in 1853, Siyyid Muḥammad could not fail to see the authority with which He was conducting the affairs of the Bábí community. Before His arrival in that country the followers of the Báb were confused and leaderless. Bahá'u'lláh, having breathed a new life into them, gave them courage and gathered them together.

Such a transformation of spirit brought about by Bahá'u'lláh further aroused the envy of Siyyid Muḥammad and increased his animosity. Being an unscrupulous schemer, he found in Mírzá Yaḥyá a willing tool who he knew could be used to oppose Bahá'u'lláh. Together, they kindled dissension among the believers, misrepresented Bahá'u'lláh and His Cause, and created a situation in which the fortunes of the Faith began to decline. It was at this point that Bahá'u'lláh left for the mountains of Kurdistán.

During His absence, the news of the martyrdom of a believer of Najaf-Ábád, Persia, reached Baghdád. This alarmed Mírzá Yaḥyá, for he thought that the authorities in Ṭihrán might look for him and, learning of his whereabouts, have him arrested in Baghdád. These thoughts forced him to change his abode. With the help of a certain Mírzá 'Alíy-i-Tabrízí, he purchased a quantity of shoes and, disguised as a Jew, proceeded to Baṣrah where he lived for some time and carried on his work as a shoe merchant. Later, he bought a consignment of silk materials which he took with him to Baghdád. There, under the assumed name of Ḥájí 'Alíy-i-Láṣ Furúsh* and changing his headgear from a hat to a large turban, he embarked on his new occupation.

Mírzá Yaḥyá's cowardly behaviour was matched only by his

* Dealer in silk.

acts of infamy which have for ever stained the annals of the Faith. While Bahá'u'lláh was absent in the mountains of Kurdistán, he committed a shameful act which inflicted dishonour upon the Báb, by marrying His second wife* and, a month later, giving her in marriage to Siyyid Muḥammad. When Bahá'u'lláh learned of this His grief knew no bounds. In a Tablet He asserts that the whole creation wept for this betrayal, and He further refers to it in the *Epistle to the Son of the Wolf* in these words:

> Reflect a while upon the dishonour inflicted upon the Primal Point. Consider what hath happened. When this Wronged One, after a retirement of two years during which He wandered through the deserts and mountains, returned to Baghdád, as a result of the intervention of a few, who for a long time had sought Him in the wilderness, a certain Mírzá Muḥammad-'Alí of Rasht came to see Him, and related, before a large gathering of people, that which had been done, affecting the honour of the Báb, which hath truly overwhelmed all lands with sorrow. Great God! How could they have countenanced this most grievous betrayal. Briefly, We beseech God to aid the perpetrator of this deed to repent, and return unto Him. He, verily, is the Helper, the All-Wise.[1]

Another act which brought untold suffering and grief upon Bahá'u'lláh was the murder of a number of illustrious Bábís by the order of Mírzá Yaḥyá. The most eminent among these was the accomplished Mírzá Asadu'lláh of Khuy, surnamed Dayyán ('One Who Rewards', or 'Judge') by the Báb. To him the Báb had referred as the repository of the trust of God and the treasury of His knowledge. He had, moreover, promised that he would be the third person to believe in 'Him Whom God shall make manifest'.

* In nineteenth-century Persia the way of life differed radically from present-day life in the West. Social and religious circumstances in Muslim countries almost required a man (especially if he were an eminent person) to take more than one wife. During His six-months' sojourn in Iṣfahán, the Báb took a second wife, Fáṭimih, who was a sister of Mullá Rajab-'Alíy-i-Qahír, a Bábí from Iṣfahán.

While Bahá'u'lláh was in Kurdistán, Dayyán, who was then living in Ádhirbáyján, wrote a letter to Mírzá Yaḥyá in which he asked certain questions. The childish and irrelevant answers which he received were sufficient to convince him of the latter's ignorance and lack of spiritual qualities. It is alleged that after this communication, Dayyán, immersed in meditation, was so carried away as to claim for himself the station of 'Him Whom God shall make manifest'.

However, in the *Kitáb-i-Badí'*, Bahá'u'lláh has refuted this allegation and asserts that Dayyán made no such claim. He mentions that Dayyán had written and circulated some prayers, a copy of which He Himself had received, but that there was nothing in them against the teachings of the Báb and His Covenant. On the contrary, Dayyán's words bore ample testimony to his humility and servitude, to his faith in God and his loyalty to the Manifestations of God. Bahá'u'lláh states that when Mírzá Yaḥyá saw these prayers he became highly jealous of Dayyán and determined to harm him.

Dayyán had also written an epistle in which he exposed Mírzá Yaḥyá's ignorance, refuted the latter's claim to be the successor of the Báb and quoted many passages from the Writings of the Báb in support of his arguments. Mírzá Yaḥyá was infuriated by this epistle and in response wrote a book entitled *Mustayqiẓ* (Sleeper Awakened). In it he severely rebuked Dayyán, together with a fellow-believer named Siyyid Ibráhím who was a close friend and admirer of Dayyán, condemned their actions, denounced the former as the 'Father of Calamities' and the latter as the 'Father of Iniquities', and called upon the Bábís in vile language to arise and take their lives.

At the same time he sent his servant Mírzá Muḥammad-i-Mázindarání to Ádhirbáyján with explicit orders to kill Dayyán. When Mírzá Muḥammad arrived there, however, he found that Dayyán had already left for Baghdád.

Upon his arrival in that city, Dayyán was confronted with a number of Bábís who, as a result of Mírzá Yaḥyá's pronouncements, were hostile to him. His life was threatened and the situation became so serious that one day, from early morning until late in the afternoon, Bahá'u'lláh called all those who were involved to His house, one by one, rebuked them for their behaviour and clearly commanded them to desist from perpetrating such a crime.

Two days later, Dayyán was honoured by meeting Bahá'u'lláh in His house. There he witnessed the fulfilment of the Báb's promise to him that he would believe in 'Him Whom God shall make manifest'. He recognized the station of Bahá'u'lláh, acknowledged His Faith and prostrated himself at His feet.

A few days after this glorious attainment, Dayyán was murdered in Baghdád by the aforementioned Mírzá Muḥammad-i-Mázindarání. This tragic event brought much sorrow to the heart of Bahá'u'lláh and to the believers. On that day a gale of exceptional fury swept over Baghdád, causing a thick layer of dust to rise and obscure the light of the sun. Darkness encompassed the city and the people, frightened and panic-stricken, had to take refuge in their homes.

After the murder of Dayyán, Mírzá Yaḥyá, turning his attention to others who admired Dayyán, issued instructions to kill them also, including Mírzá 'Alí-Akbar (a cousin of the Báb on His father's side), who was put to death by the same servant.

In *Epistle to the Son of the Wolf* Bahá'u'lláh, addressing Ḥájí Mírzá Hádíy-i-Dawlat Ábádí, the successor of Mírzá Yaḥyá, has mentioned the episode in these words:

> And likewise He [the Báb] addresseth Dayyán, who was wronged and suffered martyrdom, saying: 'Thou shalt recognize thy worth through the words of Him Whom God shall make manifest.' He, likewise, hath pronounced him to be the third Letter to believe in Him Whom God shall make manifest, through these words: 'O thou who art the third Letter to believe in Him Whom God shall make manifest!' And likewise He saith: 'Should God, however, be willing, He will make thee known through the words of Him Whom God shall make manifest.' Dayyán, who, according to the

words of Him Who is the Point*—may the souls of all else but Him be sacrificed for His sake—is the repository of the trust of the one true God—exalted be His glory—and the treasury of the pearls of His knowledge, was made by them to suffer so cruel a martyrdom that the Concourse on high wept and lamented. He it is whom He (the Báb) had taught the hidden and preserved knowledge and entrusted him therewith, through His words: 'O thou who art named Dayyán! This is a hidden and preserved Knowledge. We have entrusted it unto thee, and brought it to thee, as a mark of honour from God, inasmuch as the eye of thine heart is pure. Thou wilt appreciate its value, and wilt cherish its excellence. God, verily, hath deigned to bestow upon the Point of the Bayán a hidden and preserved Knowledge, the like of which God hath not sent down prior to this Revelation. More precious is it than any other knowledge in the estimation of God—glorified be He! He, verily, hath made it His testimony, even as He hath made the verses to be His testimony.' This oppressed one, who was the repository of the knowledge of God, together with Mírzá 'Alí-Akbar, one of the relatives of the Primal Point†—upon him be the glory of God and His mercy—and Abu'l-Qásim-i-Káshí and several others suffered martyrdom through the decree pronounced by Mírzá Yaḥyá . . .

As to Dayyán—upon him be the glory of God and His mercy—he attained Our presence in accordance with that which had been revealed by the pen of the Primal Point. We pray God to aid the heedless to turn unto Him, and such as have turned aside to direct themselves towards Him, and them that have denied Him to acknowledge this Cause, which, no sooner did it appear than all created things proclaimed: 'He that was hidden in the Treasury of Knowledge, and inscribed by the Pen of the Most High in His Books, and His Scriptures, and His Scrolls, and His Tablets, is come!'[2]

The news of Bahá'u'lláh's impending departure for Constantinople alarmed and frightened Mírzá Yaḥyá. Bahá'u'lláh

* The Báb.

† The Báb.

advised him to proceed to Persia and there disseminate the Writings of the Báb. But he was not interested in the Cause, for his major concern was his own protection. Nor did he regard Persia as a place of safety, since the authorities in that country, both civil and ecclesiastical, were determined to uproot the Cause and exterminate the Bábís.

At first his thoughts centred upon fleeing to India or Abyssinia. But later he changed his mind, and came to Bahá'u'lláh with a plan to take up residence in Huvaydar, in the vicinity of Baghdád, in a garden which belonged to Shaykh Sulṭán, a devoted Arab follower of Bahá'u'lláh.* He particularly asked that Shaykh Sulṭán be instructed by Bahá'u'lláh to build a small cottage of reeds, in which he could live apart from everyone. Bahá'u'lláh acceded to his request and Shaykh Sulṭán began to build the cottage for him. Soon afterwards, however, Mírzá Yaḥyá, feeling insecure, returned to Bahá'u'lláh to complain that the place selected was not ideal as a hiding-place; he preferred to go to Mosul before Bahá'u'lláh's departure. He made it clear that he did not wish to accompany Bahá'u'lláh's party, for he feared that once they left Baghdád, the authorities might deal treacherously with them, either by handing them over to the Persian authorities, or by killing them on the way.

Having at last come to a decision, he sent a certain Ḥájí Muḥammad-Káẓim, who resembled him, to Government-house to procure a passport for him. This was done and the passport was issued in his newly-assumed name of Mírzá 'Alíy-i-Kirmánsháhí. Disguised, and having chosen yet another name, Mírzá Yaḥyá left Baghdád with an Arab servant and proceeded towards Mosul.

Speaking of this, Bahá'u'lláh in *Epistle to the Son of the Wolf* has written:

> We especially appointed certain ones to collect the writings of the Primal Point.† When this was accomplished, We sum-

* See p. 67, n. 2.

† The Báb.

moned Mírzá Yaḥyá and Mírzá Vahháb-i-Khurásání, known as Mírzá Javád, to meet in a certain place. Conforming with Our instructions, they completed the task of transcribing two copies of the works of the Primal Point. I swear by God! This Wronged One, by reason of His constant association with men, hath not looked at these books, nor gazed with outward eyes on these writings. When We departed, these writings were in the possession of these two persons. It was agreed that Mírzá Yaḥyá should be entrusted with them, and proceed to Persia, and disseminate them throughout that land. This Wronged One proceeded, at the request of the Ministers of the Ottoman Government to their capital. When We arrived in Mossoul [Mosul], We found that Mírzá Yaḥyá had left before Us for that city, and was awaiting Us there. Briefly, the books and writings were left in Baghdád, while he himself proceeded to Constantinople and joined these servants. God beareth now witness unto the things which have touched this Wronged One, for after We had so arduously striven, he (Mírzá Yaḥyá) abandoned the writings and joined the exiles. This Wronged One was, for a long period, overwhelmed by infinite sorrows until such time when, in pursuance of measures of which none but the one true God is aware, We despatched the writings unto another place and another country, owing to the fact that in 'Iráq all documents must every month be carefully examined, lest they rot and perish. God, however, preserved them and sent them unto a place which He had previously ordained. He, verily, is the Protector, the Succourer.

Wherever this Wronged One went Mírzá Yaḥyá followed Him. Thou art thyself a witness and well knowest that whatever hath been said is the truth. The Siyyid of Iṣfahán,* however, surreptitiously duped him. They committed that which caused the greatest consternation. Would that thou wouldst inquire from the officials of the government concerning the conduct of Mírzá Yaḥyá in that land.[3]

'Abdu'l-Bahá mentions that among those who accompanied Bahá'u'lláh on the journey to Constantinople was Siyyid

* Siyyid Muḥammad-i-Iṣfahání.

Muḥammad-i-Iṣfahání, and that he would often denounce Mírzá Yaḥyá and his behaviour. It was obvious, however, that he was not sincere in this.

When Bahá'u'lláh's party reached the vicinity of Mosul, Siyyid Muḥammad informed 'Abdu'l-Bahá that he had just seen Mírzá Yaḥyá in the area and wondered whether he should bring him along. 'Abdu'l-Bahá tells us that when Mírzá Yaḥyá appeared and saw some strangers around, he pretended that he did not know Bahá'u'lláh or any of those travelling with Him. He introduced himself as Ḥájí 'Alí and said that he was returning from Mecca. Thereafter, he travelled with the party in such a way that during the day he would not associate with anyone. Only at night would he join the companions of Bahá'u'lláh, taking his rest in a tent by himself.

In this manner Mírzá Yaḥyá travelled most of the way to Constantinople. On the journey his only confidant was Siyyid Muḥammad, whom Bahá'u'lláh later expelled from His company. It was in Adrianople that the Siyyid openly joined Mírzá Yaḥyá and, as we shall see in later volumes, together they precipitated a crisis unparalleled in the history of the Faith.

One of the best testimonials to Mírzá Yaḥyá's ignorance and falsehood is to be found in his writings. Having been brought up by Bahá'u'lláh from the age of eight, he naturally knew of the Faith from his teens. As a youth, he gave a considerable part of his time to the study of the Writings of the Báb. In one of His Tablets, Bahá'u'lláh has stated that Mírzá Yaḥyá learnt everything parrot-fashion. His understanding of the Faith was therefore superficial, and many of the disciples of Bahá'u'lláh have testified to this. Men of insight who came in contact with him were disillusioned by his ignorance and shallowness.

As the nominee of the Báb, Mírzá Yaḥyá became the centre of attraction for the believers after His martyrdom, and all were anxious to see him. Shaykh Salmán was one of these. After many requests for an interview, the former agreed to meet him on a certain hill-top near Baghdád. During their entire conversation Mírzá Yaḥyá spoke of trivialities and Shaykh Salmán, who had keen insight, could not detect in him any sign of greatness. Like many other Bábís he soon realized that Mírzá Yaḥyá, whose fame as the leader of the Bábí community was widespread throughout the land, was a mere figure-head, lacking all the qualities of leadership and spirituality.

At one stage, Bahá'u'lláh had asked Mírzá Yaḥyá to transcribe some of the Writings of the Báb; for four years he was occupied in this task, as a result of which he learnt to copy the style of the Báb's handwriting. Later, when he rebelled against Bahá'u'lláh, he used this very technique to compose passages apparently similar to those of the Báb in both tone and calligraphy. In these so-called Tablets which he circulated, Mírzá Yaḥyá introduced many false statements concerning his own position in the Faith. He also corrupted, in some instances, the text of the Báb's Writings and made certain insertions in support of his claim to be the successor of the Báb.

Most of Mírzá Yaḥyá's writings are composed of strings of clumsy and meaningless words which, in turn, constitute nonsensical sentences. A mere glance at any of them reveals the ignorance, the incapacity and blindness of an ambitious man who was driven, all his life, by an indomitable passion for leadership and power.

16

The Declaration of Bahá'u'lláh in the Garden of Riḍván

His Influence on the People of Baghdád

The contrast between Bahá'u'lláh and Mírzá Yaḥyá is the contrast between light and darkness. Indeed, the Manifestation of God is exalted above humanity and there can be no comparison between the Source of all goodness and those who arise to oppose Him. Not only is this true in the spiritual sense; outwardly the Manifestation of God is endowed with a power and authority which are inherent in Him. This is especially true of Bahá'u'lláh, whose Revelation is the culmination of all the Revelations of the past.

The awe-inspiring majesty of Bahá'u'lláh's public appearances and the authority with which He spoke to both friend and foe are facts which even His greatest adversaries have acknowledged. 'Abdu'l-Bahá mentions that those who persecuted the Prophets of the past were able to deride and ridicule them. They laughed at Moses because He was a stammerer, and jeered at Christ because, in their estimation, He had no father. The barbarous people of Arabia, at the time of Muḥammad, laughed at Him, also, because of His inability to beget an heir!

But in the case of Bahá'u'lláh, His glory was so overwhelming that everyone felt inferior in His presence. Even His enemies became humble when they came in contact with His person. While He was chained and fettered in the Síyáh-Chál of Ṭihrán, the officials in that dungeon became subdued by His greatness. And when He was released from that prison and conducted to the Prime Minister's office in Ṭihrán, it was not the latter who dominated the scene; it was Bahá'u'lláh who spoke with authority and rebuked the Prime Minister for his short-sightedness and incompetence. Similarly, in Constantinople, in Adrianople and 'Akká, the enemies and the authorities both civil and ecclesiastical were confounded when they witnessed the spiritual power with which He was invested.

Before Bahá'u'lláh's arrival in Baghdád, the followers of the Báb in that city did not dare associate with each other in public for fear of being persecuted. The Faith was regarded as a heresy and its adherents ran the risk of losing their lives if they openly declared their faith. Yet, soon after His arrival there, Bahá'u'lláh decided to appear in public. He often went into the streets and bazaars of Baghdád and frequented certain cafés. Although He was well-known as a leading figure of the newly-born Faith, the people of Baghdád were charmed by His innate love and dignity, and many of them became His admirers.

Through His majesty which was born of God the enemies of the Cause were humbled. To cite a single example: In the early days of His sojourn in Baghdád, on one occasion, Bahá'u'lláh passed by the estate of Prince 'Alí Sháh, the Ẓillu's-Sulṭán,* in company with a few believers. There he overheard a disparaging remark about the Faith from some men who were attached to the household of the Prince. Immediately Bahá'u'lláh turned back, rebuked them severely for their behaviour and demanded that they be punished by their master. He further told the crowd to remind the Prince that neither the pomp and might of the sovereign, Náṣiri'd-Dín Sháh, nor all the persecutions he had inflicted, had made any impression upon the followers of the Báb, and they had failed to break their spirit. How much less, then, would they be affected by the Prince's opposition. So potent were His words that the haughty Prince punished his people and sent his son Shujá'u'd-Dawlih to Bahá'u'lláh to convey his apologies.

* Not to be confused with the eldest son of Náṣiri'd-Dín Sháh, Prince Mas'úd Mírzá, also known as the Ẓillu's-Sulṭán, who was stigmatized by Bahá'u'lláh as the 'Infernal Tree'.

For no less than eight years the supreme Manifestation of God lived freely among the inhabitants of Baghdád. He walked among them, sat with them and poured out His affection and bounties upon them. Although He did not disclose His station to them, yet multitudes of people from all walks of life were attracted to His person and longed to attain His presence, to hear His words, or even catch a glimpse of Him as He walked in the streets or paced along the bank of the Tigris rapt in meditation.

During this period, also, many Bábís from Persia came in contact with Bahá'u'lláh, and some became great heroes of His Faith. To those already mentioned should be added two brothers who were among the most illustrious of Bahá'u'lláh's apostles. These two were honoured with the appellations of 'King of the Martyrs' and 'Beloved of the Martyrs' by His pen.

The Festival of Riḍván

The love and admiration of the people for Bahá'u'lláh was fully demonstrated on the day of His departure from His 'Most Great House' in Baghdád. Then His majesty and greatness were evident to both friend and foe. The news of His forthcoming departure for Constantinople had spread rapidly among the inhabitants of Baghdád and its neighbouring towns, and large numbers wished to attain His presence and pay their last tributes to Him. But soon it became apparent that His house was too small for the purpose. When Najíb Páshá, one of the notables of the city of Baghdád heard of this, he immediately placed his garden-park, Najíbíyyih, at the disposal of Bahá'u'lláh. This beautiful garden, designated by His followers as the Garden of Riḍván (Paradise), was situated on the outskirts of Baghdád, across the river from Bahá'u'lláh's house.

Thirty-one days after Naw-Rúz, on 22 April 1863,* in the

* Thirty-one days after Naw-Rúz (21 March) normally falls on 21 April. Occasionally, as in the year 1863, when the vernal equinox takes place after sunset, Naw-Rúz is celebrated on 22 March.

afternoon, Bahá'u'lláh moved to this garden, where He remained for twelve days. On the first day He declared His Mission to His companions.* These twelve days are celebrated by the Bahá'ís as the Festival of Riḍván.

The departure of Bahá'u'lláh from His house witnessed a commotion the like of which Baghdád had rarely seen. People of all walks of life, men and women, rich and poor, young and old, men of learning and culture, princes, government officials, tradesmen and workers, and above all His companions, thronged the approaches of His house and crowded the streets and roof-tops situated along His route to the river. They were lamenting and weeping the departure of One Who, for a decade, had imparted to them the warmth of His love and the radiance of His spirit, Who had been a refuge and guide for them all.

When Bahá'u'lláh appeared in the courtyard of His house His companions, grief-stricken and disconsolate, prostrated themselves at His feet. For some time He stood there, amid the weeping and lamentations of His loved ones, speaking words of comfort and promising to receive each of them in the garden later. Bahá'u'lláh in a Tablet mentions that when He had walked some way towards the gate, amidst the crowds, a child† of only a few years ran forward and, clinging to His robes, wept aloud, begging Him in his tender young voice not to leave. In such an atmosphere, where emotions had been so deeply stirred, this action on the part of a small child moved the hearts and brought further grief to everyone.

The scenes of lamentation and weeping outside the house, of those who did not confess to be His followers, were no less spectacular and heart-rending. Everyone in the crowded street sought to approach Him. Some prostrated themselves at His feet, others waited to hear a few words, yet others were content with a touch of His hands, a glance at His face. A Persian lady

* This is stated by 'Abdu'l-Bahá in a talk given at Bahjí on 29 April 1916.[1]

† He was Áqá 'Alí, the son of Ḥájí Mírzá Kamálu'd-Dín-i-Naráqí, to whom reference was made on p. 56.

of noble birth, who was not herself a believer, pushed her way into the crowd and with a gesture of sacrifice threw her child at the feet of Bahá'u'lláh. These demonstrations continued all the way to the bank of the river.

Before crossing the river, Bahá'u'lláh addressed His companions who had gathered around Him, saying:

> O My companions, I entrust to your keeping this city of Bag͟hdád, in the state ye now behold it, when from the eyes of friends and strangers alike, crowding its housetops, its streets and markets, tears like the rain of spring are flowing down, and I depart. With you it now rests to watch lest your deeds and conduct dim the flame of love that gloweth within the breasts of its inhabitants.[2]

Bahá'u'lláh was then ferried across the river accompanied by three of His sons: 'Abdu'l-Bahá, Mírzá Mihdí (the Purest Branch) and Muḥammad-'Alí, who were eighteen, fourteen and ten years of age, respectively. With them also was His amanuensis, Mírzá Áqá Ján. The identity of others who may have accompanied Him, or of those in the garden who had pitched His tent and were making preparations for His arrival, or of those who might have followed Him on that day, is not clearly known.

The call to afternoon prayer was raised from the mosque and the words 'Alláh'u'Akbar' (God is the Greatest) chanted by the *mu'ad͟hd͟hin** reverberated through the garden as the King of Glory entered it. There, Bahá'u'lláh appeared in the utmost joy, walking majestically in its avenues lined with flowers and trees. The fragrance of the roses and the singing of the nightingales created an atmosphere of beauty and enchantment.

The companions of Bahá'u'lláh had, for some time, known the Declaration of His station to be imminent. This realization came to them not only as a result of many remarks and allusions made by Him during the last few months of His sojourn in Bag͟hdád, but also through a noticeable change in His de-

* Muezzin: the one who calls to prayer.

meanour. Another sign which unmistakably pointed to its approaching hour was the adoption, on the day of His departure from His house in Baghdád, of a different type of headdress known as *táj* (tall felt hat), which He wore throughout His ministry.

'Abdu'l-Bahá has described how, upon His arrival in the garden, Bahá'u'lláh declared His station to those of His companions who were present, and announced with great joy the inauguration of the Festival of Riḍván.*

Sadness and grief vanished and the believers were filled with delight at this announcement. Although Bahá'u'lláh was being exiled to far-off lands and knew the sufferings and tribulations which were in store for Him and His followers, yet through this historic Declaration He changed all sorrow into blissful joy and spent the most delightful time of His ministry in the Garden of Riḍván. Indeed, in one of His Tablets, He has referred to the first day of Riḍván as the 'Day of supreme felicity', and has called on His followers to 'rejoice, with exceeding gladness' in remembrance of that day.[3]

The manner of the Declaration of Bahá'u'lláh's Mission is not clear, neither is the identity of all who heard Him. One thing, however, is clear. During His ten-years' sojourn in 'Iráq, although Bahá'u'lláh had alluded to His station, and identified Himself with the utterances of God revealed in His Tablets, He had never designated Himself as 'Him Whom God shall make manifest'. It was in the Garden of Riḍván that, in the course of His Declaration, He unequivocally did so, announcing Himself as the One Whose advent the Báb had proclaimed, for Whose sake He had sacrificed Himself and for Whom He had established a covenant with His followers. That day was one of the most eventful in the life of Bahá'u'lláh. The whole day He was occupied with important affairs, which culminated in the Declaration of His Mission—the most momentous event of His ministry.

One of the differences between the Manifestation of God and

* See p. 260, n. 1.

man is that the latter becomes easily overwhelmed when afflicted by sufferings and faced with insurmountable obstacles. Under such circumstances, even men of outstanding ability show their weakness and reveal their incompetence. Their minds can cope only with one problem at a time, and they often seek the help of experts and advisers when they make a decision.

This is not so with the Manifestation of God. In the first place, He acts independently and no individual can ever assist Him. His soul is not bound by the limitations of the world of humanity and His mind is not overwhelmed when He is faced with a large number of simultaneous problems. In the midst of calamities, when the ablest of men succumb under pressure, He can remain detached and channel His thoughts to whatever He desires. This is one of the distinguishing characteristics of the Manifestation of God, and Bahá'u'lláh in the *Kitáb-i-Íqán* has explained this by quoting the celebrated Islamic passage: 'Nothing whatsoever keepeth Him from being occupied with any other thing'.[4] For instance, when Bahá'u'lláh declared His station, the believers who were in His presence became ecstatic. Their thoughts must have been focused only upon that momentous statement. But Bahá'u'lláh turned His attention to the events of a decade before, to the heroism and self-sacrifice of the followers of the Báb in the small town of Nayríz, in the province of Fárs in Persia.

Lawḥ-i-Ayyúb

He did this by revealing the *Súriy-i-Ṣabr* (Súrih of Patience), otherwise known as *Lawḥ-i-Ayyúb* (Tablet of Job), which is equal in length to almost one-quarter of the *Kitáb-i-Íqán*. This Tablet, in Arabic, was revealed in honour of Ḥájí Muḥammad-Taqí, a native of Nayríz, upon whom Bahá'u'lláh bestowed the title of Ayyúb (Job).

He was a man of wealth and culture, highly respected by his fellow citizens, who reposed such trust in him that they would deposit their savings with him and often exchange his receipts instead of money. When in 1850 Vaḥíd arrived in Nayríz, awakening a spiritual turmoil far-reaching in its consequences, a considerable number of devoted souls were deeply affected, rallied around Vaḥíd and embraced the Faith of the Báb.* Foremost among these was Ḥájí Muḥammad-Taqí, who offered to provide the means for the propagation of the Cause in that area.

Zaynu'l-'Ábidín Khán, the Governor of Nayríz, was alarmed by the tumultuous reception accorded to Vaḥíd by the people of the town, and was shocked and angered when he saw that great numbers were entering the Faith within the span of a few days. He decided to take immediate action, and ordered the army to wipe out the newly-formed community and kill its leader. Soon there was a great upheaval and the followers of the Báb were forced to take refuge in an old fort outside the town. Though vastly outnumbered by the army, and in spite of their lack of training, these defenders of the fort of Khájih fought with such courage and heroism that their enemies suffered humiliating defeat and were forced to withdraw in terror.

Having realized the futility of his armed intervention, Zaynu'l-'Ábidín Khán resorted to deception and treachery. Cunningly, he raised the cry of peace, sent a message in writing to the defenders of the fort to invite Vaḥíd and other leaders to visit him in the army camp, and pledged his word to investigate the truth of the Cause of the Báb and to end all bloodshed and strife. In order to beguile those simple and pure-hearted men, he and his staff affixed their seal to the *Qur'án* and sent it with this message as a testimony of their honesty and truthfulness. Vaḥíd knew their treachery, but to honour the *Qur'án* he emerged from the fort and went to the camp, where he was at first ceremoniously received. There he rebuked the authorities for their tyranny and blindness and called on them to investigate and embrace the new-born Faith of God. So penetrating were his words that the Governor and his men were confounded by the force of his argument. Recognizing the profundity of his knowledge and the sincerity of his beliefs, the Governor be-

* See Appendix III concerning Vaḥíd.

came apprehensive lest some of his men transfer their allegiance to Vaḥíd. Within three days, through deceit and treachery, the Governor succeeded in evacuating the fort. But its heroic defenders walked into a trap, and most were massacred by the army. Vaḥíd was shamefully put to death and his body was dragged through the streets and bazaars of Nayríz to the accompaniment of drums and cymbals, while men and women danced merrily around him.

Vaḥíd's martyrdom shed an imperishable lustre upon the Faith of God. The story of his life adorns the pages of the history of the Cause and the example he has left will guide and inspire countless generations throughout the ages. He was peerless in the realm of learning and knowledge, indomitable in his faith, challenging in his public discourse, heroic in the defence of the Cause of God and unsurpassed in his love for the Báb.

In the *Súriy-i-Ṣabr* Bahá'u'lláh describes the proclamation of the Faith by Vaḥíd and the circumstances which led to the upheaval in Nayríz. He recounts, at some length, the events which led to the incarceration of the believers and lauds their heroism, self-sacrifice, and eventual martyrdom. He portrays the agony and sufferings which were inflicted upon the survivors, mainly women and children, who were forced to accompany the heads of the martyrs which were carried aloft on lances to Shíráz and paraded in the streets and bazaars of that city.* He severely condemns the perpetrators of such atrocities and warns them not to rejoice in their actions, but to fear the wrath of an almighty God who will justly, in the next world, punish them for the cruelties they have inflicted upon His loved ones.

Three years after the first upheaval, another massacre more brutal than the first came upon the believers of Nayríz. In his narrative, Nabíl has briefly recorded some of the events associated with it:

> I shall not attempt to record the various circumstances that led to the carnage which marked the termination of that

* See p. 77, n.1.

episode. I would refer my reader to the graphic and detailed account which Mírzá Shafí'-i-Nayrízí has written in a separate booklet, in which he refers with accuracy and force to every detail of that moving event. Suffice it to say that no less than one hundred and eighty of the Báb's valiant disciples suffered martyrdom. A like number were wounded and, though incapacitated by their injuries, were ordered to leave for Ṭihrán. Only twenty-eight persons among them survived the hardships of the journey to the capital. Of these twenty-eight, fifteen were taken to the gallows on the very day of their arrival. The rest were thrown into prison and made to suffer for two years the most horrible atrocities. Though eventually released, many of them perished on their way to their homes, exhausted by the trials of a long and cruel captivity.

A large number of their fellow-disciples were slain in Shíráz by order of Ṭahmásb-Mírzá. The heads of two hundred of these victims were placed on bayonets and carried triumphantly by their oppressors to Ábádih, a village in Fárs. They were intending to take them to Ṭihrán, when a royal messenger commanded them to abandon their project, whereupon they decided to bury the heads in that village.

As to the women, who were six hundred in number, half of them were released in Nayríz, while the rest were carried, each two being forced to ride together on an unsaddled horse, to Shíráz, where, after being submitted to severe tortures, they were abandoned to their fate. Many perished on their way to that city; many yielded up their lives to the afflictions they were made to endure ere they recovered their freedom. My pen shrinks in horror in attempting to describe what befell those valiant men and women who were made to suffer so severely for their Faith. The wanton barbarity that characterised the treatment meted out to them reached the lowest depths of infamy in the concluding stages of that lamentable episode.[5]

The traditions of Islám record many signs concerning the appearance of the Promised One. In one of these, it is prophesied that the heads of some of His followers would be decapitated and used as gifts by the enemy. This prophecy was literally fulfilled during the two bloody massacres of Nayríz. Bahá'u'lláh has quoted this tradition in the *Kitáb-i-Íqán*:

> . . . Even as it hath been recorded . . . in the 'Tablet of Fáṭimih', concerning the character of the Qá'im: 'He shall manifest the perfection of Moses, the splendour of Jesus, and the patience of Job. His chosen ones shall be abased in His day. Their heads shall be offered as presents even as the heads of the Turks and the Daylamites. They shall be slain and burnt. Fear shall seize them; dismay and alarm shall strike terror into their hearts. The earth shall be dyed with their blood. Their womenfolk shall bewail and lament. These indeed are my friends!'[6]

In the *Súriy-i-Ṣabr* Bahá'u'lláh extols the station of Vaḥíd in words no pen can befittingly describe. He pays glowing tribute to the staunchness of his faith and the loftiness of his vision, declares that he had remained faithful to the Covenant of God and affirms that he had fulfilled his pledge to his Lord. He bids him rejoice among the 'Concourse on high'* for being remembered in this Tablet, a Tablet so exalted that the Holy Books of the past had derived their essence from it.

Bahá'u'lláh also addresses the believers of Nayríz in this Tablet, with words of encouragement and praise. He asks them to recall their earlier days of heedlessness and ignorance, when God showered His favours upon them through the person of Vaḥíd, enabled them to recognize His Manifestation, and guided them to the Ocean of Knowledge. He urges them to appreciate this wonderful gift, to thank the Almighty for having been made the recipients of His grace and to rejoice at the lofty station which He has conferred upon them. Should this station be revealed to the eyes of men, He states, they would unhesitatingly offer up their lives to attain it. The wisdom of its concealment is that men may be tested, that good may be distinguished from evil and the righteous from the wicked. With great love Bahá'u'lláh exhorts the believers of Nayríz to mani-

* See p. 81, note.

fest in their lives the attributes of God, to sanctify their souls from the dross of this world, and to be firm in faith and steadfast in the face of opposition.

The history of the martyrs of Nayríz demonstrates the devotion and heroism of the believers in that town. For several generations, these souls have been subjected periodically to bitter persecution by unrelenting enemies; yet they have remained faithful to the Cause of God, enduring with exemplary patience the tribulations heaped upon them.

It is interesting to note that Vaḥíd and his companions sacrificed their lives in His path just ten days before the Báb was publicly executed. Almost sixty years later, on Naw-Rúz 1909, when the remains of the Martyr-Prophet were laid to rest on Mount Carmel, eighteen believers were assassinated in Nayríz by the vicious assault of the bloodthirsty Shaykh Zakaríyyá.* 'Abdu'l-Bahá has testified that the interment of so sacred a trust as the holy remains of the Báb called for a sacrifice, which was realized in the martyrdom of these believers; and He has paid warm tribute to the Bahá'ís of Nayríz for having won, by their sacrifice, a great honour.

In the *Súriy-i-Ṣabr*, Bahá'u'lláh pays glowing tribute to Ḥájí Muḥammad-Taqí. He recalls the major role he played in the upheaval of Nayríz, the material help he extended to Vaḥíd, the fortune he expended in defence of the fort and the sufferings he bore with resignation and self-sacrifice. When the believers took refuge in the fort of Kh͟ájih, their food and other necessities were provided by Ḥájí Muḥammad-Taqí. Without his material aid, the Bábís would not have been able to defend themselves against the army. Ḥájí Muḥammad-Taqí was one of the survivors of the siege. The Governor of Nayríz, knowing that he was one of the key figures responsible for the spread of the Faith in that town, confiscated all his properties and imprisoned

* He entered Nayríz with a number of armed men, occupied the town and, among other things, launched a brutal attack against the Bahá'ís. Not only did his men seek out the Bahá'ís to kill them, but he offered to pay one hundred *túmáns* for the decapitated head of a Bahá'í.

him, intending to torture him to death, with a few others, including Siyyid Ja'far, the learned divine of Yazd, whom we mentioned earlier.

An account of Ḥájí Muḥammad-Taqí's sufferings in prison, his subsequent release and his journey to Baghdád, culminating in his attaining the presence of Bahá'u'lláh, has already been given.* Referring to the spirit of resignation and forbearance shown by him during the massacre of Nayríz, Bahá'u'lláh states that the Almighty will always assist those who willingly sacrifice their possessions to promote the Cause of God, and who patiently endure trials in His path. Such souls, He states, never complain when afflicted with calamities; rather, they welcome hardships and persecution in the path of their Lord.†

There are many mysteries hidden in God's creation. One of these is the mystery of suffering. In his life, man experiences many trials and tribulations, but often does not understand their purpose. Although the full significance of suffering cannot be fully appreciated in this world, its effects upon the individual can be readily observed.

In the world of nature most objects are affected by external influences. For instance, a piece of iron left on its own is cold and becomes rusty. As a result of friction, however, it produces heat, its surface becomes shiny, and by increasing the force of friction it can become even a luminous body. But only pressure from without will cause these characteristics, which are latent within the iron, to be manifested.

Similarly, within a human being there are many qualities and virtues which remain dormant. Often, suffering helps to release

* See pp. 139–41.

† When Ḥájí Muḥammad-Taqí travelled to Baghdád, he was accompanied by his wife, son and daughter. This son, Muḥammad-'Alí, while still a youth, was killed in Baghdád. He himself died a few years later in that city and Bahá'u'lláh honoured him by attending his funeral. Knowing that Ḥájí Muḥammad-Taqí's wife was grief-stricken at the tragic loss of both son and husband, Bahá'u'lláh arranged for a certain Aḥmad 'Alí, a youth of beautiful character, to go with her to Nayríz and live there as an adopted son.

the potentialities within man, bringing to the surface noble qualities which had hitherto remained concealed. History has shown that many eminent men have achieved greatness merely by facing hardships and difficulties. Through perseverance and steadfastness they have overcome obstacles, demonstrated their strength of character and revealed the hidden powers latent within them. In contrast, the weak and feeble have often succumbed to such difficulties and perished. Clearly, suffering reveals the strength, the character and the faith of every human being. The greater the cause, the more strenuous are the tests and trials to which the individual is subjected. In this Dispensation, from amidst the blood-baths of martyrdom, great heroes have emerged whose lives have illumined the history of the Cause of God by their courage and self-sacrifice.

In the *Súriy-i-Ṣabr* Bahá'u'lláh recounts in great detail the story of Job, one of the Prophets of Israel. He states that God conferred upon Job the mantle of prophethood. He was wealthy, owned a vast area of land, and lived with his wife and family in great luxury and comfort. Having been entrusted by God to guide the people to righteousness and truth, he dedicated his life to fulfilling this mission among his community. He summoned them all to the Cause of God, but they became jealous and accused him of insincerity, saying that his devotion to God was due solely to his wealth and material possessions.

In order to manifest his truthfulness to the eyes of men, God surrounded him with tribulations. Every day a fresh calamity descended upon him. First, his sons were taken from him, all his possessions were removed and his crops burnt. Then he was taken ill and his body was afflicted with disease and covered with boils. In spite of all these calamities, he remained thankful to his Lord and patiently endured hardships with a spirit of resignation and detachment. Yet his afflictions did not end there, for he was forced out of his village with no one to help him except his wife, who believed in him and did all she could to alleviate his pain. In the end he became destitute and was without food for many days.

Bahá'u'lláh asserts that Job was so patient and resigned to the will of God that his thankfulness and devotion to his Lord increased with his trials. At last, having proved his detachment from earthly possessions, God again bestowed upon Job all that was taken from him. His teachings spread and his words penetrated into the hearts of the sincere, enabling them to recognize and acknowledge his station.

With this story in the *Súriy-i-Ṣabr* Bahá'u'lláh throws light upon patience, one of the most important virtues which God has bestowed on man. He extols the station of those believers who endured hardships and calamities with patience and resignation. Through their fortitude and constancy, their forbearance and long-suffering, these souls attained to such a lofty position that the Concourse on high seek their companionship and long for their blessings.

Bahá'u'lláh urges the people of the *Bayán* to do likewise, counselling them to adorn their beings with the mantle of resignation, to be steadfast in the Cause of God, and never to be dismayed or disheartened by adversity. And He reminds them that, whereas God rewards every good deed in accordance with its merit, in the case of patience and long-suffering, as attested in the *Qur'án*, the recompense is limitless.*

These virtues God bestowed upon His Manifestations in a covenant with each of Them, Bahá'u'lláh states. Man should follow Their example. First, he should be patient with himself and learn to withhold himself from passion and desire and from deeds which are forbidden by God. Secondly, he should endure with fortitude any suffering which is inflicted upon him in this life and be steadfast in the Cause of God. Finally, he should be forbearing and patient with the believers and, for the sake of God and His religion, bear any ordeal which they may bring upon him.

This Tablet, revealed on the eve of Bahá'u'lláh's departure from 'Iráq, had a tremendous effect upon the believers in that

* 'Those who patiently persevere will truly receive a reward without measure.' (*Qur'án* xxxix. 10. Translated by Abdullah Yusuf Ali.)

country. It prepared them for the days of test and trial which Bahá'u'lláh had been foreshadowing for some time. It also gave them faith and courage to bear the ordeal of separation from their Lord with a spirit of resignation and fortitude.

Referring to His departure from 'Iráq, Bahá'u'lláh alludes to the future rebellion of Mírzá Yaḥyá and warns that, after the setting of the sun, 'the birds of night' would take to the air, meaning that in His absence satanic souls would arise and propagate their evil whisperings among the faithful. He exhorts His followers to protect the Cause of God from division and to remain firm and immovable as the mountain.

In this Tablet Bahá'u'lláh rejects the man-made doctrine of finality of religion, explains the meaning of the 'Seal of the Prophets',* upholds the principle of the continuity of Divine Revelation and states that God will send His Manifestations till the end which has no end. He moreover condemns the divines and the learned of Islám for their blindness and claims that they had never partaken of true knowledge nor discovered the mysteries of the Cause of God, and were wandering in the wilderness of self and passion. He rebukes them for denying the truth of the Revelation of the Báb and for putting Him to death, extols His station, testifies that He manifested the beauty of God, and states that ere long the whole of mankind will recognize Him.

He makes a similar statement concerning the future victory of the Cause in another passage in which He rebukes those who have repudiated the Faith and arisen against it. He warns them that all their efforts to uproot the tree of the Cause of God will ultimately fail, and again prophesies that the day will come when all the peoples of the world will embrace His Faith.

In one of the Tablets of Bahá'u'lláh there is a statement that God has prescribed for Himself the task of assisting those who arise to serve Him. It indeed staggers the imagination, that God should lay upon Himself any specific task. Yet another instance is to be found in this Tablet, for Bahá'u'lláh asserts that God

* See p. 66.

has pledged to gather the whole of the human race under the shadow of the tree of His Cause. This, Bahá'u'lláh states, is an irrevocable decree.

Like many Tablets of Bahá'u'lláh, the *Súriy-i-Ṣabr* may be described as an ocean containing wonderful gems of knowledge and wisdom. Revealed on the momentous occasion when its Author had just disclosed His station to His loved ones, when the hopes and visions of countless Prophets throughout the ages had been fulfilled, and when the sorrows and agonies of His companions had been turned into blissful joy, this Tablet stands out as an eternal monument to that Day of Days.

A few passages in this Tablet allude to Bahá'u'lláh's Declaration and reveal glimpses of the unveiling of His glory in the Garden of Riḍván. In one of these He calls upon Himself to tear asunder the veils which had hitherto hidden His beauty from the eyes of men, to shed abroad the fragrances of the spirit which had remained sealed from the beginning of time, and to manifest His glory through the power of the Almighty. In another passage, referring to suffering which had been inflicted upon Him, He designates His own person as the 'Manifestation of God Himself'. He extols the day, the hour and the moment of His Declaration, and asserts that in that very instant He addressed the whole of creation from the city of Baghdád, so that each being might receive that share of God's glory which God had decreed for him. He further affirms that on that day all created things were illumined by the rising of the Sun of Truth from 'Iráq.

The Significance of Riḍván

In a number of Tablets, most of which have not yet been translated, Bahá'u'lláh has extolled the sacredness and glory of the days of Riḍván. One of these, revealed a few years after His Declaration, has been rendered into English by Shoghi Effendi. The following are some excerpts:

The Divine Springtime is come, O Most Exalted Pen, for the Festival of the All-Merciful is fast approaching. Bestir thyself, and magnify, before the entire creation, the name of God, and celebrate His praise, in such wise that all created things may be regenerated and made new. Speak, and hold not thy peace. The day star of blissfulness shineth above the horizon of Our name, the Blissful, inasmuch as the kingdom of the name of God hath been adorned with the ornament of the name of thy Lord, the Creator of the heavens. Arise before the nations of the earth, and arm thyself with the power of this Most Great Name, and be not of those who tarry . . .

This is the Day whereon the unseen world crieth out: 'Great is thy blessedness, O earth, for thou hast been made the foot-stool of thy God, and been chosen as the seat of His mighty throne.' The realm of glory exclaimeth: 'Would that my life could be sacrificed for thee, for He Who is the Beloved of the All-Merciful hath established His sovereignty upon thee, through the power of His Name that hath been promised unto all things, whether of the past or of the future.' This is the Day whereon every sweet smelling thing hath derived its fragrance from the smell of My garment—a garment that hath shed its perfume upon the whole of creation. This is the Day whereon the rushing waters of everlasting life have gushed out of the Will of the All-Merciful. Haste ye, with your hearts and souls, and quaff your fill, O Concourse of the realms above!

Say: He it is Who is the Manifestation of Him Who is the Unknowable, the Invisible of the Invisibles, could ye but perceive it. He it is Who hath laid bare before you the hidden and treasured Gem, were ye to seek it. He it is Who is the one Beloved of all things, whether of the past or of the future. Would that ye might set your hearts and hopes upon Him! . . .

The Best-Beloved is come. In His right hand is the sealed Wine of His name. Happy is the man that turneth unto Him, and drinketh his fill, and exclaimeth: 'Praise be to Thee, O Revealer of the signs of God!' By the righteousness of the Almighty! Every hidden thing hath been manifested through the power of truth. All the favours of God have been sent down, as a token of His grace. The waters of everlasting life have, in their fullness, been proffered unto men. Every single cup hath been borne round by the hand of the Well-Beloved. Draw near, and tarry not, though it be for one short moment . . .

Rejoice with exceeding gladness, O people of Bahá, as ye call to remembrance the Day of supreme felicity, the Day whereon the Tongue of the Ancient of Days hath spoken, as He departed from His House, proceeding to the Spot from which He shed upon the whole of creation the splendours of His name, the All-Merciful. God is Our witness. Were We to reveal the hidden secrets of that Day, all they that dwell on earth and in the heavens would swoon away and die, except such as will be preserved by God, the Almighty, the All-Knowing, the All-Wise.

Such is the inebriating effect of the words of God upon Him Who is the Revealer of His undoubted proofs, that His Pen can move no longer. With these words He concludeth His Tablet: 'No God is there but Me, the Most Exalted, the Most Powerful, the Most Excellent, the All-Knowing.'[7]

During the twelve days that Bahá'u'lláh remained in the Garden of Riḍván, great numbers came to pay their respects to Him. Among them were notables and dignitaries of the city of Baghdád, men of learning and culture, as well as the mass of the people who were His admirers. As to the believers, Bahá'u'lláh would summon a number of His companions to come to Him each day and would dismiss them in the evening. Only those without family ties were allowed to remain for the night, when some of them would keep vigil around His tent.

Nabíl has left to posterity the following vivid description of the joyous atmosphere of that historic time:

Every day ere the hour of dawn, the gardeners would pick the roses which lined the four avenues of the garden, and would pile them in the centre of the floor of His blessed tent. So great would be the heap that when His companions gathered to drink their morning tea in His presence, they would be unable to see each other across it. All these roses Bahá'u'lláh would, with His own hands, entrust to those whom He dismissed from His presence every morning to be delivered, on His behalf, to His Arab and Persian friends in the city . . . One night, the ninth night of the waxing moon, I happened to be one of those who watched beside His blessed tent. As the hour of midnight approached, I saw Him issue from His tent, pass by the places where some of His companions were sleeping, and begin to pace up and down the moonlit, flower-bordered avenues of the garden. So loud was the singing of the nightingales on every side that only those who were near Him could hear distinctly His voice. He continued to walk until, pausing in the midst of one of these avenues, He observed: 'Consider these nightingales. So great is their love for these roses, that sleepless from dusk till dawn, they warble their melodies and commune with burning passion with the object of their adoration. How then can those who claim to be afire with the rose-like beauty of the Beloved choose to sleep?' For three successive nights I watched and circled round His blessed tent. Every time I passed by the couch whereon He lay, I would find Him wakeful, and every day, from morn till eventide, I would see Him ceaselessly engaged in conversing with the stream of visitors who kept flowing in from Baghdád. Not once could I discover in the words He spoke any trace of dissimulation.[8]

In one of His talks* 'Abdu'l-Bahá states that the enemies of the Faith, determined to extinguish the fire of the Cause, did everything in their power to banish Bahá'u'lláh from Baghdád. They did not realize that this banishment would bring victory to His Faith. However, when Bahá'u'lláh moved to the Garden of Riḍván, they saw the greatness of His Cause, and were dismayed and disheartened by the marks of honour and respect which the inhabitants of Baghdád and its notables showered upon Him. 'Abdu'l-Bahá adds that, whereas banishment is normally a sad occasion, Bahá'u'lláh turned it into the most

* This talk was given on the ninth day of Riḍván 1916, at Bahjí, 'Akká.

joyous event in His life. The days of Riḍván became the Most Great Festival, celebrating the Declaration of His Mission to His followers.

The Declaration of Bahá'u'lláh in the Garden of Riḍván may be regarded as the climax of ten years of His Revelation and the consummation of the first phase of His ministry. On that day the Hand of Omnipotence removed a 'myriad veils of light' from His countenance, vouchsafing to men a glimpse of His power and glory, and opening before them a new chapter in their life on this planet. Bahá'u'lláh has stated that on that day 'the breezes of forgiveness were wafted over the entire creation', and 'all created things were immersed in the sea of purification'.[9]

In the Tablet just quoted (pp. 274–5) Bahá'u'lláh extols the glories of the Festival of Riḍván and describes its significance in these terms:

> Verily, We have caused every soul to expire by virtue of Our irresistible and all-subduing sovereignty. We have, then, called into being a new creation, as a token of Our grace unto men. I am, verily, the All-Bountiful, the Ancient of Days.[10]

In one of His prayers revealed in Adrianople, Bahá'u'lláh refers to this new creation in these words:

> How great is Thy power! How exalted Thy sovereignty! How lofty Thy might! How excellent Thy majesty! How supreme is Thy grandeur—a grandeur which He Who is Thy Manifestation hath made known and wherewith Thou hast invested Him as a sign of Thy generosity and bountiful favour. I bear witness, O my God, that through Him Thy most resplendent signs have been uncovered, and Thy mercy hath encompassed the entire creation. But for Him, how could the Celestial Dove have uttered its songs or the Heavenly Nightingale, according to the decree of God, have warbled its melody?
>
> I testify that no sooner had the First Word proceeded, through the potency of Thy will and purpose, out of His mouth, and the First Call gone forth from His lips than the

whole creation was revolutionized, and all that are in the heavens and all that are on earth were stirred to the depths. Through that Word the realities of all created things were shaken, were divided, separated, scattered, combined and reunited, disclosing, in both the contingent world and the heavenly kingdom, entities of a new creation, and revealing, in the unseen realms, the signs and tokens of Thy unity and oneness.[11]

The spiritual energies released at the time of Bahá'u'lláh's Declaration bestowed a fresh capacity upon the human race, enabling every individual regardless of race, colour, education or background to recognize the Message of God for this day, and to play his part in the establishment of a world-embracing divine civilization for mankind.

Three Important Statements by Bahá'u'lláh

Although the manner of His Declaration is not clear, there is a Tablet in the handwriting of Mírzá Áqá Ján, addressed to a certain Áqá Muḥammad-Riḍá, which throws light on some of Bahá'u'lláh's utterances. According to this Tablet, on the first day of Riḍván Bahá'u'lláh made three particularly important statements to His followers.*

The first was to forbid the use of the sword † in His Dispensation. During the ministry of the Báb the believers defended themselves against their persecutors; Bahá'u'lláh clearly forbade this. In many Tablets He counselled His followers to teach the Cause with wisdom and prudence and not to arouse the antagonism of a fanatic enemy. He enjoined caution when teaching those who were determined to uproot the foundation of the Faith and harm its adherents. At one stage in His ministry He particularly exhorted His followers to guard against falling into the hands of enemies, but if faced with

* It is not clear, however, whether these were part of the declaration of His station, as 'Him Whom God shall make manifest', or not.

† By this was intended any kind of arms or weapon.

martyrdom, to lay down their lives in the path of their Faith rather than kill their persecutors. The tongue of the believer who teaches the Cause, He stated in one Tablet, is the mightiest sword he possesses, for his utterances are endowed with a power that can remove veils of ignorance from the hearts of men. Soon, as a result of such counsels and exhortations, the attitude of the believers was radically changed, and swords and other weapons were put away never to be used again. During the ministries of Bahá'u'lláh and 'Abdu'l-Bahá great numbers of Bahá'ís were martyred in Persia, but they did not resort to violence.* They gave their lives willingly, and many testified in the hour of martyrdom that their life-blood proclaimed the truth of the Cause of God for this age.

It was never intended, however, that the followers of Bahá'u'lláh should stand idly by and make no defence of their lives. Justice is one of the most important teachings in this Dispensation and the believers have used every lawful means to protect themselves against the onslaughts of enemies. During the days of Bahá'u'lláh and 'Abdu'l-Bahá, Bahá'ís could do little to stay the hands of oppressors, because those in authority often supported or took part in their heinous crimes. At present, when most of the nations of the world are becoming conscious of the principles of human rights, whenever Bahá'ís have been persecuted on grounds of religious belief, the Bahá'í World Community has appealed for justice and governments concerned have, in many cases, extended their protection.

The second statement made by Bahá'u'lláh on the first day of Riḍván, as attested in the aforementioned Tablet, was that no other Manifestation of God would appear before the expiration of a thousand years. In the *Kitáb-i-Badí'*, which He revealed in

* This attitude must not be confused with pacifism which is not in conformity with Bahá'í Teachings. Indeed, Bahá'u'lláh advocates the use of force on an international scale, if needed to stay the hand of an aggressor. Addressing the kings and rulers of the world He writes: '. . . Should any one among you take up arms against another, rise ye all against him, for this is naught but manifest justice.'[12]

Adrianople, Bahá'u'lláh confirmed this statement, and later in the *Kitáb-i-Aqdas* He referred to it again in these words:

> Whoso layeth claim to a Revelation direct from God, ere the expiration of a full thousand years, such a man is assuredly a lying impostor. We pray God that He may graciously assist him to retract and repudiate such claim. Should he repent, God will, no doubt, forgive him. If, however, he persisteth in his error, God will, assuredly, send down one who will deal mercilessly with him. Terrible, indeed, is God in punishing! Whosoever interpreteth this verse otherwise than its obvious meaning is deprived of the Spirit of God and of His mercy which encompasseth all created things. Fear God, and follow not your idle fancies. Nay, rather follow the bidding of your Lord, the Almighty, the All-Wise.[13]

Bahá'u'lláh's third statement on the first day of Riḍván was that, the moment He uttered those words, all the names and attributes of God were fully manifested within all created things. By this He implied the advent of a new Day and the infusion of a fresh capacity into all beings.

The Báb's Prophecies Fulfilled

With the Declaration of Bahá'u'lláh the prophecies of the Báb concerning the appearance of 'Him Whom God shall make manifest' were fulfilled. The Báb had alluded in His Writings to the scene of Bahá'u'lláh's Declaration in 'Riḍván' and to the wafting of the breezes of His Revelation from 'Baghdád'. He had also foretold in the Persian *Bayán* that He would be manifested on the completion of the first Váḥid (nineteen years) of the Bábí Dispensation, which began in 1844. In the first chapter of the *Qayyúmu'l-Asmá'*, which was revealed when the Báb communicated His Message to Mullá Ḥusayn, He referred to the 'people of Bahá' as the only 'companions of the Crimson-Coloured Ark' moving upon the 'Crimson Sea'. The 'Crimson Ark' was a reference to the Cause of Bahá'u'lláh, which was launched on the first day of Riḍván. The community of the Most Great Name emerged on that day, when the followers of Bahá'u'lláh acknowledged His station.

Of the twelve days that Bahá'u'lláh stayed in the Garden of Riḍván, three are regarded as Holy Days: the first day on which He declared Himself, the ninth day when all His family joined Him and rejoiced at His Declaration, and the twelfth day when He left that garden.

Bahá'u'lláh's Departure from the Garden

A memorable account of Bahá'u'lláh's departure has been given by Shoghi Effendi, Guardian of the Faith:

> The departure of Bahá'u'lláh from the Garden of Riḍván, at noon, on the 14th of Dhi'l-Qa'dih 1279 A.H. (May 3, 1863), witnessed scenes of tumultuous enthusiasm no less spectacular, and even more touching, than those which greeted Him when leaving His Most Great House in Baghdád. 'The great tumult,' wrote an eye-witness, 'associated in our minds with the Day of Gathering, the Day of Judgment, we beheld on that occasion. Believers and unbelievers alike sobbed and lamented. The chiefs and notables who had congregated were struck with wonder. Emotions were stirred to such depths as no tongue can describe, nor could any observer escape their contagion.'
>
> Mounted on His steed, a red roan stallion of the finest breed, the best His lovers could purchase for Him, and leaving behind Him a bowing multitude of fervent admirers, He rode forth on the first stage of a journey that was to carry Him to the city of Constantinople. 'Numerous were the heads,' Nabíl himself a witness of that memorable scene, recounts, 'which, on every side, bowed to the dust at the feet of His horse, and kissed its hoofs, and countless were those who pressed forward to embrace His stirrups.' 'How great the number of those embodiments of fidelity,' testifies a fellow-traveller, 'who, casting themselves before that charger preferred death to separation from their Beloved! Methinks,

that blessed steed trod upon the bodies of those pure-hearted souls.' '*He* (God) *it was,*' Bahá'u'lláh Himself declares, '*Who enabled Me to depart out of the city* (Baghdád), *clothed with such majesty as none, except the denier and the malicious, can fail to acknowledge.*'[14]

17

The Journey to Constantinople

As Bahá'u'lláh was leaving the Garden of Riḍván, the call of *adhán** was raised outside and the words 'Alláh'u'Akbar' (God is the Greatest), which had greeted Him on His arrival, reverberated throughout that district again. Many people, including non-believers, paid their last homage by walking beside His horse as He went.

There was a man by the name of Shaykh 'Abdu'l-Ḥamíd who had a tremendous love for Bahá'u'lláh. He was a Muslim and never became a believer, but his devotion to Bahá'u'lláh knew no bounds. As a token of respect he escorted Him out of Baghdád by running a distance of about ten miles in front of His horse. One of his sons, Shaykh Muḥammad-i-'Arab, became a Bahá'í and some years later walked all the way to 'Akká, attained the presence of Bahá'u'lláh, and then went to Persia where he served the Faith with distinction as a teacher.

A notable disciple who travelled with Bahá'u'lláh was Mírzá Áqáy-i-Káshání, whom He surnamed Ismu'lláhu'l-Muníb. As a youth he became attracted to the Cause of the Báb and joined the ranks of the Bábís. His father was a merchant of note in Káshán and was very hostile to this new-born Faith. On learning that his son had embraced the Cause of the Báb, he decided to kill him. One day he took him to a lonely desert near the town and was about to carry out his sinister design when his son convinced him that the Bábís of Káshán would not stand idly by, if his father killed him, but would take action to punish him for his crime. So his father released him on condition that he leave home for good.

* The Muslim call to prayer.

After this tragic incident, Jináb-i-Muníb travelled to Baghdád where he attained the presence of Bahá'u'lláh and was permitted to remain there for some time. He was an accomplished youth, keen and perceptive, full of charm and grace, handsome, well educated, a distinguished calligrapher and gifted poet. His radiant personality coupled with great spiritual capacity enabled him to become a worthy recipient of the outpourings of Bahá'u'lláh's Revelation in Baghdád. His heart was so filled with the love of Bahá'u'lláh that all his thoughts and actions were wholly dedicated to Him. He used to live alone in a humble house with very little to eat, spending his time in transcribing the Writings. His own writings are lucid, inspiring and full of spirit, and his teaching exploits were truly remarkable.

After some time in Baghdád, about the year 1859, Bahá'u'lláh sent Jináb-i-Muníb to Persia, where he visited the believers in Ṭihrán, Qazvín and Tabríz. He then returned to Baghdád and was there at the time of Riḍván. When he was honoured to accompany Bahá'u'lláh to Constantinople, he decided to walk all the way instead of riding with his Lord. 'Abdu'l-Bahá describes how, many nights, He and Jináb-i-Muníb walked one on either side of the howdah* of Bahá'u'lláh. Another task on which he prided himself was to carry a lantern in front of Bahá'u'lláh's howdah.

Those who accompanied Bahá'u'lláh to Constantinople were members of His family including Áqáy-i-Kalím and Mírzá Muḥammad-Qulí, His faithful brothers, and twenty-six of His disciples. As mentioned previously, two people joined the party *en route*, Nabíl-i-A'ẓam and Mírzá Yaḥyá.

Shoghi Effendi has described the journey to Constantinople in these terms:

> A caravan, consisting of fifty mules, a mounted guard of ten soldiers with their officer, and seven pairs of howdahs, each pair surmounted by four parasols, was formed, and wended

* The origin of the word is Arabic. It is a litter consisting of a pair of panniers in which two individuals can ride, and is carried by a beast of burden, in this case a mule.

its way, by easy stages, and in the space of no less than a hundred and ten days, across the uplands, and through the defiles, the woods, valleys and pastures, comprising the picturesque scenery of eastern Anatolia, to the port of Sámsún, on the Black Sea. At times on horseback, at times resting in the howdah reserved for His use, and which was oftentimes surrounded by His companions, most of whom were on foot, He, by virtue of the written order of Námiq Pá<u>sh</u>á, was accorded, as He travelled northward, in the path of spring, an enthusiastic reception by the válís, the mutiṣarrifs, the qá'im-maqáms, the mudírs, the <u>sh</u>ay<u>kh</u>s, the muftís and qáḍís, the government officials and notables belonging to the districts through which He passed.* In Karkúk, in Irbíl, in Mosul, where He tarried three days, in Níṣíbín, in Márdín, in Díyár-Bakr, where a halt of a couple of days was made, in <u>Kh</u>árpút, in Sívas, as well as in other villages and hamlets, He would be met by a delegation immediately before His arrival, and would be accompanied, for some distance, by a similar delegation upon His departure. The festivities which, at some stations, were held in His honour, the food the villagers prepared and brought for His acceptance, the eagerness which time and again they exhibited in providing the means for His comfort, recalled the reverence which the people of Ba<u>gh</u>dád had shown Him on so many occasions.[1]

Those who have travelled in the deserts or the valleys and uplands of the Middle East on the backs of mules and horses know how slow and monotonous the pace is. For miles there is no sign of life and those who travel in the party are not always able to talk and communicate easily with each other. Under these circumstances nothing can be more exhilarating than to hear a pleasant voice singing beautiful songs. Jináb-i-Muníb was one of those whose melodious voice, chanting various odes and

* The titles of these officials and notables may be translated as follows: válís, governors; mutiṣarrifs, provincial governors; qá'im-maqáms, viceregents; mudírs, district prefects; <u>sh</u>ay<u>kh</u>s, elders or chiefs; muftís, expounders of Muslim law who rule on points of religious jurisprudence; qáḍís, judges.

poems, rang out through the open fields and mountains of Turkey and brought joy and relaxation to those who travelled with Bahá'u'lláh. The odes that he sang were all indicative of his love for Bahá'u'lláh, and the prayers he chanted in the dead of night were a testimony to the yearning of his heart for his Lord.

Jináb-i-Muníb was among the companions of Bahá'u'lláh in Constantinople until His departure for Adrianople, when He summoned him to His presence and instructed him to go to Persia, where he could teach and spread the glad-tidings of the Declaration of Bahá'u'lláh to the Bábís. In fact, it took some time for the news of Bahá'u'lláh's Declaration to reach the believers in Persia. In the first place, methods of communication were still primitive. Secondly, the dissemination of such important news had to be carried out with wisdom. Only the insight and devotion of Bahá'u'lláh's disciples could bring this about, which is one of the reasons that Bahá'u'lláh sent a number of the ablest among them to Persia to teach His Cause there.

When Jináb-i-Muníb arrived in Ṭihrán, he began to intimate the station of Bahá'u'lláh to some of the Bábís, at first very discreetly. After a short while Bahá'u'lláh sent him a Tablet from Adrianople, known as the *Súriy-i-Aṣḥáb*, which was addressed to him for his guidance and support. When Jináb-i-Muníb received this Tablet, he began to unveil the station of Bahá'u'lláh to the mass of the believers in that land. This is a lengthy Tablet in which Bahá'u'lláh speaks about the greatness of His Cause and, alluding to Mírzá Yaḥyá, warns the people of the *Bayán* to beware of those who deny it. (More detail of this significant Tablet will be given in the next volume.)

During this period Jináb-i-Muníb rendered memorable services to the Faith in Persia, especially in Ṭihrán. After this, he journeyed to Adrianople, attained the presence of Bahá'u'lláh again, and was in that city when Bahá'u'lláh was exiled to 'Akká. About that time, however, he was taken ill and badly needed treatment. In spite of this, he begged Bahá'u'lláh to permit him to join in His exile as he longed to be with his Lord.

Eventually, his request was granted and he managed to reach Gallipoli with the others, but he was so weak that three men had to carry him aboard the steamer which was to take the exiles to 'Akká. Soon after this his condition deteriorated and the captain forced him to leave the ship at Smyrna.

Many times Jináb-i-Muníb had indicated to Bahá'u'lláh that his greatest desire in life was to sacrifice himself in His path. Now at last the time had come. Before being carried out of the ship he managed, in spite of his weakness, to drag his frail body before Bahá'u'lláh. He threw himself at His feet and with tearful eyes begged Him for the last time to accept his sacrifice. This Bahá'u'lláh did and his hopes and aspirations were finally fulfilled. He was taken to a hospital in Smyrna where, shortly afterwards, his soul took its flight to the immortal realms of the spirit.

Bahá'u'lláh, in a Tablet describing these events, says that when Jináb-i-Muníb's spirit ascended to his abode in the eternal worlds of God, all the angelic souls and the Concourse on high rushed forward to receive him with eagerness and love. 'Abdu'l-Bahá, one of those who carried him from the steamer to hospital, later asked the believers to try to locate his grave so that pilgrims might visit his resting-place and become inspired by his example.[2]

There were other disciples who accompanied Bahá'u'lláh to Constantinople. Among these was Áqá Muḥammad-Ṣádiq of Iṣfahán, who embraced the Faith in Baghdád, where he lived close to the house of Bahá'u'lláh. He had an extraordinary spiritual perceptiveness and recognized the truth of the Faith the moment he heard it.[3] Another was Áqá Muḥammad-'Alí of Iṣfahán, a devoted believer who accompanied Bahá'u'lláh yet further, to Adrianople and to 'Akká.[4] There was also Áqá Muḥammad-'Alíy-i-Ṣabbágh of Yazd, who stayed for about two years in Constantinople to assist the believers as they passed through the city. He then went to Adrianople and was exiled with Bahá'u'lláh to 'Akká.[5]

'Abdu'l-Ghaffár-i-Iṣfahání, being the only person among the

entire company of exiles who spoke Turkish well, served as interpreter throughout the journey. He was one of Bahá'u'lláh's companions in Adrianople who accompanied Him on His exile to 'Akká. But when the steamer reached Haifa, the authorities chose him as one of the four Bahá'ís to be exiled with Mírzá Yaḥyá to Cyprus. 'Abdu'l-Ghaffár was so distressed by this that he threw himself into the sea, preferring to die rather than be separated from Bahá'u'lláh. The officers in charge dragged him out and in spite of his strong objections forcibly sent him to Cyprus. He was imprisoned in Famagusta, but managed to escape and hastened to 'Akká, where he basked again in the sunshine of Bahá'u'lláh's presence.[6]

Áqá Muḥammad-Ibráhím-i-Amír was another devoted believer who accompanied Bahá'u'lláh to Constantinople. He was a survivor of the upheaval in Nayríz, a brave and courageous man who remained in the service of Bahá'u'lláh day and night and was exiled further to Adrianople and 'Akká.[7]

Áqá Mírzá Maḥmúd of Káshán, together with Áqá Riḍá of Shíráz, walked all the way to the port of Sámsún, ahead of the howdah of Bahá'u'lláh. They took up the task of preparing and cooking the food for the party at each halting-place. These two souls were so dedicated that, in spite of the fatigue and rigours of the journey, they were constantly engaged until each midnight in serving the friends with great devotion. Not only did they cook the meals and wash the dishes, but they ensured that every person was comfortable and had sufficient rest. They were the last to retire at night and the first to arise in the morning, rendering this vital service with an exemplary dedication each day of the journey from Baghdád to Constantinople.

'Abdu'l-Bahá has said that these two were the embodiments of detachment from this world and that Bahá'u'lláh always showered His blessings upon them. They lived in Baghdád in the utmost poverty, together with five other believers, in a single small room. This company of seven used to pool their modest earnings every day in order to buy their evening meal. 'Abdu'l-Bahá has recalled an occasion when only one of them had earned any money and for that night they could buy only a handful of dates. Yet despite their poverty, Áqá Mírzá Maḥmúd and Áqá Riḍá were content and happy. Their faces beamed with eternal joy and their hearts were filled with the love of Bahá'u'lláh. Their sole desire was to attain His good pleasure and their only aim was to serve Him.

Later, they were exiled to 'Akká where they continued to serve their Lord with sincerity and love. After the passing of Bahá'u'lláh they served 'Abdu'l-Bahá with the same devotion and loyalty and were His trusted companions upon whom He relied during the darkest hours of His ministry. He has praised their humility and lowliness and has said that throughout their long years of service, they never uttered a word which had to do with self.[8]

Another soul who was truly enamoured of Bahá'u'lláh was Darvísh Ṣidq-'Alí. He begged Bahá'u'lláh to allow him to join the party travelling to Constantinople, and when permission was granted he undertook to serve as groom on the journey. He used to walk all day beside the convoy, singing poems which brought joy to the friends, and at night he attended to the horses. From Constantinople he accompanied Bahá'u'lláh on His exile to Adrianople, and then to 'Akká. He was originally a dervish who embraced the Faith in Baghdád and became detached from the things of this world. From then on he spent his time in the service of the believers, and till the end of his life was the recipient of the blessings of Bahá'u'lláh.[9]

Yet another who performed a difficult task on this journey was Mírzá Ja'far-i-Yazdí, who was a learned divine.* After recognizing the truth of the Faith he came to Baghdád, attained the presence of Bahá'u'lláh and became filled with a new spirit. He gave up his position, discarded his clerical attire, put on a layman's hat and engaged in working as a carpenter. In spite of his great learning he was humble and self-effacing, and for some time served in the household of Bahá'u'lláh in Baghdád. On the way to Constantinople he served the friends in every possible

* Not to be confused with Siyyid Ja'far-i-Yazdí. (See pp. 137–41.)

manner. While they were resting or sleeping at a stopping-place, Mírzá Ja'far and 'Abdu'l-Bahá used to go to surrounding villages to purchase straw and other provisions for the mules and horses. Sometimes this would take hours as there was a famine in the area and it was very difficult to obtain food. Mírzá Ja'far remained in the service of Bahá'u'lláh in Adrianople and was exiled with Him to the Most Great Prison in 'Akká.

Speaking of Mírzá Ja'far, 'Abdu'l-Bahá has recounted the following story:

> The Prison was a garden of roses to him, and his narrow cell a wide and fragrant place. At the time when we were in the barracks he fell dangerously ill and was confined to his bed. He suffered many complications, until finally the doctor gave him up and would visit him no more. Then the sick man breathed his last. Mírzá Áqá Ján ran to Bahá'u'lláh, with word of the death. Not only had the patient ceased to breathe, but his body was already going limp. His family were gathered about him, mourning him, shedding bitter tears. The Blessed Beauty said, 'Go; chant the prayer of Yá Sháfí—O Thou, the Healer—and Mírzá Ja'far will come alive. Very rapidly, he will be as well as ever.' I reached his bedside. His body was cold and all the signs of death were present. Slowly, he began to stir; soon he could move his limbs, and before an hour had passed he lifted his head, sat up, and proceeded to laugh and tell jokes.
>
> He lived for a long time after that, occupied as ever with serving the friends. This giving service was a point of pride with him: to all, he was a servant. He was always modest and humble, calling God to mind, and to the highest degree full of hope and faith.[10]

Some years later a similar incident happened to Mírzá Ja'far. Ḥájí Muḥammad-Ṭáhir-i-Málmírí was present on that occasion and has recorded the event in his memoirs. The following is a translation of his notes:

> When Bahá'u'lláh was staying in the Mansion of Mazra'ih,

it was customary every night for Mírzá Ja'far, one of the servants of the household, to leave a jug of water outside the bedroom of the Ancient Beauty* on the upper floor of the Mansion. This was done in case He needed water during the night. In front of the Mansion there was a large balcony† and the Ancient Beauty often used to pace up and down it. One night, approximately four hours after sunset, Mírzá Ja'far as usual was carrying the jug of water up the stairs. That night was very dark and, through an error of judgement, he fell with the jug from the edge of the roof down into the garden below. This part of the garden was not in use and usually no one went there.

Early every morning, Mírzá Ja'far would first milk the cows and then attend to other housework. But that morning there was no sign of him and the friends looked everywhere but could not find him. Eventually they had to milk the cows, bring the milk to the household and attend to the other duties of Mírzá Ja'far. That day about three hours after sunrise the Blessed Beauty came upon the balcony to walk. He went straight to the very spot from which Mírzá Ja'far had fallen and called his name. Mírzá Ja'far immediately arose, picked up the empty jug and came out of the garden in perfect health. Whenever the friends asked Mírzá Ja'far to recount the incident, he would say, 'I lost consciousness as soon as I fell from the roof with the jug in my hand. It was not until the Ancient Beauty called my name that I regained consciousness.'‡[11]

Apart from the notorious Siyyid Muḥammad-i-Iṣfahání who was travelling with Bahá'u'lláh, and Mírzá Yaḥyá who joined Him on the way, the disciples of Bahá'u'lláh on this journey, as always, demonstrated such love, devotion and humility towards

* Bahá'u'lláh.

† The rooms which were added to the Mansion in later years have altered some features of the building, as it was in the days of Bahá'u'lláh.

‡ This and similar episodes should not be regarded as miracles, nor as proofs of the authenticity of Bahá'u'lláh's Message. He has deprecated the attributing of miracles to Himself, as this would degrade the station of the Manifestation of God.

Him as no pen can ever describe. The inestimable privilege conferred upon them of accompanying Him to Constantinople had completely overwhelmed them. Joy and contentment so inspired them that the hardships of the journey, whether on foot or by mule, had very little effect upon their health.

The marks of respect and veneration which were shown to Bahá'u'lláh by the people along the way continued until He reached the port of Sámsún. From there He travelled by sea to Constantinople. Shoghi Effendi has recounted this in *God Passes By*:

> In Sámsún the Chief Inspector of the entire province, extending from Baghdád to Constantinople, accompanied by several páshás, called on Him, showed Him the utmost respect, and was entertained by Him at luncheon. But seven days after His arrival, He, as foreshadowed in the Tablet of the Holy Mariner, was put on board a Turkish steamer and three days later was disembarked, at noon, together with His fellow-exiles, at the port of Constantinople, on the first of Rabí'u'l-Avval 1280 A.H. (August 16, 1863). In two special carriages, which awaited Him at the landing-stage He and His family drove to the house of Shamsí Big, the official who had been appointed by the government to entertain its guests, and who lived in the vicinity of the Khirqiy-i-Sharíf mosque. Later they were transferred to the more commodious house of Vísí Páshá, in the neighbourhood of the mosque of Sulṭán Muḥammad.
>
> With the arrival of Bahá'u'lláh at Constantinople, the capital of the Ottoman Empire and seat of the Caliphate (acclaimed by the Muḥammadans as 'the Dome of Islam,' but stigmatized by Him as the spot whereon the '*throne of tyranny*' had been established), the grimmest and most calamitous and yet the most glorious chapter in the history of the first Bahá'í century may be said to have opened. A period in which untold privations and unprecedented trials were mingled with the noblest spiritual triumphs was now commencing. The day-star of Bahá'u'lláh's ministry was about to reach its zenith. The most momentous years of the Heroic Age of His

Dispensation were at hand. The catastrophic process, foreshadowed as far back as the year sixty by His Forerunner in the Qayyúmu'l-Asmá', was beginning to be set in motion.

Exactly two decades earlier the Bábí Revelation had been born in darkest Persia, in the city of Shíráz. Despite the cruel captivity to which its Author had been subjected, the stupendous claims He had voiced had been proclaimed by Him before a distinguished assemblage in Tabríz, the capital of Ádhirbáyján. In the hamlet of Badasht the Dispensation which His Faith had ushered in had been fearlessly inaugurated by the champions of His Cause. In the midst of the hopelessness and agony of the Síyáh-Chál of Ṭihrán, nine years later, that Revelation had, swiftly and mysteriously been brought to sudden fruition. The process of rapid deterioration in the fortunes of that Faith, which had gradually set in, and was alarmingly accelerated during the years of Bahá'u'lláh's withdrawal to Kurdistán, had, in a masterly fashion after His return from Sulaymáníyyih, been arrested and reversed. The ethical, the moral and doctrinal foundations of a nascent community had been subsequently, in the course of His sojourn in Baghdád, unassailably established. And finally, in the Garden of Riḍván, on the eve of His banishment to Constantinople, the ten-year delay, ordained by an inscrutable Providence, had been terminated through the Declaration of His Mission and the visible emergence of what was to become the nucleus of a world-embracing Fellowship.[12]

18

'Him Whom God Shall Make Manifest'

Never before in history, until the appearance of the Báb, has one Manifestation of God heralded another Who was His contemporary. The Báb was two years younger* than Bahá'u'lláh, and They lived about five hundred miles apart, the Báb in Shíráz and Bahá'u'lláh in Ṭihrán.

The Báb was an independent Manifestation of God Who inaugurated the Bábí Dispensation, abrogated the laws of Islám, formulated new laws and, like other Prophets, founded an independent religion which spread very rapidly throughout Persia and 'Iráq. His advent closed, on the one hand, the Prophetic Cycle in which several Manifestations of God had appeared and given their visions and prophecies concerning the Day of God, and opened, on the other, the Cycle of Fulfilment whose Central Figure is Bahá'u'lláh. He has been acclaimed by Bahá'u'lláh as the 'King of the Messengers', the 'Point round Whom the realities of the Prophets and Messengers revolve', and One Whose 'rank excelleth that of all the Prophets', Whose 'Revelation transcendeth the comprehension and understanding of all their chosen ones'.[1] His Mission was to prepare men for

* The Báb, Whose name was Siyyid 'Alí-Muḥammad, was born on the first day of Muḥarram 1235 A.H., and Bahá'u'lláh on the second day of the same month in 1233 A.H. These dates are in accordance with the lunar calendar used in the Islamic world. There is a tradition which attributes to Imám 'Alí, the successor of Muḥammad, this saying: 'I am two years younger than my Lord'. (The comparable dates in the Christian calendar are, for the Báb, 20 October 1819, and for Bahá'u'lláh, 12 November 1817.)

the coming of Bahá'u'lláh, the Supreme Manifestation of God Whose advent has been promised in all the sacred Scriptures of the past.

The station of Bahá'u'lláh is so exalted that He was heralded by the Báb, Himself a Manifestation of God, Who paved the way for His coming, established a mighty Covenant concerning His Revelation and reared a new race of men worthy to meet Him and embrace His Cause.

The announcement of 'Him Whom God shall make manifest', which the Báb gave to His followers, was firm and irrevocable, more clear and emphatic than that given by any Manifestation of God before Him. In past Dispensations the signs of the coming of the next Manifestation were always wrapped in mystery and expressed in allegorical terms. But the Báb gave no such signs. Rather, He indicated that the glory of 'Him Whom God shall make manifest' would be so strikingly apparent that there would be no need of signs. Yet none could recognize Him through his own knowledge, He warned, nor judge Him by his own standards, nor adduce proofs to establish His authenticity, for He would be exalted above the recognition of His servants and known only through Himself and His Revelation. The sole testimony to His truth would be that which He Himself would reveal, and not that which men might produce. In one of His Writings extolling Bahá'u'lláh, the Báb affirmed that 'Certitude itself is ashamed to be called upon to certify His truth . . . and Testimony itself is ashamed to testify unto Him'.[2]

Throughout His ministry, the Báb continually emphasized the pre-eminence of the Supreme Manifestation Who would follow Him. In one of His prayers communing with Bahá'u'lláh, He revealed these words:

> Exalted art Thou, O my Lord the Omnipotent! How puny and contemptible my word and all that pertaineth unto me appear unless they be related to Thy great glory. Grant that through the assistance of Thy grace whatsoever pertaineth unto me may be acceptable in Thy sight.[3]

In another passage He wrote:

> Of all the tributes I have paid to Him Who is to come after Me, the greatest is this, My written confession, that no words of Mine can adequately describe Him, nor can any reference to Him in My Book, the Bayán, do justice to His Cause.[4]

The Báb's Mission, His teachings, laws and exhortations revolved around 'Him Whom God shall make manifest'. In the *Bayán*, the Mother Book of His Dispensation, the Báb states that His aim in revealing its each and every letter was to enable His followers to recognize and obey 'Him Whom God shall make manifest'. In another passage of the same Book He included these words:

> The Bayán is, from beginning to end, the repository of all of His attributes, and the treasury of both His fire and His light.[5]

The *Bayán*, He declared, was dependent upon 'Him Whom God shall make manifest', Who, through one word of His mouth, could accept or reject all the laws ordained in it. The Báb mentions that the *Bayán* derives its glory from 'Him Whom God shall make manifest', Who, in truth, revealed it and Who alone could fully understand the inner meaning of all it contained. In another passage the Báb confirmed that only 'Him Whom God shall make manifest', and those whom He would teach, would be able to understand the significance of all the Holy Books of past Dispensations.

The Báb categorically asserted that He was a Messenger sent by 'Him Whom God shall make manifest', a lowly servant at His threshold. He warned His followers that, unless they recognized 'Him Whom God shall make manifest', they would be unfaithful to the *Bayán* and unworthy in His sight. He explained in the *Bayán* that those who followed Him and faithfully obeyed the ordinances of God, as revealed in that Book, were the true believers in God. When, however, 'Him Whom God shall make manifest' would come, the spirit of faith would be taken from them unless they recognized Him and embraced His Faith. In another passage He gave the example of one well versed in the *Bayán*, who had memorized all its verses, had an immense knowledge and was the possessor of every virtue. Should such a man hesitate for one moment to accept the truth of the Cause of 'Him Whom God shall make manifest', his belief in the *Bayán* would be nullified and his faith in God would become void. Addressing Vaḥíd, one of the most illustrious among His disciples, the Báb uttered this warning:

> By the righteousness of Him Whose power causeth the seed to germinate and Who breatheth the spirit of life into all things, were I to be assured that in the day of His manifestation thou wilt deny Him, I would unhesitatingly disown thee and repudiate thy faith . . . If, on the other hand, I be told that a Christian, who beareth no allegiance to My Faith, will believe in Him, the same will I regard as the apple of Mine Eye.[6]

In many of His Writings the Báb expressed grief and agony at the thought of those among His followers who might reject the Promised One of the *Bayán*. Referring to the Revelation of 'Him Whom God shall make manifest', He proclaimed:

> . . . If on the day of His Revelation all that are on earth bear Him allegiance, Mine inmost being will rejoice, inasmuch as all will have attained the summit of their existence . . . If not, My soul will be saddened. I truly have nurtured all things for this purpose. How, then, can any one be veiled from Him?[7]

Because He was a Manifestation of God, the Báb had true knowledge of the station of Bahá'u'lláh, a knowledge which is beyond the reach of all humanity. His vision of the omnipotence and grandeur of the One who was destined to follow Him was so majestic that no mortal mind can hope to attain it. It is for this reason that the utterances of the Báb in praise of Bahá'u'lláh stagger the imagination of those who are not in some degree aware of His exalted station. The Revelation of Bahá'u'lláh, as portrayed by the Báb, is so glorious and awe-inspiring that He allows no excuse to those who reject it. To the Báb, the advent of Bahá'u'lláh was as clear and evident as the sun and, therefore, He counselled His followers to permit no doubt to enter their minds when informed of the Message of 'Him Whom God shall make manifest'. Should their hearts waver in His Cause, the wrath of God would descend on them so long as such doubts remained.

Repeatedly in His Writings, the Báb called on His followers to beware lest anything in this world, including the *Bayán* and all other Holy Books, should become a barrier between them and 'Him Whom God shall make manifest'. These are some of His words:

> Suffer not the Bayán and all that hath been revealed therein to withhold you from that Essence of Being and Lord of the visible and invisible.[8]

And in another passage He revealed:

> Beware, beware, lest in the days of His Revelation the Váḥid of the Bayán* shut thee out as by a veil from Him, inasmuch as this Váḥid is but a creature in His sight.[9]

And again He addressed His followers:

> O congregation of the Bayán, and all who are therein! Recognize ye the limits imposed upon you, for such a One as the Point of the Bayán Himself hath believed in Him Whom God shall make manifest before all things were created. Therein, verily, do I glory before all who are in the kingdom of heaven and earth.[10]

Many times the Báb alluded to the 'year nine' as the date for the coming of 'Him Whom God shall make manifest'. The Báb's Mission began in the year 1260 A.H. (A.D. 1844). The 'year nine' was 1269 A.H., which opened about the middle of October

* The Báb and the eighteen Letters of the Living.

1852, when Bahá'u'lláh had already been imprisoned for two months in the Síyáh-Chál of Ṭihrán, the scene of His transcendent Revelation.

Here are additional words gleaned from the Arabic *Bayán* and other Epistles which the Báb wrote to some of His disciples:

> In the year nine, ye shall attain unto all good.
>
> In the year nine, ye will attain unto the presence of God.*
>
> After Ḥín † a Cause shall be given unto you which ye shall come to know.
>
> Ere nine will have elapsed from the inception of this Cause, the realities of the created things will not be made manifest. All that thou hast as yet seen is but the stage from the moist germ until We clothed it with flesh. Be patient, until thou beholdest a new creation. Say: 'Blessed, therefore, be God, the most excellent of Makers!'
>
> Wait thou, until nine will have elapsed from the time of the Bayán. Then exclaim: 'Blessed, therefore, be God, the most excellent of Makers!'[11]

On the other hand, the Báb also referred to the year nineteen, a year coinciding with the Declaration of Bahá'u'lláh in Baghdád, which occurred at the end of nineteen lunar years from the inception of the Bahá'í Era. Here is what the Báb wrote:

> The Lord of the Day of Reckoning will be manifested at the end of Váḥid ‡ and the beginning of eighty. §[12]

* The Báb explained in His Writings that attaining 'unto the presence of God', as promised in the Holy Books, would be none other than attaining the presence of 'Him Whom God shall make manifest'.

† Numerically, Ḥín is equal to 68, which means the year 1268. 'After Ḥín' indicates the beginning of the year 1269. This prophecy concerning Bahá'u'lláh originated from Shaykh Aḥmad-i-Aḥsá'í.

‡ Nineteen.

§ 1280 A.H. (A.D. 1863).

Concerning the date of the coming of 'Him Whom God shall make manifest', the Báb, in the Persian *Bayán*, called upon His followers to be attentive from the inception of His own Faith until the number of Váḥid, and to hearken to the new Messenger whenever He appeared. Although the Báb frequently referred to the years nine and nineteen, He nevertheless clearly stated that the time of the coming of 'Him Whom God shall make manifest' was entirely in His own hands. Whenever He chose to manifest Himself all must turn to Him and obey His commandments. From the fortress of Máh-Kú, the Báb made this weighty pronouncement:

> Were He to appear this very moment, I would be the first to adore Him, and the first to bow down before Him.[13]

The Báb lauded in glowing terms the greatness of the Revelation of Bahá'u'lláh. He stated that nothing in the world of creation could give as much pleasure as hearing and understanding the utterances of 'Him Whom God shall make manifest', and remarked that 'A thousand perusals of the Bayán cannot equal the perusal of a single verse to be revealed by "Him Whom God shall make manifest"'.[14] In one of the chapters of the *Bayán* the Báb proclaimed that the most evident testimony to the truth of 'Him Whom God shall make manifest' would be the revelation of His words. That His followers might be aware of the exalted character of the new Revelation, and to prepare them for the coming of 'Him Whom God shall make manifest', the Báb ordained that once in every nineteen days His followers should read this particular chapter and meditate upon it.

Referring to those who might arise and announce themselves as the Promised One of the *Bayán*, the Báb confidently asserted that should anyone falsely claim this station He would be powerless to sustain it, as he would be unable to reveal the Word of God which is the greatest proof of 'Him Whom God shall make manifest'. Nevertheless, for the sake of honouring the station of 'Him Whom God shall make manifest', He ordained that if a person were to claim this station, he should be left to himself; no one should oppose him or object to his words.

Anxious to protect Bahá'u'lláh, the Báb forbade His followers to engage in heated argument and controversy, as practised among the divines of Islám, which could only result in contention and discord among them. He urged them to be chaste in their writings and courteous in their speech, especially when expressing their views or adducing proofs during discussion. His purpose in these exhortations was to ensure that the words or deeds of His followers would in no way give offence to the person of 'Him Whom God shall make manifest'. Moreover, as a token of respect for the Supreme Manifestation of God, Who would be exalted above any question His creatures might put to Him, He admonished His followers not to ask Him any questions except those worthy of His station. But Bahá'u'lláh annulled this prohibition in the *Kitáb-i-Aqdas* and permitted the believers freely to question Him.

To read the Writings of the Báb, especially the *Bayán*, is to realize that He prepared His followers in every possible way for the coming of 'Him Whom God shall make manifest'. Not only did He give them a true understanding of His station and reveal the spiritual prerequisites of worthiness to receive His Revelation, but He also instructed them on their behaviour. They should, He advised them, not only purify their inner beings from attachment to this world, but, in addition, should pay attention to their appearance and clothing so as not to offend Him.

In several passages in the *Bayán* and other Writings, the Báb mentioned Bahá'u'lláh by name and alluded to Him as 'Him Whom God shall make manifest'. All these references clearly indicate Bahá'u'lláh as the Promised One of the *Bayán* and the object of the adoration of the Báb. A striking example is to be found in the Persian *Bayán* where, in the course of a reference to 'Him Whom God shall make manifest', the Báb anticipated the establishment of a new Order by Bahá'u'lláh. These are His words:

> Well is it with him who fixeth his gaze upon the Order of Bahá'u'lláh and rendereth thanks unto his Lord! For He will assuredly be made manifest. God hath indeed irrevocably ordained it in the Bayán.[15]

Many were the tributes which the Báb paid in His Writings to the inconceivable greatness of the Revelation of 'Him Whom God shall make manifest' and numerous were the expressions of His loyalty and self-effacement towards its Author. Having recognized Him to be the Source of His inspiration, the Revealer of His Revelation, and the Object of His adoration, the Báb often craved to lay down His life as a sacrifice in the path of 'Him Whom God shall make manifest'. In the *Qayyúmu'l-Asmá'*,* described by Bahá'u'lláh as the 'first, the greatest and mightiest'[16] of the books revealed by the Báb, we find the following references to Bahá'u'lláh—'Him Whom God shall make manifest':

> Out of utter nothingness, O great and omnipotent Master, Thou hast, through the celestial potency of Thy might, brought me forth and raised me up to proclaim this Revelation. I have made none other but Thee my trust; I have clung to no will but Thy will . . . O Thou Remnant of God! I have sacrificed myself wholly for Thee; I have accepted curses for Thy sake, and have yearned for naught but martyrdom in the path of Thy love. Sufficient witness unto me is God, the Exalted, the Protector, the Ancient of Days . . .
>
> And when the appointed hour hath struck, do Thou, by the leave of God, the All-Wise, reveal from the heights of the Most Lofty and Mystic Mount a faint, an infinitesimal glimmer of Thy impenetrable Mystery, that they who have recognized the radiance of the Sinaic Splendour may faint away and die as they catch a lightening glimpse of the fierce and crimson Light that envelops Thy Revelation.[17]

The Báb in His Writings portrayed the person of 'Him Whom God shall make manifest' as majestic, awe-inspiring,

* The first chapter of this book was revealed by the Báb on the night of the Declaration of His Message to Mullá Ḥusayn, on 22 May 1844.

incomparable and infinitely glorious. Their study enables one to acquire a better grasp of the verities of the Faith of Bahá'u'lláh, although bringing to light man's inadequacy fully to appreciate the significance of His Revelation, comprehend the potency of His words, or recognize the loftiness of His station.

It was perhaps owing to this inadequacy that, at one stage during the ministry of Bahá'u'lláh, there were two major schools of thought among the believers concerning His station. Some believed Him to be the Supreme Manifestation of God, while others went further than this. When Bahá'u'lláh was asked about His station, He confirmed that as long as individuals were sincere in their beliefs, both views were right, but if they argued among themselves or tried to convert each other, both were wrong. This indicates that man because of his finite mind will never be able to understand the true station of the Manifestation of God. The criteria are sincerity and faith. Knowing man's limitations, God accepts from him what he is able to achieve.

Despite this divergence of view among the early followers of Bahá'u'lláh as to His station, attributable solely to their varying capacities to grasp so exalted a concept, it is of immense significance that the central purpose of His Revelation to bring unity to mankind was never deflected. From its earliest days the Bahá'í community was protected from division and discord, and has continued throughout its eventful history to demonstrate the cohesive and unifying influence which motivates it. Those who recognize Bahá'u'lláh and embrace His Faith come under the shelter of a unity which is spiritual in nature, which surpasses all human limitations, and is derived from the power of God's Covenant for humanity in this age.

In the Writings of the Central Figures of the Bahá'í Faith there are many references to the exalted nature of the Revelation of Bahá'u'lláh. Shoghi Effendi, the Guardian of the Faith, also elucidated this theme. Indeed, it may be said that one of his major contributions to the consolidation of the Faith was his clear explanation concerning the significance of the Revelation of Bahá'u'lláh. In his momentous work, *The Dispensation of Bahá'u'lláh*, he placed in right perspective every aspect of the Revelation: its Founders, its institutions, its guiding principles, its aims and purposes and its ultimate destiny. Prior to his elucidation and guidance, no coherent pattern was available to Bahá'ís for the proper and systematic study of their Faith. It was Shoghi Effendi who adapted the stupendous Revelation of Bahá'u'lláh to the limited capacity of man in this age, helped to canalize the outpourings of its spiritual energy, and enabled the believers to bring into focus their vision of the Faith, and to understand its workings.

The following is an extract from one of Shoghi Effendi's masterly expositions concerning the Revelation of Bahá'u'lláh and His station:

> He* Who in such dramatic circumstances was made to sustain the overpowering weight of so glorious a Mission was none other than the One Whom posterity will acclaim, and Whom innumerable followers already recognize, as the Judge, the Lawgiver and Redeemer of all mankind, as the Organizer of the entire planet, as the Unifier of the children of men, as the Inaugurator of the long-awaited millennium, as the Originator of a new 'Universal Cycle,' as the Establisher of the Most Great Peace, as the Fountain of the Most Great Justice, as the Proclaimer of the coming of age of the entire human race, as the Creator of a new World Order, and as the Inspirer and Founder of a world civilization.
>
> To Israel He was neither more nor less than the incarnation of the 'Everlasting Father,' the 'Lord of Hosts' come down 'with ten thousands of saints'; to Christendom Christ returned 'in the glory of the Father,' to Shí'ah Islám the return of the Imám Ḥusayn; to Sunní Islám the descent of the 'Spirit of God' (Jesus Christ); to the Zoroastrians the promised Sháh-Bahrám; to the Hindus the reincarnation of Krishna; to the Buddhists the fifth Buddha.

* Bahá'u'lláh.

In the name He bore He combined those of the Imám Ḥusayn, the most illustrious of the successors of the Apostle of God—the brightest 'star' shining in the 'crown' mentioned in the Revelation of St. John—and of the Imám 'Alí, the Commander of the Faithful, the second of the two 'witnesses' extolled in that same Book. He was formally designated Bahá'u'lláh, an appellation specifically recorded in the Persian Bayán, signifying at once the glory, the light and the splendour of God, and was styled the 'Lord of Lords,' the 'Most Great Name,' the 'Ancient Beauty,' the 'Pen of the Most High,' the 'Hidden Name,' the 'Preserved Treasure,' 'He Whom God will make manifest,' the 'Most Great Light,' the 'All-Highest Horizon,' the 'Most Great Ocean,' the 'Supreme Heaven,' the 'Pre-Existent Root,' the 'Self-Subsistent,' the 'Day-Star of the Universe,' the 'Great Announcement,' the 'Speaker on Sinai,' the 'Sifter of Men,' the 'Wronged One of the World,' the 'Desire of the Nations,' the 'Lord of the Covenant,' the 'Tree beyond which there is no passing.' He derived His descent, on the one hand, from Abraham (the Father of the Faithful) through his wife Katurah, and on the other from Zoroaster, as well as from Yazdigird, the last king of the Sásáníyán dynasty. He was moreover a descendant of Jesse, and belonged, through His father, Mírzá 'Abbás, better known as Mírzá Buzurg—a nobleman closely associated with the ministerial circles of the Court of Fatḥ-'Alí Sháh—to one of the most ancient and renowned families of Mázindarán.

To Him Isaiah, the greatest of the Jewish prophets, had alluded as the '*Glory of the Lord*,' the '*Everlasting Father*,' the '*Prince of Peace*,' the '*Wonderful*,' the '*Counsellor*,' the '*Rod come forth out of the stem of Jesse*' and the '*Branch grown out of His roots*,' Who '*shall be established upon the throne of David*,' Who '*will come with strong hand*,' Who '*shall judge among the nations*,' Who '*shall smite the earth with the rod of His mouth, and with the breath of His lips slay the wicked*,' and Who '*shall assemble the outcasts of Israel, and gather together the dispersed of Judah from the four corners of the earth*.' Of Him David had sung in his Psalms, acclaiming Him as the '*Lord of Hosts*' and the '*King of Glory*'. . .

To Him Jesus Christ had referred as the '*Prince of this world*,' as the '*Comforter*' Who will '*reprove the world of sin, and of righteousness, and of judgment*,' as the '*Spirit of Truth*' Who '*will guide you into all truth*,' Who '*shall not speak of Himself, but whatsoever He shall hear, that shall He speak*,' as the '*Lord of the vineyard*,' and as the '*Son of Man*' Who '*shall come in the glory of His Father*' '*in the clouds of heaven with power and great glory*,' with '*all the holy angels*' about Him, and '*all nations*' gathered before His throne. To Him the Author of the Apocalypse had alluded as the '*Glory of God*,' as '*Alpha and Omega*,' '*the Beginning and the End*,' '*the First and the Last*.' Identifying His Revelation with the '*third woe*,' he, moreover, had extolled His Law as '*a new heaven and a new earth*,' as the '*Tabernacle of God*,' as the '*Holy City*,' as the '*New Jerusalem, coming down from God out of heaven, prepared as a bride adorned for her husband*.' To His Day Jesus Christ Himself had referred as '*the regeneration when the Son of Man shall sit in the throne of His glory*'. . .

To Him Muḥammad, the Apostle of God, had alluded in His Book as the '*Great Announcement*,' and declared His Day to be the Day whereon '*God*' will '*come down*' '*overshadowed with clouds*,' the Day whereon '*thy Lord shall come and the angels rank on rank*,' and '*The Spirit shall arise and the angels shall be ranged in order*' . . .

The plenitude of His glory the Apostle of God* had, moreover, as attested by Bahá'u'lláh Himself, compared to the '*full moon on its fourteenth night*.' His station the Imám 'Alí, the Commander of the Faithful, had, according to the same testimony, identified with '*Him Who conversed with Moses from the Burning Bush on Sinai*.' To the transcendent character of His mission the Imám Ḥusayn had, again according to Bahá'u'lláh, borne witness as a '*Revelation whose Revealer will be He Who revealed*' the Apostle of God* Himself . . .

The Báb had no less significantly extolled Him as the '*Essence of Being*,' as the '*Remnant of God*,' as the '*Omnipotent Master*,' as the '*Crimson, all-encompassing Light*,' as '*Lord of the visible and invisible*,' as the '*sole Object of all previous Revelations, including the Revelation of the Qá'im Himself*.' He had formally designated Him as '*He Whom God shall make manifest*,' had

* Muḥammad.

alluded to Him as the '*Abhá Horizon*' wherein He Himself lived and dwelt, had specifically recorded His title, and eulogized His '*Order*' in His best-known work, the Persian Bayán, had disclosed His name through His allusion to the '*Son of 'Alí, a true and undoubted Leader of men*,' had, repeatedly, orally and in writing, fixed, beyond the shadow of a doubt, the time of His Revelation, and warned His followers lest '*the Bayán and all that hath been revealed therein*' should '*shut them out as by a veil*' from Him. He had, moreover, declared that He was the '*first servant to believe in Him*,' that He bore Him allegiance '*before all things were created*,' that '*no allusion*' of His '*could allude unto Him*,' that '*the year-old germ that holdeth within itself the potentialities of the Revelation that is to come is endowed with a potency superior to the combined forces of the whole of the Bayán*.' He had, moreover, clearly asserted that He had '*covenanted with all created things*' concerning Him Whom God shall make manifest ere the covenant concerning His own mission had been established. He had readily acknowledged that He was but '*a letter*' of that '*Most Mighty Book*,' '*a dew-drop*' from that '*Limitless Ocean*,' that His Revelation was '*only a leaf amongst the leaves of His Paradise*,' that '*all that hath been exalted in the Bayán*' was but '*a ring*' upon His own hand, and He Himself '*a ring upon the hand of Him Whom God shall make manifest*,' Who '*turneth it as He pleaseth, for whatsoever He pleaseth, and through whatsoever He pleaseth*.' He had unmistakably declared that He had '*sacrificed*' Himself '*wholly*' for Him, that He had '*consented to be cursed*' for His sake, and to have '*yearned for naught but martyrdom*' in the path of His love. Finally, He had unequivocally prophesied: '*Today the Bayán is in the stage of seed; at the beginning of the manifestation of Him Whom God shall make manifest its ultimate perfection will become apparent*.' '*Ere nine will have elapsed from the inception of this Cause the realities of the created things will not be made manifest. All that thou hast as yet seen is but the stage from the moist-germ until We clothed it with flesh. Be patient until thou beholdest a new creation. Say: Blessed, therefore, be God, the Most Excellent of Makers!*'

'*He around Whom the Point of the Bayán* (Báb) *hath revolved is come*' is Bahá'u'lláh's confirmatory testimony to the inconceivable greatness and preeminent character of His own

Revelation. '*If all who are in heaven and on earth,*' He moreover affirms, '*be invested in this day with the powers and attributes destined for the Letters of the Bayán, whose station is ten thousand times more glorious than that of the Letters of the Qur'ánic Dispensation, and if they one and all should, swift as the twinkling of an eye, hesitate to recognize My Revelation, they shall be accounted, in the sight of God, of those that have gone astray, and regarded as "Letters of Negation."*' '*Powerful is He, the King of Divine might,*' He, alluding to Himself in the Kitáb-i-Íqán, asserts, '*to extinguish with one letter of His wondrous words, the breath of life in the whole of the Bayán and the people thereof, and with one letter bestow upon them a new and everlasting life, and cause them to arise and speed out of the sepulchres of their vain and selfish desires.*' '*This,*' He furthermore declares, '*is the king of days,*' the '*Day of God Himself,*' the '*Day which shall never be followed by night,*' the '*Springtime which autumn will never overtake,*' '*the eye to past ages and centuries,*' for which '*the soul of every Prophet of God, of every Divine Messenger, hath thirsted,*' for which '*all the divers kindreds of the earth have yearned,*' through which '*God hath proved the hearts of the entire company of His Messengers and Prophets, and beyond them those that stand guard over His sacred and inviolable Sanctuary, the inmates of the Celestial Pavilion and dwellers of the Tabernacle of Glory.*' '*In this most mighty Revelation,*' He, moreover, states, '*all the Dispensations of the past have attained their highest, their final consummation.*' And again: '*None among the Manifestations of old, except to a prescribed degree, hath ever completely apprehended the nature of this Revelation.*' Referring to His own station He declares: '*But for Him no Divine Messenger would have been invested with the Robe of Prophethood, nor would any of the sacred Scriptures have been revealed.*'

And last but not least is 'Abdu'l-Bahá's own tribute to the transcendent character of the Revelation identified with His Father: '*Centuries, nay ages, must pass away, ere the Day-Star of Truth shineth again in its mid-summer splendour, or appeareth once more in the radiance of its vernal glory.*' '*The mere contemplation of the Dispensation inaugurated by the Blessed Beauty,*' He furthermore affirms, '*would have sufficed to overwhelm the saints of bygone ages—saints who longed to partake for one moment of its great glory.*'[18]

Bahá'í Writings contain several references to Bahá'u'lláh as the universal Manifestation of God, Who inaugurated a new and universal cycle in human history. 'Abdu'l-Bahá has explained this in answer to a question:

> Briefly, we say a universal cycle in the world of existence signifies a long duration of time, and innumerable and incalculable periods and epochs. In such a cycle the Manifestations appear with splendour in the realm of the visible, until a great and universal Manifestation makes the world the centre of His radiance. His appearance causes the world to attain to maturity, and the extension of His cycle is very great. Afterwards other Manifestations will arise under His shadow, who according to the needs of the time will renew certain commandments relating to material questions and affairs, while remaining under His shadow.[19]

Not only is Bahá'u'lláh the Author of the Bahá'í Dispensation whose duration, according to His own testimony, will be at least one thousand years, but He is also the Inaugurator of a universal cycle which is referred to as the Bahá'í Cycle. 'Abdu'l-Bahá mentions that the duration of this cycle will be at least five thousand centuries. During this period several Manifestations of God will appear, Who, while founding independent religions, will yet derive their inspiration from Bahá'u'lláh. In a Tablet 'Abdu'l-Bahá has made the following statement:

> Concerning the Manifestations that will come down in the future 'in the shadows of the clouds', know verily that in so far as their relation to the source of their inspiration is concerned they are under the shadow of the Ancient Beauty.* In their relation, however, to the age in which they appear, each and every one of them 'doeth whatsoever He willeth'.[20]

In the light of the above statements it becomes clear that Bahá'u'lláh, through His own Revelation, is the source of spiritual life for mankind during the Bahá'í Dispensation. He will also remain the motivating force in future Dispensations

* Bahá'u'lláh.

and will release progressively, through the advent of other Manifestations of God, spiritual energies for the advancement of the human race throughout the Bahá'í Cycle. It is a central tenet of Bahá'í belief that the reality of the Manifestations of God is one and the same and that They differ only in the intensity of Their Revelations, each One manifesting the attributes of God in accordance with the capacity and receptivity of the people of His age. At first sight, this belief may not seem to accord with the statement that future Manifestations will be under the shadow of Bahá'u'lláh, while yet bringing new laws and teachings for mankind, each One inaugurating a new era within the Bahá'í Cycle. But let us look more closely.

The coming of a Manifestation of God may be likened to the appearance of spring in the physical realm. In the same way that the world of nature receives new life at each springtime, so humanity becomes refreshed and revivified by the advent of each Manifestation of God. We observe in nature that, as a result of the succession of seasons year after year, a tree grows progressively until it reaches a stage when it bears fruit for the first time. This is an event of great consequence, for the tree has reached its maturity and will throughout its life continue to produce similar fruits each year.

Similarly, man has grown progressively and step by step as a result of the appearance of the Manifestations of God. The Revelation of Bahá'u'lláh occurs in an era when mankind is destined to come of age, a stage similar to that when the tree blossoms and first gives its fruit. Therefore, whatever mankind may achieve as a result of the outpouring of the Revelation of Bahá'u'lláh, whatever fruit the tree of humanity may yield during the Golden Age of His Dispensation, will provide the foundation for progress in future Dispensations. The study of the Writings will demonstrate that the ultimate objective of Bahá'u'lláh, so far as life on this planet is concerned, is the establishment of the oneness of mankind. This will be the fruit of His Revelation in relation to the structure of human society, the furthermost goal humanity can attain on this earth.

In Dispensations to come, man, as a result of the appearance of future Manifestations of God, will continue to develop and progress. He will acquire noble qualities and will grow spiritually to such a degree that none today can visualize the heights to which he will attain; yet he will function within the framework of the oneness of mankind established by Bahá'u'lláh, and the Manifestations of God Who appear from age to age during the Bahá'í Cycle will remain under His shadow.

Bahá'u'lláh, addressing His own generation, has affirmed the nature of the enduring foundation He has laid for mankind:

> O ye children of men, the fundamental purpose animating the Faith of God and His Religion is to safeguard the interests and promote the unity of the human race . . . This is the straight path, the fixed and immovable foundation. Whatsoever is raised on this foundation, the changes and chances of the world can never impair its strength, nor will the revolution of countless centuries undermine its structure.[21]

The following illuminating passage, composed by Shoghi Effendi concerning the Revelation of Bahá'u'lláh and its significance, in which he has quoted utterances of Bahá'u'lláh, emphasizes the pre-eminent character of this august Revelation:

> The Faith of Bahá'u'lláh should indeed be regarded, if we wish to be faithful to the tremendous implications of its message, as the culmination of a cycle, the final stage in a series of successive, of preliminary and progressive revelations. These, beginning with Adam and ending with the Báb, have paved the way and anticipated with an ever-increasing emphasis the advent of that Day of Days in which He Who is the Promise of All Ages should be made manifest.
>
> To this truth the utterances of Bahá'u'lláh abundantly testify. A mere reference to the claims which, in vehement language and with compelling power, He Himself has repeatedly advanced cannot but fully demonstrate the character of the Revelation of which He was the chosen bearer. To the words that have streamed from His pen—the fountainhead of so impetuous a Revelation—we should, therefore, direct

our attention if we wish to obtain a clearer understanding of its importance and meaning. Whether in His assertion of the unprecedented claim He has advanced, or in His allusions to the mysterious forces He has released, whether in such passages as extol the glories of His long-awaited Day, or magnify the station which they who have recognized its hidden virtues will attain, Bahá'u'lláh and, to an almost equal extent, the Báb and 'Abdu'l-Bahá, have bequeathed to posterity mines of such inestimable wealth as none of us who belong to this generation can befittingly estimate. Such testimonies bearing on this theme are impregnated with such power and reveal such beauty as only those who are versed in the languages in which they were originally revealed can claim to have sufficiently appreciated. So numerous are these testimonies that a whole volume would be required to be written in order to compile the most outstanding among them. All I can venture to attempt at present is to share with you only such passages as I have been able to glean from His voluminous writings.

'*I testify before God*,' proclaims Bahá'u'lláh, '*to the greatness, the inconceivable greatness of this Revelation. Again and again have We in most of Our Tablets borne witness to this truth, that mankind may be roused from its heedlessness.*' '*In this most mighty Revelation*,' He unequivocally announces, '*all the Dispensations of the past have attained their highest, their final consummation.*' '*That which hath been made manifest in this preëminent, this most exalted Revelation, stands unparalleled in the annals of the past, nor will future ages witness its like.*' '*He it is*,' referring to Himself He further proclaims, '*Who in the Old Testament hath been named Jehovah, Who in the Gospel hath been designated as the Spirit of Truth, and in the Qur'án acclaimed as the Great Announcement.*' '*But for Him no Divine Messenger would have been invested with the robe of prophethood, nor would any of the sacred scriptures have been revealed. To this bear witness all created things.*' '*The word which the one true God uttereth in this day, though that word be the most familiar and commonplace of terms, is invested with supreme, with unique distinction.*' '*The generality of mankind is still immature. Had it acquired sufficient capacity We would have bestowed upon it so great a measure of Our knowledge that all who dwell on earth and in heaven would have found themselves, by virtue of the grace streaming from Our pen, completely independent of all knowledge save the knowledge of God, and would have been securely established upon the throne of abiding tranquillity.' 'The Pen of Holiness, I solemnly affirm before God, hath writ upon My snow-white brow and in characters of effulgent glory these glowing, these musk-scented and holy words: "Behold ye that dwell on earth, and ye denizens of heaven, bear witness, He in truth is your Well-Beloved. He it is Whose like the world of creation hath not seen, He Whose ravishing beauty hath delighted the eye of God, the Ordainer, the All-Powerful, the Incomparable!"'*[22]

These utterances of Bahá'u'lláh, testifying to the greatness of His Cause, invoke feelings of awe and wonder in the hearts of His followers as they contemplate the enormous potentialities with which His Revelation has invested the human race. It is destined to cast its light upon countless centuries and ages, stretching into the far reaches of time. Its Herald, the Báb, the Primal Point 'round Whom the realities of the Prophets and Messengers revolve',[23] sounded the trumpet-call of the dawn of the New Day and through His martyrdom shed an imperishable lustre upon it. Its Author, Bahá'u'lláh, 'the Glory of God', manifesting an 'infinitesimal glimmer' of His 'impenetrable Mystery',[24] ushered in the Day of God, brought into being a new creation, breathed into it a new life, revealed the Laws and Teachings designed to advance the interests and safeguard the unity of the human race, and laid an enduring foundation for many millenniums to come. The Centre of its Covenant, 'Abdu'l-Bahá, 'the incarnation of every Bahá'í virtue and the embodiment of every Bahá'í ideal',[25] protected it from the onslaught of the unfaithful, projected its light across the Western world and delineated the features of its Administrative Order, the nucleus and pattern of the future global Order to be established on this planet.

The rising institutions of this Administrative Order, local, national and international, are being reared upon the ruins of the old order by Bahá'u'lláh's faithful supporters, in full confidence that the creative energies dwelling within His Revelation will, through Divine power, ultimately transform human society, at present so disillusioned and unstable, into a world community united in all its aspects, and destined to attain, in centuries to come, its Golden Age, the long-awaited Kingdom of God on earth.

APPENDIX I

Mírzá Áqá Ján

Following the ascension of Bahá'u'lláh, and as a result of Muḥammad-'Alí's rebellion,* several outstanding teachers of the Faith, including some of Bahá'u'lláh's companions, broke His Covenant. They rose against 'Abdu'l-Bahá and created great havoc within the Bahá'í community. But the Covenant of Bahá'u'lláh was firmly based and many heroic souls, devoted and faithful, rallied around 'Abdu'l-Bahá to defend the Covenant against the onslaught of the unfaithful.

Among all the companions of Bahá'u'lláh, Mírzá Áqá Ján was the only one who had been in close association with Him and was privileged to be His amanuensis. Yet in spite of this great honour bestowed upon him, his pride and ambition prevented him from standing firm in the Covenant, and he opposed 'Abdu'l-Bahá and created much confusion in the minds of Bahá'ís.

Dr. Yúnis Khán-i-Afrúkhtih, a devoted believer during the ministry of 'Abdu'l-Bahá, who served the Master as secretary for several years, has left a most interesting account of the events which took place during his nine years of service in 'Akká. The following is a translation of an extract from his memoirs concerning Mírzá Áqá Ján's later years in 'Akká, around 1897:

> . . . At the time of the passing of Bahá'u'lláh, Mírzá Áqá Ján, who had fallen from grace, was living an ignominious life. However, as a result of Bahá'u'lláh's generosity, he had a reasonable income. The Covenant-breakers had secretly resolved to take his life. Probably the reason for this was either

* The reader may consult *God Passes By*, pp. 244–51, by Shoghi Effendi, for information about this situation.

to seize his properties or because Bahá'u'lláh had not been pleased with his conduct towards the end of His life. Mírzá Áqá Ján discovered their plot and went immediately to 'Abdu'l-Bahá, begged forgiveness for his misdeeds and took refuge in His house . . .

Later, the Covenant-breakers decided to take advantage of Mírzá Áqá Ján's situation to create trouble and mischief [for 'Abdu'l-Bahá] . . . They succeeded in establishing a secret link with him and urged him to help them in stirring up sedition among believers. They maintained communication with him and, over a long period, devised a plan to create discord and disturbance within the community. Since Mírzá Áqá Ján had been Bahá'u'lláh's amanuensis and had recorded the words of God as they were revealed, he was induced to arise and himself lay claim to divine revelation.

As a result of their promptings, Mírzá Áqá Ján, this ill-fated man, worked for a long time to prepare some writings. In these he claimed that in a dream he had attained the presence of Bahá'u'lláh and had become the recipient of divine revelation and inspiration. These writings contained passages which invoked the wrath of God upon certain believers and were intended to be delivered to them.

Mírzá Áqá Ján even claimed that he had received a Tablet from heaven written in green ink, in which he was commanded to save the Faith from the hands of infidels. The false accusations and calumnies with which he charged 'Abdu'l-Bahá, the Centre of the Covenant, were much worse than those which Covenant-breakers had already brought against Him. It was arranged that on a certain day, which should be the time of revolt, Mírzá Áqá Ján would hand all these papers written in the same style as his 'Revelation writings' to the Covenant-breakers who would then have them transcribed, as in the days of Bahá'u'lláh, in the handwriting of Mírzá Majdi'd-Dín* and disseminated among the Bahá'ís.[1]

* He was the son of Mírzá Músá, Áqáy-i-Kalím, Bahá'u'lláh's faithful brother, who for a time transcribed the Tablets of Bahá'u'lláh, but later became 'the most redoubtable adversary of 'Abdu'l-Bahá'. He was a staunch supporter of Muḥammad-'Alí, the arch-breaker of the Covenant.

Dr. Yúnis Khán, in his memoirs, goes on to explain that the Covenant-breakers had decided to put their plans into operation on the day of the anniversary of the ascension of Bahá'u'lláh. They knew that all the believers would then be assembled outside the Shrine of Bahá'u'lláh, and so they planned with Mírzá Áqá Ján that he should speak openly against 'Abdu'l-Bahá in that gathering, in order to create tension and unrest. At the same time the Covenant-breakers made arrangements for a certain Yaḥyá Ṭábúr Áqásí to be present on that day. He was a high-ranking government official hostile to 'Abdu'l-Bahá but friendly towards them. His function was to remain out of sight until the expected disturbances had broken out, when he and his men would appear on the scene and take action against the believers. He would then send a report against 'Abdu'l-Bahá to government authorities in Constantinople and request His banishment from the Holy Land.

The following is Dr. Yúnis Khán's description of his first meeting with Mírzá Áqá Ján and of the events which took place on the anniversary of the ascension of Bahá'u'lláh, when a great tragedy was quietly and effectively diverted:

> . . . On most occasions when we were summoned to the presence of 'Abdu'l-Bahá in His reception-room, I noticed that an old man, short in stature, with a white beard and brown complexion, arrived in the room after everyone else. First he would prostrate himself at the threshold of the room ['Abdu'l-Bahá's], then he would enter, bow to the waist and, when 'Abdu'l-Bahá acknowledged him, sit at the threshold. I was curious to know who this person was and several times it occurred to me that when I left the room I should inquire of the resident believers as to his identity. For some time, however, I forgot to ask. This was due to the fact that we were so intoxicated by the wine of the Master's bounteous utterances that when we left Him we were not in a mood to talk to each other.
>
> One day I was sitting [in the presence of 'Abdu'l-Bahá] very close to the entrance of the room. I saw the old man arriving.

At first he prostrated himself at the entrance to the corridor, then approached the room and again prostrated himself at its threshold. He then entered, bowed low before 'Abdu'l-Bahá and stood there until 'Abdu'l-Bahá indicated to him to be seated, whereupon he sat with downcast eyes near the door . . . By this time I was very curious to know who this person was, and why I had not seen him among the believers in the town.

When we all left the presence of the Master, I noticed that this man went into the inner section of the house. I asked someone about him and was told that he was Mírzá Áqá Ján . . . I questioned my friends further, asking what Mírzá Áqá Ján was doing here. Is he not, I asked, the person who was rejected by Bahá'u'lláh and whom the Covenant-breakers were intent upon murdering? They told me that he had now taken refuge in the house of the Master. In those days I often thought about Mírzá Áqá Ján, who had fallen from grace, and wondered what would happen to him in the end. How little did I know then that, in a fortnight's time, he would play an important and unforgettable role in the arena of the Cause and that I myself would be one of the spectators.[2]

In his detailed narratives, Dr. Yúnis Khán describes how on the night of the anniversary of the passing of Bahá'u'lláh, as in previous years, all the believers in the area gathered together in 'Akká and, before dawn, set out for the Shrine of Bahá'u'lláh accompanied by 'Abdu'l-Bahá. In that holy place they prayed until sunrise, and then retired to the pilgrims' quarters at Bahjí.

Here is Dr. Yúnis Khán's account of what transpired that day:

. . . After lunch we were seated for a short while . . . We noticed that the Covenant-breakers were moving actively around us and that there were also a number of strangers. It was not very long before we learned of their plans to create mischief.

Having had afternoon tea, everyone was on the point of going to the Shrine of Bahá'u'lláh, when we heard that

Mírzá Áqá Ján wished to speak and that there were chairs placed for us in front of the Mansion.

This old man who was always prostrating himself at the feet of 'Abdu'l-Bahá was now standing on a stool so that he might be seen by all . . . As he spoke I noticed that he was far from coherent and I waited to catch the import of his words, but eventually became frustrated . . . I could see that he was filled with fear and was trembling, but I could hear only a few words now and then, such as: 'As I prostrated myself, I fell asleep . . .' 'The Blessed Beauty told me . . .' 'This letter in green ink was handed to me . . .' 'Why are you sitting idle?' 'Why, why?' Having abstained from sleep the night before, and having now to listen to such ridiculous talk, I became impatient and left. Mírzá Maḥmúd-i-Káshání, a resident believer, protested to Mírzá Áqá Ján and soon there was an uproar.[3]

Dr. Yúnis Khán adds that just then one of the believers informed 'Abdu'l-Bahá of the incident. As soon as 'Abdu'l-Bahá appeared, Mírzá Áqá Ján ran towards the Shrine of Bahá'u'lláh and went inside. A certain Mírzá 'Alí-Akbar, a steadfast believer, immediately ran after him and was able to obtain from Mírzá Áqá Ján the writings which were tied in bundles around his waist and hidden inside his cloak. These papers, which were handed to 'Abdu'l-Bahá, were written in the same style as Bahá'u'lláh's writings, contained many passages attacking 'Abdu'l-Bahá, and were prepared for distribution among the believers.

As a result of 'Abdu'l-Bahá's presence the Bahá'ís were calmed within a few minutes. Mírzá Áqá Ján went to the Covenant-breakers, and the government officials who were standing behind the window of Mírzá Muḥammad-'Alí's room found no opportunity to carry out their sinister designs. After this event Mírzá Áqá Ján threw in his lot with the Covenant-breakers and became one of their ablest supporters. He died in 1901.

APPENDIX II*

Ḥájí Muḥammad-Ṭáhir-i-Málmírí

Ḥájí Muḥammad-Ṭáhir-i-Málmírí lived, laboured, and passed away in the ancient town of Yazd, Írán, a town notorious for its religious fanaticism and its large number of mullás. He was born there about the year 1852, which witnessed the inception of the mission of Bahá'u'lláh, and lived there long enough to see the centenary celebration of that Holy Year. Known to almost every citizen, no other Bahá'í in Yazd was so dearly loved and admired by the friends, and so bitterly denounced and insulted by the foes.

Fortified by his staunch faith, animated by his intense desire to serve the Cause, sustained by the guiding Hand of Bahá'u'lláh, undaunted in the face of dire sufferings, his life and conduct served to perpetuate the spirit of the apostolic age to which he belonged. His life was wholly dedicated to the Cause. The idea uppermost in his mind always was that of teaching. No power, no preoccupation, no conventional matter of daily life could ever deflect him from this high purpose. His teaching exploits were so intensive that today, a large section of the Bahá'í community of Yazd owes to his life-long effort its allegiance to the Cause.

Ḥájí Muḥammad-Ṭáhir was a brilliant debater and speaker. It is difficult to convey the pleasure one derived from his inspiring conversation which ranged from humorous trifles to weighty pronouncements. His knowledge of the history and literature of the great world religions was prodigious. He could

* This account is taken from *The Bahá'í World*, vol. XII, pp. 692–4. The transliteration of Ḥájí Muḥammad-Ṭáhir's name has been changed to conform with that used in this book.

recite almost half the Qur'án by heart, as well as hundreds of recorded Muslim traditions. Also he was extremely well-versed in the Bible and the books of other religions. The source from which he drew his energy seemed to be inexhaustible. He could speak for hours about religious matters without either feeling tired himself or boring his listeners. Rather they were fascinated by the gaiety of his conversation and by the ripple of his ready and eloquent tongue. Even the enemies of the Cause were silenced and subdued by his charm and dignity. On several occasions fanatical persons, intent on carrying out sinister plots against his life, came to his fireside meetings in the guise of seekers of truth, carrying weapons in their pockets. After coming in contact with his dominating personality, however, they changed their minds altogether, and strangely enough, a couple of them eventually became ardent believers.

But Ḥájí Muḥammad-Ṭáhir's talks were not always honeyed. There are few, if any, among the leading Muslim priests in Yazd who, at one time or another, have not felt the sting of his taunts and retorts or were not drawn into his entangling net, only to emerge with their wings clipped, utterly confounded by the amazing force of his argument.

At the height of his teaching career, almost every evening he used to attend fireside meetings which usually lasted till after midnight. Whenever he was free at night or returned home rather early, he would keep awake well into the small hours of the morning, either pacing the compound of his modest house in prayer and meditation or sitting up to read or write.

His pen was as ready and able as his tongue, and his voluminous writings are direct, lively and inspiring. Famous among his works is the *History of the Martyrs of Yazd*, a moving portrayal of one of the most revolting episodes in Bahá'í history. His *Memoirs*, written during the second World War and containing a wealth of choice reminiscences, has been designated by the beloved Guardian an interesting storehouse of information for future Bahá'í historians. Another enduring work, undertaken at the behest of the National Spiritual Assembly of Írán, is the history of the inception and growth of the Faith in his native district. Compiled in two volumes, it depicts the lives, achievements, sufferings and martyrdom of the early heroes and pioneers in that area. Also his *Fusul Arbá'ih** is a masterly exposition of proofs demonstrating the prophetic mission of the Founder and Herald of our Faith with profuse quotations from various religious books used in support of his thesis.

The crowning glory of his life was the rare privilege of attaining the presence of Bahá'u'lláh in the year 1878 in 'Akká, where he stayed for about nine months. The wonderful events and experiences associated with this momentous pilgrimage, no less than his contact with the mysterious power emanating from the person of Bahá'u'lláh, made a deep and abiding impression upon his whole being and served him as a source of inspiration and spiritual enlightenment, enabling him to steer his way steadily and triumphantly amid the perils and cross currents of his eventful life.

The remarkable feature of his interviews with Bahá'u'lláh is the fact that overcome by His dazzling greatness, he seldom dared to look at His Face or to utter a single word. Rather he would approach Him in a sense of spiritual discernment. In his thrilling *Memoirs* he states: 'Whenever I came into the presence of the Blessed Beauty if there were anything I wanted to ask, I would say it by way of the heart and He would answer me invariably. I was so deeply impressed by His supreme power that I always sat in His presence spell-bound, oblivious of myself.' Once he entreated Bahá'u'lláh that he might be granted the privilege of laying down his life for the Cause as a martyr. 'You shall live long to teach the Cause,' was His prompt reply. In fact he did live long—a hundred years—and did distinguish himself in teaching and serving the Cause with exemplary devotion. The wonderful Tablets revealed in his name by both Bahá'u'lláh and 'Abdu'l-Bahá and the letters from the beloved Guardian, all bear ample testimony to his noble life of service.

Early in 1914 Ḥájí Muḥammad-Ṭáhir went on his second

* *Fuṣúl-i-Arba'ib.*

pilgrimage to the Holy Land where he basked for four months in the sunshine of 'Abdu'l-Bahá's unbounded blessings and love.

Rank and fortune, in the material sense, never came Ḥájí Muḥammad-Ṭáhir's way. He used to earn his modest living mainly by working as a hand weaver. Yet, whenever he managed to secure some bushels of grain or other provisions for our daily use, nobody was allowed to touch them until he had set aside a substantial portion for the poor of the town as well as the needy among the martyrs' widows and orphans.

After the terrible Bahá'í massacre in Yazd which occurred soon after the turn of the century, 'Abdu'l-Bahá appointed Ḥájí Muḥammad-Ṭáhir to look after the hapless, terror-stricken remnants of the martyrs' families. For several years he devoted himself to the arduous task of organizing help for the poor, comforting the bereaved, tending the sick, and rearing and educating the children. He derived ample pleasure from giving food, money and clothing to the needy and distressed. Everybody was welcome to his home and his table. The words of praise and admiration which streamed from the Pen of 'Abdu'l-Bahá in appreciation of his beneficent work stand as a glowing testimony to his sense of love and devotion to the downtrodden.

Throughout the rugged years of his life Ḥájí Muḥammad-Ṭáhir seems to have joined in permanent wedlock with adversity. The lifelong sufferings he bore at the hands of the enemies, the insults and indignities to which he was subjected at every turn, the perilous adventures he went through, the grievous loss of three children who perished during the Bahá'í massacre in Yazd, the weight of chains and imprisonment he joyfully accepted towards the end of his life in company with the fellow-members of the Spiritual Assembly of Yazd—these together with many other distressing events, far from dampening his spirits, served to steel his energies and to reveal the true measure of his indomitable faith.

The evening of his life was dimmed by years of declining faculties and infirmity. Sinking beneath the gathering weight of old age and ill health, he laid down the burden he carried so worthily for nearly eighty years and passed away peacefully at his home on June 4, 1953. In his will he bequeathed all his possessions to the Cause . . .

—Habib Taherzadeh

APPENDIX III

Vaḥíd

Siyyid Yaḥyáy-i-Dárábí, surnamed Vaḥíd (Peerless) and referred to by Bahá'u'lláh as 'that unique and peerless figure of his age', was an outstanding divine who embraced the Cause of the Báb and became one of the greatest luminaries of His Dispensation. He was a man of great learning and erudition and was particularly gifted with a remarkable memory. Of him it is authoritatively stated that he knew almost the whole of the *Qur'án* by heart and had committed to memory no less than thirty thousand traditions of Islám. He was venerated by the public and highly esteemed and trusted in royal circles.

The impact of the Message of the Báb upon the people of Persia was so tremendous that shortly after His return from Mecca the whole country was stirred to its depths. Nabíl-i-A'ẓam in his narratives has recorded the following concerning those days:

> A wave of passionate enquiry swayed the minds and hearts of both the leaders and the masses of the people. Amazement and wonder had seized those who had heard from the lips of the immediate messengers of the Báb the tales of those signs and testimonies which had heralded the birth of His Manifestation. The dignitaries of State and Church either attended in person or delegated their ablest representatives to enquire into the truth and character of this remarkable Movement.
>
> Muḥammad Sháh himself was moved to ascertain the veracity of these reports and to enquire into their nature. He delegated Siyyid Yaḥyáy-i-Dárábí, the most learned, the most eloquent, and the most influential of his subjects, to interview the Báb and to report to him the results of his investigations.

The Sháh had implicit confidence in his impartiality, in his competence and profound spiritual insight. He occupied a position of such pre-eminence among the leading figures in Persia that at whatever meeting he happened to be present, no matter how great the number of the ecclesiastical leaders who attended it, he was invariably its chief speaker. None would dare to assert his views in his presence. They all reverently observed silence before him; all testified to his sagacity, his unsurpassed knowledge and mature wisdom.[1]

Vaḥíd was staying in Ṭihrán, as a guest of the monarch himself, when he was delegated to proceed to Shíráz and interview the Báb. It is reported that the Sháh gave him a horse, a sword and the sum of one hundred túmáns for the journey. To comply with his wishes, Vaḥíd set out immediately for Shíráz, visiting on his way his home* in Yazd where his wife and four sons were living. In that city great numbers came to hear him speak about his mission. A brief account of this meeting is reported in the *Táríkh-i-Shuhadáy-i-Yazd* (History of the Martyrs of Yazd):

> ...Vaḥíd, mounted and carrying his sword, followed by a few dignitaries arrived at Muṣalláy-i-Ṣafdar-Khán, a well known place where thousands of people had gathered to hear him. There he said: 'O inhabitants of Yazd, a certain distinguished Siyyid in Shíráz has claimed to be the Promised Qá'im. I am intending to go to Shíráz to have an interview with Him. If I find him to be an impostor, I shall deal with him with this sword but if I find His claim to be true I shall be willing to give my life in His path. I will be leaving shortly and anyone who wishes to accompany me on this journey may do so.' The crowd unanimously asserted their confidence in him and announced their feelings in these words: 'All of us here, whether learned or illiterate, high or low, rich or poor ask you to be our representative in this matter. We all testify to your knowledge and wisdom, your piety, faith and discernment. Your acceptance or rejection of this Cause is sufficient

* His ancestral home was in Dáráb where he was born. He also had a home in Nayríz.

testimony for us. Whatever your findings, we all accept your views and obey your wishes.[2]

In one of his writings Vaḥíd gives the date of his meeting with the Báb in Shíráz as the month of Jamádíyu'l-Avval in the year 1262 A.H. (April–May 1846). The following is Nabíl's vivid account of Vaḥíd's interviews with the Báb:

> Siyyid Yaḥyá met the Báb at the home of Ḥájí Mírzá Siyyid 'Alí, and exercised in his attitude towards Him the courtesy which 'Aẓím* had counselled him to observe. For about two hours he directed the attention of the Báb to the most abstruse and bewildering themes in the metaphysical teachings of Islám, to the obscurest passages of the Qur'án, and to the mysterious traditions and prophecies of the imáms of the Faith. The Báb at first listened to his learned references to the law and prophecies of Islám, noted all his questions, and began to give to each a brief but persuasive reply. The conciseness and lucidity of His answers excited the wonder and admiration of Siyyid Yaḥyá. He was overpowered by a sense of humiliation at his own presumptuousness and pride. His sense of superiority completely vanished. As he arose to depart, he addressed the Báb in these words: 'Please God, I shall, in the course of my next audience with You, submit the rest of my questions and with them shall conclude my enquiry.' As soon as he retired, he joined 'Aẓím, to whom he related the account of his interview. 'I have in His presence,' he told him, 'expatiated unduly upon my own learning. He was able in a few words to answer my questions and to resolve my perplexities. I felt so abased before Him that I hurriedly begged leave to retire.' 'Aẓím reminded him of his counsel, and begged him not to forget this time the advice he had given him.
>
> In the course of his second interview, Siyyid Yaḥyá, to his amazement, discovered that all the questions which he had

* One of the disciples of the Báb, a learned divine and intimate friend of Vaḥíd, who had advised the latter to exercise the utmost consideration towards the Báb lest he should come to regret some act of discourtesy towards Him.

intended to submit to the Báb had vanished from his memory. He contented himself with matters that seemed irrelevant to the object of his enquiry. He soon found, to his still greater surprise, that the Báb was answering, with the same lucidity and conciseness that had characterised His previous replies, those same questions which he had momentarily forgotten. 'I seemed to have fallen fast asleep,' he later observed. 'His words, His answers to questions which I had forgotten to ask, reawakened me. A voice still kept whispering in my ear: "Might not this, after all, have been an accidental coincidence?" I was too agitated to collect my thoughts. I again begged leave to retire. 'Aẓím, whom I subsequently met, received me with cold indifference, and sternly remarked: "Would that schools had been utterly abolished, and that neither of us had entered one! Through our little-mindedness and conceit, we are withholding from ourselves the redeeming grace of God, and are causing pain to Him who is the Fountain thereof. Will you not this time beseech God to grant that you may be enabled to attain His presence with becoming humility and detachment, that perchance He may graciously relieve you from the oppression of uncertainty and doubt?"

'I resolved that in my third interview with the Báb I would in my inmost heart request Him to reveal for me a commentary on the Súrih of Kawthar.* I determined not to breathe that request in His presence. Should He, unasked by me, reveal this commentary in a manner that would immediately distinguish it in my eyes from the prevailing standards current among the commentators on the Qur'án, I then would be convinced of the Divine character of His Mission, and would readily embrace His Cause. If not, I would refuse to acknowledge Him. As soon as I was ushered into His presence, a sense of fear, for which I could not account, suddenly seized me. My limbs quivered as I beheld His face. I, who on repeated occasions had been introduced into the presence of the Sháh and had never discovered the slightest trace of timidity in myself, was now so awed and shaken that I could not remain standing on my feet. The Báb, beholding

* *Qur'án*, cviii.

my plight, arose from His seat, advanced towards me, and, taking hold of my hand, seated me beside Him. "Seek from Me," He said, "whatever is your heart's desire. I will readily reveal it to you." I was speechless with wonder. Like a babe that can neither understand nor speak, I felt powerless to respond. He smiled as He gazed at me and said: "Were I to reveal for you the commentary on the Súrih of Kawthar, would you acknowledge that My words are born of the Spirit of God? Would you recognise that My utterance can in no wise be associated with sorcery or magic?" Tears flowed from my eyes as I heard Him speak these words. All I was able to utter was this verse of the Qur'án: "O our Lord, with ourselves have we dealt unjustly: if Thou forgive us not and have not pity on us, we shall surely be of those who perish."

'It was still early in the afternoon when the Báb requested Ḥájí Mírzá Siyyid 'Alí to bring His pen-case and some paper. He then started to reveal His commentary on the Súrih of Kawthar. How am I to describe this scene of inexpressible majesty? Verses streamed from His pen* with a rapidity that was truly astounding. The incredible swiftness of His writing,† the soft and gentle murmur of His voice, and the stupendous force of His style, amazed and bewildered me. He continued in this manner until the approach of sunset. He did not pause until the entire commentary of the Súrih was completed. He then laid down His pen and asked for tea. Soon after, He began to read it aloud in my presence. My heart leaped madly as I heard Him pour out, in accents of unutterable sweetness, those treasures enshrined in that sublime commentary. I was so entranced by its beauty that three times over I was on the verge of fainting. He sought to revive my failing strength with a few drops of rose-water which He

* According to the Báb's testimony, He revealed the Word of God at the rate of one thousand verses in six hours.

† According to the "Kashfu'l-Ghiṭá" (p. 81), no less than two thousand verses were revealed on that occasion by the Báb. The bewildering rapidity of this revelation was no less remarkable in the eyes of Siyyid Yaḥyá than the matchless beauty and profound meaning of the verses contained in that commentary. (Ed.)

caused to be sprinkled on my face. This restored my vigour and enabled me to follow His reading to the end.

'When He had completed His recital, the Báb arose to depart. He entrusted me, as He left, to the care of His maternal uncle. "He is to be your guest," He told him, "until the time when he, in collaboration with Mullá 'Abdu'l-Karím, shall have finished transcribing this newly revealed commentary, and shall have verified the correctness of the transcribed copy." Mullá 'Abdu'l-Karím and I devoted three days and three nights to this work. We would in turn read aloud to each other a portion of the commentary until the whole of it had been transcribed. We verified all the traditions in the text and found them to be entirely accurate. Such was the state of certitude to which I had attained that if all the powers of the earth were to be leagued against me they would be powerless to shake my confidence in the greatness of His Cause.'[3]

Vaḥíd wrote a detailed account of his interviews with the Báb to Mírzá Luṭf-'Alí, the King's chamberlain, for submission to Muḥammad Sháh. When the latter heard of Vaḥíd's conversion to the Bábí Faith, he is reported to have said to his prime minister: 'We have been lately informed that Siyyid Yaḥyáy-i-Dárábí has become a Bábí. If this be true, it behoves us to cease belittling the Cause of that siyyid.'*[4] Vaḥíd also wrote a letter to the people of Yazd informing them of the truth of the Mission of the Báb.

His recognition of the station of the Báb was whole-hearted and complete. From the time that he was dismissed from the presence of the Báb till the end of his eventful life, he dedicated himself to the service of His Faith. The zeal and enthusiasm with which he arose to promote the Cause of the Báb were exemplary and of the highest degree. He travelled throughout the land and taught the Faith publicly among the multitudes.

It was in the course of these journeys that he attained the presence of Bahá'u'lláh in Ṭihrán. From there he travelled towards the south until he reached the city of Yazd. Carrying his

* The Báb.

sword and mounted on the steed that had once taken him there on his way to Shíráz, he arrived at the scene of his previous meeting, the Muṣalláy-i-Ṣafdar-Khán, where thousands heard his eloquent discourse proclaiming the advent of the Promised One of Islám. Great numbers from the crowd readily embraced the Faith of the Báb. Among them were such eminent personalities as Mullá Muḥammad-Riḍá surnamed Raḍa'r-Rúḥ; his three brothers who were later martyred in Manshád; Ḥájí Mullá Mihdíy-i-'Aṭrí, the father of Varqá, the distinguished martyr of the Faith; Mírzá Ja'far-i-Yazdí who, as mentioned in a previous chapter, accompanied Bahá'u'lláh from Baghdád to 'Akká; Siyyid Ja'far-i-Yazdí, a noted divine who accompanied Vaḥíd to Nayríz and whose services have been mentioned previously. These outstanding men, together with many more, became the pillars of the Faith in Yazd and through their teaching endeavours, devotion and self-sacrifice the Cause flourished in that city.

Vaḥíd was eventually driven out of Yazd by his enemies. He proceeded to Nayríz where he proclaimed the Cause with great courage and fortitude and in the end laid down his life in the path of His Lord.

APPENDIX IV

Ḥájí Mírzá Karím Khán

Ḥájí Mírzá Karím Khán,* who had assumed the leadership of the Shaykhí community after the death of his illustrious teacher Siyyid Káẓim-i-Rashtí, was one of the divines of Islám whom Bahá'u'lláh admonished in the *Kitáb-i-Íqán.*

His assumption of such a position was clearly in conflict with the instructions of Siyyid Káẓim who had repeatedly exhorted his followers to abandon their studies after his passing, detach themselves from earthly things and scatter far and wide in search of the Promised One. A number of ambitious men, however, did not follow this exhortation and Ḥájí Mírzá Karím Khán was one of these. His unfaithfulness and insincerity were clear to many, especially to Siyyid Káẓim. Nabíl-i-A'ẓam has recorded these words in his Narratives:

> I have heard Shaykh Abú-Turáb † recount the following: '. . . As to Ḥájí Mírzá Karím Khán, who for years sat at the feet of Siyyid Káẓim and acquired from him all his so-called learning, in the end he obtained leave from his master to settle in Kirmán, and there engage in the promotion of the interests of Islám and the dissemination of those traditions that clustered round the sacred memory of the Imáms of the Faith.
>
> 'I was present in the library of Siyyid Káẓim when, one day, an attendant of Ḥájí Mírzá Karím Khán arrived, holding a book in his hand, which he presented to the Siyyid on behalf of his master, requesting him to peruse it and to signify

* His full name was Ḥájí Mírzá Muḥammad-Karím Khán-i-Kirmání.

† One of the leading disciples of Siyyid Káẓim; he died as a Bábí in the prison of Ṭihrán.

in his own handwriting his approval of its contents. The Siyyid read portions of that book, and returned it to the attendant with this message: "Tell your master that he, better than anyone else, can estimate the value of his own book." The attendant had retired when the Siyyid, with sorrowful voice, remarked: "Accursed be he! For years he has been associated with me, and now that he intends to depart, his one aim, after so many years of study and companionship, is to diffuse, through his book, such heretical and atheistic doctrines as he now wishes me to endorse. He has covenanted with a number of self-seeking hypocrites with the view of establishing himself in Kirmán, and in order to assume, after my departure from this world, the reins of undisputed leadership. How grievously he erred in his judgment! For the breeze of divine Revelation, wafted from the Day-Spring of guidance, will assuredly quench his light and destroy his influence. The tree of his endeavour will eventually yield naught but the fruit of bitter disillusion and gnawing remorse. Verily I say, you shall behold this with your own eyes. My prayer for you is that you may be protected from the mischievous influence which he, the antichrist of the promised Revelation, will in future exercise." '[1]

No sooner did Ḥájí Mírzá Karím Khán announce his leadership of the Shaykhí community than a considerable number of Shaykhís throughout the country followed him and began their campaign of opposition against the newly-born Faith of God.

This ambitious man, lusting for fame and leadership, claimed for himself an exalted position in the Faith of Islám, namely, that he was the Rukn-i-Rábi', the 'fourth pillar' of that Faith.* This pretentious claim, however, evoked the wrath of the divines and he was forced to withdraw by publishing a statement in two of his epistles.

The Báb, soon after His Declaration, sent an envoy to Ḥájí

* The other three pillars are God, the Prophet Muḥammad and the Holy Imáms.

Mírzá Karím Khán informing him of His station as the Báb and summoning him to embrace His Faith. But he persisted in his denunciation of it, published some books against the Cause, and till the end of his life tenaciously persevered in his determination to uproot its foundation. In the eyes of the Bábís, Ḥájí Mírzá Karím Khán stood as the embodiment of all the forces of darkness opposing the Army of Light.

On several occasions Bahá'u'lláh in His Writings has referred to Ḥájí Mírzá Karím Khán and condemned his actions. The well-known *Lawḥ-i-Qiná'* * (Tablet of the Veil), condemnatory in tone, was addressed to him. In the *Kitáb-i-Íqán* Bahá'u'lláh mentions him in these words: '. . . a certain man, reputed for his learning and attainments, and accounting himself as one of the pre-eminent leaders of his people, hath in his book denounced and vilified all the exponents of true learning.' Further, He has denounced him as a man who was 'following the path of self and desire, and was lost in the wilderness of ignorance and folly.'

Referring to his reputed knowledge Bahá'u'lláh states:

> . . . I swear by God that not one breath, blowing from the meads of divine knowledge, hath ever been wafted upon his soul, nor hath he ever unravelled a single mystery of ancient wisdom. Nay, were the meaning of Knowledge ever to be expounded unto him, dismay would fill his heart, and his whole being would shake to its foundation. Notwithstanding his base and senseless statements, behold to what heights of extravagance his claims have reached!
>
> Gracious God! How great is Our amazement at the way the people have gathered around him, and have borne allegiance to his person! Content with transient dust, these people have turned their face unto it, and cast behind their backs Him Who is the Lord of Lords. Satisfied with the croaking of the crow and enamoured with the visage of the raven, they have renounced the melody of the nightingale and the charm of the rose.[2]

* This Tablet will be referred to in a later volume.

A remarkable interpretation by Bahá'u'lláh of certain verses of the *Qur'án* demonstrates that almost twelve hundred years before, Muḥammad had denounced Ḥájí Mírzá Karím Khán. These are the words of Bahá'u'lláh in this connection:

> And as to this man's attainments, his ignorance, understanding and belief, behold what the Book* which embraceth all things hath revealed: 'Verily, the tree of Zaqqúm† shall be the food of the Athím'.‡ And then follow certain verses, until He saith: 'Taste this, for thou forsooth art the mighty Karím!'§ Consider how clearly and explicitly he hath been described in God's incorruptible Book! This man, moreover, feigning humility, hath in his own book referred to himself as the 'athím servant': 'Athím' in the Book of God, mighty among the common herd, 'Karím' in name![3]

Ḥájí Mírzá Karím Khán wrote several books, all of which portray him as a haughty and vainglorious man proud of his learning and devoid of true understanding and wisdom. His unrelenting hostility to the Faith of the Báb features prominently in these books. He died in the year 1288 A.H. (A.D. 1873) on his way to the Holy Shrines of the Imáms in 'Iráq.

* *Qur'án*.

† The infernal tree.

‡ Literally, 'sinner'. (*Qur'án* XLIV. 43–4.) Ḥájí Mírzá Karím Khán for reasons of false modesty has referred to himself as 'Athím' in his writings.

§ *Qur'án* XLIV. 49. 'Karím', which can be translated as 'noble', 'honourable' or 'bountiful', has been understood by commentators on the *Qur'án* to represent an attribute, but Bahá'u'lláh states that, in this verse, it was intended as the name of a man, Karím.

BIBLIOGRAPHY

'ABDU'L-BAHÁ. *Memorials of the Faithful.* Translated from the original Persian text and annotated by Marzieh Gail. Wilmette, Illinois: Bahá'í Publishing Trust, 1971.

—— *Some Answered Questions.* Collected and Translated from the Persian of 'Abdu'l-Bahá by Laura Clifford Barney. London: Kegan Paul, Trench, Trubner & Co. Ltd., 1908. Chicago: Bahá'í Publishing Society, 1918. London: Bahá'í Publishing Trust, 1961. Wilmette, Illinois: Bahá'í Publishing Trust, rev. edn. 1964.

AFRÚKHTIH, DR. YÚNIS KHÁN. *Kháṭirát-i-Nuh-Sáliy-i-'Akká.* Memories of Nine Years in 'Akká. Written in the year 99 B.E. (A.D. 1942). Ṭihrán.

Áhang-i-Badí'. Persian Bahá'í Youth Magazine. Ṭihrán: National Bahá'í Youth Committee, 126 B.E. (A.D. 1969).

Bahá'í News and Reviews. Journal of the National Spiritual Assembly of the Bahá'ís of Írán. Ṭihrán.

Bahá'í Prayers. A selection. London: Bahá'í Publishing Trust, 1945; rev. edn. 1967.

Bahá'í World, The. A Biennial International Record. Wilmette, Illinois: Bahá'í Publishing Trust, 1956. Vol. XII, 1950–54.

BAHÁ'U'LLÁH. *Epistle to the Son of the Wolf.* Trans. by Shoghi Effendi. Wilmette, Illinois: Bahá'í Publishing Trust, rev. edn. 1953.

—— *Gleanings from the Writings of Bahá'u'lláh.* Trans. by Shoghi Effendi. Wilmette, Illinois: Bahá'í Publishing Trust, 1935; rev. edn. 1952. London: Bahá'í Publishing Trust, 1949.

—— *The Hidden Words.* Trans. by Shoghi Effendi with the

assistance of some English friends. First published in England 1932. London: Bahá'í Publishing Trust, 1949. Wilmette, Illinois: Bahá'í Publishing Trust, rev. edn. 1954.

—— *The Kitáb-i-Íqán. The Book of Certitude.* Trans. by Shoghi Effendi. Wilmette, Illinois: Bahá'í Publishing Trust, 1931; 2nd edn. 1950. London: Bahá'í Publishing Trust, 2nd edn. 1961.

—— *Prayers and Meditations by Bahá'u'lláh.* Compiled and trans. by Shoghi Effendi. New York: Bahá'í Publishing Committee, 1938. Reprinted Wilmette, Illinois: Bahá'í Publishing Trust. London: Bahá'í Publishing Trust, 1957.

—— *The Proclamation of Bahá'u'lláh* to the kings and leaders of the world. Haifa: Bahá'í World Centre, 1967.

—— *The Seven Valleys and The Four Valleys.* Translated by Ali-Kuli Khan (Nabílu'd-Dawlih), assisted by Marzieh Gail. Wilmette, Illinois: Bahá'í Publishing Trust, 1945; rev. edn. 1952.

BALYUZI, H. M. *'Abdu'l-Bahá. The Centre of the Covenant of Bahá'u'lláh.* London and Oxford: George Ronald, 1971; repr. 1972.

BLOMFIELD, LADY (Sitárih Khánum). *The Chosen Highway.* London: Bahá'í Publishing Trust, 1940. Wilmette, Illinois: Bahá'í Publishing Trust, 1967.

FÁḌIL-i-MÁZINDARÁNÍ, ASADU'LLÁH, MÍRZÁ. *Asráru'l-Áthár.* A glossary of Bahá'í terms. Ṭihrán: Bahá'í Publishing Trust. Vol. I, 124 B.E. (A.D. 1967); Vol. V, 129 B.E. (A.D. 1972).

FAIZÍ, MUḤAMMAD-'ALÍ. *Khánidán-i-Afnán.* A biography of some members of the Afnán family. Ṭihrán: Bahá'í Publishing Trust, 127 B.E. (A.D. 1970).

GIACHERY, UGO. *Shoghi Effendi—Recollections.* Oxford: George Ronald, 1973.

ḤAYDAR-'ALÍ, ḤÁJÍ MÍRZÁ. *Bihjatu'ṣ-Ṣudúr.* Reminiscences and autobiography. Bombay: 1913.

ISHRÁQ KHÁVARÍ, 'ABDU'L-ḤAMÍD. *Má'idiy-i-Ásamání,* A compilation of Bahá'í Writings. Ṭihrán: Bahá'í Publishing Trust. Vol. II, 129 B.E. (A.D. 1972).

—— *Muḥáḍirát.* An account of discussions on Bahá'í subjects. Ṭihrán: Bahá'í Publishing Trust, 120 B.E. (A.D. 1963).

——*Risáliy-i-Ayyám-i-Tis'ih.* The history of the nine Bahá'í Holy Days together with a compilation of relevant Tablets. Ṭihrán: Bahá'í Publishing Trust, 103 B.E. (A.D. 1946); 3rd repr. 121 B.E. (A.D. 1964).

NABÍL-i-A'ẒAM (Muḥammad-i-Zarandí). *The Dawn-Breakers.* Nabíl's Narrative of the Early Days of the Bahá'í Revelation. Wilmette, Illinois: Bahá'í Publishing Trust, 1932. London: Bahá'í Publishing Trust, 1953.

SHOGHI EFFENDI. *The Advent of Divine Justice.* First published 1939. Wilmette, Illinois: Bahá'í Publishing Trust, rev. edn. 1963.

—— *God Passes By.* Wilmette, Illinois: Bahá'í Publishing Trust, 1944.

—— *The Promised Day Is Come.* First published 1941. Wilmette, Illinois: Bahá'í Publishing Trust, rev. edn. 1961.

—— *The World Order of Bahá'u'lláh.* First published 1938. Wilmette, Illinois: Bahá'í Publishing Trust, rev. edn. 1955.

Star of the West. The Bahá'í Magazine. Published from 1910 to 1933 from Chicago and Washington, D.C., by official Bahá'í agencies. Vol. XIV, April 1923–March 1924.

SULAYMÁNÍ, 'AZÍZU'LLÁH. *Maṣábíḥ-i-Hidáyat.* Biography of some of the early Bahá'ís. Ṭihrán: Bahá'í Publishing Trust. Vols. I and II, 121 B.E. (A.D. 1964); Vol. VI, 125 B.E. (A.D. 1968).

TOWNSHEND, GEORGE. *Christ and Bahá'u'lláh.* London and Oxford: George Ronald, 1957; 4th repr. 1971.

YUSUF ALI, ABDULLAH. *The Holy Qur-an.* Text, Translation & Commentary. Lahore, Pakistan: Sh. Muhammad Ashraf, 1938; repr. 1969.

REFERENCES

Full details of authors and titles are given in the bibliography. Page numbers are given for both the American and British editions of *Kitáb-i-Íqán* and *The Dawn-Breakers*. See Notes and Acknowledgements, xiii-xiv, regarding translations from Persian texts and the numbering of verses in the *Qur'án*.

INTRODUCTION

1. Bahá'u'lláh, *Kitáb-i-Íqán*, pp. 63–4 (Brit.), p. 98 (U.S.).

CHAPTER 1: THE BIRTH OF THE REVELATION

1. Bahá'u'lláh, *Epistle to the Son of the Wolf*, p. 22.

CHAPTER 2: BAHÁ'U'LLÁH IN EXILE

1. Blomfield, *The Chosen Highway*, p. 45.
2. Shoghi Effendi, *God Passes By*, p. 118, for the words of Bahá'u'lláh.
3. Blomfield, *The Chosen Highway*, p. 40.
4. Shoghi Effendi, *God Passes By*, p. 185.

CHAPTER 3: THE WORD OF GOD

1. Bahá'u'lláh, *The Proclamation of Bahá'u'lláh*, p. 57.
2. Shoghi Effendi, *God Passes By*, p. 171.
3. *Bihjatu'ṣ-Ṣudúr*, p. 247.
4. Bahá'u'lláh, 'Tablet of Visitation' and 'Long Obligatory Prayer', included in most Bahá'í Prayer Books.
5. Bahá'u'lláh, *Gleanings from the Writings of Bahá'u'lláh*, section lxxiv.
6. Shoghi Effendi, 'The Dispensation of Bahá'u'lláh', included in *The World Order of Bahá'u'lláh*, p. 107.
7. Bahá'u'lláh, *Gleanings from the Writings of Bahá'u'lláh*, section lxxxix.

8. *Maṣábíḥ-i-Hidáyat*, vol. VI, pp. 446–7.
9. Bahá'u'lláh, *The Proclamation of Bahá'u'lláh*, p. 57.
10. 'Áhang-i-Badí'', vol. XXIV, nos. 7–8.
11. Unpublished memoirs of Ḥájí Muḥammad-Ṭáhir-i-Málmírí.
12. *ibid.*
13. *Muḥáḍirát*, vol. I, p. 453.
14. *Asráru'l-Á͟thár*, vol. I, p. 33.
15. Bahá'u'lláh, *Kitáb-i-Íqán*, p. 30 (Brit.), p. 46 (U.S.).
16. *Star of the West*, vol. XIV, p. 114.

CHAPTER 4: THE FIRST EMANATIONS OF THE SUPREME PEN

1. Bahá'u'lláh, *Kitáb-i-Íqán*, p. 63 (Brit.), p. 98 (U.S.).
2. Bahá'u'lláh, *Gleanings from the Writings of Bahá'u'lláh*, sections lxiii, lxiv, and lvi, for the words quoted in this sentence.
3. *ibid.*, section lvi.
4. *ibid.*, section lxiii.
5. *ibid.*, section lv.
6. Bahá'u'lláh, *Epistle to the Son of the Wolf*, pp. 169, 171.
7. Shoghi Effendi, *God Passes By*, p. 109.

CHAPTER 5: THE EARLY TABLETS IN 'IRÁQ

1. Bahá'u'lláh, *Kitáb-i-Íqán*, p. 160 (Brit.), p. 251 (U.S.).
2. *Qur'án*, iii. 93 (according to the Arabic text numbering).
3. Shoghi Effendi, *God Passes By*, p. 118.
4. Shoghi Effendi, 'The Dispensation of Bahá'u'lláh', included in *The World Order of Bahá'u'lláh*, p. 113.
5. *ibid.*, p. 113.
6. A Muslim tradition cited by Bahá'u'lláh, *Epistle to the Son of the Wolf*, p. 43.
7. Shoghi Effendi, *God Passes By*, p. 120, for the words quoted in this sentence.
8. Bahá'u'lláh, *Kitáb-i-Íqán*, p. 160 (Brit.), pp. 250–51 (U.S.).
9. Shoghi Effendi, *The Advent of Divine Justice*, p. 65, for this quotation.
10. *ibid.*, p. 64, for this quotation.
11. Shoghi Effendi, 'The Dispensation of Bahá'u'lláh', included in *The World Order of Bahá'u'lláh*, p. 115.
12. Bahá'u'lláh, 'Tablet of Aḥmad', included in most Bahá'í Prayer Books.

13. Shoghi Effendi, 'The Dispensation of Bahá'u'lláh', included in *The World Order of Bahá'u'lláh*, pp. 106–7.
14. *ibid.*, p. 107.
15. Shoghi Effendi, *God Passes By*, p. 133.
16. *ibid.*, p. 138.

CHAPTER 6: *The Hidden Words*

1. Bahá'u'lláh, *The Hidden Words*, introduction to the Arabic version.
2. Bahá'u'lláh, *Gleanings from the Writings of Bahá'u'lláh*, section cliii.
3. Shoghi Effendi, *The Advent of Divine Justice*, p. 28, for the words quoted.
4. Bahá'u'lláh, *The Hidden Words*, no. 53, from the Persian version.
5. *ibid.*, the closing words of the Persian version.
6. *ibid.* The words quoted in this paragraph are taken (in this order) from the Arabic and Persian versions, as indicated: no. 1 Arabic, nos. 26 and 57 Persian, nos. 12, 14 and 32 Arabic, nos. 32, 74, 82, 81, 17, 64, 63, 53 and 76 Persian.
7. *ibid.*, no. 13, Arabic version.
8. *ibid.*, no. 19, Persian version.
9. Shoghi Effendi, *God Passes By*, p. 238, for the words quoted in this sentence.
10. Bahá'u'lláh, *The Hidden Words*, no. 71, Persian version.
11. *ibid.*, no. 79, Persian version.
12. *ibid.*, prefatory words preceding nos. 20 and 48, Persian version.
13. *ibid.*, no. 77, Persian version.
14. The interpretations given by 'Abdu'l-Bahá, and cited in these paragraphs, are taken from His Tablets as quoted in *Asráru'l-Á<u>th</u>ár*, vol. v, pp. 36–40, and in *Má'idiy-i-Ásamání*, vol. II, p. 37.
15. Shoghi Effendi, 'The Dispensation of Bahá'u'lláh', included in *The World Order of Bahá'u'lláh*, p. 116, for the words quoted.

CHAPTER 7: SOME EARLY BELIEVERS

1. *Maṣábíḥ-i-Hidáyat*, vol. I, p. 216.
2. 'Bahá'í News and Reviews', a Journal of the National Spiritual Assembly of the Bahá'ís of Írán, no. 12, September 1948. The account was written by Habib Taherzadeh.

3. Shoghi Effendi, *God Passes By*, p. 143, for the words quoted.
4. Mullá Muḥammad-Ṣádiq-i-Khurásání is described by 'Abdu'l-Bahá in *Memorials of the Faithful*, pp. 5–8, and by Nabíl in *The Dawn-Breakers* (consult the index).
5. *Maṣábíḥ-i-Hidáyat*, vol. I, pp. 446–9.

CHAPTER 8: *The Seven Valleys*

1. Bahá'u'lláh, *The Seven Valleys*, p. 5.
2. *ibid.*, p. 7.
3. *ibid.*, p. 11.
4. *ibid.*, p. 15.
5. *ibid.*, p. 12.
6. *ibid.*, p. 18, for the quotations in this paragraph.
7. *ibid.*, p. 29.
8. Blomfield, *The Chosen Highway*, p. 166.
9. Bahá'u'lláh, *The Seven Valleys*, p. 32.
10. *ibid.*
11. *ibid.*, p. 41.
12. *ibid.*, p. 36.
13. Shoghi Effendi, *God Passes By*, pp. 136–7.
14. Bahá'u'lláh, *The Four Valleys* (published with *The Seven Valleys*), pp. 54 and 57–8, for the words quoted in this paragraph.

CHAPTER 9: SOME OUTSTANDING TABLETS

1. Unpublished memoirs of Ḥájí Muḥammad-Ṭáhir-i-Málmírí.
2. Bahá'u'lláh, *Prayers and Meditations by Bahá'u'lláh*, no. 184.
3. *ibid.*, no. 88.
4. Bahá'u'lláh, *Gleanings from the Writings of Bahá'u'lláh*, section xxiv.
5. Balyuzi, *'Abdu'l-Bahá*, p. 141.
6. Shoghi Effendi, 'The Unfoldment of World Civilization', included in *The World Order of Bahá'u'lláh*, p. 168, for the lines quoted.
7. *ibid.*, p. 169, for the lines quoted.
8. *ibid.*
9. Bahá'u'lláh, *Gleanings from the Writings of Bahá'u'lláh*, section lxxiv.
10. *Star of the West*, vol. XIV, p. 112.
11. Unpublished memoirs of Ḥájí Muḥammad-Ṭáhir-i-Málmírí.

12. Shoghi Effendi, *God Passes By*, pp. 248–9, for the words quoted.
13. Shoghi Effendi, 'The Dispensation of Bahá'u'lláh', included in *The World Order of Bahá'u'lláh*, p. 134.
14. *ibid.*, p. 135.
15. Nabíl-i-A'ẓam, *The Dawn-Breakers*, p. 367 (Brit.), pp. 496–8 (U.S.).
16. 'Bahá'í News and Reviews', a Journal of the National Spiritual Assembly of the Bahá'ís of Írán, no. 7, December 1947. This account was written by Habib Taherzadeh and has been edited by the author.
17. Shoghi Effendi, *God Passes By*, p. 142.
18. *ibid.*, p. 144.
19. *ibid.*
20. *ibid.*, p. 141, for the words quoted in this paragraph.
21. Bahá'u'lláh, *Gleanings from the Writings of Bahá'u'lláh*, section cxiii.
22. *Qur'án*, vi. 35 (according to the Arabic text numbering).
23. Bahá'u'lláh, *Gleanings from the Writings of Bahá'u'lláh*, section xlv.
24. Bahá'u'lláh, *The Hidden Words*, no. 51, Arabic version.
25. Bahá'u'lláh, *Epistle to the Son of the Wolf*, pp. 52–3.
26. *ibid.*, pp. 85–6.
27. Bahá'u'lláh, *Kitáb-i-Íqán*, p. 17 (Brit.), pp. 25–6 (U.S.).

CHAPTER 10: *The Kitáb-i-Íqán*

1. *Khánidán-i-Afnán*, pp. 25–6.
2. *ibid.*, pp. 32–5.
3. *ibid.*, pp. 42–3.
4. Bahá'u'lláh, *Kitáb-i-Íqán*, p. 161 (Brit.), p. 252 (U.S.).
5. Shoghi Effendi, *God Passes By*, pp. 138–9.
6. *Daniel*, xii. 9.
7. Bahá'u'lláh, *Kitáb-i-Íqán*, p. 3 (Brit.), p. 3 (U.S.).
8. *ibid.*, p. 9 (Brit.), pp. 12–13 (U.S.).
9. *ibid.*, pp. 10–11 (Brit.), p. 15 (U.S.).
10. *ibid.*, p. 105 (Brit.), p. 164 (U.S.).
11. *ibid.* This quotation is taken from pp. 15, 16–17 (Brit.) and from pp. 22, 24–5 and 26 (U.S.).
12. *ibid.* These extracts are taken from pp. 21, 19, 20 and 21 (Brit.) and from pp. 32, 29, 30 and 31 (U.S.).

13. *ibid.* These extracts are taken from pp. 22, 24, 25 and 27 (Brit.) and from pp. 33–4, 36, 37, 38 and 41 (U.S.).
14. *ibid.*, pp. 40–1 (Brit.), p. 63 (U.S.).
15. *ibid.*, p. 42 (Brit.), p. 65 (U.S.).
16. *ibid.*
17. *ibid.*, p. 43 (Brit.), pp. 66–7 (U.S.).
18. *ibid.*, p. 46 (Brit.), pp. 71–2 (U.S.).
19. *ibid.*, p. 51 (Brit.), pp. 79–80 (U.S.).
20. *ibid.*, p. 52 (Brit.), pp. 80–1 (U.S.).
21. *ibid.*, pp. 52–3 (Brit.), pp. 81–2 (U.S.).
22. *ibid.*, pp. 44–5 (Brit.), pp. 68–9 (U.S.).
23. *ibid.*, p. 32 (Brit.), p. 49 (U.S.).
24. *ibid.*, pp. 33, 34 (Brit.), pp. 50–1 and 52 (U.S.).
25. *ibid.*, pp. 35, 36 (Brit.), pp. 53–4 and 55–6 (U.S.).
26. *ibid.*, pp. 36–7 (Brit.), pp. 56–7 (U.S.).
27. *ibid.*, pp. 63–4 (Brit.), pp. 98–9 (U.S.).
28. *ibid.*, pp. 64–5 (Brit.), pp. 99–100 (U.S.).
29. *ibid.*, pp. 66–7 (Brit.), p. 103 (U.S.).
30. *ibid.*, pp. 97–9 (Brit.), pp. 152–4 (U.S.).
31. *ibid.*, p. 113 (Brit.), pp. 176–7 (U.S.).
32. *ibid.*, p. 102 (Brit.), p. 159 (U.S.).
33. *ibid.*, pp. 114–15 (Brit.), pp. 177–9 (U.S.).
34. *ibid.*, pp. 69–70 (Brit.), pp. 106–8 (U.S.).
35. *ibid.*, pp. 79–80 (Brit.), pp. 123–4 (U.S.).
36. *ibid.*, pp. 85–6 (Brit.), pp. 132–3 (U.S.).
37. *ibid.*, p. 73 (Brit.), pp. 112–13 (U.S.).
38. *ibid.*, p. 74 (Brit.), p. 114 (U.S.).
39. *ibid.*, pp. 76–7 (Brit.), pp. 118–19 (U.S.).
40. *ibid.*, p. 92 (Brit.), pp. 143–4 (U.S.).
41. *ibid.*, p. 120 (Brit.), pp. 187–8 (U.S.).
42. *ibid.*, p. 135 (Brit.), p. 211 (U.S.).
43. *ibid.*, pp. 123–6 (Brit.), pp. 192–6 (U.S.).
44. *ibid.* These quotations are taken from pp. 129, 130, 131 (Brit.) and from pp. 202, 203 and 204–5 (U.S.).
45. *ibid.*, pp. 127–8 (Brit.), pp. 199–200 (U.S.).
46. *ibid.*, p. 138 (Brit.), pp. 216–17 (U.S.).
47. *ibid.*, pp. 142–3 (Brit.), pp. 222–4 (U.S.).
48. *ibid.*, p. 147 (Brit.), pp. 230–1 (U.S.).
49. *ibid.*, p. 149 (Brit.), pp. 233–4 (U.S.).

50. *ibid.*, pp. 149–50 (Brit.), pp. 234–5 (U.S.).
51. *ibid.*, p. 59 (Brit.), p. 92 (U.S.).
52. *ibid.*, pp. 112–13 (Brit.), pp. 175–6 (U.S.).
53. *ibid.*, p. 159 (Brit.), pp. 249–50 (U.S.).
54. *ibid.*, p. 159 (Brit.), p. 250 (U.S.).
55. *ibid.*, p. 39 (Brit.), pp. 60–1 (U.S.).

CHAPTER 11: OTHER EARLY BELIEVERS

1. *Kh͟ánidán-i-Afnán*, pp. 111–12.
2. Shoghi Effendi, *The World Order of Bahá'u'lláh*, p. 17, for the words quoted.
3. Nabíl-i-A'ẓam, *The Dawn-Breakers*, from the Preface.
4. Shoghi Effendi, *God Passes By*, p. 135.
5. *ibid.*, p. 137, for the passage quoted.

CHAPTER 12: BAHÁ'U'LLÁH'S APPROACHING DECLARATION

1. Shoghi Effendi, *God Passes By*, p. 360, for the passage quoted.
2. Townshend, *Christ and Bahá'u'lláh*, from chap. 8.
3. Bahá'u'lláh, *Kitáb-i-Íqán*, p. 155 (Brit.), p. 243 (U.S.).

CHAPTER 13: FRIENDS AND FOES

1. *Maṣábíḥ-i-Hidáyat*, vol. II, pp. 489–91.
2. *ibid.*, pp. 504–6.

CHAPTER 14: *Tablet of the Holy Mariner*

1. Shoghi Effendi, *God Passes By*, p. 147.
2. British *Bahá'í Prayers*. These words of 'Abdu'l-Bahá's are a preface to the Tablet.
3. *ibid.*, pp. 51–7.
4. Shoghi Effendi, *The Advent of Divine Justice*, p. 64, for the words quoted.
5. Shoghi Effendi, 'The Dispensation of Bahá'u'lláh', included in *The World Order of Bahá'u'lláh*, p. 111, for the words quoted.

CHAPTER 15: MÍRZÁ YAḤYÁ AND SIYYID MUḤAMMAD-I-IṢFAHÁNÍ

1. Bahá'u'lláh, *Epistle to the Son of the Wolf*, pp. 176–7.
2. *ibid.*, pp. 174–7.
3. *ibid.*, pp. 167–8.

CHAPTER 16: THE DECLARATION OF BAHÁ'U'LLÁH IN THE GARDEN OF RIḌVÁN

1. *Risáliy-i-Ayyám-i-Tis'ih*, p. 330.
2. Shoghi Effendi, *God Passes By*, p. 149, for the lines quoted.
3. *ibid.*, p. 154, for the words quoted.
4. Bahá'u'lláh, *Kitáb-i-Íqán*, p. 43 (Brit.), p. 67 (U.S.).
5. Nabíl-i-A'ẓam, *The Dawn-Breakers*, pp. 471–2 (Brit.), pp. 643–5 (U.S.).
6. Bahá'u'lláh, *Kitáb-i-Íqán*, p. 156 (Brit.), p. 245 (U.S.).
7. Bahá'u'lláh, *Gleanings from the Writings of Bahá'u'lláh*, section xiv.
8. Shoghi Effendi, *God Passes By*, p. 153, for the passage quoted.
9. *ibid.*, p. 154, for the words quoted.
10. Bahá'u'lláh, *Gleanings from the Writings of Bahá'u'lláh*, section xiv.
11. Bahá'u'lláh, *Prayers and Meditations by Bahá'u'lláh*, no. 178.
12. Bahá'u'lláh, *Gleanings from the Writings of Bahá'u'lláh*, section cxix.
13. *ibid.*, section clxv.
14. Shoghi Effendi, *God Passes By*, p. 155.

CHAPTER 17: THE JOURNEY TO CONSTANTINOPLE

1. Shoghi Effendi, *God Passes By*, p. 156.
2. See 'Abdu'l-Bahá, *Memorials of the Faithful*, pp. 145–7.
3. *ibid.*, pp. 77–9.
4. *ibid.*, pp. 23–5.
5. *ibid.*, pp. 57–9.
6. *ibid.*, pp. 59–61.
7. *ibid.*, pp. 94–5.
8. *ibid.*, pp. 39–41.
9. *ibid.*, pp. 36–8.
10. *ibid.*, pp. 156–8, for an account of Mírzá Ja'far, including this quotation.
11. Unpublished memoirs of Ḥájí Muḥammad-Ṭáhir-i-Málmírí.
12. Shoghi Effendi, *God Passes By*, pp. 157–8.

CHAPTER 18: 'HIM WHOM GOD SHALL MAKE MANIFEST'

1. Shoghi Effendi, *God Passes By*, p. 57, for the words quoted, except for the first title which comes from the 'Tablet of Aḥmad'.
2. *ibid.*, p. 30, for the words quoted.

3. Shoghi Effendi, 'The Dispensation of Bahá'u'lláh', included in *The World Order of Bahá'u'lláh*, p. 101, for the passage quoted.
4. *ibid.*, p. 100, for the passage quoted.
5. Shoghi Effendi, *God Passes By*, p. 29, for the words quoted.
6. Shoghi Effendi, 'The Dispensation of Bahá'u'lláh', included in *The World Order of Bahá'u'lláh*, p. 101, for the passage quoted.
7. Shoghi Effendi, *God Passes By*, pp. 30–1, for the passage quoted.
8. *ibid.*, p. 29, for the passage quoted.
9. *ibid.*
10. *ibid.*
11. *ibid.*, for the five passages quoted.
12. *ibid.*, for the words quoted.
13. *ibid.*, pp. 29–30, for the words quoted.
14. Shoghi Effendi, 'The Dispensation of Bahá'u'lláh', included in *The World Order of Bahá'u'lláh*, p. 100, for the words quoted.
15. *ibid.*, pp. 146–7, for the passage quoted.
16. *ibid.*, p. 101, for the words quoted.
17. *ibid.*, for the passage quoted.
18. Shoghi Effendi, *God Passes By*, pp. 93–9.
19. 'Abdu'l-Bahá, *Some Answered Questions*, chap. XLI.
20. Shoghi Effendi, 'The Dispensation of Bahá'u'lláh', included in *The World Order of Bahá'u'lláh*, p. 111, for the passage quoted.
21. Shoghi Effendi, 'The Unfoldment of World Civilization', included in *The World Order of Bahá'u'lláh*, pp. 202–3, for the passage quoted.
22. Shoghi Effendi, 'The Dispensation of Bahá'u'lláh', included in *The World Order of Bahá'u'lláh*, pp. 103–4.
23. Shoghi Effendi, *The Promised Day is Come*, p. 6.
24. Shoghi Effendi, 'The Dispensation of Bahá'u'lláh', included in *The World Order of Bahá'u'lláh*, p. 101.
25. Shoghi Effendi, *God Passes By*, p. 283.

APPENDIX I: MÍRZÁ ÁQÁ JÁN

1. Dr. Yúnis Khán, *Khátirát-i-Nuh-Sáliy-i-'Akká*, pp. 89–90. For an account of the author's life see *The Bahá'í World*, vol. XII, pp. 679–81.
2. *ibid.*, pp. 54–6.
3. *ibid.*, pp. 84–5.

APPENDIX III: VAḤÍD

1. Nabíl-i-A'ẓam, *The Dawn-Breakers*, pp. 122–3 (Brit.), pp. 170–1 (U.S.).
2. Ḥájí Muḥammad-Ṭáhir-i-Málmírí, *Táríkh-i-Shuhadáy-i-Yazd*, p. 5.
3. Nabíl-i-A'ẓam, *The Dawn-Breakers*, pp. 124–6 (Brit.), pp. 173–6 (U.S.).
4. *ibid.*, p. 127 (Brit.), p. 177 (U.S.).

APPENDIX IV: ḤÁJÍ MÍRZÁ KARÍM KHÁN

1. Nabíl-i-A'ẓam, *The Dawn-Breakers*, pp. 29–30 (Brit.), pp. 39–40 (U.S.).
2. Bahá'u'lláh, *Kitáb-i-Íqán*, pp. 120–1 (Brit.), pp. 188–9 (U.S.).
3. *ibid.*, pp. 121–2 (Brit.), p. 190 (U.S.).

INDEX

Part I of this index consists of the titles of Tablets and Writings of Bahá'u'lláh described or mentioned by the author, including a few which were revealed after 1863. Part II contains all other entries. Titles of Tablets and books are italicized. Footnotes are indicated by the abbreviation n. after the page number; if the name or subject occurs both in the text and in a note, this is indicated by 'p. – and n.'. Principal themes are shown by bold figures.

I. TABLETS AND WRITINGS OF BAHÁ'U'LLÁH

Alwáḥ-i-Maryam, 13
Az-Bágh-i-Iláhí (ode), 211, 218–20

Epistle to the Son of the Wolf, quoted, 10, 50, 249, 251–2, 253–4

Four Valleys, The, 104

Halih-Halih-Yá-Bishárat (ode), 211, 219
Hidden Words, The, ch. 6; *see* Part II of index for further references
Ḥúr-i-'Ujáb (The Wondrous Maiden), 211, 218
Ḥurúfát-i-'Álín (The Exalted Letters), 122–5
Also titled *Muṣíbát-i-Ḥurúfát-i-'Álíyát*

Javáhiru'l-Asrár (The Essence of Mysteries), 151–2

Kitáb-i-'Ahdí (The Book of My Covenant), 37, 80, 134, 137
Kitáb-i-Aqdas (The Most Holy Book), 26, 60, 153, 160, 212, 301; quotations from, 47, 124, 134, 280
Kitáb-i-Badí', 102, 250, 279
Kitáb-i-Íqán (The Book of Certitude), ch. 10; *see* Part II of index for further references

Lawḥ-i-Áyiy-i-Núr (Tablet of The Verse of Light), 125–8
Also titled *Tafsír-i-Ḥurúfát-i-Muqaṭṭa'ih*
Lawḥ-i-Ayyúb (Tablet of Job), see *Súriy-i-Ṣabr*
Lawḥ-i-Bulbulu'l-Firáq (Tablet of the Nightingale of Bereavement), 244–5
Lawḥ-i-Fitnih (Tablet of the Test), 128–9, 135–6
Lawḥ-i-Ghulámu'l-Khuld (The Youth of Paradise), 211, 213–14
Lawḥ-i-Ḥikmat (Tablet of Wisdom), 20–21
Lawḥ-i-Ḥúríyyih (Tablet of the Maiden), 125
Lawḥ-i-Kullu'ṭ-Ṭa'ám, (Tablet of All Food), 55–60 *passim*
Lawḥ-i-Malláḥu'l-Quds, see *Tablet of The Holy Mariner*
Lawḥ-i-Qiná' (Tablet of the Veil), 334 and n.
Long Obligatory Prayer, 30

Madínatu'r-Riḍá (City of Radiant Acquiescence), 108–9
Madínatu't-Tawḥíd (The City of Unity), 109, 113, 114, 116, 117–19; quoted, 118

Muṣíbát-i-Ḥurúfát-i-'Álíyát, see *Ḥurúfát-i-'Állín*

Qaṣídiy-i-Varqá'íyyih (poem), 62–4, 84–5

Questions and Answers, on the laws of the *Kitáb-i-Aqdas*, 26

Rashḥ-i-'Amá (poem), 45–6, 51

Ṣaḥífiy-i-Shaṭṭíyyih (Book of the River), 105–8

Sáqí-Az-Ghayb-i-Baqá (poem), 64

Seven Valleys, The, ch. 8; *see* Part II of index for further references

Shikkar-Shikan-Shavand, 147–50

Subḥána-Rabbíya'l-A'lá, 211–13

Súratu'lláh (Súrih of God), 244–5

Súriy-i-Aṣḥáb, 286

Súriy-i-Ghuṣn (Tablet of the Branch), 135

Súrihs of Ḥajj (Pilgrimage), 212

Súriy-i-Haykal (Súrih of the Temple), 42, 121–2

Súriy-i-Mulúk (Súrih of the Kings), 146–7

Súriy-i-Nuṣḥ, 137, 142, 146

Súriy-i-Qadír (Súrih of the Omnipotent), 119–22

Súriy-i-Ṣabr (Súrih of Patience), *see* Part II of index

Also titled *Lawḥ-i-Ayyúb*

Tablet of The Holy Mariner, 228–43

Tablet of Visitation, 30, 206 and n.

Tafsír-i-Ḥurúfát-i-Muqaṭṭa'ih (Interpretation of the Isolated Letters), see *Lawḥ-i-Áyiy-i-Núr*

II. GENERAL INDEX

Ábádih, 77 and n., 266
'Abbás Effendi, *see* 'Abdu'l-Bahá
'Abbás, Mírzá (Mírzá Buzurg), father of Bahá'u'lláh, 7, 19, 305
'Abbás, Mírzá (Qábil), of Ábádih, 77–8
'Abbás, Sháh (reigned 1589–1627), 117
'Abdu'l-Bahá ('Abbás Effendi): as a child, 9, 13, 100; spiritual titles of, 13–14, 100, 132, 134–5; His services to Bahá'u'lláh, 25, 159; appointed by Bahá'u'lláh, 134–5; Exemplar of Teachings, 14, 100, 134; Centre of the Covenant, 14, 24, 80, 130, 135, 240, 241; station of, 14, 134–5, 313; Tablets of, 50, 77, 80–81, 91, 95, 127 n., 201, 239; statements by, 62, 100, 120, 127, 208, 214, 230, 254–5, 257, 260 and n., 262, 268, 276–7, 284, 288–9, 290, 309; interpretations by, 81–2; in the Garden of Riḍván, 261–2; pays tribute to Bahá'u'lláh, 308; Covenant-breakers, 132–3, 315–19; mentioned, 16, 19, 29, 35, 40, 41–2, 199–201 *passim*, 205, 206, 212, 219
'Abdu'l-Ghaffár-i-Iṣfahání, 287–8
'Abdu'l-Ḥamíd, Shaykh, 283
'Abdu'l-Ḥusayn-i-Ṭihrání, Shaykh, 142–7 *passim*, 225; stigmatized by Bahá'u'lláh, 148
'Abdu'l-Karím-i-Qazvíní, Mullá, 53–4, 330
'Abdu'l-Majíd-i-Shírází, Ḥájí, 94, 155, 157
'Abdu'lláh, Ḥájí Mírzá, 41, 42
'Abdu'r-Raḥmán-i-Karkúkí, Shaykh, 62, 104
Abraham, 7
Abú-Bakr, Caliph, 127
Abú-Lahab, 156 and n.
Abú-Turáb-i-Qazvíní, Shaykh, 205, 332
Abu'l-Faḍl, Mírzá, of Gulpáygán, 7, 221
Abu'l-Qásim, servant of Mírzá Yaḥyá, 247
Abu'l-Qásim-i-Hamadání, servant of Bahá'u'lláh, 62, 67
Abu'l-Qásim-i-Káshí, 252
Adrianople (Edirne), Bahá'u'lláh in, 17, 24, 37, 97, 246, 255; His Writings, 102, 279–80; Bahá'ís in, 27, 28, 203, 287–8
Afnán (the Báb's kindred), 134 and n., 155, 158–9, 198–9
Aghṣán (male descendants of Bahá'u'lláh), 134 and n.
Aḥmad-i-Aḥsá'í, Shaykh, 169 n., 204, 221, 299 n.
Aḥmad-i-Azghandí, Mírzá, 194
'Akká: traditions about, 32 n.; Bahá'u'lláh's exile and imprisonment, 17, 24, 27, 42, 98, 204, 286–9 *passim*; 'Abdu'l-Bahá in, 100, 132, 201; resident Bahá'ís, 26, 27, 29, 35, 39, 204, 287–91 *passim*; Bahá'í pilgrims, 37, 48, 50 n., 111, 131–2; Covenant-breakers, 201, 315–19
'Alí, Ḥájí Mírzá Siyyid, uncle of the Báb, 153, 154, 327, 329
'Alí, Imám ('Alí ibn Abí Ṭálib), 11, 34, 71, 126–8, 294 n., 305; refers to Bahá'u'lláh, 306

'Alí-Akbar, Mírzá, cousin of the Báb, 251 252
'Alí-Muḥammad, Siyyid, *see* Báb, The
'Álí Páshá, Turkish Prime Minister, 225, 227, 244
'Alí Sháh, Prince, 258
'Alíy-i-Afnán, Ḥájí Siyyid, 41
'Alíy-i-Basṭámí, Mullá, 222–3
'Alíy-i-Sayyáḥ, Mírzá, 220
'Ancient Beauty', a title of Bahá'u'lláh, 83, 148, 291
Animal(s): kingdom, 2, 3, 58; kindness to, 188
Anísá, Tree of, 81
Apostles, of Bahá'u'lláh, 16, 26, 27 and n., 36, 41 n., 95, 202, 259
Áqá Ján, Mírzá (Khádimu'lláh), amanuensis of Bahá'u'lláh, 24, 35–8, 40, 69, 157, 205, 228, 278; 'Revelation writing', 24–5, 35–6; biography, 24, 40–41; his important testimony, 42; breaks Bahá'u'lláh's Covenant, 315–19; mentioned, 92, 131
Áqá Khán, Mírzá, Persian Prime Minister, 10–11
Áqá Riḍá, of Shíráz, 288–9
Áqáy-i-Kalím, *see* Músá, Mírzá
Áqáy-i-Káshání, Mírzá (Ismu'lláhu'l-Muníb), 283–7 *passim*
Áqáy-i-Rikáb Sáz, Mírzá, 125
Arab(s), 22, 214–15
Arabic, language, 19, 26, 34 n., 48, 62, 215; used by Bahá'u'lláh, 22, 60, 62
Arms, use of forbidden, 278–9 and n.
Asadu'lláh, Mírzá, of Khuy, *see* Dayyán
Asadu'lláh-i-Qumí, Siyyid, 35; quoted, 35–6, 87–9
Ásíyih Khánum (Navváb), wife of Bahá'u'lláh, 12, 15, 19
'Aẓím, 327 and n., 328

'B' and 'E' (letters), 30
'B' and 'H' (letters), 83
Báb, The (Siyyid 'Alí-Muḥammad): birth, 294 n.; family of, 153–9 *passim*, 198–201 *passim*, 206 n., 249, 251; mother of, *see* Fáṭimih-Bagum; House of, 211–12; in Mecca and Búshihr, 154, 200, 221, 223; in Shíráz, 200, 327; in Iṣfahán, 102; Herald of Bahá'u'lláh, 7–8, 217; spiritual titles of, 60, 67, 221, 222 and n., 294. 307; early days of His Dispensation, 222–3, 327–30; Revelation of, 81, 108 and n., **190–4**, 329 and n.; Writings of, 23 and n., 34, 48, 54, 55, 60, 68, 102, 116–17, 207, 251–2, 255–6, 280, **294–303**, **307**; station of, 214, 223, 294–5, 313; extolled by Bahá'u'lláh, 119, 190–93, 214, 272, 294; extols Bahá'u'lláh, 294–303 *passim*, 307; martyrdom of, 53–4, 67, 154, 268; Shrine of, 15, 200, 206; mentioned, 3, 20, 56, 61, 169, 207, 213, 325, 326
Bábí(s), 39 n., 56, 84, 92, 101–2, 142, 169 n., 191 n., 194, 202; community in Persia, 84, 253, 286; persecutions and martyrs, 7, 11, 138, 264–8, 278–9; community in 'Iráq, 53–5, 61, 67–70, 144, 195, 202, **206–10**, 225–6, 248, 258–62 *passim*; community divided, 68, 248–51; Bahá'u'lláh declares His mission to, 261–2
Bábí Dispensation, 23 n., 34, 93 n., 191 and n., 280, 293, 294
Backbiting, 79, 187
Badasht, conference at, 8, 293
Badí' Calendar, of the Bahá'í Dispensation, 116–17, 228 n.
Badí'u'lláh, Mírzá, son of Bahá'u'lláh, 131–2
Baghdád: Bahá'u'lláh's sojourn, 16, 165 258–9; His House, 94, **211–12**, 259, 260; absents Himself, 55, 57; returns from Kurdistán, 41, 63, 67–9 *passim*; 'Abdu'l-Bahá in, 13, 16, 25; events in, 142–7, **206–10**, 219–20, 225–7, 228–9; Mírzá Yaḥyá's actions, 54–5, 247–54; visitors to, 39 and n., 56, 68, 84, 85, 91–2, 97, 102, 128, 141, 150, 151, 153, 156–7, 198, 202, 206, 269 and n., 284, 289; Garden of Riḍván, 53, 109 n., 259–60, 262; Bahá'u'lláh departs, 55, 57, 97, 203,

260–62, 281–2; mentioned, 17, 25, 62, 104, 105, 108, 119, 125, 137, 148, 149, 215, 219, 244, 246, 255, 280, 287, 288; *see* 'Iráq
Bahá: Bahá'u'lláh, 33, 83, 158; attribute and name of God, 48, 116, 117; *see* Jináb-i-Bahá
Bahá'í(s): 'people of Bahá', 47, 94, 238–9, 275, 280; Bahá'u'lláh's communication with, 109–10, 113, 203, 244; persecuted, 268, 279; their unity, 303; teachers, 86, 107, 162, 203, 279, 283; in Cyprus, 27, 288; in 'Ishqábád, 199; mentioned, 22, 88, 90
Bahá'í Archives, International, 19, 159
Bahá'í Cycle, 309–11
Bahá'í Dispensation, 216–18, 279, 309–14
Bahá'íyyih Khánum (the Greatest Holy Leaf), daughter of Bahá'u'lláh, 12, 14–15, 19
Bahá'í World Community, 279; community of Most Great Name, 242, 281
Bahá'u'lláh (Mírzá Ḥusayn-'Alí): lineage of, 7, 305; youth, 19–20; education, 19, 20, 22, 62–3; family of, 8–16 *passim*, 122–3, 130, 284, 305; brothers of, 10, 11, 15, 16; sisters of, 49–51; spiritual titles of, 8, 12, 42, 66, 77, 83, 109, 134, 148, 236, 304–9 *passim*, 313; in Karbilá, 223–4; persecution in Ṭihrán, 8–14, 46, 51, 224; imprisonment, *see* Síyáh-Chál, dungeon of, Prison; birth of Revelation, 7, 10, 12, 299; banishment from Persia, 11, 13, 16–17, 51–2, 224; in Baghdád, 16, 53–5, 85, 92–5, 210, 225–9, 259, 273; retirement to Kurdistán, 16, 40, 53, 55, 57, 60–4 *passim*, 248, 249; return from Kurdistán, 25, 63, 67–9 *passim*, 84, 96; in the Garden of Riḍván, 259–62 *passim*, 275–6, 281–2; declaration of Mission, 17, 53, 109 n., 142, 208, 210, 260–63 *passim*, 273–8, 286, 293, 299; important statements at Riḍván, 278–80; departure from Baghdád, 16, 97, 225–7, 243–4, 281–2, *see* Baghdád; to Constantinople, 16, 97, 243–4, 283–92 *passim*; in Constantinople, 17, 292; to Adrianople, 17, 102, 203; proclamation of Mission, 17, 109 n.; to 'Akká, 17, 204, 286–9 *passim*; station of, 10, 66–7, 295, 304–9, 313; alludes to His own station, 119, 142, 194–6, 210, 213, 218. 245, 273, 307–8; extolled by the Báb, 295–8, 300, 301–3, 307; relationship to other Manifestations, 64–6, 308–9; man's relationship to, 73–4, 79–80; recognition of, 56, 68, 84, 91, 95; His effect on people, 94, 101–3, 145, 198, 206–9, 220, 257–9; companions of, 27, 40, 95, 96–7, 206–9, 218; His majesty, 148, 257–9, 282; His innate knowledge, 18, 20; His sufferings, 10, 12–13, 51–2, 57, 61, 63, 148–9, 195–6, 249; Mírzá Yaḥyá's opposition to, 37, 54–5, 107, 120, 130, 133, 136, 195–6, 218, 241–2, 246–56; ascension of, 24, 132–3, 205; Shrine of, 206; *see* Adrianople, Apostles of Bahá'u'lláh, 'Him Whom God shall make manifest', Revelation of Bahá'u'lláh, Word of God revealed by Bahá'u'lláh, Writings of Bahá'u'lláh
Bahjí, Mansion of, 24, 276 n., 319; Bahá'u'lláh's Shrine, 206 and n., 318–19
Bayán: Mother Book of Bábí Dispensation, 296; its purpose, 296; anticipates and gives signs of 'Him Whom God shall make manifest', 296–302; 'Point' of, 298, 307; 'Váḥid' of, 298–300 *passim*; 'Letters' of, 308; 'Witnesses' to, 93 n.; 'year nine', 298–300; Bahá'u'lláh addresses people of, 109, 194–5, 245, 271, 286; mentioned, 23, 68, 85, 93 n., 190, 280
Bíbí Ṣáḥib, 39–40
'Blessed Beauty', a title of Bahá'u'lláh, 12 n., 77, 90, 200, 205, 230

Book of Certitude, The, *see Kitáb-i-Íqán*
'Branch', *see* 'Abdu'l-Bahá; Mihdí, Mírzá
Buddha, 3
Bukhárá, 95
Búshihr (Bushire), 154, 156, 200, 221
Buzurg, Mírzá, of Núr, *see* 'Abbás, Mírzá
Buzurg Khán, Mírzá, Persian consul-general, in Baghdád, 143, 146–7, 225, 226

Caliphs, of Islám, 127, 128, 215
Carmel, Mount, 15, 19, 29, 200, 268
Cause of God: features of, 129, 133, 137; is irresistible, 105–6, 148–9, 192, 201; its world mission, 217, 272–3; opposition to, 142–7, 242; how to teach it, 161, 278–9
Chains, in Síyáh-Chál, 9 and n., 10, 51
Christ (Jesus), 3, 20, 58, 64, 67, 174, 178–9, 182, 257, 267; words of, 107, 120, 182, 184; signs of return, 165–9; refers to Bahá'u'lláh, 306
Christian Faith, civilization, 214
'Cities', of spiritual attainment, 151–2; of God, 189; of certitude, 190
Clergy, *see* Divines
'Concourse on high', 81 and n., 82, 267
Constantinople (Istanbul): Bahá'u'lláh's departure for, journey and arrival, 16, 97, 203, 227, 259, 281–2, ch. 17; Bahá'ís in, 27, 28, 287–9
Contentment, 99–101, 187; three aspects of, 108
Covenant: of God, 72, 79, 242; of Bahá'u'lláh, 24, 29, 79, 80–2, 229–30, 242, 315; tests believers, 137, 238; *see* Covenant-breakers, Will and Testament of Bahá'u'lláh
Covenant-breakers, 10, 16, 24, 27, 29, 41, 130–33 *passim*, 137, 230, 240–42, Appendix I; *see* Yaḥyá, Mírzá, Muḥammad-'Alí (son of Bahá'u'lláh)
Creation, 1–3, 98–9, 101, 114, 122, 123, 269

Cyprus, 27, 288

'Day of God', 45–6, 64–7, 119, 129, 152, 213, 236–8, 275, 308
'Day of Resurrection', 171, 184–5
Dayyán (Mírzá Asadu'lláh of Khuy), 249–52
Death, 79, 123–5, 152, 183, 184
Detachment, 75–80 *passim*, 99–100, 108, 162, 187, 212–13, 239; example of Job, 270–71
Dhabíḥ, *see* Ismá'íl, Siyyid, of Zavárih
Divine civilization, 120–21, 217–18, 278
Divines, Muslim, 18–20, 39 and n., 78, 92, 144–5, 155 n., 163–4, 185–6, 194, 301; of 'Akká, 32; of Sulaymáníyyih, 62; Bahá'u'lláh's encounters with, 20, 144–6; mujtahids, 25–6, 91 and n., 144
Ḍíyá'u'lláh, Mírzá, son of Bahá'u'lláh, 131–2

Egypt, 28, 203, 204
'Elders' (twenty-four), 201 and n.

Fáḍil-i-Mázindarání, Jináb-i-(Asadu'lláh, Mírzá), 42
Faith, of a believer, 238, 243; unfaithfulness, 243
Famagusta, 288
Farídu'd-Dín-i-'Aṭṭár, 96
Fáris Effendi, 204
Fatḥ-'Alí Sháh (reigned 1798–1834), 128
Fáṭimih, daughter of the Prophet Muḥammad, 71–2; 'Hidden Book' of, 71
Fáṭimih, the Báb's second wife, 249 and n.
Fáṭimih Khánum-i-Afnán, 159
Fáṭimih-Bagum, mother of the Báb, 154–7 *passim*, 159, 200
Fu'ád Páshá, Turkish Foreign Minister, 225
Fúrúghíyyih, daughter of Bahá'u'lláh, 41
Fuṣúl-i-Arba'ib, 322 and n.

Gabriel, Angel, 71
Gallipoli, 27, 287
Ghulám-Riḍá Khán, 88
God: the Unknowable, 1, 46, 114–15, 152, 175–6; attributes of, 1–3, 30–1, 44, 46, 59, 73, 99, 114, 116–18, 119, 122, 125, 152, 176–8, 180–1; oneness of, 113–15; Bahá'u'lláh describes, 114–16; worlds of, 57–9, 64, 72–5 *passim*; nearness to, 96; presence of, 185, 299; pledges Himself, 272–3; *see* Word of God, Cause of God, Day of God, Kingdom of God
Gospels (New Testament), quoted and explained by Bahá'u'lláh, 165–9, 184; mentioned, 151, 190
Greatest Branch, *see* 'Abdu'l-Bahá
Greatest Holy Leaf, *see* Bahá'íyyih Khánum
'Greatest Name', 28, 48, 117, 274
Greece, 214

Ḥabíbu'lláh, Ḥájí Mírzá (Afnán), 155
Hádí, Ḥájí Mírzá, 211
Ḥadíth (Traditions), *see* Traditions
Hádíy-i-Dawlat Ábádí, Ḥájí Mírzá, 251
Ḥáfiẓ, poems, 11 and n.
Háhút, spiritual world of, 58
Haifa, 29, 41, 131, 201 n., 288
Ḥamíd, Mullá, of Sulaymáníyyih, 62
Hand(s) of the Cause, 36, 241 and n.
Ḥasan, Imám, 71
Ḥasan-'Alí, Ḥájí Mírzá, uncle of the Báb, 156–7, 159
Ḥasan-i-'Ammú, Ḥájí Mullá, 144–5
Ḥasan-i-Mázindarání, cousin of Bahá'u'lláh, 50 and n.
Ḥasan-i-Zunúzí, Shaykh, 205, 207–8
Ḥavvá, cousin of Bahá'u'lláh, 122, 124–5
Ḥaydar-'Alí, Ḥájí Mírzá, 28–9
Hidden Words, The: ch. **6**; manner of its Revelation, 71; major themes of, 72, 75, 77, **78–80**; potential influence of, 77; Bahá'u'lláh's reference to, 78; interpretations of 'Abdu'l-Bahá, 80–3; various subjects: backbiting, 79; Bahá'u'lláh's prescription for man, 78–80; calamity, 79, 149; Covenant of Bahá'u'lláh, 80–2; Covenant of God with man, 72, 79; death, 79; detachment, 74–7, 79–80; love, 79, 80; 'Maid of heaven', 83; prayer, 79; pride, 77, 79, 81; purity of heart, 79; soul of man, 72–5, 78–80; 'wings' and 'comb', 82; mentioned, 107 n.; *see* 'Tree of Anísá', 'Ruby Tablet', Mount Párán, Sadratu'l-Muntahá, 'Tablet of Paradise'
'Him Whom God shall make manifest': **249–303**; declaration of Bahá'u'lláh's station, 17, 206, 262; Báb's prophecies fulfilled, 207, 217, 249, 251, 280–81; false claimants, 68, 202, 300; mentioned, 38, 56, 84, 93 n., 105, 152, 194 n.
History of the Martyrs of Yazd, 321, 326
Hizdr Baytí, Lawḥ-i-, 127 n.
Holy Books (of former religions), 151, 161, 162, 190, 296; interpretations of, 166–71, 183–5; *see* Old Testament, Gospels, *Qur'án*, Terms in Holy Writings
Holy Days, Bahá'í, 281
Holy Spirit, 28, 63, 71, 148, 184, 189; *see* Most Great Spirit
House, of Bahá'u'lláh in Baghdád, 211–12, 259, 281
Ḥusayn, Imám, 56, 71, 127, 156 n., 182, 305; on Bahá'u'lláh's mission, 306
Ḥusayn, Mírzá, of Iṣfahán, *see* Mishkín-Qalam
Ḥusayn-'Alí, Mírzá, *see* Bahá'u'lláh
Ḥusayn-i-Bushrú'í, Mullá, 150, 191 and n., 280, 302 n.
Ḥusayn Khán, Ḥájí Mírzá, 225, 226
Ḥusayn-i-Mutavallí, 147, 149–50
Ḥusayn-i-Zanjání, Mírzá, quoted, 89–91

Ibn-i-Fáriḍ, poet, 62
Ibráhím, Siyyid, 250
Imáms, 60, 71, **126–8**, 156 n., 185, 335; traditions by, 48n., 193–4, 327, 332; *see* 'Alí, Imám and Ḥusayn, Imám

Írán, *see* Persia
'Iráq: Bahá'u'lláh's exile to and sojourn in, 13, 16, 51, 53–5, 67–70, 146–7, 211, 228–9, 243–4, 246, 248, 253–4; Báb's family in, 154–7; dissemination of Writings from, 28, 110; Muslim Shrines, 156–7; *see* Bábís, in 'Iráq; Baghdád
Isaiah, prophecies of, 305
Iṣfahán, 26, 28, 249 n., 287
'Ishqábád, 95, 199, 200
Islám: 23, 30, 43, 116, **126–8**, **214–6**, 333 and n.; laws of, 19, 26, 57; traditions of, 32 n., 34, 46, 48 n., 59, 63, 83 n., 117, 119 n., 130, 152, 162, 180, 193–4, 216, 266–7, 294 n.; divisions within, 128; *see* Divines, Imáms, *Qur'án*, Shaykhís, Shí'ahs, Sunnís
Ismá'íl, Shaykh, of Sulaymáníyyih, 61
Ismá'íl, Siyyid, of Zavárih (Dhabíḥ), 101–3, 205
Ismá'íl-i-Azghandí, Ḥájí Siyyid, 111–12
Ismá'íl-i-Vazír, Mírzá, 15

Jabarút, spiritual world of, 58
Ja'far, Mullá, of Naráq, 56
Ja'far-i-Yazdí, Mírzá, 289–91, 331
Ja'far-i-Yazdí, Siyyid, 137–42, 331
Jamál-i-Mubárak (Blessed Beauty), a title of Bahá'u'lláh, 12
Javád-i-Karbilá'í, Ḥájí Siyyid, 155 and n., 157, 220, **221–4**
Jerusalem, 173
Jesus, *see* Christ
Jew(s), 57, 107, 182, 214
Jináb-i-Bahá (His Honour Bahá), a designation of Bahá'u'lláh, 8 and n., 158, 224
Job, 267, 270–71
John the Baptist, 169

Karbilá, 142, 154, 156 n., 157, 221, 222, 224; Bahá'u'lláh in, 24, 207, 247
Karím Khán, Ḥájí Mírzá, 186 n., **332–5**
Káshán, 24, 56, 283
Katurah, 7
Kawthar, 178, 196 and n.; Súrih of *Qur'án*, 328, 329
Káẓim, Shaykh (Samandar), 36
Káẓim-i-Rashtí, Siyyid, 169 and n., 191 n., 204–5, 221, 332
Káẓimayn, 94, 156 n.
Khadíjih Bagum, wife of the Báb, 155, 206 n.
Khájih, fort of, 264, 265, 268
Khán-i-Súq-i-Abiyaḍ, 'Akká, 131
Khánum Buzurg, 50–51
Kingdoms, of existence, 1–3, 58
Kingdom of God, 5, 59, 82, 121, 314
Kirmán, 92, 332, 333
Kirmánsháh, 226, 246–7
Kitáb-i-Íqán (The Book of Certitude), **ch. 10**, *see* **Table of Contents**; additionally, *see*: former title, 158; written for a Muslim, 162; original copy, 159; importance of, 153, 197; effect on reader, 158–9, 161–2; dissemination of, 160; various subjects: backbiting, 187; contentment, 187; fellowship with righteous, 187; interpretation of former Scriptures, 162, 164–6, 171–2; knowledge, 172–3, 185–6; love, 187; pride, 187; purity of heart, 172, 187; 'seal' on Holy Books, 160–1; unity of religions, 160–61; mentioned, 152, 263, 332. *See also* Detachment, Holy Spirit, Manifestations of God, Qá'im, Terms in Holy Writings, Tests, True Seeker
Knowledge, 20, 31, 43, 60, 126, **216–18**; Bahá'u'lláh's, 18, 20; true knowledge, 43–4, 98–9, 172–3, 186, 217–18
Krishna, 3
Kurdistán, 16, 25, 40, 53, 55, 57, **60–64** *passim*, 67, 84
Kamálu'd-Dín, Ḥájí Mírzá, 55–6, 60, 260 n.

Láhút, spiritual world of, 58
League of Nations, 212
Letters of the Living, 60 and n., 93, 128 n., 153; *see* Quddús; Ḥusayn-i-Bushrú'í, Mullá; Ṭáhirih

London, 120, 216
Love, 2, 79, 96–7, 102–3, 187
Luṭf-'Alí, Mírzá, 330

Máh-Kú (Mákú), 56, 300
Maḥmúd, Áqá Mírzá, 288–9
Maḥmúd, Ḥájí Mírzá, an Afnán, 199
Maḥmúd, Mírzá, nephew of Bahá'u'lláh, 9, 10
Maḥmúd, Shaykh, divine of 'Akká, 32 and n., 33
Maḥmúd-i-Káshání, Mírzá, 319
'Maid of Heaven', 63, 82, 83, 125, 213, 218, **242**
Majdi'd-Dín, Mírzá, 316
Malakút, spiritual world of, 59
Man: his nature, 58, 72, 133–4; purpose of his creation, 73, 240; stages of spiritual journey, 96, 151–2, *see* ch. 8; developing spiritual qualities, 74, 80, 96, 107; his potentialities, 80, 119, 122; Bahá'u'lláh's counsels, 78–9; *see* Detachment, Pride, Suffering, Resignation
Manifestation(s) of God, 1–5, 28, 36, 58, 63–7 *passim*, 97, 237; relationship to God, 58–9, 63–4, 114–16, 117–18, 142, 161, 175–6, 179–80; relationship to each other, 64–7, 117–18, 142, 160–61, 177–8, 309–10; attributes of, 167, 179–80, 262–3, 271; powers of, 107, 263; sovereignty of, 180–3; forces released by, 4–5, 31–2, 167, 176, 184, 211, 213–18, two stations of, 59, 129, 177–80; unity of, 118–19, 161, 176–8; distinctiveness of, 119, 178–9, 309–10; signs of the advent of the next, 164–71; proof of, 106–7, 189–90; relationship to man, 58, 59, 97, 118–19; man's inadequacy to recognize, 303; man's rejection of, 163–6; opposed by leaders of religion, 163–4, 171–2; sufferings of, 163, 182–3, 194–6; the Universal, 309; the Supreme, 10, 95, 117, 125, 295–6, 301; future, 280, 309–11; *see also* Recognition of God's Messengers
Martyrs, Martyrdom, 270, 279; in Nayríz, 265–8
Maryam, cousin of Bahá'u'lláh, 12–13, 61, 122, 124
Mashriqu'l-Adhkár, 86 and n., 199
Mas'úd Mírzá, Prince (Ẓillu's-Sulṭán), 258 n.
Mázindarán, 54, 246, 305
Mazra'ih, mansion of, 290–91
Mazra'iy-i-Vashshásh, 228
Mecca, 154, 173
Mihdí, Ḥájí Mullá, 56
Mihdí, Mírzá (the Purest Branch), son of Bahá'u'lláh, 19, 261
Mihdíy-i-'Aṭrí, Ḥájí Mullá, 331
Miracles, 106–7, 145–6, 291 n.
Mishkín-Qalam (Mírzá Ḥusayn), 26–8
Moses, 3, 20, 58, 64, 67, 107, 168, **174**, 214, 236, 257, 267
'Most Great Spirit', 34, 45, 63, 242
Most Holy Book, The, see *Kitáb-i-Aqdas*
Mosul, 26, 254, 285
Muḥammad, Darvísh (assumed name of Bahá'u'lláh, 67
Muḥammad, Ḥájí Mírzá Siyyid, uncle of the Báb, 153–9; Bahá'u'lláh addresses, 186–9; also 180, 189, 198 n.
Muḥammad, Prophet of Islám, 3, 20, 22, 23, 32 n., 48 n., 59, 71, 126–7, 148, 156 n., 169, 173, 182, 189, 190, 193, 257; 'Seal of the Prophets', 66; refers to Bahá'u'lláh, 306; *see* Fáṭimih; 'Alí, Imám
Muḥammad, Siyyid, of Yazd, 39
Muḥammad Sháh (reigned 1835–48), 11 and n., 138 n., 325–6, 330
Muḥammad-'Alí, Áqá, of Iṣfahán, 287
Muḥammad-'Alí, Ḥájí Mírzá, cousin of the Báb, 198
Muḥammad-'Alí, Mírzá, son of Bahá'u'lláh, 131–3, 136, 261, 315, 316 n., 319
Muḥammad-'Alíy-i-Ṣabbágh, Áqá, 287
Muḥammad-Ḥasan, Mírzá, faithful half-brother of Bahá'u'lláh, 11, 16

Muḥammad-Ḥasan, Mírzá ('King of the Martyrs'), 103 n., 259
Muḥammad-Ḥasan-i-Sabzavárí, Shaykh, 39
Muḥammad-Ḥusayn, Mírzá ('Beloved of the Martyrs'), 103 n., 259
Muḥammad-i-'Arab, Shaykh, 283
Muḥammad-Ibráhím-i-Amír, Áqá, 288
Muḥammad-Ibráhím-i-Káshání, Áqá, 131
Muḥammad-i-Iṣfahání, Siyyid, Antichrist of the Bahá'í Revelation, 27 and n., 54–5, 68, 107, 220, 223 and n., 224, **246–9**, 254–5, 291
Muḥammad-Ja'far-i-Tabrízí, Ḥájí, 97–8
Muḥammad-i-Mázindarání, Mírzá, 250–51
Muḥammad-i-Qá'iní, Mullá (Nabíl-i-Akbar), 91–5, 145 n.
Muḥammad-Qulí, Mírzá, faithful half-brother of Bahá'u'lláh, 15–16, 284
Muḥammad-Riḍá, Áqá, 102, 103, 278
Muḥammad-Riḍá, Mullá, of Manshád, *see* Raḍa'r-Rúḥ
Muḥammad-Riḍá, Mullá, of Muḥammad-Ábád, 84–91
Muḥammad-Ṣádiq, Áqá, of Iṣfahán, 287
Muḥammad-Ṣádiq-i-Khurásání, Mullá (Muqaddas), known as Mullá Ṣádiq, 92–3
Muḥammad-Ṭáhir-i-Málmírí, Ḥájí, biography, **320–24**; receives Tablet, 37–40; writings, 38 n., 321–2; memoirs, 111–13, 131–2, 290–91; father of author, 37 n.
Muḥammad-Taqí, Ḥájí (entitled Ayyúb), of Nayríz, 139–41, 263–4, 268–9 and n.
Muḥammad-Taqíy-i-Afnán, Ḥájí Mírzá, cousin of the Báb, 158, **198–201**
Muḥammad-i-Vazír, Mírzá, cousin of Bahá'u'lláh, 122–3
Muḥammad-i-Zarandí, Mullá, *see* Nabíl-i-A'ẓam
Muḥyi'd-Dín, Shaykh, 96
Mujtahids, *see* Divines
Mulk-Ará, Prince, 92
Mullás, *see* Divines
Muníb, Jináb-i-, *see* Áqáy-i-Káshání, Mírzá
Murtiḍáy-i-Anṣárí, Shaykh, 91–2, 144
Músá, Mírzá (Áqáy-i-Kalím), most faithful brother of Bahá'u'lláh, 15–16, 53, 67 n., 131, 144, 205, 228, 247, 284, 316 n.
Músáy-i-Javáhirí, Ḥájí Mírzá, 211, 212–13
Mushíru'l-Mulk, 112–13
Mustayqiẓ (Sleeper Awakened), 250
Muẓaffari'd-Dín Sháh (reigned 1896–1907), 90

Nabíl-i-Akbar, *see* Muḥammad-i-Qá'iní, Mullá
Nabíl-i-A'ẓam (Mullá Muḥammad-i-Zarandí), 41, 48, 69, 91 n., 117 n., 131, 132, **202–6**, 212, 221, 284; quoted, 138, 204–5, 209, 220, 228–9, 265–6, 275–6, 281, 325–6, 327–30
Najaf, 156 n., 157
Najaf-Ábád, 25, 248
Najíb Páshá, 259
Najíbíyyih (Garden of Riḍván), 259
Námiq Páshá, Governor of Baghdád, 226, **229**, 244, 285
Náṣiri'd-Dín Sháh (reigned 1848–96), 8, 10, 11, 13 and n., 26–7, 37, 40–1, 225, 258 and n.
Násút, realm of, 59
Naw-Rúz, 228 and n., 259 and n.
Nayríz, upheavals in, 138–9, 263–9; Bahá'u'lláh praises believers, 267–8; mentioned, 77 n., 288, 331
Níyávarán, 8
Núr, province of, 7, 8, 10, 11, 50, 122
Núru'd-Dín, Áqá Mírzá, 155

Old Testament, 152, 161
Ottoman Government, 16, 17, 147, 225, 227, 229, 254

Párán, Mount, 81
Patience, 109, 187, 271; *see* Job
Pen, of the Most High, 34–5, 94, 128 and n., 252; Exalted Pen, 34, 35 n., 81; Supreme Pen, 45, 133
Persia, Persians (19th century): education, 18–19; language, used by Bahá'u'lláh, 22–3, 26, 48, 63, 64; writing, 35 n.; government, 16, 146, 225–7; officials, 18–20; Bahá'ís, 160, 217, 279; Bahá'u'lláh's contact with, 28, 110–13 *passim*, 203, 284, 286; mentioned, 11
Philosophers, Greek, 214
Pillars, of Shí'ah Islám, 333 and n.
Prayer, 30, 79, 116, 187, 188; prayers by Bahá'u'lláh, 51–2, 114–16
Pride, 77, 79, 81, 108, 120, 130, 152, 187
Prison, of 'Akká, 17, 98, 290
Promised One of Islám, *see* Qá'im
Prophets, *see* Manifestations of God
Purity of heart, 79, 96, 107, 172, 186, 187

Qá'im (He Who arises), 126, 128 n., 152 and n., 155, 156, 158, 169 n., 180–81, 326, 331; traditions about, 185, 194, 216, 267
Qaṣídiy-i-Tá'íyyih, 62
Qayyúmu'l-Asmá', 280, 293, 302 and n.; quoted, 302
Qazvín, 68, 284
Quddús (Ḥájí Mullá Muḥammad-'Alíy-i-Bárfurúshí, 60, 68, 150, 208
Qur'án: Word of God, 22, 23, 34, 126, 189, 190; knowledge of, 19, 126; Súrihs of, *see* Kawthar, V'al-'Aṣr, Va'sh-Shams; quoted, 56, 164, 171, 177–9, 183–5, 188–90, 271 n., 335; foretells Bahá'u'lláh, 119 n.; Bahá'u'lláh interprets, 48, 60, 125–6, 171, 177–9, 185, 335; used treacherously, 264; mentioned, 69, 86, 88, 90, 109 n., 202, 214

Raḍa'r-Rúḥ (Mullá Muḥammad-Riḍá), of Manshád, 39–40, 84–5, 331
Rajab-'Alíy-i-Qahír, Mullá, 249 n.
Recognition of God's Messengers: 107, 123, 152, 161, 208 238, 240; man's first goal, 96; prerequisites of, 162–3; obstacles to, 91, 162–6, 171–2, 183–4; tests associated with, 129–31, 173–5; *see* Manifestations of God
Religion(s), birth, 4; progressive revelation, 65–6, 272, 309–10; unity of, 161–2; opposition of clergy, 163–4, 171–2; purpose of, 311
Resignation (attribute), 98, 108, 269
Revelation of Bahá'u'lláh: His initial experience, 10, 12, 20, 21; its nature, 21; released spiritual energies, 4–5, 18, 23, 45; its greatness, 18, 23, 64–7, 121–2, 213, 218, 236–7, 245, 301–2, 307–8, 311–14; lauded by the Báb, 295–8, 300–301, 301–3, 307; brings tests, 129; *see* Bahá'u'lláh, His effect on people
Riḍá-Qulí, Mírzá, half-brother of Bahá'u'lláh, 12
Riḍván (Paradise), 109, 183; Garden, 109 n., 229, 259–62 *passim*, 275–6, 293; Festival, 259–60, 262, 277; Báb alludes to, 280; significance, 273–8; first day, 260, 262, 278, 280, 281; ninth day, 276 n., 281; twelfth day, 281
'Ruby Tablet', 82
Rukn-i-Rábí' (Fourth Pillar), of Shí'ah Islám, 333
Rúz-bih (Salmán), companion of Muḥammad, 109, 113, 169

Sabzih-Maydán (Ṭihrán), 9, 11
Sacrifice, 97, 101–3
Sadratu'l-Muntahá, 3, 82, 83, 135
Sa'íd Khán, Mírzá, Persian Foreign Minister, 225–6
Sakínih Khánum (Ṭallán Khánum), half-sister of Bahá'u'lláh, 50
Salmán, Shaykh, of Hindíyán, 109–113, 255–6
Samandarí, Ṭarázu'lláh, Mírzá, 36–7
Sámarrá, 156 n.

Sámsún, 285, 292
Sar-Galú, 60
Sárih Khánum, faithful sister of Bahá'u'lláh, 49–50
Sásáníyán kings, (A.D. 226–651), 7
'Seal of the Prophets' (Muḥammad), 66
Seals of Bahá'u'lláh, 25 and n.
Servitude, 133–4, 179–80, 239–40
Seven Martyrs of Ṭihrán, 9, 153
Seven Valleys, The, 96–103, 151: Search, 96; Love, 96–8; Knowledge, 98–9; Unity, 99; Contentment, 99–101; Wonderment, 101; True Poverty and Absolute Nothingness, 101
Sháh Sulṭán Khánum (Khánum Buzurg), half-sister of Bahá'u'lláh, 50–51
Shams-i-Jihán, Princess (entitled Fitnih), 128–9
Shaykh Bahá'í, 117
Shaykhís, 169 n., 221, 222, 247, 332, 333
Shí'ah(s), 46, 71, 116, 128 and n., 193–4, 222 n., 304
Shidád (Stress), years of, 136 and n.
Shíráz: the Báb's Declaration, 193, 293; House of the Báb, 155, 212; mentioned 111–12. 223, 265–6, 294
Shoghi Effendi, Guardian of the Bahá'í Faith, 15, 36, 38 n., 78 and n., 137, 159. 202, 229, 241 n., 303–4; quoted, 133, 143–4, 160, 208–9, 281–2, 284–5, 292–3, 304–8, 311–13
Shujá'u'd-Dawlih, 258
Ṣidq-'Alí, Darvísh, 289
Síyáh-Chál, dungeon of, 7, 8–11, 25, 45, 46, 54, 207–8, 224, 225, 246, 257, 293, 299
Soul of man, 72–5, 80, 187; journey of, 96–101, 151–2; immortality of, 72, 79, 123–4
Spirit of faith, 73–4
Spiritual worlds, *see* Worlds of God
Súdán, 28
Suffering (and tribulation), mystery and purpose of, 98–9, 148, 269–70; of Manifestations of God, 148–9, 163–4, 182–3; of Job, 270–71
Ṣúfís, 96 and n.
Sulaymáníyyih, 61, 62, 67, 96, 104, 293
Sulṭán, Shaykh, of Karbilá, 67 and n., 220, 253
Sunnís, 128, 193
Súrih of V'al-'Aṣr, 34, 102
Súrih of Va'sh-Shams, 32
Súrihs, *see* Kawthar; Tablets and Writings of Bahá'u'lláh (Index, Part I)
Ṣabr, Súriy-i- (Súrih of Patience), also titled *Lawḥ-i-Ayyúb* (Tablet of Job), 141 and n., 263–73 *passim*; story of Job, 270–71; effect upon Bábís, 271–2

Ṭabarsí, Shaykh, fort of, 149–50
'Tablet of Paradise', fifth, 82
Tabríz, 284, 293
Ṭábúr Áqásí, Yaḥyá, 317
Ṭáhirih (Qurratu'l-'Ayn), 68, 128 and n., 207
Tákúr, 50
Ṭallán Khánum, *see* Sakínih Khánum
Terms in Holy Writings explained by Bahá'u'lláh: 'angels', 171; 'ark', 236; 'clouds', 170; 'comb' and 'wings', 82; 'crimson-coloured Ark', 280–81; 'crimson sea', 280–81; 'food', 59–60; 'heaven', 170; 'hell', 183–4; 'life' and 'death', 183–4; 'moon', 167–8, 170; 'oppression', 165–7; 'signs of the Son of Man', 168–71; 'sovereignty', 180–82; 'stars', 167–8, 169–70; 'sun', 167–8, 170; *see also* Holy Books; 'B and E', letters of; 'concourse on high'; 'Day of God'; 'Day of Resurrection'; 'Elders (twenty four)'; 'Kawthar'; 'Maid of heaven'; 'Sadratu'l-Muntahá'; 'soul of man'
Tests, associated with Divine Revelations, 129–30, 135–7, 173–5; *see* Resignation, Suffering
Tigris, river, 71, 259
Ṭihrán: Bahá'u'lláh in, 7–13, 17, *see* Síyáh-Chál; addressed by Bahá'u'-

lláh, 46–9; court of Sháh, 26–7, 41, 326; mentioned, 51, 86, 202, 266, 286; *see* Seven Martyrs of Ṭihrán
'Tongue of Grandeur', a designation of Bahá'u'lláh, 42
Townshend, George, quoted, 214–16
Traditions, *see* Islám
True believer, 237–9, 243
True seeker, qualifications of, 162–3, 186–9
Trumpet-blast, 45, 109 and n.

'Ulamás, *see* Divines
'Umar, Caliph, 127
Universal House of Justice, 201 and n., 241

Vahháb-i-Khurásání, Mírzá (Mírzá Javád), 254
Vaḥíd (Siyyid Yaḥyáy-i-Dárábí), 264–5, 268, **325–31**; addressed by the Báb, 297; praised by Bahá'u'lláh, 191, 267; mentioned, 138
Varaqih (Leaf), 14 n.
Varaqiy-i-'Ulyá, *see* Bahá'íyyih Khánum
Varqá (Mírzá 'Alí-Muḥammad), 41 and n., 331

Will and Testament, of 'Abdu'l-Bahá, 137, 241 n.
Will and Testament of Bahá'u'lláh, see *Kitáb-i-'Ahdí*
'Witnesses', see *Bayán*
Word of God: Manifestations reveal, 3, 20–22, 30–32, 36–7; progressive nature, 32, 65–6, 106; proof of Prophethood, 106, 189–90; spirit and form, 21–2; independent of learning, 20, 23; its power, 31–2, 181–3; is creative, 30–31; infinite meanings, 32–4, 57; source of knowledge, 33–4, 44; *see* Word of God as revealed by Bahá'u'lláh
Word of God as revealed by Bahá'u'lláh, 18, 21, 42–3, 46; manner of revelation, 22–5, 28–9, 34–7, 40–42, 55, 64; rapidity of revelation, 23, 29, 35–6, 62, 158; power of, 29, 30–31, 62–3, 83, 102, 210; creativeness, 30–31; vastness of Revelation, 23–4, 25, 69
World Order, New, 120–21, 217
Worlds of God, 57–9, 64, 72–5 *passim*
Writings of Bahá'u'lláh, xv, 22; style and classes of, 21–5, 40, 43, 60, 62–3, 96, 147, 160, 213, 218–19; in His hand, 34–5, 37; transcription, 25–6, 27, 160; some destroyed, 69; *see* Word of God as revealed by Bahá'u'lláh

Yaḥyá, Mírzá (Ṣubḥ-i-Azal), half-brother of Bahá'u'lláh, **53–6**, **246–56**. *See also*: his opposition to Bahá'u'lláh, 16, 37, 130; Bahá'u'lláh's allusions to, 195–6, 218, 241–2, 244, 272; his Cyprus exile, 27, 288; his followers, 10, 50, 68, 203; other mentions, 40–41, 133, 136, 257, 284, 291
Yaḥyáy-i-Dárábí, Siyyid, *see* Vaḥíd
Yazd, believers and martyrs, 37–9 *passim*, 84, 85, 320, 321, 323, 331; citizens, 198, 199, 320; Vaḥíd in, 326, 331
Yúnis Khán-i-Afrúkhtih, Dr., 315–19
Yúsuf-i-Sidihí, Siyyid, 151

Zakaríyyá, Shaykh, 268 and n.
Zaynu'l-'Ábidín, Mullá (surnamed Zaynu'l-Muqarrabín), 25–6
Zaynu'l-'Ábidín Khán, Governor of Nayríz, 138–41 *passim*, 264–5, 268; wife of, 141
Zaynu'l-'Ábidín Khán, Prince, 144, 145
Zoroaster, 3, 7

www.ingramcontent.com/pod-product-compliance
Lightning Source LLC
Chambersburg PA
CBHW021828220426
43663CB00005B/169
* 9 7 8 0 8 5 3 9 8 0 5 7 5 *